History and Tradition in Melanesian Anthropology

STUDIES IN MELANESIAN ANTHROPOLOGY

General Editors

Donald F. Tuzin
Gilbert H. Herdt
Rena Lederman

History and Tradition in Melanesian Anthropology

EDITED BY

James G. Carrier

UNIVERSITY OF CALIFORNIA PRESS

Berkeley   Los Angeles   Oxford

University of California Press
Berkeley and Los Angeles, California

University of California Press
Oxford, England

Library of Congress Cataloging-in-Publication Data

History and tradition in Melanesian anthropology/edited by James G.
Carrier.
    p. cm.—(Studies in Melanesian anthropology; 10)
    Includes bibliographical references and index.
    ISBN 0-520-07523-4 (cloth)
    1. Ethnology—Melanesia—Methodology. 2. Ethnology—Melanesia—
Philosophy. 3. Melanesia—Social life and customs. I. Carrier,
James G. II. Series.
GN668.H57   1992
306'.0995—dc20   91-38223
                                      CIP

Printed in the United States of America

1 2 3 4 5 6 7 8 9

The paper used in this publication meets the minimum requirements of American National
Standard for Information Sciences—Permanence of Paper for Printed Library Materials, ANSI
Z39.48-1984 ∞

CONTENTS

PREFACE

This collection developed out of a growing frustration with the way anthropologists have thought and written about Melanesian societies.

In the Introduction I lay out that frustration in academic language and with proper regard for academic form. But underneath what I say there, motivating my arguments, has been a growing sense that what many were writing about Melanesia did not resemble, describe, or even really refer to what I saw in my own fieldwork, on Ponam Island, in Manus Province, Papua New Guinea, together with a growing sense that what I saw there may not have been all that unusual.

What did I see? I saw a society that was firmly situated in the late twentieth century, a set of people who were not at all the inward-facing and isolated villagers who seem to populate the societies presented in so much Melanesian ethnography. Certainly Ponams were fit subjects for conventional ethnographic presentation. They had elaborate kinship organization, extensive ceremonial exchange, clouds of ancestral spirits, and all the rest. But to present them this way would have been to stress the separation between me and them, between Western society and village life, and to ignore the institutions, practices, habits, beliefs, and constraints that contradicted that separation, that made them not alien people in an alien place and time but that made them something more prosaic: another set of people living in the world.

This reaction to the partiality of conventional anthropological description is not one that I could have predicted, for that partiality did not really become apparent until I thought anthropologically about Ponam Island, and hence until I had to try to reconcile what I confronted with what I had read about Melanesian societies. Of course I was aware of the anthropological oral tradition of villagers disappointed with the researcher whose conventional camera did not produce photographs in the 30 seconds to which they were accustomed and whose recording equipment was not of sufficiently high fidelity. Of course I knew that villagers near urban areas had become urban villagers and those from farther afield had experience as migrant workers and as temporary urban residents. But I was also aware—rightly or wrongly— that these were overlays, a thin frosting on a cake that was traditional. After all, the man who was a circular migrant was only in town long enough to save the money that would allow him to go back to the village, carry out a fully traditional exchange, and take up a fully traditional life. Real Melanesia and the real issues in Melanesian anthropology lay not in the towns but in the hinterlands, and real research meant focusing on the latter and ignoring the former.

It was this presumption whose existence, force, and partiality became apparent when I tried to fit life on Ponam Island into Melanesian ethnography.

Between 1980 and 1986 I taught anthropology and sociology at the University of Papua New Guinea in Port Moresby, the capital of the country. While I was there I had the chance to talk to a number of the anthropologists passing through town on their way to and from their field sites. Many of these were doctoral students, less sure of what they were there to find, and several of them seemed to experience the disorientation that I had once had. Clearly my experience was not unique.

In early 1987, having just returned to the United States, Achsah Carrier and I went to the annual meeting of the Association for Social Anthropology in Oceania, held in Monterey, California. It seemed the right circumstance to sound out other Melanesian anthropologists systematically about their experience. Reactions ranged from bewilderment to enthusiasm, but enough were enthusiastic, or at least willing to listen, that I decided to try to persuade people to contribute to a collection dealing with the issue.

This is the result.

Certainly the points made in it, both in my own Introduction and in the various papers, are not original. There is a long tradition of concern about the tendency of anthropologists to treat village societies as though they were locked in a timeless, traditional present, though this concern has become more insistent in the past few years. So perhaps this collection is best considered as a reminder, rather than as a novel statement.

Is the reminder necessary? The answer varies. Some say that Melanesian anthropology has already abandoned the orientations against which this collection is directed. Yes and no. Some Melanesian anthropologists may have done so, but it remains the case that many important books and articles, written by important scholars and published by important academic presses and journals, continue to portray a timeless, traditional Melanesia. To the degree that the core of the discipline continues with this orientation, then to the same degree is the reminder necessary.

ACKNOWLEDGMENTS

I must acknowledge first my debt to Martha Macintyre. At the meeting in Monterey she encouraged me to develop what was an incoherent idea into a real project. After the meeting, she spread her enthusiasm among her colleagues in Australia, who form the core of this collection.

I am grateful also to Roger Keesing and Margaret Jolly. They agreed to do what may be the most onerous job arising from collections, writing the conclusion. They could not begin until the collection was complete, which meant until the editor and other contributors were anxious to finish the project and get it off to the publisher.

As well, I am grateful to Achsah Carrier. She encouraged me when I was discussing this project in Monterey. She listened to and commented on various parts of the Introduction while I was writing it in London at the time when she was awaiting the *viva voce* for her doctorate. Her own research on Ponam Island, on which I was an inevitable and fortunate collaborator, was an important source of many of the ideas in the Introduction and my own contribution.

Finally, I have a long-standing debt to Joel Kahn. His concern to see and describe Minangkabau society as it is linked to and shaped by the outside world in the present, like his concern to trace the history of those links and influences, inspired my own work in ways he could not have guessed. This is as good a place as any to acknowledge that debt.

J. G. C.

Introduction

James G. Carrier

Over the past decade and more it has become increasingly obvious that anthropology is in trouble.[1] At the practical level, funds to support conventional anthropological fieldwork became more and more scarce. Those anthropologists able to get funds found it more and more difficult to gain permission to carry out fieldwork in the Third World countries that traditionally were their hunting grounds. And in those countries more and more universities were striking anthropology from the list of courses they offered.

This buffeting of conventional anthropology has occurred at the intellectual level as well. Anthropology has been criticized as being little more than an academic accessory of British imperialism. The spread of world systems theory has raised questions about the adequacy of the conventional anthropological focus on small village societies as relatively self-contained units of study. The spread of Marxist scholarship led many influential researchers to focus on aspects of the states in which villagers found themselves: colonization, urbanization, revolution, state formation, and the like have appeared to challenge the conventional ethnographer's understanding of how things are.

Within anthropology itself have come challenges to the very core of the anthropologist's method: fieldwork and ethnography. With the failing faith in the possibility of straightforward description has come a rising awareness that people in villages not only may have their own view of things but also may end up writing critical analyses of what the anthropologist publishes. Taking this as their justification, critics within the discipline have come to argue that fieldwork needs to be recast as a collaborative effort, in which the anthropologist no longer is the discoverer who imposes order on, and authoritatively presents, an alien society. Instead, the New Model Anthropologist is a facilitator, the recorder of divergent voices and viewpoints.

The various criticisms that have been made about conventional anthropology, from within and without the discipline, range from those that seem to suggest only minor modifications to the ways that anthropologists go about their business to those that demand the wholesale rejection of much of the discipline. The spirit of the papers in this collection lies at neither extreme. They do not reject anthropology as a discipline, and in fact they see much value in it. However, they do think there can be improvement in the ways that anthropologists think about and portray the societies and people they study.

The papers in this collection are about Melanesia, and certainly Melanesia has had its share of conventional ethnography. This is particularly true of its largest and most populous part, Papua New Guinea. For many, this is the last outpost of the primitive and isolated society, the place to go when Western influence is too obvious everywhere else, just as for many expatriates this was the last outpost of Empire, the place to go when African countries decided it was time to localize their civil service and university establishments. After all, Papua New Guinea is the place where Fredrik Barth found people who were never quite sure that the beings on the other side of the valley were human; the place where the notion of the discovery of a new "lost tribe" in the early 1980s was conceivable, even if improbable (see, e.g., Boyd 1989; Gorecki 1984; *Research in Melanesia* 1985).

Those who want to paint Papua New Guinea as I have just done can find much that appears to buttress their view. The country is full of small, isolated societies: its linguistic and cultural diversity are legendary and bewildering, and would appear to justify fully Margaret Mead's assertion that it constituted a natural laboratory in which one could study the range of human possibility.[2] The central Highlands region, ringed by difficult, high mountains, was not even known to the Australian colonialists in the early 1920s, and it was opened to significant Western penetration only around World War II. The bulk of the population is less tightly tied to the outside world than seems to be the case in, for instance, much of Africa: the country is relatively unurbanized and most of the people still appear to fit the general category of subsistence producers. The reappearance of tribal warfare in the Highlands in the 1970s and 1980s suggested to many that colonial and national pacification of the core of the country was only partial, that the modern world lay lightly on Highlanders. Less obvious, but perhaps equally important, Papua New Guinea never had a national, anticolonial revolution of the sort that was so common in Africa and Asia (see Nelson 1982, chap. 24). This has meant that racial and political attitudes have not been fired to the degree that they might have been (for the region as a whole, see, e.g., MacDonald 1986). Perhaps as a consequence, scholars have not produced the spate of studies focused on colonial history, the towns, colonization, rebellion, and revolution of the sort that African scholars have written in the past decade or two (e.g., Ellis 1985; Peel 1983).

Thus, more than is the case in some other regions, anthropology in

Melanesia has been able to ignore the criticisms that I have mentioned. It is true that some countries within the region, and some provinces within some countries, refuse to let anthropologists in, and some resident and national academics distrust anthropology. Nonetheless, anthropology departments in Western universities continue to send students to Melanesia to study village societies, and governments in Melanesia continue to grant the necessary visas and permissions. If the winds of change are blowing among anthropologists who study the region, they would appear to be breezes rather than cyclones.

This volume of papers is an attempt to freshen some of those winds somewhat. As I already mentioned, contributors to this collection do not seek the abolition of anthropology. Instead, they urge a continuation, and a strengthening of the rethinking that has been going on in the discipline, of the way anthropologists go about understanding the societies they study. And in particular, they challenge an unreflective acceptance of the tacit idea that anthropology in Melanesia can offer us the study of alien societies that are fairly untouched by Western social forces. Instead, as these papers will show, those societies are affected by colonial and postcolonial impact in subtle ways, and the anthropologists who would study them are affected by their disciplinary and cultural values in subtle ways.

AS WE STUDY THEM

The charge made against anthropologists, that they tend to interpret and present the societies they study as if they were alien entities that are pure beings isolated from Western influence, is a charge that is made against most of the Western academic disciplines that study non-Western societies. And many of these charges can be made against anthropology in Melanesia. In this section I discuss two books that present criticisms that are relevant to the points made by the papers in this collection. Necessarily this involves ignoring some insightful criticisms of anthropological work done in the region. Selectivity is necessary, however, if this Introduction is not to grow into a book of its own. Necessarily also my discussion here implies that these criticisms apply to all anthropologists. This is not my intent. There are a number of anthropologists whose work does not justify the sort of criticisms that have been made of anthropology generally, some of whom are mentioned later in this Introduction.

Anthropology has been identified in many different ways. One identification seems particularly apt, however: as one of the disciplines by which Westerners study non-Western societies. Viewed this way, anthropology revolves around the juxtaposition of We and They, reporting to Us about how They do things Out There. That one part of our conceptual universe and activity should be concerned with such things is entirely unexceptionable. After all, just about everyone else worries about the same problem. Why should we be any different? Even though this concern with Them, with an Other, is routine enough and shared among many disciplines, the ways that this concern is embodied in research and writing can have consequences that are more problematic.

Orientalism

Some of these consequences are described in Edward Said's influential *Orientalism*, his analysis of Oriental Studies in Western academic life over the past two centuries.[3] Oriental Studies is not anthropology, but the two disciplines face many of the same problems, many of the criticisms that Said makes appear to be pertinent to a discussion of anthropology, and his arguments have been reflected in criticisms made of the discipline. For these reasons it is appropriate to begin with his study of an important thread in Western intellectual life over several centuries, the concern with the Orient, as classically defined.

Briefly, Said argues that the modern Western discipline of Oriental Studies is the latest manifestation of the ancient concern with the nature of the Orient, and especially what we now call the Middle East, as distinct from the Occident, historically Western Europe. This concern took on a special urgency during the period of Islamic expansion, when it served to transform an alien and threatening set of people into a known and hence less threatening form. In the process, Said argues, Western intellectuals created the Orient. That is, they took a real, empirical set of people, situated in diverse and historically specific social and economic locations, and converted them into a single, unified and reified category: Orientals, who live in the Orient and who are fundamentally different from Westerners. He says, in other words, that Western intellectuals "Orientalized" the region.

For Said, modern Orientalism is not only a conceptual error. In addition it has a distinctly political dimension, because Western knowledge and construction of the Orient inevitably reflects political forces. Said argues that the rise of Oriental Studies as a scholarly field in the nineteenth century was embedded in, and thus necessarily reflected, Western imperial influence. As he puts it (1978, 11):

> I doubt that it is controversial . . . to say that an Englishman in India or Egypt in the later nineteenth century took an interest in those countries that was never far from their status in his mind as British colonies. To say this may seem quite different from saying that all academic knowledge about India and Egypt is somehow tinged and impressed with, violated by, the gross political fact—and yet *that is what I am saying*.

(Of course, this issue has been thrashed out repeatedly in anthropology, especially following the publication in 1973 of Talal Asad's collection, *Anthropology and the Colonial Encounter*.)

While this power imbalance affected the substance of Orientalist studies and the uses to which those studies are put, it also affected the more fundamental ways that Orientalists learned about, thought about, and represented the region they studied. One such result is what Said calls textualism. He says that the Orient is a textual creation, that it arises from, and is contained in, the texts that intellectuals produce. This is so in two senses. First, Oriental Studies acted as the representative of the Orient: because European empire was so much more powerful than the Orient, it itself was reduced to silence. "Flaubert's encounter with an Egyptian courtesan produced a widely influential model of the Oriental woman; she never spoke of herself. . . . *He* spoke for and represented her" (Said 1978, 6). Consequently, "the Orientalist . . . makes the Orient speak, describes the Orient, renders its mysteries plain for and to the West" (1978, 20–21). Second, and related to this, is what Said (1978, 92) calls "a *textual* attitude," the notion that, as the Orient is silent, its reality is in the text. In this, the proper process of investigation is reversed. The texts are not judged against the object described, but the object is judged against the texts. Those events and actions that do not accord with the texts are taken to be inauthentic, and so are explained away as Western corruptions, or else simply ignored as not worthy of serious investigation. Consequently, these "texts can *create* not only knowledge but also the very reality they appear to describe" (1978, 94).[4]

The point is not that these texts create the entity being described, the Orient, out of whole cloth. Rather, and facilitated by the impotent silence of Orientals themselves, it is that they define what is authentically Oriental, what is valid or real in the alien entity, what is worthy of notice, as distinct from what is merely accidental and insignificant.

As a result of this Orientalization, certain traits appeared in the scholarly work that Orientalists produced. Two of these are contained in Said's observation (1978, 96) that "Orientalism assumed an unchanging Orient, absolutely different . . . from the West," and I want to deal with them in turn.

The first of these traits is that the Orient became essentialized, came to be seen as eternally manifesting certain attributes simply because it was the Orient. Consequently, scholars wanted to show how specific acts or situations demonstrated this Oriental nature or essence, or were concerned to explain what factors blocked such a demonstration. Of course this made this essentialist view of the region almost unassailable. The result, according to Said (1978, 70), was a "self-containing, self-reinforcing . . . closed system in which objects are what they are *because* they are what they are, for once, for all time, for ontological reasons that no empirical matter can either dislodge or alter." And as this ontological essence is timeless, the past and the present collapse into each other: "an observation about a tenth-century Arab poet multiplied itself into a policy towards (and about) the Oriental mentality in Egypt, Iraq, or Arabia. Similarly, a verse from the Koran would be considered the best evidence of an ineradicable Muslim sensuality" (1978, 96). This essentialism is made possible in part because of something I have mentioned already, the power of texts to constitute the Orient. In defining what is real and worthy of attention, texts also can impose their own transhistorical durability on those definitions. This makes the Orient itself, or at least the "real Orient" that Orientalist texts define, essential and timeless.[5]

The second of these two traits was a bifurcation of the world into the Orient and the Occident. The Orient was conceived of as an alien other, made exotic, romantic, repellent, and always different. Thus, "Orientalism was ultimately a political vision of reality whose structure promoted the difference between the familiar (Europe, the West, 'us') and the strange (the Orient, the East, 'them')" (Said 1978, 43). There are many reasons for this alienation of the Orient. One is political, for it facilitated empire, but Said identifies more universal reasons as well. For instance, he says (1978, 55) that "there is no doubt that imaginative geography and history help the mind to intensify its own sense of itself by dramatizing the distance and difference between what is close to it and what is far away."

Orientalism presents a single, powerful example of the problems that can arise when people attempt what anthropologists have long sought to do: identify, describe, and characterize a society or region that is alien and relatively weak, and hence likely to be mute. As I said, not all of Said's criticisms apply to anthropology, and it is obvious that Said has much more to say than I have summarized here. Moreover, Said himself exempted anthropology from his complaint. In part, this is because the sheer scope of Oriental Studies, a scope that dwarfs that of anthropology, seems to be part of the problem (Said 1978, 50), and in part this is because he seemed to see in at least some anthropology a way to dissolve the structures that Orientalism created (1978, 326). In spite of Said's charitable view of anthropology, however, anthropologists themselves have been quick to charge the discipline with something very much like Orientalism. Indeed, Said himself subsequently recanted his exemption of anthropology (see Richardson 1990, 17).

For instance, it is undeniable that anthropology has been associated with relatively weak alien areas that are far removed from the urban Western centers in which professional anthropologists normally live. This was undoubtedly true when anthropologists confined themselves largely to village societies in the Third World. And it remains true today. For most of the discipline, "real anthropology" is still village fieldwork, however much this has become an ideal that a decreasing number of anthropologists really achieve (e.g., Bloch 1988). And this is more true of the research associated with the powerful realm of anthropological theory than it is of the more common but less prestigious body of descriptive ethnography, much less applied anthropology. Even when anthropologists work in Western societies, the work they do that gets published or reviewed in central journals in the discipline tends to be that which focuses on smaller, weaker, peripheral groups: the Celtic Fringe or dying village life in the British Isles (e.g., Cohen 1982; Fox 1978; M. Strathern 1981*b*), poor rural societies in the Mediterranean basin (e.g., Cassia 1982; Gilmore 1982; Sanmartin 1982, all from a single issue of *Man*),[6] or regions like Appalachia in the United States (e.g., Batteau 1982). In an important sense, then, anthropology still is concerned with weak alien societies, whether or not they exist in Western countries: almost no anthropologists study their own groups within their own societies.

And this concern with the exotic appears in Melanesian anthropology. It is true that some anthropologists within the region have described areas or processes that are more "Western": urban life, wage labor, migration, electoral politics, Christianity, nation-building, and the like. But it is also true that however important these areas or processes may be to Melanesians, however much they may be topics of informal conversation among Melanesianists, they remain peripheral to the core anthropological construction of Melanesia, which remains dominated by a view of isolated societies full of exotica—big men, subsistence agriculture, exchange cycles, bride price, spirit cults, cargo cults, and the rest—and by texts that focus on what is taken to be essentially Melanesian.

Of course, concern with areas or processes that are more "Western" appears to be greater in more recent anthropological work on Melanesia. However, this appearance may be a consequence more of selective disciplinary memory than of changing disciplinary interests. In the 1960s and 1970s, for example, one could make the same comment about greater recent concern with these topics among those concerned with Papua New Guinea. After all, this was the heyday of the Waigani Seminars and the New Guinea Research Unit, both concerned with innovative cross-disciplinary studies of important contemporary topics. And in that time, commentators made points critical of conventional anthropology that were substantially the same as those made in this collection and by other recent critics. (This is recounted depressingly in Clarke and Ogan [1973], which contains much more than I allude to here.) The sense of *déjà vu* is understandable when it is remembered that Melanesianists do not only construct the object they study in part by eliding the inauthentic or peripheral, they construct their own discipline the same way. Thus the sense of greater recent interest may be the result of little more than the systematic forgetting of a constant stream of such work in the less recent past, always forgotten because always peripheral.

Time and the Other

Even if anthropologists are predisposed to investigate alien societies, those societies need not be represented in the way that Said criticizes, a way that stresses or heightens the sense of exotic distance and radical separation from the society of those doing the fieldwork and representation. But this sense of separation is common, and it is embodied in different ways. One device that generates it is temporal markers, in particular the ethnographic present. This has been discussed by Johannes Fabian in *Time and the Other*.

Fabian says that in Western culture, the culture that pervades anthropology, there is a conflation of space and time: "relationships between parts of the world . . . can be understood as temporal relations. Dispersal in space reflects directly . . . sequence in Time" (1983, 11–12; Kuper 1988 explores this). This conflation carries with it the dimension of power, in the sense that for Europeans "here" is Western Europe, the seat of power, and "there" is the subordinate place to be studied. Put together, these elements state that the farther away one is from Western Europe, the seat of cultural power, the farther back one is in time.

To complicate this, Fabian points out that in the West time is not neutral. Underlying our conceptions of time is the notion of evolutionary progress, so that going away in space is not only equivalent in some sense to going back in time, it is also equivalent to going back to a lower, more primitive level of existence. "Civilization, evolution, development, acculturation, modernization . . . are all terms whose conceptual content derives, in ways that can be specified, from evolutionary Time" (Fabian 1983, 17). He says that although the discipline is overtly concerned to treat the societies it studies objectively, this valorization of space and time pervades anthropology.

> It is not the dispersal of human cultures in space that leads anthropology to "temporalize" . . . ; it is naturalized-spatialized Time which gives meaning . . . to the distribution of humanity in space. The history of our discipline reveals that such use of Time almost invariably is made for the purpose of distancing those who are observed from the Time of the observer. (Fabian 1983, 25)

This being the case, it is no surprise to Fabian that anthropologists face a problem, that of denying that they and the people they study live in the same Time. This denial is especially poignant because the sheer fact that anthropologists undertake fieldwork means that they *must* share Time with the people they study. Fabian calls this denying of common Time the "denial of coevalness. By that I mean a persistent and systematic tendency to place the referent(s) of anthropology in a Time other than the present of the producer of anthropological discourse" (1983, 31, emphasis omitted). It is in this denial of coevalness that anthropologists are able to maintain their separation from the people they study, a separation that is important given the valorization of space and time.

Fabian's argument on this point is extensive and at times difficult. For my purposes, however, it is useful because it points out that anthropologists tend to think in terms of, and produce in their writing, a radical separation of themselves and their own society on the one hand, and the people and societies they study on the other. This echoes some of what concerned Said in *Orientalism* and bears on some of the points made in this collection. The denial of coevalness is a device that, however unintentionally, further separates Western society from village life, and so further maintains the idea of a radically different and radically alien world that anthropologists can study.[7]

CRITIQUE OF ANTHROPOLOGY

Although Said and Fabian criticize different disciplines, they both make the same general point: our concern with an Other has led us to see societies in terms of a dichotomy of Us and Them. At the simplest level, we tend to lump the unfamiliar into the category of the alien. For Said, this is manifest in the notion of the Exotic or Mysterious Orient. For Fabian, this is manifest in the denial of a common Time. For both, this leads to an unrealistic view of the societies that we study, and the tendency to modify, select, or interpret the evidence to make them fit our preconceptions. This modification can take the form of eliding from our perception or our presentation of the alien societies we study any signs of Western influence, for these signs of the ways that We and They are linked and have shaped each other are seen as inauthentic and hence insignificant, not worthy of serious attention. This modification can take the form of deciding that certain topics are more worthy of discussion than others, that certain issues are more interesting to pursue than others. In general, this modification takes the form of shaping our knowledge of the alien societies we study to make them conform to our image of what they ought to be. (The parallels with Thomas Kuhn's [1970] notions of paradigms and scientific communities should not need elaboration.)

This tendency is not unique to anthropologists and Orientalists. For instance, Bernard Smith describes it in *European Vision and the South Pacific*, his study of European artistic representations of the South Pacific made on early voyages of discovery. Smith found that initial working sketches, usually by trained illustrators and naval draughtsmen, appear to have been quite accurate. However, these sketches were transformed as they were reworked into finished paintings, and particularly as they were rendered into woodcuts for book illustrations by publishers. Their initial accuracy gradually was displaced, so that they became stylized, made to conform to, and hence made to reproduce, the cultural images that were part of the repertoire of Western Europe: Dark savage, Noble savage, World turned Upside Down.[8] A strikingly similar point has been made with regard to the process of ethnographic writing. Exponents of the New Ethnography argue that what is learned and observed in fieldwork increasingly becomes transformed and stylized as it gets written in field notes and then prepared for publication (e.g., Clifford and Marcus 1986). What James Clifford (1986a, 7) says about ethnographic writing applies as well to the paintings described by Smith: these representations contain "powerful 'lies' of exclusion and rhetoric. Even the best ethnographic texts . . . are systems, or economies, of truth. Power and history work through them, in ways their authors cannot fully control."

The biases that Bernard Smith finds creeping into visual representations, like those Clifford sees creeping into written ones, reflect the values and orientation shaping those doing the representing. Said suggests that disciplines like anthropology are oriented in part by a need to identify an alien entity as the object of study, and Fabian states that anthropology places a value on this alien by defining it as primitive, long ago rather than just far away. The search for and creation of such alien entities can serve many purposes beyond those peculiar to academic anthropologists pursuing a career. Particularly, they fulfill the need to strengthen the sense of who "We" are by opposing us to "Them."

As anthropologists have pointed out, this is a need we have in common with many other people. For example, according to John Middleton (1960, chap. 5), the Lugbara conceptual universe puts normal people ("Us" to the Lugbara) in the center, and populates the far away with people of inverted values and habits. Thus, like us, the Lugbara tend to define those from far away in terms of themselves, and do so in moral, evaluative terms. Similarly, Howard and Frances Morphy have described how the Ngalakan, of the Roper Valley in the Northern Territory of Australia, use the image of their own, precontact past to define a world turned upside down. They use this image to distance themselves from their own past, and to identify and value themselves in their present world. Finally, while I can only speculate, it seems plausible that this was one of the reasons the pseudo discovery of a "Lost Tribe" in the Papua New Guinea Highlands in the early 1980s attracted so much interest, including two provincial premiers ready to fly in by helicopter to help bring civilization to the benighted.

In the West this need has been manifest for centuries, as the alien other was seen to offer us a special insight on ourselves. One of Bernard Smith's purposes in *European Vision and the South Pacific* is to describe the ways that eighteenth- and nineteenth-century Europeans used the newly discovered exotic people of the South Pacific to help define Europeans themselves. This is played out more subtly in Marilyn Strathern's *The Gender of the Gift*. Western feminists see gender relations in Melanesia as a vehicle for understanding gender relations in the West. Strathern sees her own work as aimed at those feminists and drawing meaning from their interests. And she points out that, as a result of her analysis, they are no longer confronted with "example after example" of male domination in Melanesia, each needing to be countered, accounted for, and weighed in the balance. Instead, she offers what is much less daunting, "varieties or versions of a 'single' instance" (M. Strathern 1988, 341).

Of course, the way we conceive of the alien society will affect the way that our presentation of it can allow us to reflect on ourselves. A modern view of alien peoples, reflecting the modern concern with the ill effects of predatory, expansionist capitalism, sees the alien as underdog. Like the earlier imagery of the Dark savage and the Noble savage, this allows a special critical function to the alien.[9] This echoes our tendency to allow the underdog a privileged position in understanding the nature of Western capitalist society. In Marxism, the proletariat are, by their very subordinate position, uniquely able to understand what capitalism is like; during the Civil Rights movement in the United States, blacks were held to be especially able to view and understand the racist nature of American society; under feminism, women are especially able to understand the nature of sexism in modern society. In all of these cases there is a set of people who are, by their subordinate position, made outsiders, excluded from the dominant core of society. And all these outsiders—proletariat, black, woman, and savage—possess a special location from which to view and understand "our own" society. Analysts who can study and come to understand these outsiders are able to participate in that unclouded, objective vision (a classic analysis of the complexities of this issue, with particular regard to race, is in Merton 1972; a fine example of the assertion that women and the proletariat have a privileged, unclouded view of modern, masculinist, capitalist society is in Hartsock 1985, esp. 63).

Orientalism and *Time and the Other* illustrate elements of a core criticism of the way that anthropologists approach, interpret, construct, and present the societies they study, a criticism of the way that anthropologists are predisposed to study the *authentic* alien society. Unpacked a bit, this criticism is that anthropologists tend to think in terms of a reified, radically non-Western, and primitive society, a society that is "untouched," and indeed in its reified timelessness is in important ways untouchable. We want to find, study, and present an authentic village society, and, more critically, our wanting leads us willy-nilly to create such societies in our research and writing. This criticism says that anthropologists are prone to look at the world in a way that heightens the untouched alien aspect of the societies they study, which leads to a systematic denial of the fact that villages are themselves fully located in the same late twentieth century that the anthropologist inhabits, and which leads to a systematic failure to consider how villages may participate in and be shaped by many of the social processes and changes that touch the researcher.

Elements of the Critique

I have described a critique of anthropology that centers on the way the discipline conceives, investigates, and represents the societies it studies. Although it necessarily involves oversimplifying, I want to lay out in a summary form the elements of conventional anthropology that are the focus of the critique.

These elements support and imply each other, and hence to some degree the list is one massive redundancy: identifying one element in it identifies, or at least implies, all elements. Further, I need to repeat a point I made earlier. These elements do not appear in all the work of all anthropologists. Rather, they are tendencies, in two senses. They are tendencies in one sense because they tend to characterize anthropological work, rather than necessarily being found in the writings of all anthropologists. They are tendencies in another sense because they are subtle biases or orientations, rather than overt positions to which any anthropologist could be expected to declare explicit allegiance.

Because these are only tendencies, my descriptions are inevitably exaggerations. This has the advantage of enabling me to render in clear terms something that is subtle and often partly obscured. However, it has the disadvantage that my exposition begins to look like caricature. Certainly this is not my intent.

Authenticity. This is the concern to discover and describe an authentic Them, a radically alien and different society that is free from the corrupting influence of contact with Us; I list this first because it is the core of the conventional anthropological concern, as identified by the critics, and because the notion of authenticity contains most clearly many of the other elements of this critique. A concern with authenticity means that things that are identified as authentic are more noticed, esteemed, and presented than are things that are identified as inauthentic. The concern with authenticity thus entails a covert hierarchization and evaluation of what is observed in research and described in writing. Of course the pitfall of authenticity, like the other elements of this critique, does not arise solely from the anthropologist's imaginings. All can dwell as well in the minds of those being studied, either as elements of an overtly politicized notion of local tradition or as the more routine problem of the purification and distortion of the memories of those who are asked to recall their early lives.

The greater visibility of the authentic is illustrated in the difference between two treatments of marriage exchange in Papua New Guinea. One is Marilyn Strathern's invited paper in *Annual Review of Anthropology*. This journal is often treated as a reference work, consulted regularly by those interested in current anthropological thought, and papers in it are likely to have an extensive readership and significant impact. Strathern's paper focuses on "understanding the role of exchanges in items other than persons when these items are part of or move in conjunction with . . . exchanges of persons" (1984, 42). However, it does not deal with the prime Western contribution to "items other than persons" that appears routinely in Melanesian marriage exchange: money. Regardless of the reason for this avoidance, the result is the portrayal of a timeless and authentic Melanesia, and its publication in *Annual Review* inevitably tends to define this portrayal as authoritative. The other paper is Colin Filer's (1985) analysis of letters to the editor in Papua New Guinea's main newspaper, the *Post-Courier*. Filer's paper is the mirror image of Strathern's. It portrays an inauthentic Melanesia, dealing precisely with the ways that many urban and rural people see marriage exchange as linked with money, and the ways that they generate definitions of both of these in the context of a range of issues and processes that are associated with money in contemporary Papua New Guinea: wage labor, remittance, urbanization, prostitution, and so on (see A. Carrier and J. Carrier 1991, conclusion). This presentation, however, is unlikely to have the influence of Strathern's paper, for it appeared in *Mankind*, a journal that is much less authoritative than *Annual Review*.

This brief example illustrates how the discipline's concern with authenticity tends to be self-reproducing. Anthropology tends to conceive of alien societies in terms of authenticity. As a consequence, works like Strathern's, that embody that conception, are more likely to be published by important journals or presses. Alternatively, works like Filer's, that do not embody that conception, are more likely to be published in less important places. Anthropologists trained on those publications will be socialized into that more authoritative conception, and so will be predisposed to reproduce it in their own publications. This process is hardly unique to anthropology, of course. It is merely one way that a dominant paradigm is maintained in an intellectual discipline, a necessary activity if the discipline is to progress in its ability to define, describe, and explain its subject matter (Kuhn 1970). Equally, the process is never perfectly efficient. Alternative conceptions do emerge and can become dominant; authoritative presentations can be forgotten and marginal ones elevated to paradigmatic status. In short, members of a discipline can change their minds.

Essentialization, or Dreamtime. This is the tendency to hypostasize the Other, to bestow upon the alien society a timeless concreteness, which indeed is one aspect of the construction of the notion of authenticity. As a part of this, anthropologists tend to see the societies they study in terms of states of being, rather than in terms of contingencies and historical processes. In other words, a consequence of constructing alien societies in essentialistic terms is the tendency to focus on the essence, and hence to see and represent the society or culture being studied in synchronic terms.

This essentialism is, of course, widely criticized as a key shortcoming of classic structural functionalism, but it is important to note its more subtle forms. A peculiar variant of it is manifest in debates about whether this or that earlier anthropologist Got It Right or, instead, Misunderstood. In Melanesia, this is most obvious in the cottage industry that reevaluates, using modern fieldwork, Malinowski's work in the Trobriands. Those who produce such reevaluations often make the Dreamtime assumption that the aspects of life that concern them did not change between World War I, Malinowski's time in the field, and whenever they did their own fieldwork. This is as problematic as criticizing an early twentieth-century analysis of gender relations in American society, for example, on the basis of research in the 1970s.

Essentialization occurs more visibly when researchers treat colonization as a kind of ontic rupture that ends the village's old, authentic, static state, and reconstitutes it in a new, inauthentic, and often equally static form— a view that some villagers seem to hold as well (see J. Carrier 1987). The essentialism of this view is most apparent when a researcher seeks to elicit and describe traces of the old state in order to recover the stable precolonial order, just as an earlier, evolutionist anthropologist might seek "survivals" to uncover a society's primordial state (Kuper 1988).[10]

This synchronic essentialism occurs as well, albeit less obviously, when researchers transmute local understandings of the past into manifestations of timeless social structure or timeless cultural values and categories, as well as when they subsume change under stasis. That is, when they treat change in terms of endlessly repeating cycles or oscillations, such as are contained in the time of structural cycles: life cycles, exchange cycles, domestic cycles, cycles of social reproduction. The changes are subordinated to the theoretical constructs that define these essentialist cycles, and they need bear no relation to the actual course of events (this is discussed in A. Carrier and J. Carrier 1987). In fact, it seems plausible that the very notion of the Society and Culture of the x is likely to carry with it a synchronic air.

At a more concrete level, the tendency to essentialization can produce in anthropologists an unwillingness to focus on aspects of society that are recent innovations, under the assumption that because they have not been present for a very long time, they must be transient and illegitimate, inauthentic. This view of legitimacy as longevity produces an inevitable bias among anthropologists in Melanesia, an area that has experienced extensive Western influence for a relatively short and recent period of time. Because the relatively new is the relatively inauthentic, there is pressure to treat as illegitimate those things associated with colonial administration or the emerging national state. Thus, the conventional anthropological approach is likely to result in a double predisposition to slight the effects of Western impact. Not only does their Western taint make them inauthentic, but the fact that the effects of this impact are recent also means that they are inauthentic.

In identifying this trait as a focus of criticism, I am not arguing that we can do away with essentialization. Instead, I accept Kenneth Burke's Kantian view that essentialization "is a form of the mind (or, in my narrow usage, an inevitable aspect of linguistic placement)" (quoted in Holland 1959, 36). It would be foolish to expect researchers to be wholly open to all that they perceive, and wholly naive to be dismayed to find that description, much less analysis, entails essentialization of one sort or another. Equally, it is certain that many of the people that anthropologists study essentialize themselves, as do people in the societies that produce anthropologists (e.g., Schneider 1979). Thus, criticizing someone purely for essentializing something is missing the point. Instead, the questions that ought to be asked need to deal with the consequences of different essentializations. Do they mislead or obfuscate rather than help and reveal? And perhaps more importantly, have we so reified our essentializations that we forget that they are *our* essentializations and mistakenly take them as real? For many critics, the old anthropological essentialism has become too reified and is no longer helpful and revealing.

Isolationism and Passivism. These are variants of each other, isolationism being the stronger of the two. Isolationism is the tendency to put a conceptual *cordon sanitaire* between Us and Them, and it follows in part from the desire for authenticity and the essentialization of the alien society. This *cordon sanitaire*, intended perhaps to mark off clearly the village society being studied, has the effect of making it difficult to think in terms of generative interaction between the alien village and the more familiar outside and Westernized world. This isolationism can be a subtle and pervasive aspect of conventional anthropology.

The weaker form of isolationism, passivism, is found even among anthropologists who are concerned with contact between Western and village society. This appears in the tendency on the part of many of those anthropologists to focus on the ways that contact leads to acculturation, Westernization, or the other ways that We displace Them by turning them into Us (Modernization: they become like us), or just a part of Us (Underdevelopment: they become like our proletariat). In other words, We impose ourselves on Them, and they accept that imposition. There may be resistance to this imposition, but this is simply a passive resistance, a surly withdrawal, not a creative process or interaction. In these cases, the passivist orientation is evident in the focus on displacement and the failure to see any real interaction.

Unidimensionality. This is the tendency to see Us and Them as all there is in the universe of study, as defining the two poles of the dimension that contains all possible states of the alien society being studied. Given this view, any change that follows Western contact and influence can only be Us-ification, a movement from the Them pole along the path toward the Us pole. Unidimensionality thus resembles the old discredited models of unilinear evolution produced by nineteenth century anthropologists and sociologists (Kuper 1988, esp. chap. 1).

Acceptance of unidimensionalism makes it difficult to grasp the idea that

They can change without becoming some variant of Us, which helps explain why anthropological theories of change are rarely more sophisticated than those of acculturation or Westernization. Unidimensionality, together with passivism, is manifest in common understandings of cargo cults in Melanesia. These tend to be seen either as reactive reassertions of a precontact order or as acculturative attempts to become like the colonizers. Relatively rarely are they seen as attempts to appropriate and transform elements of colonial and village life to generate new syntheses.

This unidimensionality is erroneous because societies can be exposed to Western influence and can change without becoming simply Westernized: modernized or underdeveloped. Because of their simplistic approach to change, those who accept unidimensionalism are predisposed to associate the alien with the untouched. After all, unidimensionality assumes that any change brought about by Western contact and influence leads to Westernization. Therefore, the fallacious reasoning goes, the absence of Westernization proves the absence of significant contact. The risk to which this exposes conventional anthropologists is what Pierre Bourdieu (1977) calls misrecognition. Unidimensionalist anthropologists look at the less self-evident consequences of Western influence as they are manifest in the society and culture being studied, but they see them as elements of traditional, alien, and non-Western social life. This masks the consequences of Western influence, and so strengthens the lure of unidimensionality.[11]

Mirroring.   This is the tendency to read Them in terms of Us, and to some degree it follows from the argument about unidimensionality. After all, that implies the tendency to define the two poles of the single dimension as opposites of each other. And as a practical matter, the imbalance in power between the West and the village means that the potential symmetry between the two poles is not likely to be realized. Instead, the Western pole will be taken as the point of reference, with the alien pole defined in terms of it, so that the alien society will end up being our "own society . . . seen in a distorting mirror" (Kuper 1988, 5). As Roy Pearce (1965, 232) put it, summarizing early American writings on North American Indians, "It turned out, as it had to, that what Indians signified was not what they were, but what Americans should not be. Americans were only talking to themselves about themselves." This process is complicated somewhat by the fact that defining Them as "opposite" of Us allows more than one possible construction of Them. For example, mirroring can involve seeing Them as a sort of proto-Us, in which case We are thereby naturalized and to some degree universalized. However, it can involve seeing Them as a sort of anti-Us, in which case We can be rendered partial and contingent, and to some degree artificial and illegitimate. In each instance, however, They are seen in terms of Us, and not in their own terms.

To understand this process of mirroring adequately it would be necessary to investigate a topic as interesting as the Orientalizing of village societies. That is the way that anthropologists Occidentalize the West, the way that they frequently and unreflectively invoke a naive, essentialist notion of their own societies (this process is pursued in J. Carrier n.d. and illustrated in Gewertz 1990). This Occidentalizing is less visible than Orientalizing, because usually anthropologists write explicitly only about their field sites. Often, however, it is striking in the implicit and oral renderings of Western industrial capitalism by anthropologists, which at times are so simplistic that anyone making comparably naive and stereotyped statements about a Melanesian society would be drummed out of the discipline.[12]

Like every other intellectual endeavor, anthropology involves the attempt to make sense of the object of study. As such, anthropologists necessarily impose their own interests and orientations on village life. In spite of the occasional shock with which anthropologists are charged with something other than pure and lucid descriptivism, and in spite of the belief of many Melanesians that anthropology consists of little more than being told and writing down a village's story, anthropology is not the undigested representation of the sensory impressions that impinge on the fieldworker. After all, the discipline is made of practitioners seeking to make sense of aspects of village life, which means interpreting those aspects to themselves and to their colleagues, whether in terms of positivist laws of social organization or interpretative frames of coherence and meaning. In this sense, mirroring is, like many other parts of this critique, an unavoidable aspect of anthropology, for "making sense" unavoidably means rendering the experiences and observations of fieldwork in familiar language and in terms of familiar concerns and interests. Perhaps what James Clifford (1986b) calls "ethnographic allegory" is better called "inevitable allegory."

To attempt to avoid this altogether is to attempt to see the object of study purely in its own terms. Not only is such positivism impossible in practice, it is pointless because it strips away the motivation to do research. Adam Kuper (1988, 148), for instance, suggests that Boas's critique of evolutionism, successful as critique, failed ultimately as anthropology for just this reason: "Yet the very triumph of the Boasian critique left it vulnerable to the charge that it was merely destructive and that it offered no positive new theory to replace the old orthodoxy." The same can be said of New Model Anthropology. Its concern with the complexities of rhetoric and representation easily becomes a withdrawal from engagement with and efforts to understand the lives and societies that anthropologists have claimed for their focus. The discipline becomes so self-referential that the sorts of issues addressed in this collection become meaningless. The discipline merely parasitizes villagers in order to provide the real object of interest, ethnographic text. But there is no motive to go and do the research that results in the production of these texts. For these reasons and others, it seems unlikely that any discipline can totally avoid subordinating its object to its theoretical interests.

Moreover, it is not clear that there is anything inevitably wrong with imposing ourselves on what we study. Certainly if we are to move beyond a simple reflectionist view of knowledge we must recognize that one of the purposes of intellectual activity is to answer questions. And *whose* questions are we to answer, after all, but *our* questions? Those are the only questions we have, and necessarily they will reflect our viewpoint and our position in the world. The problem arises when we attempt to argue, or even to assume, that the knowledge we produce is free of this self-referential influence.[13]

BRINGING THE OUTSIDE IN[14]

The critics have charged that conventional anthropology is an essentialist anthropology whose practitioners are prone to look for and present authentically alien village societies. It follows that reorientating anthropology would involve breaking down this essentialism. In broad terms, it would involve recognizing the ways that the society that an anthropologist may study is not an alien essential being waiting to be revealed and described, but is instead a consequence of influences and processes at work outside the present place and time—a place that is both the physical place of the village and the conceptual place of reified, essentialized village society; a time that is both the present of the ethnographer's experience and the conceptual time of the far away and long ago. We need to understand how these outside influences and processes affect the societies we study and the events we see, and in that understanding we will be better able to see and make sense of the ethnographic world we confront, just as we will be better able to address the theoretical issues that concern us.

The papers in this collection show, in their different ways, the nature of that essentialism and what such a reorientation might entail. In this section I will describe only briefly what seems to me to be the most straightforward route to reorientation, the strengthening of a concern with history in Melanesian anthropology.[15] Edmund Leach's (1989, 141) criticism is appropriate: "Why should anthropologists take it for granted that history never repeats itself but persuade themselves that, if left alone, ethnographic cultures never do anything else?" However, I want to extend "history" to mean not just the history of those we study but also anthropology's history. Each history allows us to relativize the present that we confront when we are in the field and that we inhabit as members of our discipline, and allows us to see how the present that we inhabit shapes the ways that we perceive and render the present that we confront.

The sort of linear history punctuated by events that I refer to is, of course, itself problematic, a creature of specific social situations (see J. Carrier 1987).

However, my purpose here is not to engage in historiographic debate, nor is it to prescribe history as a panacea. Instead, I mean to suggest that it can be useful for the task at hand, being a powerful lever for prying open the sealed units that are an essentialized village society and an unreflective anthropology. Certainly the historical approach has pitfalls of its own, including its own variety of essentialization: unthinking historicism. The defense against these pitfalls is not the abandonment of history but its judicious invocation.

The Present We Confront

Conventional anthropology presupposes a village society that, like Said's Orient, is in dreamtime, always there and always the same. It presupposes a world of custom and tradition. Recently, however, the very notion of traditional life and society, of the customary round, has become problematic in a way that is disruptive of conventional anthropology. Studies of the use of the concept of custom in Melanesian societies (e.g., Keesing and Tonkinson 1982), like similar studies concerned with other parts of the world (e.g., Gill 1983; Hobsbawm and Ranger 1983), raise questions about the notion of traditional society. They do not only show that what appears customary may be much more recent than it would seem at first glance. They show as well that tradition itself is often a politically charged notion, a resource that can be manipulated by competing groups in society in their dealings with one another, with the outside world or with the anthropologist. Hence it is something that is likely to require an historical and social subscript. These studies should make anthropologists uneasy about stalking what has been for many the core concern of study, traditional social life. And what is probably of greater significance, they raise questions about the very existence of a set of people, relationships, and practices sufficiently stable to justify being called "a society." After all, if what the people of x village do turns out to be historically fluid, malleable, then what are we to understand by the notion of x society or x culture? These notions may be useful mnemonics, but as I have argued previously in this Introduction, it is wrong to assume that they have an ontic status that is independent of and prior to the researchers who present them and the discipline that validates them.

Authenticity, essentialism, and their attendant tendencies are likely to be made problematic not just by historical studies of the emergence and use of custom and tradition, but by attention to history more generally. Radcliffe-Brown's assertion (e.g., 1952, 3) that accessible historical evidence was lacking for most of the societies that anthropologists study was broadly correct for many of the societies that concerned anthropologists in the early part of this century. (A more dispassionate discussion of why Radcliffe-Brown rejected history, and what this rejection entailed, is in Thomas [1989, 18–24]). However much researchers may have wanted to take a historical approach, data were lacking and it would not do to fabricate historical sequences in the conjectural way that he criticized, sequences that were as much ahistorical as is conceptual time. With the passage of time, however, an antihistorical or nonhistorical approach has become less reasonable. For one thing, that very passage of time has meant that the period for which historical evidence exists has been increasing: every year, another year's worth of historical records and raw materials is being produced.[16] Also important, however, has been the fact that historians themselves have been taking increasing interest in the history of Western expansion and colonization, and so have made that history increasingly accessible to those who are not themselves historians. In Melanesia this has appeared as the increasing interest in Pacific history.

With the increasing availability of historical evidence, it has become possible to question the degree to which the authentic, essential societies that anthropologists study really are what they seem to be: alien Others. It seems likely that a growth in the use of historical information will end up breaking down anthropological essentialism by showing in what ways village societies, seemingly pristine, have been shaped by their contact with the intruding outside world. Eric Wolf's *Europe and the People without History* is probably the most influential work in this regard. Ultimately, of course, this will challenge the very idea that there are authentic, alien societies in the way that many critics assert that anthropologists presently seem to think of them, and thus this will raise questions about just what it is that anthropologists ought to study.

The Present We Inhabit

With the passage of time has come a growing body of Melanesian ethnography. But this body contains not just an expanding record of Melanesian societies, it contains as well a record of past issues within the discipline and past conceptions of what those societies are like.[17] Just as anthropological essentialism shapes what ethnographers see and write, so the succession of topics that have moved through the discipline leave their mark. Approaching anthropological texts in terms of theme and chronology, rather than in terms of geographic subarea, helps reveal how disciplinary fashion shapes ethnographic presentation. With the passage of time, then, not only has it become possible to gain increasing historical information about the societies we study, but it has become possible to gain increasing historical information about our understanding of those societies. Not only is it easier to put an historical subscript on the world we study, it is easier to put an historical subscript on our studies.

In making this point I am not referring to the way that the passage of time provides us with the opportunity to produce a verdict, however tentative, on anthropological theories and predictions, though it is nice to have this opportunity. Rather, I am referring to the fact that the passage of time allows anthropologists to approach their discipline's work more dispassionately.

Theories and concepts advanced in the discipline's past with great fervor as self-evident truths existing in the data in the past are likely to excite less passion in the present, and on reflection may appear to be more problematic, or even unsatisfactory impositions on, or partial renderings of, the data. Thus, the passage of time makes it easier for anthropologists to be self-aware, to see the ways that their theories and representations of Melanesian villages change with the passage of the seasons in the West, rather than just with the changing circumstances of Melanesia. By allowing us to relativize our own conception of the alien people and societies that we study, this history will also help allow us to see in what ways the discipline's essentialist conception is faulty.

ABOUT THE COLLECTION

The papers in this collection illustrate the dimensions of a reorientation of anthropology in different ways. Their geographical focus ranges throughout Melanesia and even beyond; their temporal focus ranges from the beginnings of colonial penetration to the present; their topical focus ranges from literature through ethnography to anthropological theory. This breadth is appropriate. For one thing, the essentialism that these papers seek to criticize and displace has extensive bases and ramifications that resist narrow treatment. For another, a range of papers helps us to avoid a common failing of critiques of anthropology, a critical scrutiny of existing works coupled with an absence of positive examples of how we might do things differently. We should not, after all, forget Thomas Kuhn's by-now-venerable observation in *The Structure of Scientific Revolutions* that criticism that is fruitful goes beyond mere complaint: it contains as well positive statements and concrete examples of an alternative.

As the concrete examples in this collection will show, this reorientation is much less radical and dogmatic than that proposed by some of the recent destructive criticisms of anthropology as a discipline or as a method of investigation. Anthropology has been bombarded by these over the past decade, each part of a new criticism, many of which seem intended to destroy the discipline, either directly or, more coyly, by insisting that we recognize that destruction has taken place already. Thus, this collection is not intended as the notification of the demise of anthropology. Neither is it the programmatic statement of a new theoretical position on the nature of the discipline and its knowledge or on the nature of Melanesian societies. Such statements are almost certain to be premature if they are developed in the absence of extensive scholarly work that embodies, tests, and shapes the emerging approach. The papers in this collection are only a start toward such a body of work, so that we must leave it to the theorists to draw whatever theoretical conclusions they may.

Instead, the purpose here is more modest and reconstructive. This Introduction and these papers are intended as examples of how anthropologists can be more careful about thinking about the societies they study, and so help them avoid some of the errors of the past. Moreover, this collection is not intended to herald a radically new approach to the study of Melanesian societies. The criticisms of anthropology that I have described in this Introduction are, as I have noted from time to time, in no way applicable to all anthropologists all the time. It is not my intention to paint all previous anthropology or all previous anthropologists in the same color of inadequacy. Regard for the work of others, past and present, not only recognizes the contribution of different anthropologists to the task of increasing our knowledge of Melanesian societies, it also helps us avoid the error of thinking that we have invented the wheel. Here I can only allude to the body of this work by mentioning some of it; but while an adequate description of it would have to be voluminous, my point is that an adequate description of its recognition by and impact on core regional scholarship could, sadly, be brief. Classic studies such as Cyril Belshaw's *The Great Village*, A. L. Epstein's *Matupit*, Peter Lawrence's *Road Belong Cargo*, and Richard Salisbury's *Vunamami*, as well as the more recent work of anthropologists like Andrew Strathern (e.g., 1982, 1984) and Deborah Gewertz (e.g., 1983), to mention only some of the people who have worked in only one of the countries in the region, demonstrate that what this collection is intended to encourage is not an innovation but the greater attention to issues that have already been addressed in Melanesian anthropology.[18]

The Papers

The first two papers in this collection deal with a common problem: the ways that a failure to take careful account of the historical impact of colonization can lead people to form essentialist images of village societies, though they do so in different ways and in terms of different issues.

The first of the two is Margaret Jolly's "Banana Leaf Bundles and Skirts: A Pacific Penelope's Web?" She is concerned with the presentation and analysis in anthropology of women of the Trobriand Islands of Papua New Guinea, kula country. Her particular focus is Annette Weiner's influential discussion of banana leaf bundles: Trobriand women's wealth and the medium of special ceremonial exchange, especially in mortuary distributions. In these, according to Weiner, women exercise their control over the traditional Trobriand cosmological domain and so distinguish themselves from men, who control the traditional Trobriand social domain. Extending earlier critical discussions of Weiner's work (most notably, M. Strathern 1981a), Jolly argues that the analysis of women's ceremonial exchange needs to be undertaken with caution if one is to avoid the pitfall of essentializing women and the order of Trobriand society.

She points out that Weiner has succumbed to the idea of an unchanging Trobriand order. Though Weiner is aware of changes in the Trobriands in this century, brought about by colonization and Western influence, she sees these as minor markings on the skin of a body of social order and social practice that itself remains substantially the same. Jolly's criticism is pertinent, for Weiner's essentialist view allows her to treat women's wealth and women's exchange in terms of what she presents as the timeless essentials of Trobriand society and cosmology. Jolly points out that this ahistorical view is inadequate, because it ignores the fact that since the onset of colonization Trobriand women's wealth and women's exchanges have come to exist in a world that is larger than Trobriand society itself, a world that helps define the context in which these women fashion their wealth and carry out their exchanges. Using discussions of the emergence of women's exchange in the Highlands of Papua New Guinea, Jolly argues that it is important to see that Trobriand women's wealth draws its meaning from more than just its relationship to men's wealth and exchange, the focus of Weiner's inward-looking analysis. In addition, it is a vehicle for defining and expressing indigenous views of traditional life, and so it draws its meaning from its relationship to the world that lies beyond the Trobriands. Thus, Jolly argues that placing Trobriand women in their proper modern context allows us to see that there is much more at issue than the balance and conflict between women and their cosmological domain, and men and their social domain.

The second of this pair of papers concerned with essentialism is Nicholas Thomas's "Substantivization and Anthropological Discourse: The Transformation of Practices into Institutions in Neotraditional Pacific Societies." While Jolly is concerned with how Western academics impose an essentialist image on alien society, Thomas is concerned with indigenous essentialism, which can feed into anthropology if the fieldworker adopts those indigenous concerns and preoccupations uncritically, and so recreates them and their distortions in the study and representation of village life. This essentialism is the way that village people select or fix on certain practices and ideas as characterizing their own lives, an essentialization that can be as partial and as fertile as anthropological essentialization, though springing from very different contexts and concerns. As Thomas points out, in thus picking out certain practices as key to or characteristic of their society, villagers are not in fact identifying themselves in the abstract, in isolation. Instead, like anthropological essentialism, they are likely to be essentializing those practices that define an opposition between Western and indigenous life. This opposition can be a basic element of the creation of a village society's identity in the new field in which it exists, one that includes Western colonization.

Thomas illustrates this with an analysis of three groups: the Wamira people of Papua New Guinea, indigenous Hawaiians, but especially Fijians and their practice of *kerekere*, an ethic of sharing and informal exchange. He argues that while something like it may have existed long before Western contact, kerekere was not taken to be a central Fijian institution until late in the nineteenth century. Thomas then goes on to reject the idea that this is simply a further case of the invention of tradition in the Pacific. He does so by arguing that such a perspective tends to root the institutions that it defines as neotraditional primarily in terms of indigenous society, tends to explain the appearance of those elements only in terms of the structure and processes of indigenous life. He says this perspective ignores the ways that the impact of colonization itself leads some aspects of indigenous life, such as kerekere, rather than others to be singled out for special attention and special meaning, both by indigenous villagers themselves and their Western colonizers.

Thus, Thomas is making the same general point as Jolly. That is, it may be that the importance of practices and customs that come to be markers of a particular way of life cannot be explained without understanding the colonial history that elevated them to salience and the social processes that lead villagers to construct themselves and their societies partly in opposition to what they see of, and how they interpret, the Western world that impinges upon them. One consequence of this argument is that studies of cultural systems, ethos, discourse, and the like, studies that rely on key images, metaphors, and interests in village life, must consider the facts of colonization, for these are likely to shape what it is that becomes key. The study of village culture must incorporate the study of colonial history if it is not to reproduce the essentialistic timelessness that dogs anthropology.

The next paper is concerned with the ways that history can, and can not, be used to avoid the problems of conventional anthropology. It is Bronwen Douglas's "Doing Ethnographic History: The Case of Fighting in New Caledonia." This paper is particularly pertinent because it is written by a Pacific historian rather than an anthropologist, and hence is written by someone who is aware, as anthropologists tend not to be, of the problematic nature of the "history" that has been so glibly invoked in this Introduction. The somewhat disheartening point this paper makes is that if anthropologists want to avail themselves of history—either by rifling published works or doing their own research—they need to be wary of just the sort of shortcomings that have been identified in conventional anthropology.

Douglas helps explain this point by warning us of the danger of the causal approach to history, and her warning is an important qualification to the stress on the impact of colonization that appears throughout this collection. The causal approach is one with which we are most comfortable: we know how history came out, we know what the big forces and changes at play were, therefore we have a ready-made framework at hand to make sense of the past. Unfortunately, Douglas reminds us, this causal approach can impose a unidimensionality that is likely to hide more than it reveals. The people who acted in the events in the past that might interest us, that might help explain how the societies we study in the present came to be as they are—these people did not know what the big forces and changes at play were because they had not read to the end of the book, they did not know how it was all going to come out.

Douglas addresses this issue through the analysis of descriptions of fighting in New Caledonia in the nineteenth century. Conventionally this fighting is understood primarily in terms of the encroaching French power in the region. Government officers, missionaries, later anthropologists, and modern Kanak advocates identify that fighting as response, reaction, resistance, rebellion—always orbiting around French colonialism. However, such a rendering presupposes the outcome of French encroachment and French assertions of power, which may have clear meaning in the present but which were much more tentative, fluid at the time. Thus, Douglas shows that the Melanesians in the fray frequently were responding to a very different array of issues and concerns. The French colonial presence was not the massive, self-evident new force at work that later commentators took it to be. Instead, people saw it more ambiguously and interpreted it in terms of concerns that were more local. They allied with the French against each other or allied with each other against the French in their own time and for their own reasons. In making this point, Douglas cautions us. The present that we see in our research may be rooted in the past, but that past should be understood in its own terms, it should not be subordinated to the present that it brought about.

The next three papers in this collection, my own and those by John Barker and Roger Keesing, share an important concern: how anthropologists construct village societies as relatively authentic, untouched by contact with Western influences. The papers do so by looking at different topics within anthropology: articulation, religion, big men under colonization.

My paper, "Approaches to Articulation," looks at the ways anthropologists have tried, over the past few decades, to deal with the issue of articulation, the relationship between traditional village societies and the West. Attention to approaches to articulation is important for understanding the anthropological construction of alien societies, for it is in dealing with articulation that anthropologists most directly confront and construct the separation between, and relationship of, Us and Them, an area that is a key focus of the critique of conventional anthropology.

The paper begins by looking at the changing predictions that some anthropologists have made about the impact of Western contact on villages in Papua New Guinea. It shows that an initial pessimism was replaced by the optimistic view that village societies were more resilient than was thought by the earlier pessimists. However, it appears as though this optimism was based on a highly selective unidimensionalist view of tradition and the impact of the West, one that took the absence of overt signs of Westernization as evidence of the persistence of precolonial social forms. I then look at three influential programmatic statements about articulation that appeared at about the same time that ethnographers were becoming more optimistic: Claude Meillassoux's *Maidens, Meal and Money*, and two works dealing specifically with Papua New Guinea, Peter Fitzpatrick's *Law and State in Papua New Guinea* and Chris Gregory's *Gifts and Commodities*. Briefly, I argue that these statements, explicitly concerned to describe links between traditional and Western realms, adopted, reproduced, and reinforced a highly unidimensionalist view of Western influence. I argue that they did so because they denied, either directly or by their silence, that village societies are capable of generative interaction with Western influences. In the paper I then demonstrate the nature of such a generative interaction by describing the impact of colonization on the Admiralty Islands, and especially Ponam Island. Looking particularly at the realm of kinship and exchange, I show that colonization and the spread of the national monetary economy in Papua New Guinea brought profound changes, but that the result is no more recognizably Western than the older order.

The second of these papers is "Christianity in Western Melanesian Ethnography," by John Barker. Barker directly confronts the problem of the desire for authenticity among anthropologists and the ways that this affects their perceptions and representations of the people they study. He does so by questioning the anthropological understanding of Christian religion in Papua New Guinea. As he notes, anthropologists generally have denied legitimacy to Christianity, assuming that Christian villagers are not "real natives" and hence are incapable of supporting serious ethnography, which reduces Christian Melanesians to silence and Christian institutions, beliefs, ideas, and symbols in Melanesia to invisibility. In his paper he points out the inadequacy of this approach and the tangles into which it leads scholars. Thus, for example, he shows that anthropologists have conceived of Christianity unidimensionally, in terms of a dyadic opposition between missionary and villager that can have only three outcomes: conversion, and the destruction of indigenous religion; rejection, and the maintenance of indigenous religion; or syncretism, a blending of the two in a sort of evolutionary middle stage. This viewpoint preserves the essentialization of pagan indigenous societies by allowing anthropologists to treat Christianity as an inauthentic overlay that needs to be recognized primarily in order that it may be stripped away. There is no creative, complex interaction between indigenous and Christian religion.

Barker says it is important to orient our thinking away from our old categories of pagan versus Christian, Melanesian versus Western, and authentic versus inauthentic. Instead, we need to look anew at the totality of people's religious concerns and practices, things that do not reflect these rigid dichotomies but instead change over the course of people's lives and their societies' histories. And we need to see how Christianity appears in these concerns and practices, just as we need to see how more indigenous religious elements appear. Further, Barker argues that these Christian and indigenous elements will not appear as totalities that can be used to essentialize a people's religion. Instead, they will mix and interpenetrate in different ways as each is modified or interpreted in terms of the other, and they will coexist within the same culture as each is used to address different concerns. In short, God, gods, ghosts, and men in Melanesia need to be approached as aspects of people's lives. As those lives transcend the simple distinctions between village and West, pagan and Christian, so the use people make of the religious elements that surround them also transcends those simple distinctions.

The last of this trio of papers is Roger Keesing's "Kwaisulia as Culture Hero." While my paper and Barker's analyzed anthropology to describe the shortcomings of the discipline's constructions of authentic Melanesian societies, Keesing demonstrates the shortcomings by presenting the history of Kwaisulia, a big man from Malaita, in the Solomon Islands. Briefly, Kwaisulia rose to prominence at the end of the nineteenth century as a village headman and colonial government agent. Although Europeans called him a chief, he was not descended from chiefs, and his power appears to have had no real basis in traditional social structure. Instead, he worked his way into a series of positions of power and authority which depended on relations with the growing colonial apparatus. Thus, building on his own experience as a migrant worker in Queensland, he became a passage master in the labor trade. This gave him control of significant amounts of European wealth, which he was able to use to establish his own political faction. This gave him control over a substantial geographical area and consequently made him a useful ally for the British Protectorate administration. Although some of his private dealings angered the British, he remained powerful to the day, in 1909, when he accidentally blew himself up while dynamiting fish.

Keesing says that anthropologists generally are reluctant to deal with figures like Kwaisulia. This man, after all, laid no valid claim to traditional bases of power; neither did he conform to the standard model of the Melanesian big man, for he did not generate his power through the adroit manipulation of indigenous resources and relations. No chief or big man, Kwaisulia and leaders like him pass through the anthropological net: they are not anthropologically legitimate, but they straddle the two worlds that are worlds apart. Kwaisulia based his power on his ability to interpose himself between colonizers and villagers, and in fact this is the way that present-day Lau speakers remember him.

Keesing argues that the failure on the part of anthropologists to recognize and attend to those who, like Kwaisulia, draw their strength precisely from the untraditional and illegitimate mixture of the village and the West, means that they find it that much harder to understand the nature of political power in the societies that they study. Moreover, he suggests that in failing to attend to the ways that village power is linked to changing external circumstance, they expose themselves to the risk that they will misperceive and misrecognize the sorts of power that they do study, treating as traditional and indigenous what was shaped by the growing colonial presence and the ability of indigenous leaders to manipulate that presence to serve their own ends.

The final paper in this collection is the least conventional, for on its face it is not about anthropology. It is "Gone Native in Isles of Illusion: In Search of Asterisk in Epi," by Michael Young. In this paper, Young looks at *Isles of Illusion*, a book about the South Seas that came out in England in 1923. This was a collection of letters written by Robert Fletcher, an Englishman who spent several years in Melanesia, to his friend Bohun Lynch, who edited and published them under the pseudonym of "Asterisk" without Fletcher's knowledge. The book was popular in England, was reprinted there, and was translated into French, attracting favorable attention among Parisian intellectuals and anthropologists.

Isles of Illusion (and its successor, *Gone Native*, a popular piece of fiction that Fletcher wrote after he returned to England) is appropriate as a topic to end this collection, for Fletcher experienced earlier and more intensely the ambiguities and dilemmas that confront Western anthropologists in Melanesia, and the letters he wrote express earlier and more intensely the essentialization of indigenous life and the chasm between Westerner and Villager that, the critics argue, has been a feature of Melanesian ethnography.

Fletcher saw the life he led as a plantation manager on Epi, in the New Hebrides, as being on the border between two worlds that were worlds apart. One was Europe, a world he had already rejected, as he rejected its local manifestation in the colonial establishment of government officials, missionaries, and entrepreneurs. The other was the village, a world he also rejected. Even though he married a village woman and fathered her child, she and her world were the land of lotus for Fletcher, a life that attracted him but was too alien to his own to be a world he could inhabit. And he reserved his greatest scorn for the half-castes, the métis, who seemed to him impossible beings devoid of the virtues of either side of their inheritance. Even his own half-caste child could not hold him in Epi. Though clearly Fletcher loved him, the boy was too much of the lotus to offer the satisfaction of a true child to his father. Instead, he was only part of an interlude, ultimately rejected by Fletcher, who returned to England and stayed single until he died.

In describing Fletcher's work, Young describes the anthropologist's plight: standing uneasily between the Village and the West. And he describes as well the anthropologist's response: a construction of the reified, essentialized worlds of Us and Them, worlds that do not mingle in any but the most distasteful ways. Fletcher's letters and his subsequent writing allow us to see how one man experienced and reflected upon his precarious position, and allow us to see one of the works that shaped English understanding of Melanesia in the early part of this century. And Young's reflection on the reasons he was so attracted to *Isles of Illusion* helps explain how anthropologists at work in the field, separated from the world of friends and colleagues that awaits their return, try to reconstruct themselves and their work in the light of those who have "gone native" before them.

In their "Epilogue," Roger Keesing and Margaret Jolly explore the prospects and problems of some of the different ways that, the critics of conventional anthropology have suggested, can be used to extricate the discipline from the impasse in which it finds itself.

Like Michael Young, Keesing and Jolly were drawn to the exotica of Melanesia, for they sought to discover an authentic alien society. They ask why they carried this essentialistic view with them into the field and why they were tempted to use it to filter what they saw when they arrived. The answer they propose is a simple one: because that is what they had learned. The textual criticisms of New Model Anthropology are largely correct. Melanesian anthropology has generally (though certainly not always) elided the social and historical contingencies that the fieldworker confronts, instead presenting an abstracted, essentialist construction of a timeless and self-contained alien village society. Those who are inducted into the discipline learn what Melanesia is like through the filter of the classic texts, and so absorb their biases. However, while Keesing and Jolly see the problem as one that is embodied in anthropological texts, they are cautious about the textual solutions that many critics have proposed.

They look at three proposed solutions: the use of self-accounts or life-histories of villagers, a greater reliance on the use of history to understand and present village societies, a more adequate rendering of the disjunctures and uncertainties of fieldwork and village life. However, they note that these can offer no proof against the essentialist vision. Instead, they may even make that vision more pervasive, for each tactic only *seems* to remove a layer of authorial intervention in, and hence disciplinary control over, the representation of village life. Self-accounts, historical sources, even a sense of discontinuity, do not appear unbidden in the text. They need to be elicited, translated, edited—made relevant to the fieldworker's purposes, investigations, analyses, and writings.

In other words, and against some of the critics of conventional anthropology, they warn us that our perception of authoritative essentialization in anthropological texts is correct, but that the problem can not be resolved at the level of the text. Instead, it must be addressed more generally, in the ways that anthropologists conceive Melanesian societies, and more generally yet, in the political and social framework in which Melanesian anthropology exists.

Each paper in this collection, like this Introduction, deals with the ways anthropologists go about their business in Melanesia. However, if the criticisms and suggestions made are to be more than philosophical or idealized statements cast only in generalities, they must attend to more than just how that business is gone about—as in fact they do. In making their criticisms and suggestions, most of the contributors juxtapose an existing presentation of Melanesian lives and societies with an alternative. It is only in doing so that they can move beyond simple criticism to the proposing of alternative approaches to the study of Melanesian societies.

Inevitably, then, these papers are ethnographic to a degree, though none really fits the standard model of the ethnographic report. And just as inevitably, the criticisms and suggestions that they make depend to a degree on their ethnographic basis, and particularly the degree to which Western impact has affected life in the various parts of Melanesia that the papers describe. It thus becomes pertinent to ask how typical are the sorts of colonial and postcolonial intrusions and consequences to which so many of these papers refer. The short answer is that ethnographers need to assume they are there in all circumstances, for this is the surest way to assure that ethnographers will look for them carefully.

This does not mean, of course, that these intrusions and consequences will be of equal strength everywhere, or that the mechanisms that transmit, and the practices that reflect, those intrusions will be the same everywhere. There are regions in the Highlands of Papua New Guinea that have been under government control for only a few decades, in contrast to regions of coastal and island Melanesia which have had extensive contact for much more than a century. Societies in these different regions will have experienced those intrusions and will manifest those consequences differently. Equally, there are societies in Melanesia that have been relatively isolated from their neighbors, relatively self-contained, while there are other societies that have long depended on extensive interaction with neighboring societies in local and regional integrating networks. Societies of these different sorts will have experienced those intrusions and will manifest those consequences differently. Likewise, societies differ in their histories of Western intrusion: some have met with intense missionary activity, some have met with intense labor recruiting, some have met with intense plantation activity. Societies differ in their own internal states at the onset of intrusion: some were more hierarchical, some more fluid, some more oriented toward trade and exchange, some more oriented to cosmology. And so on. This list could be extended to cover as many variables as one likes.

But however long the list, the points it makes are relatively straightforward. There is no reason to assume that there is a uniform Western impact in Melanesia, that all societies experience and deal with Western intrusion in the same ways. What is described for particular societies in these papers needs to be taken to be as particular as those societies. But at the same time, there is even less reason to assume that one can make sense of the societies that we study in Melanesia without attending to that intrusion and its consequences. Thus, what occurred in the particular societies described in these papers needs to be taken as particular instances of more general processes.

And as these papers show, these processes of intrusion and reaction challenge the timeless essentialism that commonly colors anthropological renderings of the region, just as they challenge the common anthropological goal of uncovering the authentic Melanesian society.

NOTES

1. This Introduction was first written in London in the summer of 1987, and I thank Achsah Carrier for setting aside her preoccupation with her upcoming *viva voce* repeatedly to pay attention to my half-formed ideas. I also thank Eugene Ogan for bringing Clarke and Ogan (1973) to my attention, Donald Tuzin for bringing Pearce (1965) to my attention, and Fitz Poole for his close reading and comments. I have taken the phrase "New Model Anthropologist" from Colin Filer. The pressure of his teaching duties made it impossible for him to contribute to this volume, and it is poorer for his absence. Finally, I want to disavow the idea that the critical points made in this Introduction are particularly original. They have been expressed in different ways by anthropologists working inside and outside Melanesia, though I can refer to only a few of them in this Introduction. But while they are not original, they remain peripheral to much Melanesian ethnography, as is evident in the recent, ahistorical concern with gender and agency. This is the situation that this collection is intended to help change.

2. Indeed, this view encapsulates many of the ideas criticized in this Introduction. By stressing the idea that Melanesian societies are independent and self-contained units that can be juxtaposed only for purposes of comparison, this view diverts attention from the existence of links between societies and their broader social environment. But such links make problematic the idea that societies can be understood solely in terms of their internal states and processes, they raise the possibility that societies need to be situated in the regions of which they are a part, and they even suggest that in some areas and for some purposes regions rather than individual village societies may be the appropriate unit of analysis. Finally, attention to these links would help make researchers more sensitive to the ways that colonial impact on a village can be indirect, transmitted in transmuted form through the village's links to the region of which it is a part (a point made in Thomas 1991). Of course, a more regional perspective has been used by some anthropologists of Melanesia (e.g., Gewertz 1983; Harding 1967), and is most visible in work on the societies of Milne Bay Province (e.g., Damon and Wagner 1989; Leach and Leach 1983).

3. Orientalism is discussed and situated in Western thought briefly in Turner (1989). Said's formulation is criticized in Richardson (1990). Many of Said's general points, like many of the arguments made by Johannes Fabian, discussed later in this Introduction, were developed just after World War II by Roy Pearce in *Savagism and*

Civilization, a study of the portrayal of Indians in North America, especially in the last half of the eighteenth century and the first half of the nineteenth century.

4. Although this Introduction is concerned with the more subtle ways that what we know about alien societies shapes what we see and how we evaluate it, it is important to recognize that this can occur in more overt ways as well. Consider, for example, Adam Kuper's discussion (1988, chap. 5) of research in Australia by Fison and Howitt, and then by Spencer and Gillen, in the second half of the nineteenth century. In each case, the attention of the fieldworker (Howitt, and later Gillen) was directed by an academic anthropologist (Fison, and later Spencer), who was in turn guided by a metropolitan theorist (Morgan, and later Frazer). Kuper says (1988, 102), for example, that "Spencer was quite clear that a fieldworker required detailed guidance. Without such direction, he would simply miss what was of importance."

5. To anticipate a point made later in this Introduction, essentialization of some sort may be unavoidable, and not all essentializations are equally undesirable or unassailable. The power imbalance between Orient and Occident reduced the chance that Orientalist essentialism would be challenged by alternative constructions that could provide alternative interpretations or could fragment the monolithic construction of the Orient into a number of less encompassing images and typifications.

6. Joseph Llobera (1986) has criticized Mediterranean ethnography in terms similar to Said's criticism of Orientalists; see also the discussion of his criticism in *Critique of Anthropology* (Summer 1987). Related criticisms of Mediterranean ethnography are made by Michael Herzfeld (1987).

7. Although I have stressed the temporal distance in Fabian's *Time and the Other*, this coexists with spatial distance, and it is the pair that is important. This is apparent when temporal distance exists without spatial distance, a set of conditions that for many people defines their forebears. They may be good or evil, but they are not alien in the same way as those who are distant in both senses. Equally, Fabian's criticism draws its strength from the ways that anthropologists *use* spatio-temporal distance. That dual distance itself only predisposes one to certain evaluative forms of thought and representation, it does not require them. Some of the aspects and complexities of temporal distance are discussed by Kenneth Burke (1969, esp. 430–440) under the concept of the temporalizing of essence.

8. Pearce (1965, chap. 5) describes a similar process in writings about American Indians. An analogous process appears in Daniel Miller's story that research workers some years ago confronted old, unknown cloths of a peculiar style, "composed mainly of exuberant large blossoms with curvilinear stems, sometimes joined to trees which were no longer rooted to the earth." After trying to relate this style to the indigenous production of different Asian societies, they concluded that it was not the product of any Asian culture, but of Western conceptions of Asian culture. Early Indian indigenous designs

> were not . . . to the taste of the British at the time, who had developed a somewhat different image of Oriental peoples. The consumers' hints and suggestions, communicated over considerable distance and thereby often greatly distorted when realized by the manufacturers, resulted in changes in the cloth, which in turn prompted further comments. Gradually, through several cycles of modification and response, there emerged a style embodying an image of what the European consumers thought the Indian manufac-

turers ought to be making for themselves. This design has come to be known as the Oriental style. (Miller 1987, 123)

9. Maurice Bloch (1983, chap. 1) notes that Karl Marx, that arch worrier about the ill effects of capitalism, was interested in precapitalist societies for precisely this reason. Pearce (1965) describes a similar function in early renderings of American Indians.

10. This tendency is not peculiar to anthropologists. In *The Origins of English Individualism*, Alan Macfarlane complains that English historians validated their notion of a primordial, premodern communal and peasant system by finding traces of it in the period they study, traces that suggest it must have flourished only a century or two earlier. He says historians find such traces whether they are writing about the eighteenth or the fifteenth century.

11. In his Malinowski Lecture, "Anthropology and the Analysis of Ideology," Talal Asad made this point in a broader way, saying that anthropologists focus on a substantialist conception of a group and its culture, and so misrecognize the impact of the social and historical conditions that underlie and make possible the production of that culture.

12. Marilyn Strathern's *The Gender of the Gift* illustrates mirroring and the related processes of Orientalizing the village and Occidentalizing the West. An explicit theme of this difficult book is the juxtaposition of Them and Us. This juxtaposition entails casting "the distinctive nature of Melanesian sociality" (1988, 10) in a contrast with Western society, and it relies on the classic Maussian distinction between gift systems and commodity systems. To make this essentialistic juxtaposition she slights the question of the historical specificity and social partiality of gift relations in Melanesia (a point pursued in Thomas 1991, chaps. 1 and 2), just as she slights the question of the social partiality of commodity relations in the West (a point pursued in J. Carrier n.d. and Kopytoff 1986). She invokes these simplifications and distortions for theoretical purposes, while at the same time she denies, for example, "that 'Western' society . . . can be understood monolithically" (1988, 348; but cf. chap. 12). But these slightings necessarily call into question the adequacy of her representations of these social forms, and hence the adequacy of her conclusions. It is not yet clear whether the theoretical outcome justifies the simplifications and distortions.

13. Indeed, some of the advocates of self-referential New Model Anthropology have failed to apply their method to themselves, have failed to see that they too are answering questions that they pose themselves rather than more accurately or fearlessly recognizing the experience of fieldwork and ethnographic writing. This point has been made nicely by Frederick Errington and Deborah Gewertz (1987). More extended criticisms are by Richard Handler (1985) and Jonathan Spencer (1989).

14. Much of what is said in this section, and indeed in this Introduction more generally, is contained implicitly or explicitly in Moore (1987).

15. My discussion here is simplistic but not, I think, necessarily misleading. The complexities of history in anthropology that I omit are described by Thomas (1989). Further, in stressing history I do not mean to deny the insights that a more synchronic approach can yield, insights recently illustrated by Albert (1989) and defended explicitly by Heusch (1989).

16. The passage of time, unfortunately, makes decreasingly accessible the history that the written documents supplant. That is the history of societies before contact, a history that is denied by the essentializing view as surely as modern history is denied.

17. See, for example, the historical description of kinship theory in the region in A. Carrier (1984).

18. Bruce Knauft's more recent (1990) summary discussion of warfare in Melanesian anthropology shows how attention to the issues raised here can produce fruitful insights in the consideration of classic anthropological topics.

REFERENCES

Albert, Steven M. 1989. "Cultural Implication: Representing the Domain of *Devils* among the Lak." *Man* 24:273–289.

Asad, Talal, ed. 1973. *Anthropology and the Colonial Encounter*. London: Ithaca Press.

———. 1979. "Anthropology and the Analysis of Ideology." *Man* 14:607–627.

Asterisk [pseud. of Robert Fletcher]. 1923. *Isles of Illusion: Letters from the South Seas*. Ed. Bohun Lynch. London: Constable & Co.

———. 1925. *Gone Native: A Tale of the South Seas*. London: Constable & Co.

Barth, Fredrik. 1975. *Ritual and Knowledge among the Baktaman of New Guinea*. Oslo: Universitetsforlaget.

Batteau, Allen. 1982. "Mosbys and Broomsedge: The Semantics of Class in an Appalachian Kinship System." *American Ethnologist* 9:445–466.

Belshaw, Cyril. 1957. *The Great Village*. London: Routledge.

Bloch, Maurice. 1983. *Marxism and Anthropology*. Oxford: Clarendon Press.

———. 1988. "Interview with Maurice Bloch." Ed. Gustaaf Houtman. *Anthropology Today* 4(1):18–21.

Bourdieu, Pierre. 1977. *Outline of a Theory of Practice*. Cambridge: Cambridge University Press.

Boyd, David. 1989. "The Hagahai 'First Contact,' Incorporation and the Expansion of Moka Exchange." Presented at the American Anthropological Association Eighty-eighth Annual Meeting, Washington, D.C., November 15–19.

Burke, Kenneth. 1969 (1945). *A Grammar of Motives*. Berkeley, Los Angeles, London: University of California Press.

Carrier, Achsah H. 1984. "Structural and Processual Models in Oceanic Kinship Theory." *Research in Melanesia* 8:57–87.

Carrier, Achsah H., and James G. Carrier. 1987. "Brigadoon, or; Musical Comedy and the Persistence of Tradition in Melanesian Ethnography." *Oceania* 57:271–293.

———. 1991. *Structure and Process in a Melanesian Society: Ponam's Progress in the Twentieth Century*. London: Harwood.

Carrier, James G. 1987. "History and Self-Conception in Ponam Society." *Man* 22:111–131.

———. n.d. "Occidentalism: The World Turned Upside-Down." MS.

Cassia, Paul. 1982. "Property in Greek Cypriot Marriage Strategies: 1920–1980." *Man* 17:643–663.

Clarke, William C., and Eugene Ogan. 1973. "Assumptions and Alternatives: A Look at Recent Research by Social Scientists in Papua New Guinea." Pp. 264–290 in Joseph Fischer (ed.), *Foreign Values and Southeast Asian Scholarship*. (Research Monograph No. 11). Berkeley: University of California Center for South and Southeast Asian Studies.

Clifford, James. 1986a. "Introduction: Partial Truths." Pp. 1–26 in James Clifford and George Marcus (eds.), *Writing Culture: The Poetics and Politics of Ethnography*. Berkeley, Los Angeles, London: University of California Press.

———. 1986b. On Ethnographic Allegory. Pp. 98–121 in James Clifford and George Marcus (eds.), *Writing Culture: The Poetics and Politics of Ethnography*. Berkeley, Los Angeles, London: University of California Press.

Clifford, James, and George Marcus, eds. 1986. *Writing Culture: The Poetics and Politics of Ethnography*. Berkeley, Los Angeles, London: University of California Press.

Cohen, Anthony, ed. 1982. *Belonging: Identity and Social Organisation in British Rural Cultures*. Manchester: Manchester University Press.

Damon, Frederick H., and Roy Wagner, eds. 1989. *Death Rituals and Life in the Societies of the Kula Ring*. Dekalb: Northern Illinois University Press.

Ellis, Stephen. 1985. *The Rising of the Red Shawls: A Revolt in Madagascar 1895–1899*. Cambridge: Cambridge University Press.

Epstein, A. L. 1969. *Matupit*. Berkeley, Los Angeles, London: University of California Press.

Errington, Frederick, and Deborah Gewertz. 1987. "Of Unfinished Dialogues and Paper Pigs." *American Ethnologist* 14:367–376.

Fabian, Johannes. 1983. *Time and the Other: How Anthropology Makes Its Object*. New York: Columbia University Press.

Filer, Colin. 1985. "What Is This Thing Called Brideprice?" *Mankind* 15 (special issue): 163–183.

Fitzpatrick, Peter. 1980. *Law and State in Papua New Guinea*. London: Academic Press.

Fox, Robin. 1978. *The Tory Islanders: A People of the Celtic Fringe*. New York: Cambridge University Press.

Gewertz, Deborah. 1983. *Sepik River Societies*. New Haven: Yale University Press.

———. 1990. "We Think, Therefore They Are?—On Occidentalizing the World." Five College Twenty-fifth Anniversary Lecture, October 4, Amherst College, Amherst, Mass.

Gill, Sam D. 1983. *Mother Earth: An American Story*. Chicago: University of Chicago Press.

Gilmore, David. 1982. "Some Notes on Community Nicknaming in Spain." *Man* 17:686–700.

Gorecki, Peter P. 1984. "The Documented History of the 'Lost Tribes' of the Schrader Mountains, 1913–1984." *Research in Melanesia* 8:47–56.

Gregory, C. A. 1982. *Gifts and Commodities*. London: Academic Press.

Handler, Richard. 1985. "On Dialogue and Destructive Analysis: Problems in Narrating Nationalism and Ethnicity." *Journal of Anthropological Research* 41:171–182.

Harding, Thomas. 1967. *Voyagers of the Vitiaz Straits*. (American Ethnological Society Monograph 44.) Seattle: University of Washington.

Hartsock, Nancy C. N. 1985. "Exchange Theory: Critique from a Feminist Standpoint." Pp. 57–70 in S. G. McNall (ed.), *Current Perspectives in Social Theory*, vol. 6. Greenwich, Conn.: JAI Press.

Herzfeld, Michael. 1987. *Anthropology through the Looking-Glass: Critical Ethnography in the Margins of Europe*. Cambridge: Cambridge University Press.

Heusch, Luc de. 1989. "Kongo in Haiti: A New Approach to Religious Syncretism." *Man* 24:290–303.

Hobsbawm, Eric, and Terence Ranger, eds. 1983. *The Invention of Tradition*. Cambridge: Cambridge University Press.

Holland, L. Virginia. 1959. *Counterpoint: Kenneth Burke's and Aristotle's Theories of Rhetoric*. New York: Philosophical Library.

Keesing, Roger, and Robert Tonkinson, eds. 1982. "Reinventing Traditional Culture: The Politics of Kastom in Island Melanesia." *Mankind* 13 (special issue).

Knauft, Bruce. 1990. "Melanesian Warfare: A Theoretical History." *Oceania* 60:250–311.

Kopytoff, Igor. 1986. "The Cultural Biography of Things: Commoditization as Process." Pp. 64–91 in Arjun Appadurai (ed.), *The Social Life of Things: Commodities in Cultural Perspective*. New York: Cambridge University Press.

Kuhn, Thomas. 1970. *The Structure of Scientific Revolutions*. Chicago: University of Chicago Press.

Kuper, Adam. 1988. *The Invention of Primitive Society*. London: Routledge.

Lawrence, Peter. 1964. *Road Belong Cargo*. Manchester: University of Manchester Press.

Leach, Edmund. 1989. "Writing Anthropology." *American Ethnologist* 16:137–141.

Leach, Jerry, and Edmund Leach, eds. 1983. *The Kula: New Perspectives on Massim Exchange*. Cambridge: Cambridge University Press.

Llobera, Joseph. 1986. "Fieldwork in Southwestern Europe." *Critique of Anthropology* 6:25–33.

MacDonald, Barrie. 1986. "Decolonization and Beyond." *Journal of Pacific History* 21:115–126.

Macfarlane, Alan. 1978. *The Origins of English Individualism*. Oxford: Basil Blackwell.

Meillassoux, Claude. 1981. *Maidens, Meal and Money*. Cambridge: Cambridge University Press.

Merton, Robert. 1972. "Insiders and Outsiders: A Chapter in the Sociology of Knowledge." Pp. 9–47 in *Varieties of Political Expression in Sociology*. Chicago: University of Chicago Press.

Middleton, John. 1960. *Lugbara Religion*. London: Oxford University Press.

Miller, Daniel. 1987. *Material Culture and Mass Consumption*. Oxford: Basil Blackwell.

Moore, Sally Falk. 1987. "Explaining the Present: Theoretical Dilemmas in Processual Ethnography." *American Ethnologist* 14:727–736.

Morphy, Howard, and Frances Morphy. 1984. "The 'Myths' of Ngalakan History: Ideology and Images of the Past in Northern Australia." *Man* 19:459–478.

Nelson, Hank. 1982. *Taim Bilong Masta: The Australian Involvement with Papua New Guinea*. Sydney: Australian Broadcasting Commission.

Pearce, Roy Harvey. 1965 (1953). *Savagism and Civilization: A Study of the Indian and the American Mind*. Baltimore: Johns Hopkins Press.

Peel, J. D. Y. 1983. *Ijeshas and Nigerians: The Incorporation of a Yoruba Kingdom, 1890s–1970s*. Cambridge: Cambridge University Press.

Radcliffe-Brown, A. R. 1952. *Structure and Function in Primitive Society*. London: Routledge.

Research in Melanesia. 1985. *The University of Papua New Guinea Schrader Mountains Project* 9 (special issue).

Richardson, Michael. 1990. "Enough Said: Reflections on Orientalism." *Anthropology Today* 6(4):16–19.

Said, Edward. 1978. *Orientalism.* Harmondsworth: Penguin.

Salisbury, Richard. 1970. *Vunamami.* Berkeley, Los Angeles, London: University of California Press.

Sanmartin, Ricardo. 1982. "Marriage and Inheritance in a Mediterranean Fishing Community." *Man* 17:664–685.

Schneider, David. 1979. "Kinship, Community, and Locality in American Culture." Pp. 155–174 in Allan Lichtman and Joan Challinor (eds.), *Kin and Communities: Families in America.* Washington, D.C.: Smithsonian Institution Press.

Smith, Bernard. 1985. *European Vision and the South Pacific* (2d ed.). New Haven: Yale University Press.

Spencer, Jonathan. 1989. "Anthropology as a Kind of Writing." *Man* 24:145–164.

Strathern, Andrew. 1982. "The Division of Labor and Processes of Social Change in Mount Hagen." *American Ethnologist* 9:307–319.

———. 1984. *A Line of Power.* London: Tavistock.

Strathern, Marilyn. 1981*a.* "Culture in a Net Bag: The Manufacture of a Subdiscipline in Anthropology." *Man* 16:665–688.

———. 1981*b.* *Kinship at the Core.* Cambridge: Cambridge University Press.

———. 1984. "Marriage Exchanges: A Melanesian Comment." *Annual Review of Anthropology* 13:41–73.

———. 1988. *The Gender of the Gift.* Berkeley, Los Angeles, London: University of California Press.

Thomas, Nicholas. 1989. *Out of Time: History and Evolution in Anthropological Discourse.* Cambridge: Cambridge University Press.

———. 1991. *Entangled Objects: Exchange, Material Culture and Colonialism in the Pacific.* Cambridge, Mass: Harvard University Press.

Turner, Bryan S. 1989. "From Orientalism to Global Sociology." *Sociology* 23:629–638.

Wolf, Eric R. 1982. *Europe and the People without History.* Berkeley, Los Angeles, London: University of California Press.

ONE

Banana Leaf Bundles and Skirts
A Pacific Penelope's Web?

Margaret Jolly

In her review of the significance of cloth in Pacific polities, Annette Weiner has evoked the persona of Penelope, "weaving by day, and unweaving the same fabric by night, in order to halt time" (1986, 108).[1] This image of a Pacific Penelope halting time was inspired by Weiner's reanalysis of the Trobriand islands. In her monograph (1976), in several subsequent papers (1980, 1982*a*, 1983*a*, 1986) and in her shorter text (1988) she conclusively demonstrated that Malinowski and a host of other male observers had failed to see women's central place in Trobriand exchange: that in fixating so totally on men's exchanges of yams in *urigubu* and of shell valuables in the kula, they had ignored women's exchanges of banana leaf bundles and skirts, most importantly at mortuary distributions. In her reassessment of the relations of the sexes in the Trobriands she portrayed men as controlling events in historical time and space (the social domain) and women as controlling events in ahistorical time and space (the cosmological domain) (1976, 20). This distinction, she later observed, was an attempt to escape the connotations of two separate spheres constituted by terms like private/public or nature/culture (1986, 97).

Rather than eschewing such invidious Western dichotomies her analysis ultimately reinforces them, by articulating them with another—eternal/historical. Such Eurocentric dichotomies typically presume that the private or domestic sphere is outside history (see Jolly and Macintyre 1989) and that women's nature is not only given but eternal. Essentialist elisions in Weiner's work have already been noted (M. Strathern 1981). What is suggested here is the further point that in situating women outside history, Weiner has reproduced Eurocentric notions of an unchanging women's world. But women's worlds in the Pacific, though they may have remained virtually invisible or hidden to centuries of male observers, have certainly not persisted unchanged.

Exchanges of women's wealth have assumed an inflated and a novel significance since Malinowski's time—not only securing the regeneration of Trobriand persons but ensuring the perpetuity of Trobriand culture in the face of competing values. Perhaps Trobriand women see themselves as defending Trobriand tradition and the value of women against both monetary and male values. Women are, as Weiner has portrayed them, at the core of Trobriand traditions. But such traditions are, I contend, not unselfconscious persistences but self-conscious resistances[2] to modernity and monetary values. In the Trobriands as elsewhere in Melanesia, modernity and money are practically mediated by and symbolically associated with men.

TIME AND THE TROBRIANDS

The difference between Malinowski's and Weiner's accounts is thus not merely a contrast between an androcentric male observer and a gynocentric female observer,[3] but a difference amplified by the history between the periods of their observations. The passage in time between the fieldwork of Malinowski and of Weiner marks not only a shift in the historical context of ethnography and in the sexual politics of Europeans looking at Trobriand others, but also a transformation of Trobriand realities.

Weiner herself is not unaware of either anthropological or Trobriand history. At several points in her monograph (1976, xvi–xx, 25–33) and in later essays (e.g., 1980, 271–272, 275–276, 280) she alludes to the historical changes affecting both Trobriand and anthropological culture. But such history is often alluded to in order to deny its consequences—in order to stress constancy rather than change. For instance, Weiner presents a genealogy of Trobriand high-ranking male informants and anthropologists, which links her good friend and valued informant Vanoi (1976, xvii) with the past.

> Standing in front of Vanoi's house gave me a sense of both anthropological and Trobriand history. In the ground, ten yards in front of Vanoi's house, lies a stone marker on the grave of Touluwa, who was Malinowski's friend and the man whom Malinowski called the paramount chief of the Trobriands. Not far from this gravesite, another stone marks the grave of Mitakata, successor to Touluwa and Powell's informant in 1950. Mitakata died in 1961, and Vanoi became his heir. (1976, xix)

The rhetorical device that Weiner uses in *Women of Value, Men of Renown*, namely, heading each section with a quotation from Malinowski, does, as she suggests, highlight their historical relation, but, again, ultimately it stresses the consistency of their ethnographic questions and the constancy of Trobriand culture despite the gap in time and interpretation. The same point is made explicitly in a later essay.

> What initially astounded me upon my arrival in Kiriwina was the striking similarity between a Kiriwina village in 1971 and Malinowski's descriptions and photographs of the same village in 1922. Although superficially some things had changed (an airstrip, tourists, some Western clothing) everything else was as if nothing was changed. (Weiner 1980, 272)

The introductory notes to this later essay situate the Massim in Melanesian colonial history—cataloging the successive influences of whalers, pearlers and bêche-de-mer traders, gold prospectors, and labor recruiters from the 1850s; Christian missions from 1894; and the controls of government from the establishment of a British colonial administration post at Losuia in 1906 to the Massim's incorporation within the independent state of Papua New Guinea in 1975. However, Weiner asserts that despite more than a century of such contacts there had not been any "major significant changes in the basic structural features of the exchange system" (1980, 276; cf. Macintyre and Young 1982).

"As if nothing was changed"—change is perceived as "superficial," a patina on the body of Trobriand tradition. And change is seen only in terms of Western imports: clothing, airplanes, tourists. Changes indigenous to the system or diverging from the movement of "Westernization" are not countenanced. Change is not admitted to the core, the "basic structure" of Trobriand culture, manifest in the exchange system, which persists as before. But this excludes the possibility of transformation in the exchange system itself. It has now been conclusively demonstrated that the kula has undergone dramatic historical transformations. It has even been suggested by Macintyre (1983), Irwin (1983), and Berde (1983) that the system witnessed by Malinowski in the Trobriands was a novel integration of Massim regional trade and exchange and that the form it assumed in the period of Malinowski's fieldwork was in part the consequence of European contact. Such exchanges in the kula clearly had ramifications for women's exchanges too. Moreover there is some evidence suggestive of changes internal to *sagali*, and definitive evidence of changes in the broader context in which these exchanges transpire. This broader context situates traditional elements of Trobriand culture in relation to the ongoing processes of economic and political development (cf. Carrier and Carrier 1987).

Weiner stresses the continuity of Trobriand culture in the context of the politics of the emerging nation of Papua New Guinea. It is clear from Weiner's introduction to her monograph that she was witness to much of the turbulence of Trobriand politics in the 1970s, in particular the struggle between the Kabisawali movement and the Toneni Kamokwita movement. Her main informant Vanoi was himself caught up in this struggle, shifting his allegiance between the two main camps on several occasions. But this fight over Trobriand tradition and its relation to economic development and tourism is not a part of Weiner's study, being seen primarily as a disturbing threat to her main lines of enquiry (1976, xix–xx; but see Weiner 1982*b*).[4] These conflicts deserve to be considered, however, since as Young suggests (1979, 19), tradition itself is at issue.[5]

The intensity, subtlety, and irony of these debates about tradition is graphically revealed in the film *Trobriand Cricket*, shot in 1973, at the height of these political struggles. Here we see a unique form of the game played with local rules (e.g., an unrestricted number of players on each side, the hosts must always win). Trobriand cricket is accompanied by chants and dances derived from the ancient rites of war but dealing with eminently modern imports such as airplanes, tourists, and chewing gum. As Weiner observes (1977, 506–507; 1988, 181), this film attests to an extraordinary cultural resilience, "exuberance and pride." But we see not just persistence but innovation, adaptation, resistance to, and satire of, Western practices and values. Who can forget those extraordinary sequences when the history of Trobriand cricket is recounted, how the game as played by Methodist missionaries was seen as staid and boring, and was reinvented Trobriand style? Who failed to delight in the extraordinary burlesque of a Trobriand man, simulating the obsessive interest of a tourist with binoculars perpetually attached like an ommatophore? The film records a cricket match organized by Kasaipwalova expressly for the film, which was perceived partly as publicity for the concerns of the Kabisawali movement (Weiner 1988, 181). It is aptly subtitled: "An Ingenious Response to Colonialism." It evokes not just cultural vitality but complicated processes of acceptance, rejection, and transformation of European culture.

The very existence of such debates about tradition suggests that, as with debates about *kastom* in the Solomons and Vanuatu, it is inappropriate to see tradition as merely a persistence of the past in the preaent: tradition can be a symbol of resistance and even a way of justifying change (see Keesing and Tonkinson 1982; Hobsbawm and Ranger 1983; Handler and Linnekin 1984; Keesing 1988, 1989*a*; Linnekin and Poyer 1990). Elsewhere in Melanesia the values of tradition are primarily articulated by male politicians, and "kastom" as political symbol tends to be a male monopoly (see Mera Molisa 1987). In the Trobriands, too, as is evidenced both by the history of the Kabisawali and Toneni Kamokwita movements and the cinematic sequences of *Trobriand Cricket*, men dominate political talk. But here the value of tradition is overtly associated with women. Weiner has argued that the value accorded women and the centrality of exchanges of women's wealth have safeguarded Trobriand tradition and proved a buffer against colonization. But perhaps rather than just "stability in banana leaves," what we now witness is their expanded and novel salience, as symbols not just of the constant regeneration of Trobriand persons, but of the self-conscious regeneration of Trobriand culture in the face of external pressure. In both these processes men and women occupy a different place (cf. Keesing 1985).

Let us start then by comparing Malinowski's and Weiner's analysis of women's place in the Trobriands. We will then look at those banana leaves, the women's wealth to which Weiner directs our gaze, and in particular the salience of women's exchanges in sagali, the mortuary ceremonies. There is no doubt that these bits of ephemeral plant-fiber fluff have been disregarded, both because they seemed such unlikely candidates for wealth objects when compared to durable shell valuables and because they were wealth produced and exchanged by women. But as well as having this previously unseen significance, have they not also assumed a novel significance, a new value as symbols of tradition and the centrality of women to such tradition?[6]

WOMAN'S PLACE IN THE TROBRIANDS: FROM MALINOWSKI TO WEINER—FROM SEXUALITY TO REPRODUCTION

Malinowski's portrayal of sex and gender in the Trobriands is dispersed in several parts of his huge Trobriand corpus. But the most developed distillations are to be found in *The Sexual Life of Savages*, a text that was a self-conscious part of European debates about sexual freedom and repression in the 1920s—debates involving Freud, Russell, and Havelock Ellis, who wrote the Preface to the first edition.[7] This presents the work as a contribution to the "natural history of sexuality," a scientific investigation of the erotic life of remote peoples conducted with calm, solemnity, and scholarly precision (Malinowski 1929, vii–xii). There is no doubting the scholarly precision of Malinowski's account of Trobriand erotic life, although calm and solemnity may not have characterized his inner life during fieldwork (see Malinowski 1967; Young 1979). Such precision coupled with the flamboyant title no doubt contributed to the sensational rather than scholarly reception of the book, about which Malinowski grumbled in his Preface to the third edition.

His depictions of the sexual lives of Trobrianders from childhood to adulthood leave little doubt that these were "free and easy," certainly by the standards of sexual morality in the Europe of his time. Infants' early observations of adult sexuality, the casual inclusion of sexuality in children's games, the elaboration of the arts of physical and magical attraction, and adolescents' premarital preoccupations with lovemaking—no doubt all were shocking and titillating to the audience of his day. Although husbands and wives were supposed to be more circumspect than adolescent lovers (at least in public), the companionate ease and harmony of Trobriand marriage must have exerted an exotic allure to those Europeans whose marriages were characterized by greater formality and tension.

His depiction of Trobriand kinship, property, and power relations further highlighted this portrait of remote and exotic practices. Trobrianders were not only matrilineal but they denied the role of the father in conception. Malinowski informed his incredulous European audience that Trobrianders saw the fetus as the coming together of maternal blood and of *baloma*, matrilineal spirit. The father merely "opened the way," semen was thought to have no generative power, and physical resemblance between father and child was seen as the result of intimate nurture, not biology.[8] Malinowski recognized that this view of procreation also informed events at the other end of the life cycle: at death the physical and spiritual aspects of the person had to be separated so that the spirit might return to the land of the dead. Women's role in mortuary practices was noted, but not discussed, beyond the observation that widows had to assume an onerous burden in mourning their husbands.

Malinowski here and in several other places described the way in which matriliny attached people to the land. Women, like men, had matrilineally inherited rights in land, but because most went to live with their husbands at marriage, they did not, as their brothers did, live on and work such land. They were, however, entitled to produce from their land—the brother in particular had the responsibility to feed his sister's family by giving yams to her husband. This Malinowski called *urigubu*,[9] a prestation that he argued became tribute to a chief: chiefs had claims on yams from affines other than their wife's brother, and since chiefs were often polygynists, their yam-houses were filled from several affinal sources.

In *The Sexual Life of Savages* Malinowski adjudicated on the position of women in Trobriand society. His earlier view, enunciated in *Argonauts of the Western Pacific*, was that women, "enjoyed a very independent position, and are exceedingly well treated . . . and wield a considerable influence" (Malinowski 1922, 37). In *The Sexual Life of Savages* he qualified this by the claim that they had "rank but not power." He noted that women were "barred from the exercise of power, land ownership and many other public privileges" (Malinowski 1929, 38), including a voice in deliberations about gardening, hunting, the kula, war, or ceremonies. Moreover, he suggested that even within the family, the "real guardianship" was vested not in a woman but her brother: "a woman continues the line and man represents it" (1929, 24).

Weiner's book, *Women of Value, Men of Renown*, is of course the product of a sexual politics rather different to that of Malinowski's time. It is a self-conscious product of feminist anthropology, and is indeed an ethnography offering "one of the most compelling reappraisals from a female viewpoint" (M. Strathern 1981, 671). It demonstrates not only the thesis of women's invisibility to male observers but how much this matters in understanding men and the cultural system as a whole. Weiner is not merely adding the study of women to the study of men, but challenging the very basis on which observation and interpretation proceeds—namely, giving more time and value to male activities, on the premise that they are more central culturally. Because men are the controllers of resources and the embodiments of public authority they do not therefore necessarily represent the core of cultural value.

In Weiner's monograph (1976) the emphasis is on reproduction[10] rather than sexuality, a shift in emphasis which, in an analysis of another Melanesian society, she suggests is closer to indigenous conceptions (1983*b*, but see Weiner 1988, chaps. 4 and 5). On several points she concurs with Malinowski's depiction of the patterns of relations between women and men in the system of kinship, property, and politics, but she suggests a different interpretation of ideologies of procreation and growth and of configurations of love and power in the system of matrilineal descent and hereditary rank.

Although the father is not thought to give substance to the fetus, he is seen to contribute to the substance of the growing child by his nurture and love. The father then is not so much a stranger in the Trobriand family, peripheral to the core sibling bond of brother and sister, but a secure member because of the gifts of love, food, and valuables. Children are indebted to their father and to his matrilineage because of these gifts, and these debts entail cycles of exchanges, of both male and female wealth, culminating in the distributions at death (Weiner 1988, 6). Moreover such exchanges are basic to the legitimation of chiefly power—it is not just that chiefs are accorded special privileges by birth right, but these have to be constantly legitimated not just by the flows of shell valuables in the kula or of yams but of banana leaf bundles and skirts in sagali and other contexts.

Thus Weiner ultimately dissents from Malinowski's conclusions about the power of Trobriand women. Although women are excluded from positions of public power—from control over land, from exchanges of yams and kula valuables, from public authority such as those exerted by male chiefs and hamlet managers—she asserts that women ultimately transcend male power because of their control over the cycles of life and death. This power is objectified in the exchanges of women's wealth, exchanges that Malinowski and others overlooked.

BANANA LEAVES AS WOMEN'S WEALTH

Weiner describes the painstaking process whereby women bleach, treat, and manufacture banana leaves into bundles of skirts, thus converting seemingly inconsequential bits of plant-fiber fluff into "women's wealth." But these valuables are not only *produced* solely by women, they are also *exchanged* by them, and exchanged because of the very value of women in the Trobriands. This derives from Trobriand philosophies of life, death, and regeneration, and the central significance of maternal blood and matrilineal spirit in procreation and in deconception at death. Weiner demonstrates how the flow of yams, which passes between men in prestigious exchanges, relates to the flow of women's wealth.

A man makes yam gardens, not for himself but to give to other men— in particular his father, elder brother, and mother's brother—and also to women—in particular his daughter and sister. When a woman marries any man, her brothers are bound to supply her, and thus her husband, with yams. When a woman marries a chiefly man, not only her brothers but also father and mother's brother are enjoined to cultivate an annual yam garden for her. Since chiefly men are often polygynous, they receive far more yams than ordinary men and thus have yam-houses that are full, sometimes over-flowing with rotting yams. Husbands should, in return, assist their wives to accumulate "women's wealth." Women use the banana leaves thus accumu-lated primarily in the context of sagali, the distributions that follow the death of kin of one's own *dala*. Banana leaves flow to those to whom the deceased was indebted in life—that is, those outside their matrilineage: affines, patri-lateral kin, adopted kin, friends. Such prestations of women's wealth free the person from the debts of worldly exchanges, so that the spirit can be regener-ated as baloma and return to the spiritual pool of the dala to be reincarnated in another person. Trobriand women secure immortality through their con-trol of the identity of the dala—that is, the matrilineal clan. This power derives not from matriliny per se but from the value Trobrianders give to re-generation. "Beyond the fact of matrilineality, the Trobriand concern with regenesis gives women their primary place of value" (Weiner 1976, 231).

This, according to Weiner, is not a biological fact but a cultural value given to woman, and the value is amplified through the exchange of objects, since "the controls which women exert at the two ends of the life cycle—both at birth and at death rituals . . . are given greater significance through the objectification of their power into wealth objects: skirts and bundles" (1976, 227).

Although stone ax blades (male wealth) and yams (conjoint male and female wealth) represent some measure of regeneration, it is women's wealth that secures regenesis.

Weiner sees male control as confined to objects and persons within a present social time and space, and as perpetuating individual rather than collective identity. Thus, "male valuables made from shell and stone, the least perishable artifacts in the Trobriand corpus of exchange objects, carry a man's name only as long as he can demonstrate his power over other men" (1976, 232). Land, kula valuables, ax blades, decorations, names—all such property requires calculated control by men in order not to be lost. Women's wealth may be far more ephemeral physically, but women's identity by con-trast is not transient or contingent. Women do not rely on such temporal political strategies since they have control over the continuity of life and death: bundles of leaves and skirts may perish but human life goes on. Although women participate in both the social and the cosmic realms, the temporal and the eternal, men cannot enter the "ahistorical domain of women" (1976, 231). Weiner thus sees Trobriand women as eclipsing the power of men and the male domain of exchange.

But this opposition between ahistorical and immortal versus historical and ephemeral is not only a contrast of Trobriand women's and men's worlds but simultaneously a contrast of Trobriand and Western worlds.[11] Trobriand society is seen to give a different value to things and human persons. "Trobriand exchange objects, unlike Western money, cannot be detached from the human experience of regeneration and immortality" (1976, 231), whereas in Western society, "free from the processes of the life cycle, objects become depersonalized and a shift occurs in the relations between persons and things" (1976, 235).[12]

Weiner's account is thus animated by a double opposition—between the worlds of Trobriand women and men, and between the worlds of Trobriand values and Western values. Through the articulation of both these values Weiner develops a moral critique of Western society on the basis of the Trobriands. But there is also a real historical link between men and money in the Trobriands. Although the Trobriands may be distinctive if not unique in the range of gender relations found in Melanesia (but see Macintyre 1986), in one sense the Trobriands is like everywhere else in Melanesia—namely, the introductions of European goods, cash, and commodity values are mediated and indeed monopolized by men (cf. Gewertz 1983; A. Strathern 1979; Sexton 1982, 1986).

REINTERPRETING JOSHUA'S MESSAGE

In conversation with Weiner, Trobrianders constantly stressed the value of women's wealth by comparing it to money or by expressing the value of specific bundles in monetary terms. On her first day in Kiriwina women had told Weiner that "*Nununiga* (banana leaf bundles) are just like your money" (1986, 109, cf. 1986, 99 and Thomas [this volume], commenting on Kahn). At several points specific cash equivalents were suggested to her, for example, that the bundles accumulated for sagali are worth "hundreds of dollars" (1986, 98) or that in 1976 five bundles of banana leaves were equivalent to one stick of tobacco or 1.3 cents. There is much evidence that banana leaf bundles and skirts have become increasingly exchangeable for an expanding range of goods—not only for indigenous items such as betel nuts, coconuts, fresh fish, and shells, but also tobacco, biscuits, chewing gum, and balloons. Weiner notes that in the one hundred years of contact the value of women's wealth relative to such things has increased, that women are commanding more and more for their wealth. "The greater the opportunities for men to command any kind of wealth, the greater becomes the number of baskets of women's wealth that 'wealthy women' command" (1980, 276). Moreover, she observes that since it is often younger men who have more access to cash and commodities, it is often their young wives who are very heavily involved in the amassing and distribution of women's wealth.

In "Stability in Banana Leaves" Weiner quotes from a conversation with Joshua, a highly educated young man who had returned from college and employment elsewhere in Papua New Guinea to work at the hospital in Kiriwina. While they were driving together they observed a sagali, and although he commented approvingly on her knowledge about women's wealth, he also lamented: "We have to get those women to stop throwing their wealth, because they take our money. If the women would stop needing so many baskets of wealth . . . then men would have plenty of money to pay for other things" (1980, 274). Weiner was patently shocked by this and attributed it to the fact that "Joshua had been away too long and had learned to think in Western capitalist terms" (1980, 274). Though she admits that women's wealth is a drain on the flow of other kinds of goods, she contends that it is a "buffer to Western economic intrusions," a buffer that underwrites the power of both men and women.

This is probably true, but what Weiner fails to address is the question of why European goods and cash are classified as "male" wealth. This classification appears to reflect both male control of such wealth and the symbolic gendering of goods. Is this because, as in the rest of Melanesia, men have been the mediators of the commodity economy? From the barter associated with the first navigators, through labor migration to sandalwood depots, mines, and plantations, to patterns of contemporary wage labor, cash-cropping, and touristic development, the intrusions of European goods and values have typically been through men.

Although the economic integration of the Trobriands with the cash economy has always been distinctly peripheral, it is men who have always effected such integration. Trobriand men were not much engaged in the early forms of labor migration in the Massim region, unlike those from islands such as Goodenough, where the numbers of men recruited in the late nineteenth and early twentieth centuries constituted a high percentage of all men (see Young 1983). In the nineteenth and early twentieth centuries the main economic links were with whalers, pearlers, and bêche-de-mer traders, involving the exchange of food and local crafts for steel tools, cloth, tobacco, and other European goods. Such exchanges appear to have been a male monopoly. At the time of Malinowski's fieldwork such exchanges expanded to include locally resident missionaries, Australian colonial officials, and traders operating local stores. During Weiner's fieldwork the main source of cash was the sale of carvings to tourists, and she makes it clear that carving was a male craft and money earned through selling carvings entered internal exchanges through men. Since the collapse of the tourist boom of the early 1970s, the main source of cash is no longer the sale of carvings to tourists but remittances from those working elsewhere. Although increasing numbers of women are migrating to work in Port Moresby and other regional centers, men still constitute the majority of migrant workers and thus remain the major source of cash and commodities in the Kiriwina community.

Thus, through different periods and in different ways it is men who have consistently engaged in commodity exchanges. This asymmetrical engagement of men and women has not been without internal consequences. There is, I suggest, a tendency for male and female interests in the exchange system to diverge,[13] because of their differential engagement in the cash economy. Whereas in the precolonial and early colonial period, male and female wealth objects and realms of exchange might be reckoned to be different but complementary and mutually supportive, in the contemporary situation there is both difference and competition between the exchange interests of women and men (despite Weiner's claims that they are mutually supportive). How else can we explain Joshua's complaint that women are throwing their wealth and diverting "male" money from other purposes? How else can we interpret women's trenchant insistence that their wealth is as valuable as money? Men clearly have a choice about dividing their time between internal indigenous exchanges and external commodity transactions. According to Weiner, some Trobrianders warned that "men spent too much time carving, resulting in smaller yam harvests" (1988, 23). Given the ultimate links between yam exchanges and the flows of women's wealth, this diminution of yam harvests must have had an impact on women's exchanges too. Women's productive and exchange orientations are not similarly divided, being focused on the cultivation of crops and the manufacture of banana leaf bundles and an array of superb skirts.

It is significant that women still choose to wear these skirts—they are not just wealth objects used in ceremonial display but items of daily attire. The various styles of dress mark the social situation of women—young girls wear short red miniskirts, older married women wear longer skirts, an influential woman who is a central figure in a sagali wears an exceptionally long and flowing skirt, a woman after childbirth wears a long flowing cape also made from banana leaf fibers, and a woman in mourning wears an undyed banana fiber skirt reaching to her ankles (and the widow of the deceased a mat cloaking her body). By contrast, only a few older men routinely wear the white pandanus penis covering. Although young men usually don this for ceremonies, they routinely choose to wear shorts, trousers, or sarongs made of brightly colored cloth. Thus the differing orientations of women and men to traditional and introduced elements of Trobriand culture are signaled in the very clothes they wear.

TRANSFORMATIONS IN THE KULA

The changing historical significance of sagali and women's wealth needs to be related to the changing significance of that preeminently male domain of exchange, the kula. A number of ethnographers have reanalyzed the kula in historical terms, both in the light of prehistorical evidence of exchange in the region and in the light of transformations consequent on European colonization. From the viewpoint both of prehistory and of recent colonial history, the kula as described by Malinowski emerges as an institution unique to a particular time and place rather than a manifestation of unchanging Massim culture.

Prehistorical research suggests that the kula has developed only in the last five hundred years or so, out of rather different earlier exchange systems. Although shell valuables have a longer antiquity in the region, dating back to about 2000 BP, the development of the kula seems to have been a more recent phenomenon, associated with the specialization of craft industries such as pottery. Moreover, the precise ringlike character of exchanges of armlets for necklaces which Malinowski describes seems only to be true of this northern corner of the network and not for the southern islands such as Tubetube and Koyagaugau. In the southern islands at least, many more items entered the kula—pigs, greenstone ax blades, wooden platters, lime gourds, and spatulas—and overseas exchanges of such valuables were intimately linked to internal exchanges—rites at marriage and death, and purchases of land, canoes or magic.

Furthermore, it has been claimed that Malinowski overemphasized both the inconvertibility of kula valuables and their separation from internal exchanges in Kiriwina itself. This is obvious from his failure to discuss a central concept, found today throughout the Massim, that of *kitoma* (*kitoum*, *kitomwa* in the languages further south). This concept refers to the idea that the valuables, rather than circulating endlessly and being detached from persons, move from states of being encumbered by debts to states of being debt-free. When a valuable is unencumbered it becomes the kitoma of the person holding it, and in this state may pass into internal exchanges such as those at marriage and death. Campbell has argued, from the vantage point of Vakuta, that shell valuables can be fed into the internal exchange system "thereby securing other wealth in the form of yams, magic, land and women" (Campbell 1983, 204). In the past, kitoma valuables were used expressly for compensation payments due for injury and death sustained in warfare (Macintyre 1983, 143). It may be that this concept and this process of articulation between external and internal exchanges has itself become more developed since Malinowski's fieldwork (see Keesing n.d.). Whether this was always the case or is another instance of historical change, it means that nowadays the kula cannot be dissociated from these internal exchanges of men and women's wealth.

Not only does overseas exchange seem to be much more articulated with internal exchanges than Malinowski presumed, but it also appears that European penetration and pacification was a precondition for the emergence of the kula system as Malinowski perceived it. This historical reinterpretation has been developed by Macintyre in the following way:

> Throughout his analysis of kula Malinowski assumes an historical depth of the institution. The inheritance of the kula valuables, the value of wealth items being viewed as cumulative over time, and the permanence of the circulation along time-honoured paths are essential features of Malinowski's kula. It is my contention that such incessant circulation could only occur after pacification. The kula as closed circuit is a modern institution. (1983, 132)

Macintyre suggests that the preeminence of kula (*kune* in the southern islands) exchange as a form of political alliance was possible only after the colonial authorities abolished war, making peaceful interactions possible over a much wider area and stabilizing exchange paths.

Moreover, as Macintyre and others have demonstrated, there were profound economic changes in the kula as a result of the introduction of the steel ax and other European goods. Many wealth items disappeared from the kula or became very restricted in their circulation, such as greenstone ax blades, lime spatulas and gourds, and wooden platters. Local craft production declined with the introduction of European substitutes and this must have had an effect on the flow of such artifacts in the kula. There was an inflationary spiral in the value of shell valuables, but simultaneously there was also a process of democratization of access to kula valuables. European control radically reduced the power of the *guyau*, those high-ranking men who had dominated exchange, trade, and warfare in and between Massim communities.

It may be argued, as Weiner has done (1980), that such historical transformations affected only the domain of male prestige economy and did not affect women's exchanges. But if, as Macintyre and others have argued, overseas exchanges were intimately related to internal exchanges, and if, as Weiner herself suggests, the male and female exchange systems were intimately linked, then exchanges of women's wealth cannot have been completely insulated from such processes. Indeed, although Weiner sees women's exchanges as a buffer to colonization, it would seem that this buffer has at least absorbed the ramified impact of changes to the male prestige economy. For instance, she argues that the system of chiefly power is intimately related to the production and circulation of yams by men, which in turn is related intimately to women's exchanges of wealth. So, changes in the relative power of high-ranking men, and the loss of their monopoly over kula valuables, would logically have some effects on the patterns of women's exchanges too. The spiraling value of women's wealth, like the spiraling value of kula valuables, may be attributable to its articulation to commodity exchanges. Finally, insofar as women's wealth is measurable and convertible into cash and a range of commodities, it must be seen as related to the cash economy.

So, in the Trobriands as in the rest of Melanesia, indigenous exchange systems have become articulated with commodity exchange. What is distinctive is that in the Trobriands there is and was a sphere of exchange controlled by women, and a sphere of women's exchange which is seen as crucial to perpetuating Trobriand tradition. The particular character is clear if we compare it to similar processes in the Highlands region of Papua New Guinea. Here also gift and commodity exchanges are related, but the gendering of these exchanges is different from the Massim.

GENDERING GIFTS AND COMMODITIES IN THE HIGHLANDS AND THE MASSIM

Throughout Melanesia we witness a complicated process, not just of competition between the values of the commodity and the gift, but of mutual accommodation, integration, and substitution (see Gregory 1982; M. Strathern 1988; Carrier and Carrier 1989). Elsewhere this relation is between exchange commodities and gifts, which are both under male control. What is distinctive about the Trobriand situation is that as well as gift exchanges classified as male, such as the kula and yam exchanges, there were exchanges of women's wealth. The negotiation of values between the gift and the commodity takes on a different significance if this is perceived not just as the substitution of one kind of male wealth for another but the relation of introduced male wealth to indigenous male and female wealth (see Gewertz 1983).[14]

The special character of the Trobriand situation is clear if we briefly compare it with the situation described in parts of the Highlands of Papua New Guinea. The Highlands region differs markedly from the Trobriands because Highlands women are producers and rarely if ever transactors (though Feil [1978] has argued otherwise for the Enga). Let us take the ethnographic case that has been the most intensively described and analyzed, that of Mount Hagen, where Marilyn Strathern early pointed to the crucial distinction between women as primarily producers of sweet potatoes and pigs and men as transactors of pigs and shell valuables.[15]

What concerns us here is how the increasing importance of cash, commodities, and monetary values has affected the exclusively male domain of ceremonial exchange in the Hagen area, the moka. Andrew Strathern (1979) argues that there has been a profound alteration in the strategic relations of women and men as producers and transactors. He suggests that even though women's productive contribution to exchange goods was obscured by men in the indigenous system, women could exert some influence over the directions and uses of such goods because of moral claims deriving from their role as producers (directly in the case of pigs and indirectly in the case of shells; cf. M. Strathern 1972). Such claims are less likely to be acknowledged with the new valuables—cash, trucks, and beer—which are increasingly substituted for pigs and shells in the exchange system.

Most of these new valuables derive from coffee cultivation. Women do most of the work of clearing, planting, weeding, harvesting, drying, and porterage of beans, but men claim ownership of the produce on the grounds that they own both the land and the trees. Although women "produce" both cash and commodities through intensive work in coffee cultivation, they do not exert influence over exchanges of such goods. Indeed, Andrew Strathern suggests that men have an interest in denying women's productive contributions to their transactions. For example, in Hagen today a man may use cash to purchase a pig from another household rather than use a pig his wife has reared, seemingly to demonstrate that even pigs can be procured independently of women. However, Strathern contends (1979, 544) this is a double obfuscation: the pig has clearly been raised by a woman, even if not the purchaser's wife, and the cash used for the purchase is likely to have come from coffee production by his wife.

It is in the context of such new relations of production and transaction, and of the particular control men exert over cash as commodity and as gift, that the congeries of women's movements called *wok meri* have arisen in the Highlands of Papua New Guinea. These are widespread in the Chimbu and Chuave regions, though importantly not in the Hagen area. Sexton (1982, 1986) suggests that they derive from women's perceptions of a deterioration in their situation and protests about the economic profligacy of men in ceremonial exchange, drinking and gambling. The women's work performed by such groups is expressly about money—saving, lending, exchange. Though clearly innovative in this way, they employ traditional models for women's association derived from kinship or affinal relations.[16] Groups relate as mothers and daughters or as wife-givers and wife-takers, and idioms of growth and reproduction are applied to the cash itself. Although there is a strong element of protest against men involved, there is also a degree of co-operation from them. Perhaps male endorsement of such projects for saving and exchange derives from the fact that the small amounts of cash generated by these groups often find their way back into the circuits of male ceremonial exchange. Sexton suggests (1984) that despite this convergence with male strategies these groups are profoundly important in generating a sense of women's autonomous interest and efficacy.

Such a comparison brings into focus both the commonalities and the differences in the Trobriand case. Trobriand women have not had to forge new groups of association, since women as members of a dala have a strong sense of shared interest and efficacy. Trobriand women have not suffered, as their Highlands counterparts have, such deleterious consequences from rapid colonization and economic development based on cash-cropping and male labor migration. There are both ecological and historical differences which explain why cash-cropping is, by contrast, of minimal importance and why most cash comes into Trobriand communities from the proceeds of selling crafts to tourists and from the remittances of migrant workers.

But also crucial appears to be the way in which the gender relations of western and central Highlands systems meshed with those of the colonizing culture (see Jolly 1987). The gender relations of the Trobriands were not, as Weiner has stressed, amenable to easy integration. This is not just a matter of an exotic matrilineal system, at odds with the notions of sexuality and procreation, kinship, and property prevalent in the West. The difference resides also in the way in which the values of persons and things were articulated. In the Trobriand case all objects of economic transaction and exchange were more deeply imbedded in the human relations of kinship. All exchange goods—shell valuables, ax blades, and yams, as well as banana leaf bundles—carried messages about kinship and reproduction.[17] But in Kiriwina, according to Weiner, only a certain class of these could secure regenesis: banana leaves, the wealth of women. The valuables exchanged in the Highlands, though they were also loaded with meanings derived from human reproduction, were not associated with a culture that accorded women a central place either in biological or social reproduction. Moreover, as Marilyn Strathern (1988) has shown, Hagen male ceremonial exchange is seen to eclipse the values of kinship rather than being eclipsed by kinship, as in the Trobriands.[18]

In part, such differences in indigenous relations help to account for the divergent impact of cash and commodities in the Highlands and the Trobriands. Although their experience of these processes has been very different, the women of the Trobriands have not completely escaped the influence of the association between monetary and male values. Highlands women have perforce to try to get some control over money, while Trobriand women perhaps can counter its influence by consolidating the association of women with banana leaves, matriliny, and tradition. But in both cases we must not be misled by the character of the objects themselves. Money can be a gift as well as a commodity, and banana leaves can be a symbol of women's resistance as well as of women's persistence.

We have been inclined to ignore or underestimate the historical changes in Pacific societies, especially insofar as these changes bear on women. The tendency within anthropology to dehistoricize and essentialize the other is arguably greater when dealing with small, isolated island cultures than in dealing with great literate civilizations such as India. But perhaps my argument about the political and historical significance of women's weaving in the Trobriands can best be underlined by making a provocative comparison far beyond the region. In the fight of Indian nationalists against British hegemony, Gandhi, Naidu, and others used powerful images of mother India, derived from the Hindu mythology of Sita (Forbes 1979; Kishwar 1985; Aylett 1988). In the struggle for independence, the political significance of the family and of household production were celebrated through the symbol of the spinning wheel. The women who spun and wove and whose families wore clothing made only from homespun cloth were thereby opposing the effects of British manufacture, the imports of cheap cloth from the mills of Manchester and Birmingham. The historical and political messages of banana leaf skirts are not the same as homespun saris. But women's weaving in India and the Pacific signals not just stability and persistence but also change and resistance to European goods[19] and a world where cloth is a symbol of human regeneration and not a mere commodity. In evoking mythic women, the politicized imagery of the Indian goddess Sita, devoted wife and mother deployed against the British, may be more appropriate than that faithful wife of Greek myth, Penelope, devotedly "weaving by day and unweaving the same fabric by night in order to stop time—to neither bury her husband, marry a suitor, nor change the politics of the land" (Weiner 1982a, 240).

EPILOGUE

When we look at women's worlds in remote parts of Melanesia, our general tendencies as anthropologists to exoticize and eternalize are amplified in a remarkable way. This is not to deny the pervasive character of this in all Western discourse about others, and indeed discourse about those others of literate civilizations such as India, China, and the Middle East. As Said's *Orientalism* has so persuasively argued, even contending civilizations with a self-conscious history have been reduced to silent, inarticulate passivity by Orientalist texts emanating from Europe. The Orient is constructed as the opposite of the Occident, essentialized as unchanging, passive, and closed: she cannot speak for herself but must be spoken for.

In similar vein, Fabian (1983) suggests that anthropology is predicated on a radical separation between Us and Them, a separation that conflates the coordinates of space and time. Other cultures are seen as spatially remote, as distant from a center that centers on us. But even when we are there, when we have "penetrated" those remote regions, we may deny copresence in shared historical time. "Their" culture may be eternalized through textual fictions such as the ethnographic present, or may be seen as before, in terms of an evolutionary narrative leading to a present inhabited by us.

In looking at non-Western women such tendencies to exoticize and eternalize are even greater. Even in writings about Europe and America, women have often been located outside history, not participating in the public political events that are seen as constitutive of historical process. Instead, they are portrayed as inhabiting a world that is contained and unchanging, the "family" or the "domestic sphere." This view of women in European history has of course been challenged and changed by feminist scholarship (e.g., Tilly and Scott 1978; Davidoff and Hall 1987), but such views seem even more strongly entrenched in studies of non-Western women. Consider a recent example from another part of Melanesia.

In his review of the history of anthropological writings on Tanna (southern Vanuatu), a review that is expressly critical of decades of homocentric writings—from Speiser, Humphreys, and Guiart to Lindstom—Ron Adams (1987, 14) says:

> anthropologists—like missionaries and government officials before them—have been consistently used to present to the outside world a homocentric construction of reality, in terms of which outsiders have perceived and related to the Tannese. While the Tannese have shown themselves to be amenable to intensive investigation of virtually every aspect of the domain, the female sphere has remained hidden—and intact.

Adams's bad joke about a female perspective as a "bird's-eye view" (1987, 14) and the language of observation as "penetration" of an intact women's world seem curiously at odds with the expressed critical aim of revealing the homocentric premises of anthropology. But apart from this troubling paradox, it is an extraordinary presumption to claim that because women's worlds are not open to the gaze of the European (male) observer, then they are closed and unchanging. To suggest a view of the timeless situation of Tannese women on the basis of twentieth-century ethnography is a very problematic exercise. In this part of southern Vanuatu, there were dramatic transformations wrought in the lives of women by the combined but contradictory effects of sandalwood and bêche-de-mer trading, Protestant missionary activity and the rival British and French colonial influences dating from the middle of the nineteenth century. The documents associated with each of these colonial agents are rich in descriptions of women's lives, and in the case of missionary reports are full of messages about transformations (or "improvements") of their situation. Such colonial projects were often in tension: for traders and labor recruiters women were potential laborers and sexual partners, while missionaries strove to keep women away from plantation labor and interracial liaisons (which they labeled prostitution), in order that they might devote themselves more thoroughly to making good Christian homes. Such colonial projects were only ever partially realized, but there have been crucial changes in the patterns of women's work, in the character of households and families (Jolly and Macintyre 1989) and most spectacularly in the cessation of practices such as widow strangulation and female infanticide. Even where there has been patent persistence—as for instance in the perpetuation of male kava drinking, which women cannot drink or witness being prepared—this is in the face of decades of attempts to ban it, or at least transform its exclusivist masculine character. Again, apparent persistence may be resistance to colonial intervention.

As in the Trobriand case, women and men are differently situated in relation to tradition or kastom, as lived practice and conscious construct. This raises a nest of associated problems about conscious and unconscious aspects of tradition, about the reifications involved in constructs of tradition (cf. Thomas, this volume) and about the gendered character of tradition.

In the burgeoning literature on tradition there has been an unfortunate tendency to distinguish an authentic, unselfconscious, lived culture from a less authentic, self-conscious construct of tradition. While not denying that traditionalism draws selectively on elements of precolonial culture which then stand for the totality, I think it is important not to stress unduly the self-consciousness and novelty in this process. The very notion of invention, central to the formulations of Hobsbawm and Ranger's (1983) early influential text obscures the unselfconscious aspects and the generality of such processes in the construction of identity and ethnicity.

Although earlier writing on tradition in island Melanesia (esp. Keesing and Tonkinson 1982, which, incidentally, predates Hobsbawm and Ranger) did not draw an invidious distinction between custom and tradition (but see Hobsbawm and Ranger 1983, 2), it did perhaps distinguish too strongly between tradition as lived practice and tradition as political construct. Thus, in my earlier paper on the kastom communities of South Pentecost I distinguished sharply between those who adhered to kastom as a way of life and those who used it as a rhetorical construct in political debates about nationalism and secessionism. This was no doubt unduly influenced by the strenuous political ideologies that were promulgated by kastom communities, which distinguished their way of life as authentically ancestral, in contradistinction to those of "skin deep" kastom adherents, Christian politicians who in fact followed the ways of *skul*. Attempts at revival of lost practices by Christian or skul communities were similarly treated with derision and contempt.

But tradition is both lived practice and ideological construct in rural villages and in the national parliament. Moreover, kastom is similar in both contexts in important ways. First, as an ideology of past-present relations it tends to eternalize, to gloss over changes—to cover ruptures and discontinuities with an idea of primordial place and space: immobile, eternal black stone, in the imagery of Grace Mera Molisa, a ni-Vanuatu poet. In this indigenous construct there is a denial of historical transformation, a dehistoricizing or eternalizing just as powerful as what we have isolated in European thinking about Melanesian societies. In my own ethnographic work, I was eventually forced to recognize a complicity between indigenous constructions and my own, ahistorical analytical fictions. Similarly, in the Trobriand case I have considered here there is no doubt complicity between the indigenous eternalism of Trobriand views of life as regenerative cycle and Weiner's representation of them in her theory of social reproduction. In such an intimate dialogue, it feels unseemly to tear the interlocutors apart.

But we do need to recognize the power of the representation of tradition, both by Pacific peoples and by anthropologists (Keesing 1989*b*). In both the Solomon Islands and in Vanuatu, the right to codify tradition and perpetuate it is still primarily a male prerogative. This male power to define and control has been seen by Grace Mera Molisa (1983) as being expressly asserted against women. And yet, as Keesing (1985) has shown for Kwaio kastom adherents, women do not necessarily see themselves as excluded from conscious deliberation about tradition. They do not merely practice custom in unselfconscious ways in remote rural spaces but may themselves be strongly and consciously committed to its perpetuation, even where outsiders may perceive this as perpetuating their own domination.

Such conscious celebration of tradition is, I contend, especially possible for Trobriand women, for here "tradition" gives to them a value and a power greater than in most other parts of Melanesia. This power is in part a consequence of their indigenous situation, in part the result of the particular limits of exogenous influences. But it is a power emerging from the relation *between* the interior world of the Trobriands and the exterior world in which it is situated.

And in construing this relation between interior and exterior worlds, the power of the anthropologist in representing tradition is patent. We have often elided the histories of Pacific peoples in a way that conformed not only to Western stereotypes about isolated and timeless others but suited our disciplinary interests. But in attending to history—in stressing discontinuity rather the continuity, resistance rather than persistence, self-conscious creation rather than unselfconscious reproduction—it is imperative that we do not thereby suggest that Pacific peoples engaged in projects of historical transformation are thereby less themselves, are inauthentic because they are becoming "like us." This would be to believe our own eternalist fictions about the essence of their culture, and another equally powerful fiction, that change can only mean that local culture becomes more like that imaginary metropolis of the West.

NOTES

1. This paper develops some themes presented in an earlier paper coauthored by Martha Macintyre and myself, presented at the AAS Conference in Adelaide 1983. Though this version owes much to Martha's insights about the Massim, it is not an

elaboration she would necessarily endorse. I am also grateful for conversations with Michael Allen, Wendy Cowling, and Christine Dureau about Weiner and women's wealth, and especially to Nicholas Thomas for discussions about the uses of European things by Pacific peoples.

2. There is, I agree, a "romance of resistance" abroad in the discipline at the moment as Abu-Lughod (1990) has argued. Although I endorse her cautions about the use of this term, it does seem appropriate for these small, localized subversions by Trobriand women as well as large-scale collective insurrections. Resistance is, as Abu-Lughod has argued, best seen as a diagnostic of power.

3. The most incisive appraisal of gynocentrism in feminist anthropology is to be found in the recent work of Moore (1988, 4ff.). She notes the hazards of the simple substitution of a female view for a male view, especially if this is based on the assumption of identity between the viewpoints of a woman as analyst and a woman as subject.

4. This is less true of Weiner's more recent text (1988), in which both the colonial history of the Trobriands and the political struggles of the early 1970s are given greater attention. Here, too, she develops an analysis of Trobriand culture along lines similar to that presented here—as resistance rather than persistence.

5. The Kabisawali movement was initiated by the chief of Yalumugwa in 1968, and involved villagers raising cash for small ventures through self-imposed levies. Their attempts to opt out of the local government system led to the jailing of its leaders by Australian authorities and the return of Kasaipwalova from the University of Papua New Guinea to become its chief negotiator. The movement became an alternative local government, and although it was organized along traditional lines it promoted "development": economic cooperatives, village trade stores, a bank, and a tourist hotel. The Kabisawali Village Development Corporation purchased a tractor for agricultural improvements, a machine to facilitate the making of coral bricks, and was committed to maintaining a high influx of package tourists with the development of regular charter flights, a bus service in Kiriwina, a hotel modeled on a traditional village, and local demonstrations of dance and arts and crafts. In 1970, tourism was the major source of cash for Trobrianders, and in the following year 2,100 tourists visited (Young 1979, 19).

Kabisawali came into dramatic conflict both with the colonial administration and with local opponents. These were led by Waibadia, an older high-ranking man, rival to Vanoi, and his associate Lepani Watson (later a Member of the House of Assembly). They adopted a more conservative policy on economic and touristic development. In 1972, a fire originating in a kerosene freezer destroyed the tourist hotel. In 1973, a series of unarmed clashes between local opponents and the destruction of property occasioned intervention by riot police from Port Moresby. Young (1979, 19) suggests that Kasaipwalova was alert to the threats of tourism and economic development and aimed to preserve "Trobriand cultural uniqueness" through cultural revival, in particular competitive yam gardening and rivalrous displays at harvest festivals. Thus garden magicians resumed the prominence they had in Malinowski's time, although their efforts were being harnessed to the goals of economic development as much as competitive food production. But such successful integrations were short-lived. By 1976, Kabisawali was spent—the stores were closed and the headquarters deserted and boarded up and villagers were complaining about losing money.

Kasaipwalova was himself later jailed on charges of embezzling national government funds to establish an art school and cultural center (Weiner 1988, 24). The struggle about tourism persists to the present. The conflict generated by a recent hotel project initiated by two Australians was reported in *The Sydney Morning Herald* (12 January 1989, p. 5) under the headline "Australians Held as 'Friendly Hostages' on Islands of Love."

6. In her more comparative essays, Weiner (1985, 1989) directs our attention to a range of fibrous wealth in the Pacific: banana leaf bundles, net bags, bark cloth, and fine mats. Though the argument advanced here might be extended to embrace net bags in Papua New Guinea (see M. Strathern 1981; Mackenzie 1986), fine mats in Vanuatu and bark cloth and mats in Polynesia (see Weiner 1986; Gailey 1980; Cowling 1988), here I concentrate on the skirts and banana leaf bundles of the Trobriands. Elsewhere I consider these other examples, and especially the fine mats of Vanuatu, in more detail.

7. This was also true of *Sex and Repression in Savage Society* (1927).

8. I am here of course merely alluding to the intense debates about Trobriand ideas of procreation, and in particular the infamous "denial of physiological paternity." For some recent evaluations, see Jorgensen (1983), and for an intriguing reformulation, see Marilyn Strathern (1988, 231–243).

9. Note that this was an incorrect translation by Malinowski since *urigubu* does not apply to presentations of yams. In fact it refers to pork, areca and coconut palms, and betel pepper plants presented to the same person for whom ego cultivates a yam garden (Weiner 1976, 140, 258).

10. It should be noted here that Weiner's concept of reproduction involves much more than just biological reproduction, and a different notion of social reproduction from that used by other feminists influenced by Marxism (e.g, Edholm, Harris, and Young 1977). For her, reproduction means

> the way societies come to terms with the processes whereby individuals give social identities and things of value to others and the way in which these identities and values come to be replaced by other individuals and regenerated through generations. These identities and objects of value range from abstract categories such as kinship identities to substances such as blood and semen or material objects used in formal exchange events. . . . Rebirth, what I formally call regeneration, constitutes the replacement of these values at death so that some measure continues, i.e., is regenerated for the living. (Weiner 1982a, 56)

11. Weiner claims that the association of men with history and change, and of women with eternity and stasis, is an indigenous schema and not just her analytic construct, although how the contrast between history and eternity is conveyed in Trobriand terms is not clear (1976, 231; 1988, 165–167). The *interaction* between such indigenous constructs and the exogenous constructs of Europeans, including anthropologists, is the focus of my attention here. It must also be admitted that here I am maintaining clear distinctions between Trobriand and Western views of the sort I have criticized elsewhere. Not only is the Trobriands constructed as radically different, as opposed to "us," but the content of the West and Western values is unspecified and unanalyzed.

12. This assertion of the nature of the relations between persons and things in the West is derived in part from the analysis of commodity fetishism in Marx. A more

subtle rendering of this theory, especially in the context of a colonizing capitalism, is to be found in Taussig (1979). Recent works by Appadurai (1986), Miller (1987), and Baudrillard (1975) suggest a rather different view of the relations between people and things, especially in the processes of mass consumption in capitalist society.

13. It is hard to know whether contemporary perceptions of divergent gender interests are novel. For the Highlands, Marilyn Strathern (1987, 380–381) has criticized Sexton for projecting male-female conflicts back into the precolonial past. For the Chambri, Errington and Gewertz (1987) have argued for divergent but complementary gender interests.

14. This might be compared to Gewertz's (1983; cf. Errington and Gewertz 1987) analysis of Sepik River societies, and the differential impact cash and commodities had on male and female exchange relations, in the context of interethnic relations in this riverine region. It should be noted that here I am allowing a distinction between gift and commodity to mark a difference between indigenous and exogenous, or Melanesian and Western, systems. This is central to Marilyn Strathern's analysis in *The Gender of the Gift*, but is disputed by Thomas (1991).

15. We cannot here enter into the debates about the indigenous relations of men and women in the system and whether they are characterized by complementarity or exploitation and appropriation (but in this regard, see M. Strathern 1972, 1988; A. Strathern, 1979, 1982; Modjeska 1982; Josephides 1985; Sexton 1986; Jolly 1987).

16. These associations also owed their existence in part to women's church groups, especially within the Lutheran tradition.

17. This is not to suggest that goods were never able to be detached, alienated, or appropriated. See Damon (1982), Macintyre (1984), and M. Strathern (1988, 151–162) in this regard, and my earlier discussion of *kitoma*.

18. This is mere allusion to the complex comparative argument in Marilyn Strathern's *The Gender of the Gift*, too dense to consider here.

19. See the recent work of Keller (1988) for a similar argument about the political symbolism of plaited pandanus baskets in West Futuna, Vanuatu.

REFERENCES

Abu-Lughod, Lila. 1990. "The Romance of Resistance: Tracing Transformations of Power through Bedouin Women." *American Ethnologist* 17:41–55.

Adams, Ron. 1987. "*Homo Anthropologicus* and Man-Tanna: Jean Guiart and the Anthropological Attempt to Understand the Tannese." *Journal of Pacific History* 22:3–14.

Appadurai, Arjun, ed. 1986. *The Social Life of Things: Commodities in Cultural Perspective*. Cambridge: Cambridge University Press.

Aylett, Merrilyn. 1988. "The Liberation of Sita: Religious Symbolism in Indian Feminism." B.A. hons. thesis, Macquarie University.

Baudrillard, Jean. 1975. *The Mirror of Production*. St. Louis: Telos Press.

Berde, Stuart. 1983. "The Impact of Colonization on the Economy of Panaetai." Pp. 431–443 in Edmund Leach and Jerry Leach (eds.), *The Kula: New Perspectives on Massim Exchange*. Cambridge: Cambridge University Press.

Campbell, Shirley. 1983. "Kula in Vakuta: The Mechanics of Keda." Pp. 201–227 in Edmund Leach and Jerry Leach (eds.), *The Kula: New Perspectives on Massim Exchange*. Cambridge: Cambridge University Press.

Carrier, Achsah H., and James G. Carrier. 1987. "Brigadoon, or; Musical Comedy and the Persistence of Tradition in Melanesian Ethnography." *Oceania* 57:271–293.

Carrier, James G., and Achsah H. Carrier. 1989. *Wage, Trade, and Exchange in Melanesia: A Manus Society in the Modern State*. Berkeley, Los Angeles, London: University of California Press.

Cowling, Wendy. 1988. "Women's Production in Tonga." Unpublished paper delivered to the Women's Studies Seminar, Macquarie University, May.

Damon, Fredrick. 1982. "Alienating the Inalienable." (Correspondence.) *Man* 17: 342–343.

Davidoff, Leonore, and Catherine Hall. 1987. *Family Fortunes: Men and Women of the English Middle Class 1780–1850*. London: Hutchinson.

Edholm, Felicity, Olivia Harris, and Kate Young. 1977. "Conceptualising Women." *Critique of Anthropology* 3(9–10):101–130.

Errington, Frederick, and Deborah Gewertz. 1987. *Cultural Alternatives and a Feminist Anthropology: An Analysis of Culturally Constructed Gender Interests in Papua New Guinea*. New York: Cambridge University Press.

Fabian, Johannes. 1983. *Time and the Other: How Anthropology Makes Its Object*. New York: Columbia University Press.

Feil, Daryl. 1978. "Women and Men in the Enga *Tee*." *American Ethnologist* 5:263–279.

Forbes, Geraldine. 1979. "Women's Movements in India: Traditional Symbols and New Roles." Pp. 149–165 in M. S. A. Rao (ed.), *Social Movements in India* (vol. 2). Delhi: Manohar.

Gailey, Christine Ward. 1980. "Putting Down Sisters and Wives: Tongan Women and Colonization." Pp. 294–322 in M. Etienne and Eleanor Leacock (eds.), *Women and Colonization: Anthropological Perspectives*. New York: Praeger.

Gewertz, Deborah. 1983. *Sepik River Societies: A Historical Ethnography of the Chambri and Their Neighbors*. New Haven: Yale University Press.

Gregory, Chris A. 1982. *Gifts and Commodities*. London: Academic Press.

Handler, Richard, and Jocelyn Linnekin. 1984. "Tradition, Genuine or Spurious." *Journal of American Folklore* 97:273–290.

Hobsbawm, Eric, and Terrence Ranger, eds. 1983. *The Invention of Tradition*. Cambridge: Cambridge University Press.

Irwin, Geoffrey. 1983. "Chieftainship, Kula and Trade in Massim Prehistory." Pp. 29–72 in Edmund Leach and Jerry Leach (eds.), *The Kula: New Perspectives on Massim Exchange*. Cambridge: Cambridge University Press.

Jolly, Margaret. 1987. "The Chimera of Equality in Melanesia." *Mankind* 5 (special issue):168–183.

Jolly, Margaret, and Martha Macintyre, eds. 1989. *Family and Gender in the Pacific: Domestic Contradictions and the Colonial Impact*. Cambridge: Cambridge University Press.

Jorgensen, Dan, ed. 1983. *Conceptions of Conception. Mankind* 14 (special issue) (1).

Josephides, Lisette. 1985. *The Production of Inequality*. London: Tavistock.

Keesing, Roger. 1985. "Kwaio Women Speak: The Micropolitics of Biography in a Solomon Island Society." *American Anthropologist* 87:27–39.

———. 1988. "Colonial Discourse and Codes of Discrimination in Melanesia." Paris: UNESCO, Division of Human Rights.

———. 1989a. "Counter-Colonial Discourse in Melanesia." *Culture and History* 1. Forthcoming.

————. 1989*b*. "Creating the Past: Custom and Identity in the Contemporary Pacific." *The Contemporary Pacific* 1:16–35.

————. n.d. "New Lessons from Old Shells: Changing Perspectives on the Kula." In J. Siikala (ed.), *Culture and History in the Pacific*. Helsinki: Finnish Academy. Forthcoming.

Keesing, Roger, and Robert Tonkinson, eds. 1982. *Reinventing Traditional Culture: The Politics of* Kastom *in Island Melanesia. Mankind* 13 (special issue).

Keller, Janet D. 1988. "Woven World: Neotraditional Symbols of Unity in Vanuatu." *Mankind* 18:1–13.

Kishwar, Madhu. 1985. "Women in Gandhi." *Economic and Political Weekly* 20:40–41.

Linnekin, Jocelyn, and Lin Poyer, eds. 1990. *Cultural Identity and Ethnicity in the Pacific*. Honolulu: University of Hawaii Press.

Macintyre, Martha. 1983. "Changing Paths: An Historical Ethnography of the Traders of Tubetube." Ph.D. thesis, Australian National University.

————. 1984. "The Semi-Alienable Pig." *Canberra Anthropology* 7:109–121.

————. 1986. "Female Autonomy in a Matrilineal Society." Pp. 248–256 in Norma Grieve and Patricia Grimshaw (eds.), *Australian Women: Feminist Perspectives*. Melbourne: Oxford University Press.

Macintyre, Martha, and Michael W. Young. 1982. "The Persistence of Traditional Trade and Ceremonial Exchange in the Massim." Pp. 207–222 in Ronald J. May and Hank Nelson (eds.), *Melanesia: Beyond Diversity*. Canberra: Australian National University.

Mackenzie, Maureen. 1986. "'The Bilum is the Mother of us All': An Interpretive Analysis of the Social Value of the Telefol String Bag." M.A. thesis, Australian National University.

Malinowski, Bronislaw. 1922. *Argonauts of the Western Pacific*. London: Routledge.

————. 1927. *Sex and Repression in Savage Society*. London: Routledge.

————. 1929. *The Sexual Life of Savages in North-Western Melanesia*. London: Routledge.

————. 1967. *A Diary in the Strict Sense of the Term*. London: Routledge.

Mera Molisa, Grace. 1983. "Custom." Pp. 24 and 25 in G. Mera Molisa, *Black Stone*. Suva, Fiji: Mana Publications.

————. 1987. *Colonized People*. Port Vila: Black Stone Publications.

Miller, Daniel. 1987. *Material Culture and Mass Consumption*. Oxford: Basil Blackwell.

Modjeska, Nicholas. 1982. "Production and Inequality: Perspectives from Central New Guinea." Pp. 50–108 in Andrew Strathern (ed.), *Inequality in New Guinea Highlands Societies*. Cambridge: Cambridge University Press.

Moore, Henrietta L. 1988. *Feminism and Anthropology*. Oxford: Polity Press.

Said, Edward. 1978. *Orientalism*. Harmondsworth: Penguin.

Sexton, Lorraine. 1982. "*Wok Meri:* A Women's Saving and Exchange System in Highlands Papua New Guinea." *Oceania* 52:167–198.

————. 1984. "Pigs, Pearlshells and 'Women's Work': Collective Response to Change in Highland Papua New Guinea." Pp. 120–153 in Denise O'Brien and Sharon W. Tiffany (eds.), *Rethinking Women's Roles: Perspectives from the Pacific*. Berkeley, Los Angeles, London: University of California Press.

————. 1986. *Mothers of Money, Daughters of Coffee: The* Wok Meri *Movement*. (Studies in Cultural Anthropology 10.) Ann Arbor: UMI Research Press.

Strathern, Andrew. 1979. "Gender, Ideology and Money in Mount Hagen." *Man* 14:530–548.

———, ed. 1982. *Inequality in New Guinea Highlands Societies*. Cambridge: Cambridge University Press.

Strathern, Marilyn. 1972. *Women in Between: Female Roles in a Male World, Mount Hagen, New Guinea*. London: Academic Press.

———. 1981. "Culture in a Net Bag: The Manufacture of a Subdiscipline in Anthropology." *Man* 16:665–688.

———. 1987. Review of *Mothers of Money, Daughters of Coffee: The* Wok Meri *Movement. Man* 22:380–381.

———. 1988. *The Gender of the Gift*. Berkeley, Los Angeles, London: University of California Press.

Taussig, Michael. 1979. *The Devil and Commodity Fetishism*. Chapel Hill: University of North Carolina Press.

Thomas, Nicholas. 1991. *Entangled Objects: Exchange, Material Culture and Colonialism in the Pacific*. Cambridge, Mass.: Harvard University Press.

Tilly, Louise, and Joan Scott. 1978. *Women, Work and Family*. New York: Holt, Rinehart and Winston.

Weiner, Annette. 1976. *Women of Value, Men of Renown: New Perspectives in Trobriand Exchange*. Austin: University of Texas Press.

———. 1977. Review of "Trobriand Cricket: An Ingenious Response to Colonialism." *American Anthropologist* 79:506–507.

———. 1980. "Stability in Banana Leaves: Colonization and Women in Kiriwina, Trobriand Islands." Pp. 270–293 in M. Etienne and Eleanor Leacock (eds.), *Women and Colonization*. New York: Praeger.

———. 1982a. "Plus précieux que l'or: Relations et échanges entre hommes et femmes dans les sociétés d'Océanie." *Annales* 37:222–245.

———. 1982b. "Ten Years in the Life of an Island." *Bikmaus* 83(4):64–75.

———. 1983a. "A World of Made Is Not a World of Born: Doing Kula in Kiriwina." Pp. 147–170 in Edmund Leach and Jerry Leach (eds.), *The Kula: New Perspectives on Massim Exchange*. Cambridge: Cambridge University Press.

———. 1983b. "Sexuality among the Anthropologists, Reproduction among the Informants." *Social Analysis* 12:52–65.

———. 1985. "Inalienable Wealth." *American Ethnologist* 12:210–227.

———. 1986. "Forgotten Wealth: Cloth and Women's Production in the Pacific." Pp. 96–110 in Eleanor Leacock and H. I. Safa (eds.), *Women's Work: Development and the Division of Labor by Gender*. South Hadley, Mass: Bergin and Garvey.

———. 1988. *The Trobrianders of Papua New Guinea*. New York: Holt, Rinehart and Winston.

———. 1989. "Why Cloth? Wealth, Gender and Power in Oceania." Pp. 33–72 in Jane Schneider and Annette Weiner (eds.), *Cloth and Human Experience*. Washington, D.C.: Smithsonian Institution Press.

Young, Michael W., ed. 1979. *The Ethnography of Malinowski: The Trobriand Islands 1915–18*. London: Routledge.

———. 1983. "'The Best Workmen in Papua': Goodenough Islanders in the Labour Trade 1900–1960." *Journal of Pacific History* 18:74–95.

TWO

Substantivization and Anthropological Discourse

The Transformation of Practices into Institutions in Neotraditional Pacific Societies

Nicholas Thomas

Anthropological thought has dealt mostly with totalities, with "society" or "culture."[1] These have always been partitioned; there have always been bits of one sort or another to be contextualized. Anthropologists, naturally, have not called the components of the totalities "bits" but have drawn on a confusing array of shifting terms. At different moments we have spoken of customs, institutions, habits, rites, norms, structural principles, ethics, icons, images, statements, acts, and practices. These objects may often overlap or roughly correspond, but the inflections of many of the terms were diacritical: they expressed differentiation of approach, the privileging of features marginal to an earlier vision, or rigor as opposed to imagery and interpretation.

The concern of this chapter is with an issue that cuts across and is frequently elided by this array of words: this is the difference between practices and ideas which are simply done or thought, or simply take place, and those set up as definite entities to be reflected upon and manipulated by the people in the situation under consideration. The former—like any action or statement—always express, even if idiosyncratically, broader concerns, meanings, and social relations but are not themselves regarded as symbolic entities or socially fundamental acts. Practices that are formalized and regarded as substantial entities do not necessarily have greater social effect, but potentially have quite different uses and implications. A ceremony that is named, and thus can be conceived of as an entity separable from particular enactments, can become a vital element in the self-expression or regeneration of a group, and especially may state and mark its differentiation from other groups. Attitudes toward it, or competing constructions of it, may also register crucial lines of disagreement or conflict within a particular society. I take it to be virtually tautological to assert that elaborated and substantivized notions or practices have a political and cultural potential which implicit ideas and unreflective action do not have: to be manipulated, things must be "there" in some sense. It is of great importance whether a "custom," "code of behavior," or whatever is reified as such by those who do it and think it, or only by the anthropological analyst.

The problem is not, of course, reification or substantivization as such: the whole point of research and writing is presumably to order things and argue about them in a different way to the one in which they present themselves. Analytical reification may thus be justified or justifiable by the theoretical objective of disclosing implicit meaning. The form of substantivization is, however, consequential for an understanding of cultural dynamics, and for the interpretation of particular beliefs and statements. A conventional, unhistorical anthropological analysis may take a specific custom simply as an element in a culture, to be "explained" on the basis of its functional or signifying coherence with a totality; a particular institution or belief would be anthropologically substantivized as an expression of a "web" of signification or kinship (Hooper 1985, 13; Fortes 1949). The argument here does not deal with anthropological reification and essentialism (but see James Carrier's Introduction), but is concerned instead with the fact that indigenous reifications of culture have been passed over. I suggest that there is always a general cultural potential for substantivization, and that substantivization can be a topic of broader theoretical importance for anthropology, but the process of naming and reifying customs and beliefs takes place in a particularly marked and conspicuous fashion in the course of colonial history. Abstracted notions about practices can be invented on the basis of daily life and colonial interaction or borrowed from the practices of other groups, and come to be represented—by indigenous people or anthropologists or both—as "customs" in the strong sense, without it being recognized that their existence as such derives from the oppositional dynamics of the colonial encounter. Cultural objectification in noncolonial contexts—between saltwater and bush people in Melanesia, or rivalrous religious and migrant communities in Europe—may emerge in essentially the same manner as the type of substantivization discussed here, and could be based on a range of oppositional kinds of social difference; in the Pacific, however, the history of colonialism has been crucial to the recognition of culture and the elaboration of difference.

KEREKERE IN FIJI

In what remains one of the most detailed ethnographies of neotraditional Fijian society, Sahlins discussed transactions, reciprocity, and redistribution in the economy of Moala (in the Lau group of eastern Fiji) at considerable length. The analysis included an extended discussion of what was described as "the famous custom of *kerekere*" (Sahlins 1962, 145); this was "the prevailing form of economic transaction among kinsmen as individuals" (1962,

203). The verb from which the term derived meant "request," or, in economic contexts, "solicit": kerekere involved soliciting goods, resources, services, or use rights in goods or resources (1962, 203). Only houses and house
platforms could not be subject to kerekere; while land was inalienable, use
rights in land could be solicited, as could virtually any kind of product, food,
or service.

Sahlins drew the attention of readers to the fact that kerekere had frequently been mistranslated as "begging," which it was "most emphatically
not" (1962, 203, and cf. 441 nn. 2, 4). This was misleading because it
obscured "the essential kinship ethic [and] the implied reciprocity" (1962,
203). Kerekere stood as a kind of formal operator as opposed to certain informal transactions; it played a significant part as a "mechanism" in a system
that tended to "produce material equality in a community of kinsmen";
which "obliterate[d] the material inequality among households and regions
by transforming it into social inequality"—that is, into asymmetries based
on the prestige and superiority of givers as opposed to receivers. The singularity of kerekere is thus attributed to its place within a socioeconomic
system based on principles quite different from those of Western capitalist
economies, and we could see it being drawn into the polarities so suc-
cinctly articulated by Gregory in *Gifts and Commodities*—between clan-based
and class-based societies, between transactions based on qualitative rank,
directed at relations of social value, and those turning on quantitative
equivalence, directed at profits or use-values; I have argued elsewhere
(Thomas 1991) that Gregory's analysis provides a stimulating point of departure, but stress here that this is because his concepts outrun the limitations of these dichotomous categories. The theoretical error arises from a
failure to notice that the properties of the gift economy are simply conceptual
and ideological inversions of those of the capitalist economy, rather than
attributes derived from particular studies of gift economies that have not
been caught up in colonial entanglements. I shall argue that the peculiar
cultural and political circumstances of Fijian colonial history produced a
neotraditional system that corresponded in some of its effects and elements to
the stereotype of a clan economy structured by solidarity and reciprocity.

Fijians have differing views today about customs such as kerekere, which
have been taken to be emblematic of the "communal" character of Fijian
society, and these constructions and adjudications have also changed over
time. My point here, however, is that the reification of kerekere as a "custom" and a possible reference point for such debate is something that occurred during the colonial period; there is no evidence that kerekere existed
in this sense during the earlier phases of Fijian history. That is, kerekere
apparently did not exist as a reified custom in indigenous Fijian society during precolonial phases of its history. In the numerous accounts of Fijian culture, belief, behavior, and politics, in general and particular, as these were

observed before the formation of neotraditional Fijian culture in the years of expanded settlement and extensive official codification of early colonial rule—that is, before the 1860s—there appear to be no references to kerekere as a recognized practice, as a custom.

This statement may appear categorical, and needs to be specified and qualified in three ways. First, I am not making a claim about what was absent or present in *precontact* Fijian society, which is unknowable, but am instead contrasting the period of trading relations and contacts (roughly from 1800 to the 1860s) with the subsequent period of more extensive settlement and (from 1874) formal British administration. Second, the unsatisfactory character of evidence for a negative proposition is in this instance ameliorated by the extent and nature of ethnohistoric documentation. Third, my claim is not about the types of transactions called "kerekere," which no doubt occurred in precontact society as well as at other times. It is rather about the process of objectification.

Let us consider the problematic character of strictly negative evidence. It is true that most of the descriptions by missionaries and traders were oriented toward the spectacular, and more specifically, toward the features of indigenous life which provided ideologically useful images, such as warfare, cannibalism, and widow-strangling. This is the obvious and familiar line of criticism of preanthropological ethnographic writing, and it has some basis, especially in relation to the missionary publications that were worked up by metropolitan editors mindful of the appetites of mission supporters and the need to secure future funding; such works often seem especially laden with the burden of stereotyping and racial imagery. I have argued elsewhere, however, that the most significant distortions in missionary texts operate at a more subtle level, and that, in general, the representational value of these accounts may move beyond the apparent constraints of premises.[2] This is so especially if unpublished discursive manuscripts, rather than popular publications, are drawn upon. In fact, much of the missionary ethnography of Fiji is of a very high and detailed standard, and concerned itself with relatively mundane and unspectacular aspects of Fijian life. There was a bias toward reportage of the activities of chiefs, but it did not overwhelm entire descriptions. The manuscripts and publications of writers such as Williams (e.g., 1843–1852, 1858) and Lyth are, moreover, not the only sources; I have found no discussion of kerekere in the texts of naval visitors or beachcombers, who were from very different social backgrounds, and who of course acted and reported on the basis of very different practical interest (e.g., Wilkes 1845; Erskine 1853; Diapea 1928). Nor could it be suggested that these preanthropological writers were simply unable to notice a custom when they saw one, as there is a great contrast between the invisibility of kerekere and the extensive comments upon the rights of nephews (*vasu*), especially chiefly nephews, to appropriate anything from within the maternal uncle's domain (e.g., Williams 1843–1852, I, 61; 1858, 28; Wilkes 1845, 63; Diapea 1928 [late 1840s], 89, 110). Given that one can hardly expect to find positive evidence for the absence of a reification, the absence of reference to kerekere from extended discussions of a variety of customary usages in a substantial literature justifies my claim that kerekere was not talked about as a recognized practice in Fijian culture before the 1860s.

This is not, of course, to say that the sorts of transactions described by Sahlins in his early monograph did not take place. It is almost certain that they did. Nor do I suggest that the word "kerekere" did not exist. There is evidence from Hazelwood's dictionaries (1850, 61; 1872, 54) that it had roughly the same meanings as were noted later. The point is, rather, that the claim made in Capell's later dictionary, that kerekere was "a recognized system in Fijian society" (1957, 112) would have been unintelligible earlier. In earlier usage the word may not have had such specific associations with a particular kind of transaction; Hazelwood's reference to a "petition" implies that services or favors, rather than property, might often have been sought. Capell noted some associated usage such as "*i kere ni vanua*, ground rent paid in kind" (1957, 112); the translation may carry misleading connotations but does suggest a more diffuse pattern of meanings.

Why, then, should this practice have acquired a distinct status and become, as Sahlins put it, a "famous custom"?

The answer is connected with the singular form of indirect rule developed by the British administration in Fiji in the years immediately after cession (which took place at the request of a group of leading chiefs in October 1874). The influence of the first governor, Sir Arthur Hamilton Gordon, was crucial. He had interests in anthropology, and saw parallels between native Fijian society and the clan system which had existed in his native Scotland a few centuries earlier. He also had a unique opportunity to shape the direction of British policy in Fiji. Experience in other colonies, and especially New Zealand, had convinced him that trampling upon native rights, especially wide-scale alienation of indigenous land, produced highly undesirable conflict and instability. He was determined to avoid such developments in Fiji and, contrary to the vigorously expressed wishes of planters and settlers, he set about generating policies and establishing institutions that perpetuated what he saw as the indigenous Fijian chiefly hierarchy; more importantly, in the hands of his successors, a fabricated and homogenized but "traditional" system of corporate ownership of land by Fijian descent groups was institutionalized.

As the historian France has stressed, Gordon's construction of the basic principles of the traditional Fijian system derived less from detailed observation and inquiry than from general expectations about the nature of a society at a certain level of development; "communal ownership and inalienability" were the cornerstones of a codification which solved the political problem of the moment by precluding the free sale of land to settlers and the dispossession of the Fijians (France 1969, 102ff.). A few years later, the missionary-anthropologist Fison, in correspondence with Morgan, determined that Fijians had reached the "Middle Period of Barbarism." His 1880 discussion of Fijian land tenure, which stresses the paramount importance of communal ownership, was twice reprinted by the Administration, which used it and apparently regarded it as authoritative until at least the 1950s (France 1969, 118–119). Gordon and his successors were thus engaged in the creation of a substantivized Fijian culture, toward which they were sympathetic—Gordon in particular seeing himself as a Fijian paramount chief—but which was there to be acted upon in whichever ways were deemed necessary (see Thomas 1989*b*).

Fijian "society," or more particularly the "Fijian communal system," was thus not something that always existed, either in Fijians' own minds or in practice. This is not to say that there was no substantivizing of Fijian customs before colonialism: certain practices were indigenously identified as *vakaviti*, Fiji style, as opposed to the *vaka* Tonga; for instance, in Fiji women were tattooed, whereas in Tonga and Samoa this was done only to men. In a similar manner, particular polities (*vanua*) within Fiji had their distinctive customs of respect and ways of preparing *kava*. In some cases, what was presumably important was the specificity of local identity, rather than any oppositional concept of a type or social totality. However, where there was a broader oppositional relationship, of the kind that clearly is often characteristic of relationships between foraging and agricultural neighbors, it is clear that colonial circumstances would be conducive to the substantivization of a totality manifested in particular features, which would have lacked such salience earlier. The general idea of a Fijian customary order—which always glossed over considerable internal diversity in kinship, ritual, social structures, and language—drew on a set of basic components, which were therefore meaningfully revalued upon being incorporated as key constituents of the system in general. Some of the customs and institutions seen by European administrators and, to some extent, by other Europeans as the fundamental elements of the system were *lala*, the system of chiefly requisitions; kerekere, "begging"; the land tenure system; and *solevu*, the practice of large-scale feasting.

The question of whether chiefly requisitions for goods or services should be tolerated, regulated or proscribed by the administration was a contentious political question which fueled tempers and consumed a great deal of paper from the earliest days of the colonial administration. Lala in fact often overshadowed kerekere in debates about the desirability of retaining or modifying elements of Fijian society. Here I do not attempt to identify the origins of kerekere as a vital representation in European discourse but turn instead to a document of considerable importance in Fijian colonial history: the 1896 report on the Decrease of the Native Population.

Reflecting an ambitious, ideologically charged, pan-Pacific concern with indigenous depopulation, the inquiry attempted to map out in great detail the cause of the nineteenth-century decline in the Fijian population, as well as evaluating potential means of reducing or reversing the trend. An initial section of the report set out an array of prospective causes for consideration; the opinions of respondents—mostly Europeans in Fiji—to a circular questionnaire were summarized and evaluated, and the judgment of the commissioners was expressed. The "Communal system" was among the prospective causes specified under the general class of "predisposing" causes "tending to the Degeneracy of the People as a Race" (Fiji 1896, 6–7). More immediate causes affecting "Welfare and Stamina," such as water supplies, modes of treating the sick, "abuse" of *yaqona* (kava), and so on, were also discussed extensively.

A prefatory observation in the section on the communal system acknowledged that this was a site of contest: "This system, which is to some extent synonymous with the native policy of the Government, has been frequently referred to in criticisms of the Colonial Authorities, and has been the principal source of contention between the Government and the European Colonists" (1896, 45). The centrality of lala and kerekere in the communal system was stressed: "After *lala*—or perhaps before it—*kerekere* (the mutual appropriation of property) is the principal feature of the communal system" (1896, 47).

The statements of evidence were generally vehemently opposed to both the "system" in general and to the specific practices:

> The perpetuation of the communal system keeps the people in their primitive state. . . . A good deal is said [in the respondents' statements] about the bearing of the communal system upon native industry. If a man acquires anything, he cannot retain it. It is *lavaka*'d by his chief, or *kerekere*'d by any relative. The former he cannot deny for fear of punishment, and the latter he must appease for custom's sake. (1896, 47–48)

The last sentence shows the dependence of the specific comment upon a much larger conception of the "custom-bound" savage condition. This was expanded in the note of the commissioners' own views. It was noted that the Fijian system was not wholly communal, that private property existed in such things as pigs and canoes, and therefore that Fiji probably represented "the first stage of evolution from the state in which the proprietary unit was the tribe" (1896, 57).

> It is difficult to imagine how primitive society could exist without some such custom as communal *lala* and *kerekere* within the limits of the clan. So long as

usage prescribed an universal standard of industry the system worked well enough; it is only with the decay of that stimulus of fear that it has become mutilated. (1896, 57)

At this point it needs to be mentioned that two of the three authors of this document took a great interest in anthropology and were subsequently associated with the Royal Anthropological Institute. Both Bolton Glanville Corney and Basil Thomson wrote on aspects of Fijian customs and history, but Thomson's contribution is especially significant, as he later elaborated the theme of the "decay" of the "custom-bound" society at considerable length (Thomson 1908). In this context, the suggestion that kerekere was formerly essential and unobjectionable because a "standard of industry" was customarily enforced, but had become pernicious as "usage" had lost its force, was a neat way of expressing criticism of the particular custom without calling into question the government's overall policy of maintaining the native system: the problem was that change had brought about the "mutilation" of this specific element.

The report's recommendation on kerekere was singularly uncompromising, given that a positive view was taken of lala and that generally the authors were for administrative policy and against the settler view: "We condemn *kerekere*" (Fiji 1896, 209).

Kerekere has in fact always been alluded to, or more extensively discussed, specifically in relation to the question of the inhibition of enterprise and development (e.g., Brewster 1922, 92; Roth 1953, 36, 49; Belshaw 1964, 126; Sahlins 1970 [1960], 84). I do not suggest that this overall process of definition and inscription had particular or necessary social effects apart from upon the consciousness and behavior of the administrative actors themselves. That is, the ideological construct did not automatically lead to the refashioning of actual Fijian societies. Fijian social and cultural change was obviously a complicated process that affected different parts of Fiji unevenly (partly because administrative control was initially far more limited in some areas, such as upland Viti Levu, than elsewhere); the adoption or imposition of official models was clearly only one aspect of the process. However, the indirect rule system in general made chiefs especially, and to some extent all Fijians, complicit in the transformation of the administrative construction of Fijian society into a model of considerable practical salience. This is apparent especially in relation to land tenure, which has become firmly enshrined in Fijian custom and has developed a renewed and deeper relevance in the political conflict and rhetoric associated with the end of parliamentary democracy in 1987. The point is thus not that a certain invented or imposed tradition is "inauthentic," because through its enactment what begins as a mystification can become a genuine element of the system, a notion to be resorted to, or a model to be adduced.

The vital point is that what become elements of the system do not all have the same kind of significance; they should not be seen simply as parts of an expressive totality or functional or dysfunctional system of social relations. In the case of kerekere, such a view is inadequate because it obscures the fact that kerekere was not an isolated term, but one which operated in relation, and specifically in opposition, to others. Numerous efforts were made from about the time of the report onward to proscribe kerekere, and its true meaning and positive and negative features were extensively debated by Fijian native councils at all levels, as well as in correspondence to the government-published Fijian language gazette, *Na Mata* (Macnaught 1982, 20–21). Some Fijians, especially a few who had begun cash-cropping, supported the administrative moves to abolish or restrict the procedure; others defended it on various grounds. In one case, a provincial council in the eastern interior of Viti Levu voted overwhelmingly at one meeting to abolish kerekere for a trial period, yet at a subsequent vote were almost evenly divided. They were also confused about the application of the proscription in a particular case, and sought clarification from the white Resident Commissioner: "the people want to know whether when people kill pigs and make feasts and then ask for property if that is *kerekere*."[3]

Here, then, the Fijians needed to obtain information from Europeans about the nature of what was supposedly an important institution of their own. While the observations of many Europeans cannot be taken to reflect adequately developments in Fijian culture and consciousness, it is clear from this example that as they responded to and debated colonial regulations, Fijians had to deal with European codifications of customs such as kerekere. While indigenous objectification was not ideologically homogeneous, and did not directly mirror European invention, the disputes and debates did turn upon newly substantivized terms. Whether individuals felt that the system should be maintained or suppressed, they were talking about a recognized entity that had not previously been defined as a topic of discussion, an ideological token. The meaning of kerekere as a substantivized practice derived largely from the fact that it was the target of policies that sought to foster individualism and dismantle the communal social order. These challenges were very ineffectual, and laws against kerekere were mostly ignored (Macnaught 1982, 21). In a private comment upon one of the legislative attempts to ban kerekere, Hocart effectively sums up my argument:

> I think the government is mad or more ignorant than it imagines. There is a new law forbidding "begging"; I suppose the last governor was told that it killed initiative, and *he imagined that it was a well defined custom* like tauvu, circumcision, etc. & the result is that according to the law a Fijian who begs yams of his neighbour, to plant, or sends for a fowl to feed his guest, or brings a whales tooth and mats and asks for taro in exchange, is liable to the same penalty as a thief. The best part of the law is that it cannot be enforced. (Hocart 1912, n.p., emphasis added)

Sahlins noted that "breach of [the law] is not only common, it is a way of life" (1962, 203). This way of life, though, was not simply a pattern of behavior or an array of "well defined customs" of the type mentioned by Hocart, but a neotraditional existence that was profoundly affected by the rigidifying efforts of a paternalistic administration, and, more particularly, partly structured in opposition to the incursions of planters and a cash economy. The communal forms were recognized and magnified through contrast to what they were not, to what occasionally threatened to encroach upon them.

My point here is thus not that anthropologists have fabricated an order that did not really exist, or that they have regarded recently introduced practices or notions as manifestations of timeless tradition. An interpretive or analytic endeavor can deal with a system, irrespective of the time depth of some or all of its elements. The point should not be their origins but coherence and positional value. This sort of critique was, of course, the basis for the rejection of "historical" perspectives such as diffusionism by Radcliffe-Brown and others, and led to debates about "the relevance of past events" (Lewis 1968, xv–xx). These claims have been contested on a variety of grounds; the objection I develop here is specifically that neglect of the colonial and historical processes leads to a misconstruction of the system; it fails to recognize the factors that make some features of culture or social life more prominent or important than others. The notion that some particular theme, process, or metaphor may be seen as the big thing for a group of people is never elaborated in detail but looms large in the way anthropologists informally and implicitly try to come to grips with particular bodies of evidence, whether from their own fieldwork or that of others (see Damon 1980, 289). Certainly, if one is attempting to learn about a group of people it is presumably necessary to identify their preoccupations or central concerns. However, given that the most elementary aspect of anthropological method involves the contextualization of specific items in terms of a social or cultural totality, what is problematic is the contextualization of the "big thing" in systemic terms which fail to recognize the reactive interpenetration of local and colonial systems. This point will be developed in relation to two other cases, which will help me to draw together a set of concepts which might provide a better basis for the analysis of colonized societies.

RECIPROCITY AND WAMIRA

In discussions of economic processes in egalitarian societies, anthropologists frequently stress that food is constantly shared and redistributed beyond the boundaries of immediate domestic groups. The fact that this point is also often emphasized in television documentaries about "disappearing" peoples alerts us to the ideological import sustained by the observation: it is a way of saying that in this type of simple society we find a kind of sharing amongst kin, or amongst members of a community, which is quite unlike the privatized, impersonal, and even unpleasant interaction that pervades extrafamilial interaction in modern societies. For us, the family is a haven in a heartless world; for them, we suppose, the family is coextensive with society: pervasive kinship engenders cosy solidarity and a fuller, unfractured, and ultimately more natural existence.

The unsubtle versions of this vision, while continuing to flourish in mass-circulation anthropology, are becoming rarer in professional discourse. Everyone is attuned to the dangers entailed in projecting Western categories, either through eternalizing our forms or by romanticizing what are misrepresented as their inversion. Or rather, there is a widespread understanding at a general level that these projections are unsatisfactory; that Western hermeneutics can often lead simply to another level of tautology (e.g., Strathern and McCormack 1980). However, scepticism of this kind has been selectively directed: while some objects of anthropological discussion such as ritual have long been assumed to be complex and refractory for a Western vision, others have been taken to be transparent and relatively unproblematic. Economic transactions of the barter type have, for example, been taken to belong to a general class of straightforward exchanges of use-values (e.g., Sahlins 1972) that was not seen to demand especially complex cultural interpretation, but recent explorations of the field have led to rather drastic rethinking (see Humphrey and Hugh-Jones 1992).

I will argue that some images—such as that of the witch doctor invoked in the rationality debate, and that of tribal sharing—cannot be effectively contextualized in a way that subverts their ideological inflection without grounding in colonial history. Kahn's discussion (1986) of the attitudes of the Wamiran people (of Milne Bay province, Papua New Guinea) toward food and reciprocity permits me to elaborate this point.[4] I choose her study because it is a fine and subtle description of people's attitudes and behavior; it does not attempt to ignore or minimize the contemporary importance of Christianity, the involvement of men in wage work, or the significance of purchased commodities in the Wamiran economy. It is also a down-to-earth, particularistic work that conveys a lively sense of individuals and events, of the flow of village life. It is thus not a book that is preoccupied with symbolic abstractions, that one would obviously expect to reify and dehistoricize its cultural subject matter.

The monograph's main concern is with food symbolism. This is explored initially through elucidation of an initially paradoxical state of "famine" lacking any objective basis in actual food shortage. This is attributed to a deeper "obsession" with control. Desires for food and sex are regarded ambivalently and therefore repressed, controlled, and channeled outward in a variety of ways. The myth of Tamodukorokoro, for instance, is shown to compound the images of hunger and sexual desire: the external movements entailed in marriage involve "getting meat," which is unavailable at home; home is a place of famine and alliance is therefore "socially necessary" but difficult and stress-ridden. In another line of argument it is suggested that women's sexuality and reproductive capacities create a problem for men: they are dependent upon processes they cannot control or even (allegedly) "represent" (Kahn 1986, 74). Kahn suggests that men "solve" this problem at a metaphoric level by exchanging and symbolically manipulating pigs: in this domain of "female surrogates" men see themselves as controllers and "become independent of women" (1986, 75).

The overall analytic procedure of the text is thus to make connections between food and other aspects of social reality; once the field of such connections acquires the status of an explanatory or interpretively satisfying context, the domain of food can be seen to "express" features of kinship, affinal competition, sexual relations, and so on, which are problematic in other ways. One register of thought and practice thus resolves complications or contradictions that are inescapable within another.

We might wonder whether these symbolic transpositions actually provide solutions (a sort of functional closure) or whether, in displacing the issue to another domain, they simply express tensions or contradictions (which might be taken to meet a psychological requirement of the actors). My main concern here, however, is the way Kahn's contextualizing procedure resorts to systemic links and coherence.

It is clear from Kahn's description of Wamiran food-sharing and generosity that this is something ethically crucial: "Wamiran social etiquette centers on, and can be translated into, rules about sharing food. Generosity is accorded the highest social value. . . . The emphasis on sharing was brought to my attention within the first week of my arrival in the village" (1986, 41). Although it is noted that the moral injunctions are routinely violated in practice, and that in fact ways of hiding food, avoiding sharing, or demanding that others share, are highly elaborated, the ideals and rules are "mechanisms to control the fear of greed" and are pursued further through the deeper meanings ascribed to hunger and famine. The line of argument, however, neglects the context of many of the statements quoted: "We are not like white people, we share our food" is thus taken simply as an expression of the Wamiran view of the world, rather than as an indication of the opposition in which the statement is most salient. Kahn's account indicates that an insistence upon food transactions and sharing was constantly enunciated against an image of Western practice:

Wamirans constantly reminded me that they define their world, themselves, and their relationships in terms of food. To bring their beliefs into a framework that I could more easily grasp, they often explained, "We are taro people, but where you come from, people are money people." Time and again I was told,

"In your place people are different. They work for money. That is their life. That is who they are." (1986, 154)

The last sentence is especially revealing in that it implies that, just as in America, work for cash is identity, food and transacting food are identity in Wamira—which is clearly the ethnographer's point. I suggest that the repetition and stress upon reciprocity and sharing is contrastive in the first instance: this ideological salience can only arise in opposition to what are perceived as Western values; it is not a self-subsistent expression that could have existed in the same form prior to the recognition of the terms to which it is now opposed. In 1984, in the Marquesas Islands, I was frequently told that people there shared food, that if one could not grow or buy any, one would be looked after by others, but that they knew that where I came from, no money—no food—you die. The persistence of this type of statement across a variety of colonized situations suggests that it was more than the Wamirans' helpful effort to put their ideas "into a framework that [Kahn] could more easily grasp" that in fact motivated those resonant polarities.

EGALITARIANISM IN HAWAII

The suggestion is essentially that, in fundamental respects, modern Pacific cultures and practices are organized oppositionally. This condition can be further documented with material from contemporary traditionalist Hawaiian society, through Jocelyn Linnekin's (1985) study of a settlement on Maui. Keanae is "a taro place," a marginal settlement of about fifty households, seen both by outsiders and residents as having a "real Hawaiian" feel; it was still, in the mid-'seventies, a "reservoir of tradition" (Linnekin 1985, 18–22). This traditionalism was of course starkly different from that of anti-Christian Melanesians such as the Malaitan Kwaio and Sa speakers of Pentecost (Keesing 1982; Jolly 1982), and even from that in-scribed in Christian "kastom," because contact history in Hawaii has greater temporal depth and was marked by some savage moments of dispossession or displacement (for an overview, see Kent 1983). Continuity with early religious beliefs might be expected to be virtually nonexistent, given the celebrated chiefly abrogation of the *kapu* system in 1819 and the extent of subsequent development of various missions and indigenous churches.

Linnekin effectively demonstrates that what is now taken to be authentically Hawaiian as opposed to what is *haole* (foreign or white) is largely invented tradition:

A key concept in the organization of the cultural revival is that of *'ohana*, a term for extended family . . . [which] appears rarely in texts and archival materials from the nineteenth century, but today it refers to an idealized version of the Hawaiian family unit, characterized by cooperation (*kokua*), internal harmony, and aloha (love, affection). The word evokes Hawaiian kinship and solidarity. . . . *'Ohana* also describes an ethic of egalitarianism and thus represents the rejection of certain historical aspects of Hawaiian society [i.e., stratification and chieftainship]. (1985, 12)

This point is made in relation to contemporary and partly urban Hawaiian nationalism, but the overall pattern applies in such places as Keanae: "the egalitarian ethic does have a correlate in rural society, although aloha and *kokua* represent the ideals rather than the reality of village social relations" (1985, 12). The assertion of rural Hawaiian identity was and presumably still is thus based more on generalized notions about the importance of wide bilateral networks of relatives (in which one has aunties and uncles) and the value of gift-giving as opposed to purchase and sale, rather than upon a Melanesian-style retention of specific practices such as revalorized gender taboos and menstrual segregation.

Exchange is one of the central concerns of Linnekin's study. She notes that while Keanae Hawaiians are deeply and indisputably embedded in various capitalist relations, there is a strong ethic that within the village things, and especially food, should be given rather than sold. In practice food is offered constantly, both in the contexts of casual visiting, and in *luau*—feasts celebrating marriages, anniversaries, and the like. "The *luau* celebrates relatedness and the ideal of aloha" (1985, 114).

The larger interpretation of local gift exchange foregrounded in Linnekin's book is entangled with a knotty set of issues in the history of anthropological ideas: the Melanesia-Polynesia division, and the conflation of that pair of ethnological terms with the social conditions of "equality" and "inequality." It might seem that Linnekin's work makes a further healthy step toward undermining these tired and very misleading labels, since her suggestion is essentially that the "important people" of Keanae, those who mobilize labor and offer major luau—are like Melanesian big men (1985, chap. 8) (although certain points of contrast, and especially the fact that the Hawaiians understate prestige, are consistently noted). Yet whereas the concept of Polynesian ascribed rank has retained currency (despite its limitations), the stereotype of the egalitarian, competitive Melanesian system is now discredited (see Douglas [1979], Jolly [1987*a*] for extended critique). Linnekin's argument introduces the most dubious and problematic aspects of the Melanesian construct into the contemporary Polynesian situation.

As was the case with Kahn's book, it could not be complained that *Children of the Land* is an ahistorical work that suppresses the extent to which the people studied have been affected and indeed absolutely transformed by historical changes. It is not only an unlikely work to be flawed by colonial history; taken together with some of Linnekin's articles (e.g., 1983), it directly addresses the mutability and social basis of notions of tradition in Hawaii.

My interest here, however, is not in criticizing Linnekin's work, which more recently (1990) has included a valuable synthesis and development of the debate about tradition and identity in the Pacific; I am concerned rather with the way in which anthropologists' analytical frameworks can often obscure the oppositional character of substantivized traditions.[5] Hence the elucidation of the status of "important people" through reference to Melanesian big men, which is central to Linnekin's book, seems to deflect a more effective contextualization of Hawaiian ideology in history.

Although it is true that Melanesian big men, like chiefs (among other Pacific political figures), might be restrained or cut down to size if perceived to be despotic or overly domineering, the antihierarchical nature of Keanae egalitarianism seems to have a rather more specific character. Linnekin notes at several points that the ideology is at variance with actual inequalities of property, but that much is made in practice of diminishing these differences: "the Hawaiian social ethic demands that individuals deny their achievements, repudiate special status, and avoid differences in social position" (Linnekin 1985, 135, 142–145, 209–210, etc.). This case thus almost amounts to an inversion of what Sahlins reported from Moala, where mechanisms such as kerekere removed material inequalities by transforming them into "social" asymmetries, that is, into prestige relations associated with giving and receiving (1962, 146). In Hawaii, actual differences are sustained while equality in interaction and behavior is upheld: "the Hawaiian big-man's role is notable in its understatement and in the public denial of any special status" (1985, 212). While Linnekin discusses the contrast with Melanesian systems in this regard, it is not explained beyond further reference to "the Hawaiian ethic of egalitarianism" (1985, 235–247).

This "ethic" need not, however, be the end point of analysis; it has some singular features that are consistent with a comparative model of egalitarianism in poor and marginal societies. I refer here to Jayawardena's argument about the interrelationship between "the existence in a complex society of a local community whose members occupy a uniformly low status in the wider system" and "a dominant egalitarian ideology that provides the norms [and] the basis of social solidarity" (1968, 425, 426). The people

> are, or believe themselves to be, economically and politically under-privileged. They are not reconciled to their position and therefore are antagonistic to the social order and the upper class that represents it, whom they think are responsible for their deprivation and subjection. . . . The norms derived from the [egalitarian] ideology conflict with a degree of differentiation that actually exists [within the marginal community]. (1968, 425–426)

This argument is based primarily on Guyanese plantation workers of Indian origin who were obviously extracted from their own societies and severely oppressed in a way that was rare in the colonial Pacific (although the conditions of Chinese laborers on Hawaiian plantations were probably as severe [Kent 1983, 41]). There are few parallels to the "violent collective protests" reported by Jayawardena (1968, 418–423; see also Jayawardena 1963).

However, Jayawardena's argument becomes more appropriate to the Pacific case if the significance of egalitarian ideology is seen less in terms of its function for a lower-class community, than in terms of an oppositional cultural process whereby the ideals of a particular group are produced through an inversion of the values of the dominating external world. The members of the marginal community invert the values they perceive as the ones that energize a larger set of discriminating relations. Hence formulations such as "you are money people, we are taro people." This is part of a reactive process of positive collective self-identification within which a local group distinguishes itself, and expresses its own worth, by articulating and elaborating features of local practice which contrast with attributes of wider social relations. This process frequently operates in conjunction with a sense that the Europeans who perpetrate discrimination in workplaces or elsewhere, are also (generically) the producers of valuables, the possessors of wealth, and the means of obtaining and appropriating such valuables. The foreigners must often therefore be dealt with, perhaps through indentured labor, and are therefore represented in specific, ambivalent, and emotionally salient ways.

Partly through the influence of the "invention of tradition" paradigm, Pacific anthropologists have become aware of the extent to which traditional culture now operates as a "political symbol" (Keesing 1989), but it is important to examine the sense in which foreigners and colonizers were not a self-evident intrusion and presence but were also worked into an image by Melanesians and Polynesians, which then provided a foil for their own reactive self-identifications. The strength of fraternal (male) solidarity and egalitarianism among those who engage or have engaged in migrant labor must clearly be seen in this context (see Jolly 1987b).

Hawaiian egalitarianism has a longer history in a whole sequence of displacements and cannot be seen as an immediate reaction to specific work conditions; it is rather a generalized reversal of the principles that order the external world. Gift-giving, as one of the main elements of the asserted local culture, is not a self-subsistent category but something that is defined in opposition to the sorts of transactions conducted by outsiders:

Hawaiians say that monetary transactions have no place within the village. As one informant explained, "Keanae is a small place. The minute you sell, you going to get in trouble. You *give*, don't sell. When you give, something tastes good; but when you sell, it not going to taste so good." (Linnekin 1985, 137)

The "ethic" of egalitarianism of course upholds precisely what is absent, both in the general relationships that constitute the minority or oppressed group as such and in the differentiation within that group. Jayawardena argued that the combination of an egalitarian ideology with actual discrepancies of wealth led to "frequent disputes between individuals over real or alleged breaches of egalitarian norms" (1968, 426). It is notable that there are direct parallels between the "eyepass" disputes he reports from Guyana and a process noted by Linnekin of "talk stink": critical gossip about objectionable behavior, in reaction to unseemly status seeking, reflecting the acute disapproval of those who "act high," leading in some instances to the almost complete ostracism of offenders (1985, 146). As a Portuguese garage foreman told Linnekin, "[T]hey cannot stand the minute you little bit higher than them" (1985, 145).

Since writing the body of this paper I have spent some time in the western interior of Viti Levu, the largest island of the Fiji group. It would be inappropriate to extend the arguments of this essay with substantial ethnographic detail, but it may briefly be said that contemporary rural Fijian culture has a strong "oppositional" character of the kind postulated here. The constitution of "the Fijian way" (which has been discussed by Toren [1984] among other recent writers) places great emphasis on sharing, kinship, reciprocity, and respect. Fijian customs (*itovo*) or manners (*varau*) also entail hospitality and the welcoming of others. Here, the cruder and more rhetorically positive constructions seem to have been influenced by, or at least share imagery with, tourist constructs of "Fiji—the way the world should be." However, from the rural perspective the emergence of these values from a distinctive Fijian-Christian social order constituted both hierarchically (through chieftainship) and on the basis of *loloma* (Christian affection and kin solidarity) is more significant. The polarities are between the way of the land (*na itovo vakavanua*) and the path of money (*na calevu ni lavo*); Indians and foreigners are dedicated to the latter, and are rhetorically said to be inhospitable, indifferent to kinship, and to be concerned much more with work and the money it generates than with children and wider family ties.[6]

It should perhaps be made clear that the argument about the oppositional character of these Fijian cultures—which I think is true with permutations and to a greater or less degree of all contemporary Pacific societies—does not in some sense apply to the "whole" of Fijian culture. The reactive self-construction does influence practice in many spheres of daily life, but is particularly salient in rhetorical discussions that are specifically concerned with collective self-presentation. It follows from this that visiting foreigners, and particularly ethnographers, are extensively exposed to this form of ideological difference, but it would be wrong to suppose that these statements are made only to foreigners. Their internal relevance has, of course, been magnified as the specter of interracial political conflict has been raised over recent years—small wonder that a Fijian anthropologist should bring out a work entitled *The Fijian Ethos* in the year of the coup (Ravuvu 1987). But the contrast between the way of the land and the path of money is perhaps even more significant as a way of encoding social difference *within* the Fijian community. People of the interior and others in villages and outlying islands make much of their commitment to the way of custom, setting themselves up as the "real" Fijians in opposition to those in town, who may have done well in money terms but have abandoned their Fijian-ness. Speaking of this, a man who had fought the Japanese most of the way through the Solomons before settling for the rest of his life in a tranquil interior village, said of Fijians in town, *Eri sa qulu na itovo ni vavalagi*—they have picked up the customs of foreigners—because, he said, they watch videos. This is, of course, a stereotype: urban Fijians are no more Westernized than the lives of rural Fijians are really mirrored in the positive but highly selective constitution of "the way of the land."

A WIDER VIEW

Neotraditional customary sharing and egalitarianism is thus quite different from the condition of equality and the practice of reciprocity which might be thought to exist in "simple" societies in general. That state tends to be seen as the absence of varieties of social differentiation and inequality which are associated with more complex stages in social evolution. Although the evolutionary rhetoric is now overtly discredited, much of the intellectual baggage persists in implicit associations. Both Kahn's and Linnekin's studies are open to history, and disclose the impact of historical processes, but set up sharing and egalitarianism as elements consistent with cultural form rather than as effects of historical and cultural dynamics. Kahn neglects the extent to which the ideal of sharing is substantivized as a marker of the singularity of the Wamiran people and their difference from whites. Linnekin's study appears more conscious of the reified and abstracted character of the "ethic of egalitarianism," but takes this simply as a central theme or—although she does not use the term—"key symbol" which provides a cohesive point of reference for analysis. Practices are not quite transformed into institutions, as kerekere in Fiji was transformed into a "custom," but are substantivized as "ethics" or cultural propositions in an equivalent way. The open attitude of both texts toward history thus masks the fact that the core of the analysis depends on systematization in synchronic registers of meaning. The alternative perspective I have advocated here is not a reactive historical particularism that denies the systemic form of social and cultural phenomena, but rather a different systematization that takes process rather than coherence as its primary trope.

From this perspective certain cultural terms—such as kerekere and the practice of insisting upon sharing—are to be read at least partly as meanings predicated upon their opposites: they thus derive directly from indigenous confrontations with, and representations of, the other (i.e., intrusive foreigners). A system of positive and negative ideals may consist of items $+A$, $-B$, $+C$, $-D$, and so on, which might stand for "you must share food," "you must not 'act high'," and so on. The argument of this paper began with a query as to why some ideas should be reified and enunciated anyway, and partly answers this by stressing the dependence of the terms mentioned upon another set, $--A$, $+B$, $-C$, $+D$, and so on, which are represented by the indigenous people as the values of the system they are—to a highly variable degree—oppressed by or confronted with. This is not peculiar to colonial contexts, and might fruitfully be analyzed elsewhere, but culture contact of all kinds does produce, in a particularly powerful manner, essentialized constructs of selves and others within which particular customs and practices are emblematic.

I do not wish to abstract from Jayawardena's argument any quasi-positivistic hypothesis or an overall model for colonized Pacific societies. Substantivization is a general process, but there is, of course, a great deal of local specificity: the way of *kastom* for non-Christian traditionalists in Vanuatu and the Solomons is very different to the elite chiefs' version of the "way of the land" in Fiji or Tonga, and these differ again from reconstructions of Maori and Hawaiian culture within white-settler states. The general intellectual configuration at present is such that those who attempt to think about modern Pacific societies—and indeed tribal or marginalized societies in many parts of the world—must choose talk about power, work, exploitation, colonialism, development, and history, or opt for apparently more subtle and expressive words which bear upon culture, discourse, ethos, and metaphor. From a variety of directions, steps have been taken which enable us to break down this division, a theoretical task that seems urgent in the south Pacific, since recent upheavals in Fiji, Papua New Guinea, and elsewhere underline the political resonance of "custom" and tradition in both local "cultures" and nationalist rhetoric. The elaboration of Jayawardena's argument helps us to think differently and fashion an anthropology for these circumstances.

NOTES

1. The arguments here owe much to conversation and the writings of Margaret Jolly and Roger Keesing.

2. For a more extensive discussion of the state of ethnographic observations in the texts of nonanthropologists, see Thomas (1989a, 69–85). Many of the important

sources for nineteenth-century Fiji are listed in Thomas (1986, 69–73) and used there for quite a different analysis to that offered in this paper.

3. Minutes, Provincial Council of Colo East, April 1899, National Archives of Fiji. It is also interesting that when the motion was first introduced, "the common people shouted for it, though the chiefs were not so enthusiastic." The precise reason for this is not obvious, but it is likely that those who attended the meeting thought that some form of chiefly appropriation was being abolished. Kerekere, as subsequently understood, benefited commoners rather than chiefs in material terms.

4. My comments on Kahn's and Linnekin's texts are expanded from reviews, which can be found in *Cambridge Anthropology* (12 [1987], 90–91) and *Oceania* (57 [1986], 154–156).

5. Linnekin's 1990 essay, and a number of other recent contributions, have dealt with objectification and substantivization in a manner related to the discussion here (see also Handler 1984 for the case of Quebec). This article was initially drafted in 1987 and responded to the literature on the Pacific then available; however, I am still surprised that the oppositional character of Pacific cultures is referred to only cursorily, and by the associated neglect of indigenous reifications of outsiders. An understanding of the oppositional process must clearly link Fijians' or Samoans' substantivizations of their culture with their objectifications of what they take to be European customs or morals.

6. For further discussion, see Thomas (1989c and 1991, chap. 5). Another work is concerned in part with the significance of these cultural structures in political changes of the last few years (1990), a topic that has also been explored by Kaplan (1988).

REFERENCES

Belshaw, Cyril S. 1964. *Under the Ivi Tree*. London: Routledge.

Brewster, A. B. 1922. *The Hill Tribes of Fiji*. London: Seeley, Service and Co.

Capell, Arthur. 1957. *A New Fijian Dictionary*. Sydney: Australian Medical Publishing Company.

Damon, Frederick. 1980. "The Kula and Generalized Exchange: Considering some Unconsidered Aspects of *The Elementary Structures of Kinship*." *Man* 15:259–292.

Diapea, W. [a.k.a. W. Diaper, John Jackson]. 1928. *Cannibal Jack: The True Autobiography of a White Man in the South Seas*. London: Faber & Gwyer.

Douglas, Bronwen. 1979. "Rank, Power, Authority: A Reassessment of Traditional Leadership in South Pacific Societies." *Journal of Pacific History* 14:2–27.

Erskine, J. E. 1853. *Journal of a Cruise among the Islands of the Western Pacific*. London: Murray.

Fiji. 1896. *Report of the Commission Appointed to Inquire into the Decrease of the Native Population*. Suva: Government Printer.

Fortes, Meyer. 1949. *The Web of Kinship among the Tallensi*. Oxford: Clarendon Press.

France, Peter. 1969. *The Charter of the Land: Custom and Colonization in Fiji*. Melbourne: Oxford University Press.

Gregory, C. A. 1982. *Gifts and Commodities*. London: Academic Press.

Handler, Richard. 1984. "On Sociocultural Discontinuity: Nationalism and Cultural Objectification in Quebec." *Current Anthropology* 25:55–71.

Hazelwood, David. 1850. *A Feejeean and an English and an English and Feejeean Dictionary.* Vewa, Feejee: Wesleyan Mission Press.

———. 1872. *A Fijian and English and an English and Fijian Dictionary.* London: A. Low, Marston & Co.

Hocart, A. M. 1912. Letter to W. H. R. Rivers. MS in Rivers Papers, Haddon Collection, Cambridge University Library.

Hooper, Antony. 1985. "Introduction." Pp. 1–16 in Antony Hooper and Judith Huntsman (eds.), *Transformations of Polynesian Culture.* Auckland: The Polynesian Society.

Humphrey, Caroline, and Stephen Hugh-Jones, eds. 1992. *Barter, Exchange and Value.* Cambridge: Cambridge University Press.

Jayawardena, Chandra. 1963. *Conflict and Solidarity on a Guianese Plantation.* London: Athlone Press.

———. 1968. "Ideology and Conflict in Lower Class Communities." *Comparative Studies in Society and History* 10:413–446.

Jolly, Margaret. 1982. "Birds and Banyons of South Pentecost: Kastom in Anti-Colonial Struggle." *Mankind* 13 (special issue):357–373.

———. 1987a. "The Chimera of Equality in Melanesia." *Mankind* 17:168–183.

———. 1987b. "The Forgotten Women: A History of Migrant Labour and Gender Relations in Vanuatu." *Oceania* 58:119–139.

Kahn, Miriam. 1986. *Always Hungry, Never Greedy: Food and the Expression of Gender in a Melanesian Society.* Cambridge: Cambridge University Press.

Kaplan, Martha. 1988. "The Coups in Fiji: Colonial Contradictions and the Post-Colonial Crisis." *Critique of Anthropology* 8(3):93–116.

Keesing, Roger. 1982. "Kastom and Anticolonialism on Malaita: 'Culture' as Political Symbol." *Mankind* 13 (special issue):357–373.

———. 1989. "Creating the Past: Custom and Identity in the Contemporary Pacific." *The Contemporary Pacific* 1:19–42.

Kent, Noel J. 1983. *Islands under the Influence.* New York: Monthly Review Press.

Lewis, Ioan M. 1968. "Introduction." Pp. ix–xxvii in I. M. Lewis (ed.), *History and Social Anthropology.* London: Tavistock.

Linnekin, Jocelyn. 1983. "Defining Tradition: Variations on the Hawaiian Identity." *American Ethnologist* 10:241–252.

———. 1985. *Children of the Land: Exchange and Status in a Hawaiian Community.* New Brunswick: Rutgers University Press.

———. 1990. "The Politics of Culture in the Pacific." Pp. 149–173 in Jocelyn Linnekin and Lin Poyer (eds.), *Cultural Identity and Ethnicity in the Pacific.* Honolulu: University of Hawaii Press.

Macnaught, Timothy J. 1982. *The Fijian Colonial Experience: A Study of the Neotraditional Order under British Colonial Rule prior to World War II.* (Pacific Research Monograph 7.) Canberra: Australian National University.

Ravuvu, Asesela. 1987. *The Fijian Ethos.* Suva: Institute of Pacific Studies.

Roth, G. K. 1953. *Fijian Way of Life.* Melbourne: Oxford University Press.

Sahlins, Marshall. 1962. *Moala: Culture and Nature on a Fijian Island.* Ann Arbor: University of Michigan Press.

———. 1970 (1960). "Production, Distribution and Power in a Primitive Society."

Pp. 78–84 in T. G. Harding and B. J. Wallace (eds.), *Cultures of the Pacific*. New York: Free Press.

———. 1972. *Stone Age Economics*. London: Tavistock.

Strathern, Marilyn, and Carol P. MacCormack, eds. 1980. *Nature, Culture and Gender*. Cambridge: Cambridge University Press.

Thomas, Nicholas. 1986. *Planets Around the Sun: Contradictions and Dynamics of the Fijian Matanitu*. (Oceania Monograph 31.) Sydney: Oceania Monographs.

———. 1989a. *Out of Time: History and Evolution in Anthropological Discourse*. Cambridge: Cambridge University Press.

———. 1989b. "Material Culture and Colonial Power: Ethnological Collecting and the Establishment of Colonial Rule in Fiji." *Man* 24:41–56.

———. 1989c. "Tin and Thatch: Identity and Tradition in Rural Fiji." *Age Monthly Review* (Melbourne) 8(11):15–18.

———. 1990. "Regional Politics, Custom and Ethnicity in Fiji." *The Contemporary Pacific* 2:131–146.

———. 1991. *Entangled Objects: Exchange, Material Culture and Colonialism in the Pacific*. Cambridge, Mass: Harvard University Press.

Thomson, Basil. 1908. *The Fijians: A Study of the Decay of Custom*. London: Macmillan.

Toren, Christina. 1984. "Implications of the Concept of Development for the Symbolic Construction of 'the Fijian way.'" Pp. 39–52 in Christian Clerk (ed.), *The Effects of Development on Traditional Pacific Islands Cultures*. London: Institute for Commonwealth Studies.

Wilkes, Charles. 1845. *Narrative of the United States Exploring Expedition*. (vol. III). Philadelphia: Lea and Blanchard.

Williams, Thomas. 1843–1853. "Miscellaneous Notes Chiefly Concerning Fiji and the Fijians." MSS, Mitchell Library, Sydney.

———. 1858. *Fiji and the Fijians*. London: Heylin.

THREE

Doing Ethnographic History
The Case of Fighting in New Caledonia

Bronwen Douglas

I am a historian, not an anthropologist, whose current project is an ethnographic history of fighting in New Caledonia. I work mainly with contemporary action descriptions located in nineteenth-century texts. I aim to elucidate the varied significance of actions to observers and actors and to discern patterns of action and meanings, rather than to explain the causes of subsequent outcomes. In the context of this collection, my position is that of a friendly disciplinary next-door neighbor, concerned less in criticizing anthropological housekeeping—that has been admirably and reflexively undertaken by other contributors—than in reflecting on ways anthropologists and historians can use and misuse one another's methods and perspectives in their complementary endeavors. The historical enterprise is itself problematic and in the throes of redefinition along similar, though not identical, lines to anthropology's: social historians seek to hear, represent, and perhaps share authorial authority with voices—women's, peasants', workers', the colonized—rendered inarticulate by textual bias; for some, the morally and politically charged question "Who owns the past?" has become insistent, despite—or perhaps because of—inequalities of power and access which continue to privilege Western scholarship.

REFLECTIONS ON HISTORY AND ANTHROPOLOGY

James Carrier's exhortation to his fellow anthropologists on the need for history (see the Introduction; see also Ortner 1984, 158–159) will inspire a warm glow in the breasts of Pacific historians, but self-congratulation may be premature. There are pitfalls in a naive assumption that an injection of history is one obvious and simple corrective to anthropological essentialism. Sensitivity to the value of a historical perspective is certainly an improvement on the radical synchrony of classic functionalism and structuralism, but also necessary is a critical and reflexive awareness of what "doing history" might mean, of how other eras and other people can be known, and what such knowledge comprises; in other words, how to conceive relationships between past and present (e.g., Dening 1988; Seneviratne 1989, 4). "History" is a creative process of interpretation of relics of the past, relics that are mostly, but by no means entirely, documents. Such relics do not comprise a neutral body of inert objects, which can be neatly slotted together to reveal the past as it actually was; rather, like field notes, ethnographies and histories, oral and written, they are products of engaged human perception, conception, and communication. Reading them for content, for information, requires constant alertness to personal, cultural, rhetorical, and political dimensions of their production, survival, and interpretation. Given the contingent, contested status of knowledge, fashioned in an engaged present, an ethnographic historian must be prepared to make rigorous and imaginative use of such traces of actions, what people did and said, as are inscribed in contemporary texts. As cultural artefacts, actions have a public, symbolic dimension which enables their traces to be "read" and translated, provided one has a grasp of actors' idioms of expression and communication. That grasp is derived in part from later ethnographies and from people's present notions about their past, which may resonate with, and help give meaning and pattern to, more fleeting glimpses in contemporary texts (e.g., Clendinnen 1987, 131–138).

The disciplinary divide between history and anthropology is increasingly artificial and irrelevant: many anthropologists work in archives and ask serious questions about the past in the societies they study; some historians do ethnographic fieldwork and record vernacular texts, while many grapple creatively with anthropological concepts; a few individuals comfortably wear either or both hats. This growing synergy, however, should not obscure what are in practice often rather different concerns, giving rise to different temporal perspectives and methods of enquiry, different sins and different virtues. There are chronological and conceptual dimensions involved: some anthropologists have denied the past (and the future) by eternalizing an ethnographic present; some historians have denied the otherness of the past by collapsing it into present interests and values. While some anthropologists reify the Alien Other, as is noted in the Introduction to this collection (see also Bensa and Bourdieu 1985, 74–76), some historians reduce past others to a common human denominator by failing to acknowledge elements of difference in the past (our own, as well as those of other people) and to develop conceptual tools for dealing with them. In a historian's version of mirroring, they may unthinkingly depict past actors as acting in utilitarian, rationalist, common sense terms as if these were universal, rather than culturally and temporally defined (Philipp 1983, 347). Since assumptions of radical identity are no less distorting in their own way than the conventional anthropological assumption of radical alterity, I applaud Keesing and Jolly's call for critical and reflexive exploration of diversity (see Epilogue; see also Geertz 1986).

While in modern anthropological theory action is no longer subordinate to structure, nonetheless, as Carrier stresses in this volume, anthropologists are normally concerned with identifying systems of action, rather than focusing on contextualized actions, which are the historians' meat and drink. This collection variously demonstrates ways in which thoughtful attention to history can help dereify the icons of anthropological discourse and anchor them more firmly in worlds of acting, thinking, feeling human beings; historical analyses, in turn, can benefit from closer attention to elements of systems in the particular and the idiosyncratic and from greater conceptual rigor. An important concern for both disciplines must be development of historically grounded, ethnosensitive theories of transformation, which go beyond the merely descriptive or the logic of a particular case and privilege actions equally with structure (Sahlins 1985; in this volume, suggestive models are advanced in Barker's analyses of dynamic pluralism in Melanesian popular religion and Carrier's image of Ponam society changing "in its own way").

This chapter applies the case in point of Melanesian fighting in New Caledonia to two related ends: to display the ethnographic potential of contemporary action descriptions, notwithstanding the cultural blinkers and frequent rhetorical artifice of their authors; to illustrate some of the guises in which essentialism, ethnocentrism, and anachronism are to be variously encountered and countered in contemporary texts, histories, and ethnographies. Where appropriate I bracket action descriptions with later representations by ethnographers; each category of text can throw light on the other. Twentieth-century ethnographies mentioned fighting rarely and mainly in normative terms (e.g., Leenhardt 1930, 34–46, 262; Bensa and Rivierre 1982, 80–81, 103), but with respect to on-going, though not unchanging, dimensions of Melanesian experience, such as boundaries and alliances, they can add flesh and system to the often skeletal patterns discerned in contemporary texts. Their aptness to past contexts, however, cannot be taken for granted: to avoid anachronism an ethnographic historian must strain to read the traces of actions filtered through contemporary texts, however distorted or faint, and not preempt or bypass that reading process by prematurely closing categorical options. Since Pacific historians can scarcely edit out the colonial and postcolonial worlds which provided the archival legacies they exploit and the contexts for most of their histories, they are rarely guilty of Orientalizing the primitive in Carrier's ontological sense (see the Introduction). Typically, however, they write first chapters or introductions on "Traditional Culture and Society" (e.g., Douglas 1972, chap. 1; 1980, 25–30), which construe the past as mirroring and culminating inevitably in a later ethnographic present and adopt ethnographic categories and entities, such as "descent," "chief," "big man," "clan," "tribe," as unproblematic and automatically appropriate to past contexts.[1] This is a variety of essentialism, representing "traditional (precontact) societies" as timeless and neatly divided into enduring, usually territorially based units. It is also generally ethnocentric, depicting change as a unilinear, unidimensional, postcontact phenomenon of replacement or addition resulting from islanders' "response" or "reaction" to European "impact," "influence," or "imposition" (see Carrier and Barker, this volume).

The rubric "fighting," this paper's substantive focus, encompasses collective violence between Melanesians and between Melanesians and Europeans, which occurred regularly in New Caledonia before 1880, intermittently until 1917 and was renewed in 1984 and 1988. Almost every colonial confrontation saw some Melanesians fight as allies of the French, making a significant and sometimes critical contribution to the latter's eventual victory. To exemplify dimensions of ethnocentrism, I discuss Melanesian coalitions against, and alliances with, the French, as represented in both contemporary texts and histories. I argue that Melanesians in colonial contexts acted in creative and meaningful ways, which often belied the unilinear labels of imposition and reaction used by Europeans. Missionaries and administrators alike usually assumed that when Melanesians fought each other they were taking an explicit stance for or against the mission or the colonial regime; it can be shown that this was not necessarily so and that support for or opposition to the French often derived from, and was secondary to, local considerations. Though the colonial presence became gradually more ubiquitous and interventionist, especially after French victory in the war of 1878–79, it is ethnocentric to infer, as contemporary Europeans invariably did and historians tend to do, that Europeans were always the touchstone of Melanesian actions and conceptions of self and other; this is a variety of passivism and mirroring, which treats islanders as passive victims or recipients, implicitly gives Europeans and the West the status of dominant casual agency and ignores the complex, creative dialectics of cultural interaction, adaptation, incorporation, and transformation. Even when Melanesians did act primarily in response to Europeans, they did so in their own terms, which were rarely those intended or anticipated by Europeans. The reverse, of course, was also true: Melanesians also misconstrued and mislabeled European intentions and actions, but the traces are more obscure. In heavily colonial contexts, moreover, the concentration of power in European hands meant that their misconceptions mattered more to Melanesians than the latter's did to them: the dominated have perforce to be more sensitive to the culture, intentions, and expectations of the powerful.

Ethnocentrism and unwitting or interested present perspectives often conjoin in representations of colonial contexts to telescope the past in terms of outcomes, anticipated in contemporary texts, retrospective in political ideologies, histories, and ethnographies. Contemporary writers tended to assume the reality of paper claims to general sovereignty over annexed territories and to anticipate "European conquest," regarded as the inevitable outcome. Kanaks,[2] as well as most Europeans in New Caledonia today and some historians (Connell 1987; Dousset 1970; Dousset-Leenhardt 1976; Lyons 1986), construct causal explanations of the past which, despite political differences, project backward similar categorical assumptions about outcomes ("French conquest," "colonial control," "cultural destruction," "resistance," "collaboration"). Such assumptions, grounded in present perceptions of relative domination and power, or lack of it, may beg questions of when and how colonial hegemony was established in particular places and what it involved. They derive from a bird's-eye perspective on the past, which glosses over the actual interface of cultural exchanges in local contextualized transactions, discerned through informed attention to contemporary action descriptions. Numerous studies by Pacific historians have demonstrated how islanders might exercise significant controls over incoming Europeans for lengthy periods after the initial encounters. Gross structural power differentials in favor of colonizers often took decades to enforce and even then might be experienced intermittently by islanders, less insistently or consistently than local inequalities of power (e.g., Belich 1986; Corris 1973; Douglas 1980; Maude 1968, 134–177; Newbury 1980; Shineberg 1967). These assumptions ignore, moreover, the "ground level" ethnographic perception that the values, intentions, and practices of intruders were always subject to definition and evaluation according to local cultural premises and to manipulation in local action contexts (Ortner 1984, 143; Dening 1980; Sahlins 1981; Stephen 1979).

A desire to show how the present came to be is clearly an important human concern, in order to legitimate or deny the status quo, while such presented meanings are part of what the past is. A focus on the past as shaping or causing a later present has always been a major theme for historians and is clearly critical for antiessentialist ethnographers, intent on challenging the disciplinary tyranny of the ethnographic present. When such a focus mirrors the past in the image of the present, however, it becomes anachronistic and antithetical to an ethnographic historian's concern to explore past actions in context and the dialectical processes by which actions and meanings were transformed; like Carrier's "inevitable allegory" (see the Introduction), to be legitimate it must be reflexive.

AN ETHNOGRAPHY OF FIGHTING IN ONE
MELANESIAN CONTEXT

Given that the avowed purpose of this collection is not to discard ethnography but to suggest ways in which it can be more reflexive and sensitive to contexts, one concern of my paper is the pertinence of contemporary action descriptions as an ethnographic resource. Limitations of space, however, permit only a brief ethnographic sketch, stripped of the scholarly apparatus, the detailed evocation of episodes, and the qualifications that display how actions were sifted from rhetoric and inference transformed into reasoned argument. The result is an outline with a somewhat spurious aura of certainty and general applicability, not altogether unlike that of conventional ethnographies, which claim relevance beyond the situated logic of time and place (see the Epilogue). It must suffice to stress that the ethnography of fighting which follows is very context specific (this ethnography is drawn from Douglas 1990, 22–32).

Some of the most significant early action descriptions of Melanesians in New Caledonia referred to part of the northern region called Hoot ma Waap and focused on a place known as Balade. This was the site of earliest recorded European contacts and of most French naval and missionary activity until after annexation in September 1853. In detail and consecutiveness over protracted periods, the cluster of texts, both manuscript and published, which emerged after the settlement of French Marist missionaries among the small, autonomous Puma chiefdom of Balade in December 1843 was unmatched for more than a decade. These texts are invaluable in relation to fighting between Melanesians, since after about 1860 action descriptions of such fights became relatively unusual. European voyage reports from 1774 and 1843 described the Melanesians of Balade as a grave and tranquil people (Cook 1961, 528–546; Laferrière 1845, 63–111; Pigeard 1846, 83–129), while the official mission journal, mainly authored by Bishop Guillaume Douarre, made no mention of fighting during the first sixteen months of the missionaries' stay. These early texts belied the later conventional wisdom that "all these diverse tribes are almost constantly at war" (Leconte 1847, 822).[3] Although the potential for fighting was ubiquitous, it was neither a permanent nor unrestrained condition of Melanesian political interaction. Its dramatic impact on outsiders, informed by stereotypes of savagery (Sinclair 1977), was usually so compelling, however, as to shape their representations of the normal (e.g., Ta'unga 1968).

Traces of Melanesian fighting littered the early Balade mission texts written between April 1845 and annexation in September 1853: there were at least twenty-four fights between Melanesians, nine attacks on foreigners, and three retaliatory expeditions by the French navy. The concepts and values which informed Melanesian actions were refracted through the authors' very different cultural and rhetorical lenses, while both actions and meanings were described or implied from the special perspective of residence at Balade, among a weak, divided, and therefore vulnerable people. In accordance with the stereotype of savagery and sometimes radical discordance between European and Melanesian conceptions of political and military morality, missionaries damned virtually everything Melanesians did or did not do when fighting as contemptible or disgusting. The tone of Douarre's descriptions oscillated between a dismissive impression that most fights were limited and "not very deadly"—"their courage is not always in perfect accord with their shouts" ("Journal," 27 August 1845, 11 February 1852)—and an appalled sense of the cumulative desolation, tension, and uncertainty which resulted from recurrent violence—"they dare not go two leagues [about five miles] without trembling" ("Journal," 1 May 1845). This seeming contradiction captured something of a rhythm in Melanesian fighting, encapsulating both the banality of particular engagements and the treadmill cadence of injury, vengeance, and counter-vengeance.

My ethnography is fashioned from careful scrutiny of action descriptions, correlated with more formal images conveyed in ethnographies written by missionaries and French naval medical personnel ([Gagnière] 1905; Lambert 1900; Rochas 1862; Patouillet 1872). The two categories of contemporary text can be usefully complementary: one, extemporary and less consciously wrought, enables some unpacking of the other's abstractions, which in turn imply elements of regularity in actions described singly or even parenthetically in journals and correspondence. A pattern is suggested of widely shared Melanesian military preferences and related scenarios. They conceived vengeance for insult and injury as imperative to maintain relative equivalences, while a principle of collective responsibility meant potential liability both to suffer retaliation for the deeds of one's kinspeople, friends, and allies and to exact recompense through exchange or violence for insult or injury to the latter. They regarded performance of appropriate ritual as a pragmatic necessity in any military endeavor and shaped their actions according to omens read in immediate experience. They sought to minimize risk and human loss in fighting and thus avoided open confrontation with an alert enemy, preferring ruse, ambush, surprise raid, stealthy attack on weak and unwary individuals, destruction of property, and withdrawal; pitched battles seem to have been fairly unusual.

No contemporary author was noticeably appreciative of the restraint displayed in much Melanesian fighting, presumably because it was inconsistent with the prevailing European image, then and now, of unbridled savage violence. Those with an eye to see may read restraint as implicit in many of the actions traced in Douarre's journal, but it went unremarked by the bishop himself, subsumed as a brutish reflex triggered by fear:

> if they do not destroy each other with still more fury, it is because they reciprocally fear each other. . . . [I]f they did not . . . fear [war or vengeance], one could only compare them to dogs, which wrangle over their prey. ("Journal," 1 May 1845, 15 March 1846)

Despite such persistently negative evaluations of pagan motives and actions, Douarre also inadvertently depicted another side to fighting: nonviolent retaliation or conflict management, compensation and peacemaking. A chief notorious to the missionaries as a warmonger and cannibal was reported to have said of his enemies, "They have kept one of my women and will not give her back to me; so, to make them aware how much I despise them, I intend to return home by sea without visiting them" ("Journal," 26 October 1851)—surely a case of symbolic vengeance via diplomatic insult. Douarre detailed several instances of compensation enforced, without bloodshed, for "theft" of women or goods through the adventitious seizure of a canoe or other valuables ("Journal," 17, 24, 29 November 1851). Elsewhere he described how chiefs defused violent or potentially violent situations, usually by offering shells or other valuables to offended parties ("Journal," 29 April, 2, 9, 13 May, 19 July, 22 August 1852).

By such means Melanesians sought, ideally and often actually, to limit the scale, duration, and deadliness of their conflicts.[4] Except in the heat of actual battle, when warriors' ferocity had been stoked by fiery oratory, dance, and magic, their actions were normally less violent than their rhetoric, while particular engagements, and the anger that fueled them, were short-lived and casualties usually few. One missionary described the duration of an eighteen day "war" in 1856 as "quite extraordinary. Habitually their wars are limited to one or two encounters, and each party says: It's enough" (Villard to Supérieur-Général, 29 April 1856, *Annales des Missions de la Société de Marie*, 1, 46). As the passions of combat subsided the chiefs of the opposing parties normally made overtures for peace, negotiated exchange of compensation for casualties, and authorized the return of the vanquished or their absorption without prejudice by the victors. While whole groups were occasionally all but obliterated in surprise attacks, both through massacre and subsequent incorporation of survivors, conquest of place and expulsion of residents were fairly unusual. Though all Melanesian men might at times be warriors, none was exclusively so, and the demands of subsistence provided an ubiquitous incentive to limit and contain fighting.

ETHNOGRAPHIC HISTORY AND ETHNOGRAPHY

In my introduction I suggested that cautious correlation of contemporary action descriptions with later ethnographies can promote more systematic understanding of some aspects of Melanesian experience; it can also help bring into relief contradictions between the traces of actions inscribed in the texts and the essentialist terms in which they were construed by Europeans, as well as place ethnographic abstractions in broader temporal perspective. For example, Douarre's journal provides a rich mine for inference about lateral relations in northern New Caledonia, as seen from Balade, though his appreciation of the significance of such links was limited, as was that of Europeans generally. One manifestation of a lateral orientation was the extent of individual mobility and incorporation of strangers, implied by frequent references to small-scale visiting and resident strangers. It seems clear that the span of secure relationships in these societies could be narrowly localized and introverted, often threatened by rivalry, competition, and mutual suspicion between close kin, neighbors, and friends;[5] a corollary, however, was interest in relationships over considerable space, especially on the part of powerful chiefs, and with a wide variety of "others"—more distant kin, affines, allies ("friends"), enemies ("strangers"). This reflex of domestic insecurity in commitment to the elaboration of lateral links was enacted at Balade: on the one hand, in recurrent internal conflict between the two locally most high-ranking clan segments (nine of the twenty-four fights between Melanesians mentioned in the mission journal were intra-Puma); on the other hand, in the interest displayed by the rival parties in forging alliances with "strangers," including their neighboring enemies, the Mwelebeng of Pouébo, and the Catholic mission.

These patterns correlate with the thesis of an excellent recent ethnography by Bensa of the *cèmuhî* language zone of the center-north. He argued for the operation of a dynamic, creative tension between ideology and action: on the one hand, formal social models, usually phrased in the homogenizing idiom of consanguinity, stressed permanence, and equilibrium; on the other hand, at basic segmentary levels there was constant flux and competition for access to high-ranking names and longest-established house mounds, which meant that most groups were very diverse in actual composition (Bensa and Rivierre 1982). An emphasis on structure and entity, embedded in Western political thinking, was evident from the outset in the European tendency to depict Melanesian sociopolitical organization in terms of solidary bonds to permanent corporate political groups, assumed to occupy fixed "territories." Such images were not entirely inappropriate to Melanesian idioms and ideological representations, but they were at odds with the traces of Melanesian actions in the same texts, which provide glimpses of the countervailing pull of widely dispersed individual and small group relationships and allegiances and of extreme mutability in political practice.

A strong lateral orientation was apparent throughout New Caledonia's northern region, which Kanaks call Hoot ma Waap. Local groups were distributed, patchwork fashion, between two mutually hostile, ritually opposed groupings known as Hoot and Waap and labeled "networks of identification" by the modern French anthropologist Jean Guiart (1963, 631; 1957, 21–27; 1966, 49–53; see Bensa and Rivierre 1982, 108; 1984, 102–103). No contemporary mission text actually mentioned these names,[6] but the existence of regional patterns of alliance and enmity was implicit in the mission journal, in the authors' taken-for-granted attributions of the terms "friends," "allies," "strangers," "enemies." Fourteen of the twenty-four fights between Melanesians were "external" and only four of these involved opponents within the same network. The journal bore the repeated imprint of a web of enduring relationships in which the Puma, who were Waap, were enmeshed. In one entry Douarre differentiated guests attending a ceremony at Balade into "strangers" (enemies) and "strangers[,] friends of the tribe" (allies) ("Journal," 16 May 1852). This web of relationships appears to have encompassed the entire northern region and beyond and provided a ready, though by no means invariable, framework for escalation of quarrels beyond a local arena.

Predictably enough, early French official observers remarked only military implications of the existence of supralocal patterns of relationship in the north. In 1854, the senior officer on the New Caledonian naval detachment proposed as a "general rule" that "each tribe is the enemy of those adjacent to it," and he distinguished "enemies by birth, as the natives say, . . . irreconcilable enemies" from "accidental." The presence of mission stations at Balade and Pouébo and a French military post at Balade had, he thought, modified this "rule": the Mwelebeng and the Puma, formerly hereditary enemies, but brought together by the missionaries, now made common cause; the Puma's Arama neighbors had formed an alliance with Bondé, their "born enemy, . . . to oppose our [French] establishment on their territory," and had attacked the Puma, now their "accidental enemies." His grasp of long-standing political relationships in the environs of Balade was accurate enough: Arama and the Puma were both Waap, while Bondé and the Mwelebeng were Hoot. His unquestioned assumption of European centrality in Melanesian affairs, however, was by no means justified, since Puma chiefs had made several attempts to gain Mwelebeng support in local squabbles, while recent conflict between the normally allied people of Balade and Arama predated French annexation by nearly a decade (Douarre, "Journal," 3, 10 December 1845, 20 February 1846). Oblivious to the potential in these patterns for alliances over a wide area, including opposition to the French, he saw only "this great variety of interests, these inter-tribal hatreds . . . [which] may be useful initially if we are able to turn them to account by opposing one to another" (Tardy de Montravel to Ministre, 27 April, 25 December 1854, Archives nationales, section Outre-mer [hereinafter ANOM], Carton 40). The first governor of the colony put a name to the Hoot-Waap relationship, but accorded it limited significance; he, too, anticipated easy pickings from a colonial "divide and rule" policy. Seventy odd years later, however, with the arduous French conquest of New Caledonia finally complete, the missionary ethnographer Maurice Leenhardt reflected: "in all the struggles and rebellions of colonial history [in the north], one finds alliances or enmities between Oote and Waap" (du Bouzet to Ministre, 14 February, 20 June 1855, ANOM, Carton 40; Leenhardt 1930, 105).

The foregoing both exaggerates the coherence and oversimplifies the complexity of Hoot-Waap identifications in northern New Caledonia. The patchwork pattern of alliance and enmity implied in contemporary texts was set within the frame of a Balade-Pouébo perspective and the European tendency to divide the political landscape neatly into permanent, juxtaposed entities they labeled "tribes": these were the region's chiefdoms, assumed to exercise direct, undifferentiated political control over substantial, contiguous "territories." The histories of movements of actual groups between nodal points (house mounds) on itineraries, however, gave rise to multiple, overlapping, more or less sustainable claims to names, roles, statuses, places, and resources; to Europeans seeking to convert, control, and exploit Melanesians, the mobility, competition, and ambiguous allegiances of smaller groups throughout New Caledonia were easily dismissed or ignored, as aesthetically untidy and administratively chaotic. In the 1950s, Guiart sought to systematize hints provided by Leenhardt on the Hoot-Waap opposition, but was frustrated by lack of precision in information received. He decided that "it was not a question of an ordered institution the mechanism of which informants can describe with a great wealth of details" (1966, 49) and later concluded: "it did not involve a dualism regulating traditional enmities, but a structure organizing ritual complementarity and congealing territorial limits in such a way that war cannot end in conquest of the lands of others" (1985, 91). The relative geographical permanence and regional balance of Hoot and Waap looks therefore like another instance whereby an ideology stressing stability and equilibrium served both to contain and to legitimate the constant flux and competition of Melanesian political practice.

COALITIONS AND ALLIANCES:
ETHNOCENTRISM AND ANACHRONISM

The early Balade mission texts mentioned nine Melanesian attacks on foreigners, three of which provoked French retaliatory expeditions. They comprised only a sample of cross-cultural clashes in one region of New Caledonia during the first decade or so of intensive culture contacts, before the formal installation of a colonial regime. Yet in them can be traced patterns which anticipated significant elements in subsequent colonial encounters. Melanesians continued to place tactical emphasis on ruse and surprise attack and, except in the heat of anger against totally unwary victims, to prefer plunder to killing as a means to restore equivalence, enforce reciprocity, or exact vengeance. Just as they shunned open combat with a numerous and alert local enemy, so they generally refused to face the disciplined firepower of trained French troops; throughout the colonial period Melanesians possessed no artillery and usually had few effective firearms. Withdrawal remained their favored defensive tactic. Since the French were unable to inflict significant damage on an agile and elusive foe, stalemate normally ensued, to which the French responded with the tactic of devastation. They were usually aided by Melanesians who were prepared to fight with Europeans, as

Christians or against their own enemies. Melanesians could nurture grievances for generations and concert long-term plans for war involving substantial coalitions, as they did in preparation for the war that broke out in
1878; nonetheless, most actual attacks on Europeans, like those on other
Melanesians, were sudden, delivered in heat, and fairly short-lived, concluded once vengeance had been taken, immediate grievances redressed, or
losses suffered.

It is impossible here to do more than sketch broad categories of Melanesian political and military action during the colonial period, with qualifications as to the need to differentiate realities, intentions, and actions within
and between groups, in context and over time. Yet after annexation in 1853
Melanesian violence was usually collapsed in French official rhetoric and
later histories as "revolt" or repudiation of legitimate sovereign authority, as
indeed it was according to the logic of a colonial hierarchy; it was generally
assumed, moreover, that European presence was the ultimate mainspring of
Melanesian actions, even for unpacified groups. One example can serve both
to illustrate these tendencies and demonstrate how an informed attention to
the traces of actions contained in contemporary texts provides a corrective to
the inherent ethnocentrism of those same texts. A governor's order of the day
in 1868 referred to the implementation of a "system of aggression against our
allies" by certain inland dwellers in the central region between Houaïlou,
Canala and Bourail:

> Since November 1867, a veiled unrest spread amongst the peoples of the East
> and the North-East: its cause was soon unmasked. The natives of the interior,
> still harboring feelings of suspicion and hostility against the whites, planned
> their massacre or expulsion. . . . They wished to impose the same views on the
> natives of the seaboard, who, won over to the cause of civilization, that is to
> French sovereignty, refused to participate in the realization of this bloodthirsty
> project. (*Moniteur*, 6 September 1868)

This simple lineal interpretation has passed unchallenged into historical
orthodoxy. For example, although Alain Saussol commented on the complexity of relationships between Melanesian groups in this region, he
nonetheless labeled violence against the French and their allies in 1867–68 as
"revolt," "rebellion," and "resistance" to European settlement (1979, 106–
118). In a more extreme and strikingly anachronistic sample of the same
tendency, Roselène Dousset-Leenhardt categorized every instance of
Melanesian violence against Europeans from 1847 (i.e., six years before
annexation!) as "acts of resistance which succeeded each other in almost
uninterrupted fashion on every part of the island, as colonization progressively affirmed its economic and social hold"; this inevitable reflex of rebellion against colonialism had its logical culmination in the 1878 insurrection.
As a token of unreflective Eurocentrism and a priori categorization, her list of

so-called "revolts" actually comprised French punitive expeditions (1976, 37–38; Dousset 1970).

A less Eurocentric perspective on Melanesian intentions and relationships in the central region in 1867–68 is suggested, however, by traces of their actions inscribed in the published official reports (*Moniteur*, 2, 9, 23 August, 30 August–6 September 1868; see also Guiart 1984): the interior people had had few relations with whites; there were persistent local quarrels within and between interior and coastal groups; rumors of a hostile inland coalition alarmed the handful of European settlers and allies of the government along both coasts; this inspired a small French expedition, accompanied by numerous east coast warriors, against several inland settlements, which suffered significant losses; a respected inland chief was seized and interned by the French; a month or two later, mountain-dwellers killed two French convicts in stealthy attacks and about forty Melanesians in various raids on coastal settlements allied to the French; a subsequent series of punitive expeditions into the valleys above Bourail were at least in part motivated by the exasperation of "our friends," who threatened to take matters into their own hands and accompanied the French in strength; numerous settlements were burned and their inhabitants accepted peace on French terms.

The simple dichotomy of coastal allies-inland enemies was a metaphor encapsulating French notions of their own centrality in Melanesian affairs rather than a feature of Melanesian politics, since neither category formed a homogeneous, solidary group, and complex webs of relationship linked both coasts, their hinterlands, and the mountainous interior. So far as the interior was concerned the concept of "French sovereignty" was a legal fiction, meaningless to people who knew themselves to be autonomous and acknowledged no higher authority. Their original targets were local enemies who happened to be coast dwellers; European soldiers initially incurred their enmity as allies of the latter while isolated settlers became objects of attack in retaliation for the chief's capture and imprisonment. Some of the coastal groups involved had previously experienced punitive expeditions, others had French posts in their midst; in consequence, the French had become a meaningful element in their present political realities. The "cause of civilization," however, took unexpected shape when conceived from a Melanesian perspective. More significant to these "natives of the seaboard" than their obligations under "French sovereignty" was the potential value of the French in their relationships with other Melanesians, as useful allies in the event of attack and as political tools for conquest or for vengeance.

Although opposition to French actions or presumed intentions was often a significant element in the formation of Melanesian coalitions, especially in the 1870s, and in Melanesian violence against Europeans, especially close to colonial centers, those actions and intentions were construed by Melanesians in their own contextually and culturally meaningful ways, which analytic categories need to comprehend. A collision of rival contenders for regional domination, Melanesian and French, the latter aided by Melanesian enemies of the former, was neither resistance to imposed colonial authority nor reaction to French oppression (see below). Attempts by Melanesians to take vengeance or gain redress through violence were not necessarily intended as "revolt," rejection of colonial domination scarcely acknowledged, but as chastisement of disrespectful strangers whose actions challenged local systems of authority and reciprocity.

It is essential to grasp that only in the wake of the war of 1878–79 were the French able permanently to impose their authority on substantial areas outside the south, which had been effectively conquered by 1859. Even after 1880 the French yoke was fairly light in much of the north and French control was confirmed only with expansion of colonization in the 1890s, implementation of a repressive system of native administration, and Melanesian defeat in 1917.[7] Thus "French sovereignty" often meant different things from what colonial authorities thought it ought to mean, while there were almost always local political dimensions in confrontations between Melanesians and Europeans. Best sense is made of New Caledonia before 1880 if the French are seen as only one element, albeit potentially and often actually a powerful and dominating one, in complex, dynamic political contexts.

A persistent pattern in the colonial encounter, unsuspected by the first administrators and sometimes insufficiently appreciated by historians, was the capacity demonstrated by Melanesians to envisage and coordinate political and military action beyond a purely local domain: on occasions this promoted the formation of far-flung coalitions which collided with or opposed French expansion; it also, however, enabled contingents of warriors from widely separated places to operate effectively against other Melanesians as allies of the French. The commitment and contribution of particular groups to a coalition or French alliance could vary widely, active phases tended to be brief, and usually some groups tried to remain neutral. The French occupation of New Caledonia was a piecemeal process with many vicissitudes, far more difficult, lengthy, and costly than its initiators had dreamed. Insofar as Melanesian alliances—"collaboration" in modern parlance—were decisive, French "divide-and-rule" tactics were successful, but over a much longer run and on a wider scale than was originally anticipated (La Hautière 1869, 69).

An anatomy of Melanesian alliances with the French displays a range of motives and varying degrees of commitment depending on period, place, and past experience; it also reveals the inappropriateness of the term "collaboration," with its implication of "cooperation with the enemy," since "the enemy" was always defined in context: "New Caledonians," remarked Lambert, "are very jealous of their nationality, between tribes" (1900, 341). Some groups seeking advantage in political and exchange relationships threw in their lot with the French from the outset, notably the Bwaghea of Canala, who nonetheless remained vigorously independent. Their decision to support the French in 1878 was by no means a foregone conclusion, but a product of prolonged debate (Olry to Ministre, 2 August 1878, ANOM, Carton 43; Rivière 1881, 129–138).

Christians in general were pro-French. Mwelebeng support for France before 1866, however, was clearly incidental to the local political and religious aspirations of their powerful Christian chief (Douglas 1980, 42–46), while the Christians of Conception and St. Louis, in the south, were a special case. They comprised several hundred resettled northern converts who, provided with firearms and ammunition by the colonial authorities, fought from 1856 to 1858 with the French against a southern coalition hostile to intruders, whether European or Melanesian (Douglas 1980, 32–40). The French commandant, frustrated by his own troops' inability to come to grips with an elusive enemy, ultimately used the Christians as his military spearhead, as he explained to the mission superior:

> Our soldiers are too heavy in the behind to be able to run after the natives; the 40 or more men whom you can supply, with a detachment of soldiers in reserve and always within range, would pursue the enemy with equal speed and perhaps with success. (Testard to Rougeyron, 25 January 1858, Archivio di Padri Maristi, section Oceania, Nova Caledonia [hereinafter APM/ONC], 5 Ca 180)

Neither the French nor their opponents in the south in the 1850s were numerous: about a hundred and fifty French troops faced a total of probably no more than a thousand warriors scattered through the vast, sparsely populated southern region (Guiart 1963, 268). In this context the Christians, who must have included about a hundred men of warrior age, unrestrained by local ties, were critical to French victory. At this stage the most effective allies were strangers to the local people, but farther north hereditary enemies and defeated groups were to prove equally so.

Desire for protection or vengeance against Melanesian enemies often provided significant motives for forging an alliance with the French. The most celebrated such instances occurred in the center-north during the 1860s in response to aggressive political expansion by the war leader Gondou. Though he became notorious to the French as a bitter opponent of colonization and as a scourge of allied and "subject" people, his activities well predated his entry into French awareness in 1862. As leader of a loose military confederation, he had apparently sought to expel or dominate the residents in a wide belt of the island (*Moniteur*, 14 May 1865; Garnier 1868, 38; La Hautière 1869, 170–171; Guiart 1963, 107–110; Leenhardt 1930, 261–262; Bensa and Rivierre 1982, 131–132, 201–206). Among his victims, expelled and expropriated during the 1850s, was a west coast group, whose chief,

Mango, became an enthusiastic French ally in 1865, when a multipronged expedition converged on Gatope to avenge the killing of several Europeans. Mango implicated Gondou in the deaths and in two separate operations French troops and Melanesian warriors burned his main inland settlements and destroyed their gardens (*Moniteur*, 1, 29 October 1865). Whatever his previous opinion of the French, these attacks and their alliance with several of his bitter enemies ensured Gondou's future hostility (Patouillet 1872, 48).

In 1869, Gondou's Melanesian and European enemies combined to bring about his downfall. A man said to have been the brother of one of his victims revealed his whereabouts to the commandant of the Wagap post. This officer accompanied a party of native fusiliers and warriors inimical to Gondou, whom they surprised and killed (*Moniteur*, 14 February 1869). His death was essentially a Melanesian affair, in which advantage was taken of the existence of the post to redress local grievances. While Gondou's ultimate enmity toward the French was indisputable, he was not in "rebellion" against established colonial authority (see *Moniteur*, 11 November 1866, 24 February 1867), but became their rival for domination of a region. He remained independent and beyond the reach of French arms, except on rare occasions that they were able to penetrate inland in concert with his local enemies, and he contemptuously rebuffed repeated offers of a free pardon in return for submission to colonial authority (*Moniteur*, 29 October 1865, 11 November 1866, 24 February 1867). It is hardly surprising that two expansionist military regimes, both with designs on the same places, should eventually collide. It is interesting that the French were seen by many Melanesians as the lesser evil.[8] Gondou's aggressiveness, persistence, and territorial ambitions probably made him as unusual a phenomenon as the French in Melanesian experienced; normatively, according to Leenhardt, war leaders exercised no authority outside combat (1930, 42–43). His actions might ultimately have helped, more than hindered, the colonial cause because they inspired many Melanesians to forge the new alliance that ultimately killed him.

Among the most enthusiastic Melanesian contributors to the 1865 expeditions and several subsequent operations were Bouarate, high chief of Hienghène, and his "neighbor and friend" Kahoua of Poyes (Guillain to Ministre, 3 September 1865, Archives nationales, section Marine [hereinafter ANM], BB4 847). They exemplified another major category of French ally: formerly hostile people who chose to align with the colonial forces following setbacks or defeat suffered at the hands of Christians, the French, or the latter's allies, and who sometimes found themselves fighting their own former "friends." Bouarate and Kahoua had been leaders of successive "northern coalitions" which between 1856 and 1862 caused considerable grief to mission and Administration (Douglas 1972, 111–136, 216–224, 1979a, 47–50, 1980, 41–47), though it is clear that they were initially alliances against traditional enemies, combinations mainly of Waap against Hoot adversaries, especially the partly Christian Mwelebeng. They became bitterly antimissionary in part because the Marists supported their enemies and invoked French intervention on the latter's behalf. In 1860, the Mwelebeng achieved a series of victories against opponents as far south as Hienghène. This transformed attitudes and relationships throughout the northeast, established Mwelebeng dominance and seemed likely to ensure the rapid success of the mission (Rougeyron to Poupinel, 23 October 1862, Archives of the Province of Oceania), though Kahoua still refused to submit.

At this time the composition of alliances in the north sometimes transcended the Hoot–Waap relationship, as, indeed, they had always had the potential to do. For example, the remnants of the Puma chiefdom of Balade, occupied continuously by the French from 1853 to 1859, concluded that new circumstances demanded a new strategy and aligned firmly with the French, the only group outside the south to do so in the 1850s. They fought with them against their Waap "friends," the Bouarate of Hienghène, in 1859 and with their former enemies, the Mwelebeng, against a coalition which included several of their former "friends." In 1862, warriors from Hienghène supported the missionaries and the Mwelebeng, previously their bitter enemies and their vanquishers in 1860, against a coalition that included their former ally Kahoua as well as Gondou. Except at Balade, however, such new alignments were acknowledgments not of actual French power, but of the latter's potential in alliance with the mission to transform the regional political balance in favor of the Mwelebeng.

There was little but a supporting role for the colonial government in this scenario, until an anticlerical governor, Charles Guillain, set out after 1862 to replace Marist and Mwelebeng influence with his own and to pacify the north (Douglas 1972, 163–196, 225–312, 1979a, 51–54). His best weapons in both campaigns were pagan allies, won through "a policy of pardoning and rallying chiefs previously compromised" (*Moniteur*, 14 May, 29 October 1865). In return for "submission" to French authority, they gained opportunities to influence the direction of French repression against their enemies and to harass and plunder them during expeditions, while internally their own chiefdoms stayed virtually autonomous. Bouarate and Kahoua remained opponents of the mission but became firm government allies in several expeditions against "rebel tribes" both Christian and pagan. To officials, their actions resulted from acknowledged weakness in the face of French arms (Gaultier de la Richerie to Guillain, 3 July 1863; Guillain to Ministre, 10 August 1863, ANOM, Carton 26; Garnier 1868, 58; *Moniteur*, 14 May 1865), but their stance toward the mission-government conflict and the French seems to have been coldly pragmatic. One missionary complained that "these chiefs are not less hostile to the government than to the missionaries; but they say quite publicly that they profit from the Governor's disposition to combat Christianity" ([Forestier], Notes sur la mission de la

Nouvelle-Calédonie, [1865], APM/ONC, Documents concernant . . . le Gouverneur Guillain).

Despite Guillain's energy, much of the north remained unpacified and the French "governed" through their allies, most of whom they hardly governed at all. All the major allies between 1863 and 1870 were aggressively pagan; in the north they were all Waap, and they used their favored position to torment the Hoot, especially the Christian Mwelebeng. Indeed, Guillain's antimissionary campaign saw political alignments revert to an older pattern, as the Mwelebeng sphere of influence receded. As the latter had done, Bouarate took advantage of a new situation to extend the authority of his chiefdom over traditionally autonomous neighbors (Douglas 1979a, 54–55). Kahoua's change of camp might have been influenced by the growing threat posed by Gondou, whose ally he was in 1862 but whom he denounced to the Administration on several subsequent occasions (*Moniteur*, 29 January, 14 May 1865). He personally led the warriors of Hienghène and Poyes during the 1865 expeditions and served as guide in a surprise night-time attack on Gondou (Guillain to Ministre, 3 September 1865, ANM, BB4 847; *Moniteur*, 1 October 1865).

In 1878–79 Melanesian allies of all categories played a central role in the French victory, not least by killing two of the main war leaders, one of whom, Ataï, instigated the war and has become a key symbol for the modern Kanak nationalist movement. Fighting began with coordinated series of surprise Melanesian attacks on gendarmes, officials, and settlers at the west coast settlements of La Foa and Bouloupari, where some 120 men, women, and children died. The decision of the warriors of Canala to fight on the colonial side, combined with the neutrality, ambivalence or tardy involvement of many other groups, gave the French sufficient breathing space after the initial disasters to permit implementation of a strategy of attrition; their eventual victory at La Foa and Bouloupari was already assured before the entry into the war of groups farther north (Olry to Ministre, 28 September 1878, ANOM, Carton 43). Stanley James, an Australian correspondent in the field, was in no doubt as to the significance of the allies' contribution:

> Almost everything which has been done, except the destruction of plantations, in which the French soldiers excel, has been by the Canaque auxiliaries. . . . Indeed, in the bush fighting in the thick scrub around La Foa, it is . . . almost impossible for regular troops to operate. (*Sydney Morning Herald*, 15 October 1878)

The allies were rewarded with bounties, loot, and women and took the opportunity to absorb refugees and colonize remote areas.[9] In the Bourail region an earlier political lineup was reserved: some previously defeated inland groups used a French alliance to balance accounts with coast dwellers who, a decade earlier, had supported the French against them; these coastal people apparently felt so betrayed and threatened by the spread of penal colonization around Bourail and the brutality of local administrators that they turned against the French in 1878 (Lecouteur to Fraysse, 20 September, 22 October, 4 December 1878; Gilibert to Fraysse, 25 September 1878; Hilléreau to Pionnier, 29 November 1878, AAN, 16.2).

The pro-French, neutral or ambivalent stance adopted by so many Melanesians in 1878 meant that the warrior strength of the groups opposed to the French was exiguous: Guiart estimated their total number at fewer than seven hundred, and in the La Foa-Bouloupari region as probably no more than two hundred (1968, 118). Against this the Canala war leader Nondo at times led three hundred to five hundred warriors into the field, while the French military force in the colony at the beginning of the war totaled nearly twenty-five hundred men. They were reinforced by the end of 1878 to more than forty-five hundred, irregulars apart, though they were thinly spread and many might not have been of high quality. A victory won so hardly against so few, by Melanesian as much as European agency, scarcely demonstrated the inherent superiority of French civilization and military culture. One missionary noted the allies' significance both to the French war effort and to the articulation of Melanesian opinion on the relative worth of black and white:

> This war . . . will cause the whites to be held in contempt by all the loyal blacks, even by the *warriors* of Canala. The blacks see that the whites cannot pursue and kill them in the mountains, they see that the whites kill or spare innocent or guilty *canaques* at random, according to the whim of the moment, and unfortunately they see and they *say* that the whites need blacks to destroy blacks. (Moris to Fraysse, 1 January 1879, AAN, 16.1, emphasis in original)

By the end of 1878, a French officer could afford to deplore the presumption of Melanesian allies, in whom he discerned "a tendency[,] the danger of which I had already appreciated at Canala, . . . of wanting to monopolize devotion to our cause and to regard themselves as indispensable to our security" (cited in Olry, *Récit détaillé* . . . , 16 January–5 February 1879, ANOM, Carton 43); a few months earlier, if the allies' devotion had been no less interested, their indispensability was scarcely in doubt (Servan to colonists of Canala, 26 July 1878 [copy], AAN, 16.1).

CONTEMPORARY RHETORIC, HISTORICAL CATEGORIES

Writers of contemporary European texts had recourse to a vocabulary of savagery, both metaphoric ("ferocious beasts," "remote lairs") and explicit ("this struggle of the savage against civilized man"). Tone varied with context and interest, but was always demeaning, even in praise. In the immediate aftermath of massacres, shaken officials depicted savages as "monsters";

defeated, they were transformed into "tenacious and brave," "sometimes intelligent" opponents, worthy of their vanquishers, whose efforts deserved acknowledgment in medals and promotion. So far as missionaries were concerned, a rhetoric of anticipated conversion required denigration of the unregenerate as covetous, sly, treacherous, and vindictive, to counterpoise the transformation to generosity, frankness, reliability, and resignation wrought in the converted by the miracle of grace.[10]

As with early missionary evaluations of Melanesian fighting as uniformly despicable, so most assessments of their military action against Europeans, by both contemporaries and historians, were more or less damning, at best with faint praise.[11] In 1878, the Australian journalist James belittled Ataï's tactical sense and attributed to cowardice the Melanesian refusal to confront armed bodies of troops and their preference for surprise attack on defenseless opponents: "They were afraid of the soldiers; and really, I think the feeling was reciprocal" (Thomas 1886, 58–60, 72, 76; cf. *Sydney Morning Herald*, 17 August 1878). Words matter. What to James was cowardice looks to me like prudence, given Melanesian deficiencies in arms and, frequently, manpower. In virtually every engagement in 1878, and in many earlier ones, Melanesian warriors were markedly inferior in number to French troops and their allies, though this was rarely acknowledged officially, nor perhaps even recognized, given the indelible European image of savage hordes falling unaware on scattered, defenseless whites, an image imprinted partly by stereotype and partly by the surprise massacres that preceded every major colonial conflict. I also argue that Melanesian tactical preferences in fighting Europeans, as expressed in their actions, represented not only the prudent pragmatism of outnumbered, outgunned, part-time warriors, but also a widely shared preference for restraint, combined with belief that emotional and political dividends were to be gained from short, sharp explosions of extreme violence (e.g., Guiart 1968, 109–110).

What I see as deliberate choice has sometimes been interpreted by historians dazzled by negative outcomes as a kind of passive savage conservatism which doomed from the outset Melanesian resistance to French intrusion. In one extreme example of this genre they were depicted as anarchic reactionaries who, lacking a coherent grasp of the implications of colonialism or a capacity for coordination, clung blindly to traditional modes of fighting and political action and ensured French victory by their lack of fortitude, desperation, or sense of common interest (Latham 1978). Even Saussol, who wrote an acute and meticulous history of land matters in New Caledonia, attributed Melanesian defeat in 1878 to poor coordination and inefficient decision-making resulting from commitment to "precolonial methods" of a people incapable of envisaging more than a return to the old order. Thus "as much technically, through lack of firearms, as tactically, Melanesians were badly adapted to this new war," initial successes gained through surprise were not repeated and they became "bogged down in a hopeless guerrilla" conflict (Saussol 1979, 189, 228, 240). Though in outline the Melanesian tactical repertoire was not markedly different during the colonial era from what it had been, their flexibility and adaptability in matters of detail suggest that they were not simply locked into culturally ordained patterns. Inadequate armament is scarcely an index of failure to adapt; on the contrary, one aim of the initial attacks in each theater of the war was to obtain firearms and ammunition, as Saussol allowed (1979, 216). Melanesians handled firearms expertly when they could get them and made significant defensive tactical innovations to accommodate their use in fortified positions (Rochas 1862, 208–209; Olry, Récit détaillé . . . , 22 December 1878–16, January 1879, ANOM, Carton 43). I maintain that the tactics adopted in 1878 were the only ones possible following the critical decision to join the French taken at the outset by the warriors of Canala. Melanesian mistakes during these campaigns were tactical rather than cultural and were not "inevitable."

Though ultimately Melanesians lost this and every other colonial war, they were usually not defeated militarily, but chose or were forced to negotiate when the costs of continued fighting became unacceptable. A subsistence economy could not sustain armed mobilization indefinitely, particularly when assailed by a strategy of attrition, which brought famine and displacement as a legacy of ruined gardens and razed dwellings; furthermore, these people scorned political martyrdom and saw no virtue in fighting to the bitter end against daunting odds. There were several indices of effectiveness of Melanesian military action in colonial contexts, though they were little acknowledged, then or since: their repetition of similar tactics at different times and places; the length of time and amount of French effort it took before Melanesians decided that endurance of inequities and oppression was less destructive of their interests than violence; the arduousness for Europeans and inconclusiveness of particular campaigns; the generally heavy French reliance on Melanesian support. Most notable, perhaps, was the extent to which Melanesians forced the French, despite their superior armament and pretensions to military science, to adopt their methods. James considered in 1878 that "this war of repression on the Canaques had to be made *á la Canaque*. . . . [The French] appreciated this to a certain extent, and native manners had been adopted" (Thomas 1886, 64). Another journalist made the same point rhetorically, to justify the slow progress of repression: "the tedious process of starvation, and of black against black, are the means which must be depended upon for the reduction of this handful of agile devils" (*Sydney Morning Herald*, 3 August 1878). French reliance on Melanesian allies often forced them to tolerate actions that, when committed by enemies, produced spasms of outraged civilized sensibility. A naval doctor attached to several expeditions during the 1860s admitted that native fusiliers "indulged after combat in feasts in which enemy bodies paid the price; but it would have been both useless and impolitic to thwart the customs of these always faithful allies, and we closed our eyes on deeds which we despaired, alas! of being able to prevent" (Patouillet 1872, 50). Though French campaign reports tended to downgrade allies' military contribution to a purely auxiliary role under the direction of French officers, it is clear that allied contingents often operated autonomously under their own priest and war leader, the latter elected according to standard Melanesian procedures (Patouillet 1872, 156–159; Leenhardt 1930, 41–43).

In modern Kanak political ideology and in histories written by some European sympathizers, fighting between Melanesians and Europeans has been transformed into protonationalist resistance against colonial domination and oppression, while the war of 1878 has become a "national uprising," a "revolutionary war" (Dousset-Leenhardt 1976, 13; Guiart 1968, 109–110); analogously, opponents of independence have invested the same episodes with a very different but no less politically charged significance, as the just and inevitable triumph of civilization over savagery. A Melanesian priest writing in the 1960s captured nicely the symbolic irony, expressing asymmetry in contemporary power relationships, of such discordant ideological transformations:

A monument at La Foa piously conserves the memory of he whom the European population considers the hero of French presence in the island [i.e., the French military commander killed in ambush in 1878]. The high chief Ataï, venerated by the native population, is considered a murderer. (Anova-Ataba 1969, 215)

Symbolically, these present meanings are an important part of what the past has become (Dening 1989; Keesing 1989; Seneviratne 1989), but neither genre necessarily represents aptly the intentions and actions of past actors. "Nationalism" is a crucial ideological icon for an oppressed and partly divided people seeking radical transformation of the status quo, but an inappropriate rubric under which to lump the varied endeavors of quasi-autonomous groups in a politically heterogeneous past society.

My history is not and cannot be Kanak history, but the question of whether the two can be, or need to be, reconciled is beyond the scope of this chapter. It is *my* history that major explosions of collective Melanesian violence against Europeans during the colonial era were both redressive and assertive measures by people inclined culturally to welcome and incorporate strangers, rather than reject them: that they were intended to avenge grievances, punish derelictions, enforce reciprocity or local autonomy, and control, or perhaps expel, disrespectful newcomers when their aggression, insolence, and greed consistently transgressed the limits of acceptability. Isolated European settlers and traders in remote areas generally could not afford to misbehave and were usually welcomed, but such constraints diminished and

European confidence grew in proportion to their numbers, especially where reinforced by local penal or military administrators, themselves usually arrogant and arbitrary toward Melanesians.

For eight years after 1870 Melanesians all but disappeared from the colonial record. This apparent quiescence—what I regard as a widespread readiness to pursue peaceful coexistence to the limits of toleration, while some prepared to defend those limits with the club—enabled Noumea-based officials to ignore Melanesians in accordance with the promptings of economic stringency and wishful thinking (Gaultier de la Richerie to Ministre, 15 October 1872, ANOM, Carton 32; Reboul to Ministre, December 1873, ANOM, Carton 166; Rivière 1881, 78–79). Announcing the outbreak of war in June 1878, Governor Olry marveled that soldiers and settlers in the bush "regarded *canaques* as big children, sometimes sulky, but always inoffensive, they enjoyed a truly strange confidence, even intimacy" (Olry to Ministre, 6 July 1878, ANOM, Carton 43). Throughout this period, however, penal and free colonization had steadily expanded along the mid-west coast, with little concern for Melanesian livelihood and sensibilities; it is undoubtedly significant that the groups most active in covertly planning and initiating the 1878 war were among those most affected and outraged by their experiences at this time. In shocked retrospect the mid-1870s were redefined by Europeans as the deceptive calm before the storm, and simple savages— "big children"—underwent figurative retransformation into treacherous, inscrutable ones: "The savage! I prefer him furious to silent and pensive," announced Olry at the end of the war (Olry to Ministre, 22 August 1879, ANOM, Carton 43). As the emergency receded, however, pecuniary considerations again dictated reduction in the military forces available to police the bush, the direct French yoke eased and Melanesians disappeared from official texts, except spasmodically when their actions stirred administrative notice or the demands of colonization inspired new official onslaughts on their lands and labor (Ministre to Courbet, 12 June 1880; Courbet to Ministre, 5 December 1882, Service historique de la Marine, BB4 1577).

CONCLUSIONS

The intentions of this chapter are at once critical and advocatory: I aim to identify elements of essentialism, anachronism, and ethnocentrism in contemporary texts, histories, and ethnographies, while illustrating a historical method based primarily on contemporary action descriptions. Essentialism is apparent in contemporary European images of fixed, territorially defined Melanesian political entities. These contradict likewise indications in the same texts of contingency and fluidity in Melanesian actions and relationships, and a stress in some twentieth-century ethnographies of the significance of flux in Melanesian political practice. A major concern is with temporal aspects of mirroring, distortions induced by unreflexive present perspectives: anachronism always looms in the assumption that later ethnographic categories are automatically appropriate to past contexts, but the tyranny of the ethnographic present in anthropology is at least matched by the tyranny of outcomes in history, exemplified above with reference to the central region in 1868–69. A congruent, recurrent concern is with ethnocentrism, particularly the Eurocentric passivism of words used to represent Melanesian actions.

The question must arise as to how the rhetorical trappings of contemporary action descriptions may be recognized and penetrated. Most nineteenth-century texts on New Caledonia were written by French men; their interpretation for ethnographic purposes places a heavy burden on nuance, implication, hints, and single instances, as even the best were written with other ends in view and with a focus on prominent Melanesian males, especially "chiefs." Vivid insights often emerge from the contradictions and frustrations of refractory experience, displayed in the texts and belying the ethnocentric arrogance and a priori assumptions of their authors. To illustrate: Douarre despaired of Melanesians as a people who would not give or receive a "gift" in the spirit in which he thought it ought to be intended and whose every gesture seemed to have a materialistic double meaning. He wrote disparagingly of a Mwelebeng chief who "opened to me his two great arms to say that he loved me much, much, much; he took care, however, to add finally 'You will give me a *toqui* [piece of iron]!'" ("Journal," 20–24 February 1846). Reading emotion and value across cultures and eras is a slippery enterprise; in this case, as so often, dissonance was interpreted negatively. Though accused of materialism (e.g., Douarre, "Journal," 16 July, 20 November 1844), Melanesians set far greater store by acts of exchange and the relationships and meanings they mediated and expressed than by the objects as such, though objects were essential to maintain the flow and symbolize the rhythm of exchange relationships. A senior naval officer described aptly the peripatetic quality of objects, but dismissed it as "curious," token of a "weak . . . sense of property," which others deplored as "communism" (e.g., Leconte to Ministre, 31 March 1847, ANOM, Carton 40; Verguet 1854, 61–62):

> the possessor of whatever object, given as payment for a service rendered or as a present, parts with it almost immediately in favor of the first comer, who himself gives it to another; such that one often sees an object of great value, in the eyes of the natives, pass through a thousand hands and, from tribe to tribe, make a tour of the island. (Tardy de Montravel to Ministre, 25 December 1854, ANOM, Carton 40)

As in the case of ethnographic field notes and the working sketches of artists on early European voyages of discovery, the more immediate and less formal and overwrought the text, the more useful the action description. Unpublished mission journals and correspondence are especially valuable, since missionaries, like ethnographic historians, knew that souls, like minds, are inaccessible to mere mortals and that actions and words provide the best clues available as to what people might have thought and felt. There were also different categories of text, especially in colonial contexts, the authors of which had different, often incompatible, axes to grind. Missionaries, settlers, and administrators, for example, were often mutually critical, even hostile: their accounts derived from varied perspectives, giving opportunities for cross-checking; furthermore, in condemning opponents and rivals, they tended inadvertently to caricature their own motivations, intentions, and biases, as in the several estimations cited above of the significance of Melanesian allies to the French cause in 1878–79.

Language is transformative. The rhetorics encountered in contemporary texts and histories are varied: savagery in several guises; primitive cultural conservatism; reflex resistance to colonial domination. All shared a vision of human action—or at least Melanesian actions—as product of impersonal forces or structures. My own rhetoric derives from a philosophical inclination to see actors as intending subjects, rather than passive objects or victims of abstract causal forces (Douglas 1984; Fabian 1979, 13–14; Ortner 1984; Parkin 1982; Philipp 1983, 346–350). I aim to assess both Melanesian and colonial performance in context, in terms appropriate to actors' actions, intentions, and conceptions and the practical constraints under which they operated. I am struck at once by the range of Melanesian actions and choices and by the consistency of restraint: their enduring preference for compromise over martyrdom, their emphasis on selective, intensely psychological violence, often verbal rather than physical and aimed at property rather than persons. Two philosophically opposed ethnographers made similar points in relation to more recent events, though in somewhat essentialist terms. According to Leenhardt, fighting for Melanesians was culturally and linguistically a "corollary of anger" and they abhorred the cold persistence of Europeans: Melanesian soldiers in France during World War I were profoundly astonished "to see Whites capable of coldly making severe war on each other" (1930, 38). Bensa remarked that "*Canaques* loathe direct violence" and linked this trait to the "constantly unravelling and reforming segmentary structures" of their societies, "to which correspond ideologies of integration, of respect, of ambiguity, of contained and staged violence" (Bensa and Bourdieu 1985, 82–83). Multiplication does not transform interpretation into truth, but it is suggestive that three disparate methods of inquiry focused on very different contexts at widely separated periods should produce similar impressions of Melanesian attitudes to violence, impressions that contradict most past and present stereotypes.

NOTES

1. Anthropologists' sensitivity to the problematic status of such contexts is clearly displayed, for example, in persistent debates on the aptness of African models to Melanesian social systems (and vice versa) (e.g., Barnes 1962; Karp 1978; Keesing 1971, 1987; Strathern 1973, 1982*b*) and on social stratification in Melanesia (e.g., Douglas 1979*b*; Jolly 1987; Strathern 1982*a*). With special reference to New Caledonia, the French anthropologist Alban Bensa questioned the adequacy of the term "chief" to translate the *cèmuhî* concept *daame*, as well, by implication, as cognates in other local languages and dialects (Bensa and Rivierre 1982, 110).

2. *Canaque* became the standard French term for the indigenous inhabitants of New Caledonia (Hollyman 1959, 372–373, 1978, 39). The modern independence movement appropriated the term, given a simpler phonetic spelling, as an ironic statement about cultural identity and shared experience of dispossession under the colonial regime. I use "Melanesian" as a general label and "Kanak" with specific reference to those people who now so identify themselves.

3. I have translated all French quotations into English.

4. Douarre, "Journal," 10 December 1845, and 19, 22 July 1852; Rochas 1862, 252; Mathieu 1868, 10; Patouillet 1872, 164; Lambert 1900, 177; Durand 1900, 514; Leenhardt 1930, 38, 45–46, 52–53; cf. Ta'unga 1968, 86.

5. Bensa commented: "The most frequent wars most often develop . . . within the clan. . . . The will to segment is most often manifested within the family (quarrel between brothers) or in the bosom of a lineage between two branches nourishing divergent interests" (Bensa and Rivierre 1982, 80–81).

6. The missionary/ethnographer Pierre Lambert, who was based in the extreme north from 1856 to 1863, later remarked that "the north of New Caledonia is divided into different tribes which are grouped under two names, the Ots and the Ouaouaps. When war breaks out between two tribes, the Ouaouaps must take up the cudgels for each Ouaouap tribe, and the Ots for the Ot peoples" (1900, 173–174).

7. In 1882, Governor Courbet complained that, owing to the remoteness and rugged terrain of the north, "the effective action of the [three] military posts does not extend beyond a certain radius" and some places were rarely visited (Courbet to Ministre, 22 June 1882, ANOM, Carton 32). In 1917, Governor Repiquet reported that the people in the mountains between Koné and Tipindjé were still virtually uncontrolled (Repiquet to Ministre, 7 December 1917, ANOM, Carton 193).

8. The mining engineer Jules Garnier reported that Gondou and his ally Poindi-Patchili "gave their neighbors no respite and were detested by them. Gondou especially had amongst Kanaks a great reputation for ferocity; one native . . . told us . . . : '*Gondou he no all same man he all same poika [dog]; he look one Kanak he houo-houo [barks]; he kai kai [eats] plenty man*'" (1868, 48; see also La Hautière 1869, 170–171).

9. Various letters, Archives de l'Archevêché, Noumea (hereinafter AAN), 16.1; Olry to Ministre, 28 September 1878; Récit détaillé . . . , 16 January–5 February 1879, ANOM, Carton 43; Rivière 1881, 246, 249, 255–260; Guiart 1968, 114–115.

10. E.g., Olry to Ministre, 6 July, 2 August, 28 September 1878; Récit détaillé . . . , 16 January–5 February 1879, ANOM, Carton 43; Rochas 1862, 209; Rougeyron 1846–1849, 16; Goujon to Poupinel, 15 June 1857, APM/ONC, General

Correspondence 1857; Rougeyron, 30 November 1867, APM/ONC, Massacres de Pouébo, 1867–1868; Montrouzier to Fraysse, [1878], AAN, 16.1. The questions of the range and origins of nineteenth-century French conceptions of the "primitive" are complex and beyond the scope of this paper, but see Foucault (1966); for a general historical overview of concepts of the "savage," see Sinclair (1977).

11. The points in this and the following paragraphs are discussed in Douglas (1990, 43–45).

REFERENCES

Anova-Ataba, Apollinaire. 1969. "Deux exemples de réflexions mélanésiennes: 1. L'insurrection des Néo-Calédoniens en 1878 et la personnalité du grand chef Ataï; 2. Pour une économie humaine." *Journal de la Société des Océanistes* 25:201–237.

Archives de l'Archevêché. Noumea.

Archives nationales, section Marine. Paris.

Archives nationales, section Outre-mer, série Nouvelle-Calédonie. Paris.

Archives of the Province of Oceania. Formerly Sydney, now Rome.

Archivio di Padri Maristi, section Oceania, Nova Caledonia. Rome.

Barnes, J. A. 1962. "African Models in the New Guinea Highlands." *Man* 62:5–9.

Belich, James. 1986. *The New Zealand Wars and the Victorian Interpretation of Racial Conflict.* Auckland: Auckland University Press.

Bensa, Alban, and Pierre Bourdieu. 1985. "Quand les Canaques prennent la parole." Entretien avec Alban Bensa. *Actes de la Recherche en Sciences Sociales* 56:69–83.

Bensa, Alban, and Jean-Claude Rivierre. 1982. *Les chemins de l'alliance: L'organisation social et ses représentations en Nouvelle-Calédonie (région de Touho—aire linguistique cèmuhî).* (Langues et cultures du Pacifique 1.) Paris: SELAF.

———. 1984. "Jean Guiart et l'ethnologie." *L'Homme* 24:101–105.

Clendinnen, Inga. 1987. *Ambivalent Conquests: Maya and Spaniard in Yucatan, 1517–1570.* (Cambridge Latin American Series 61.) Cambridge: Cambridge University Press.

Connell, John. 1987. *New Caledonia or Kanaky? The Political History of a French Colony.* (Pacific Research Monograph 16.) Canberra: National Centre for Development Studies, Australian National University.

Cook, James. 1961. *Journals* II, ed. J. C. Beaglehole. Cambridge: Cambridge University Press for the Hakluyt Society.

Corris, Peter. 1973. *Passage, Port and Plantation: A History of Solomon Islands Labour Migration 1870–1914.* Melbourne: Melbourne University Press.

Dening, Greg. 1980. *Islands and Beaches: Discourse on a Silent Land, Marquesas 1774–1880.* Melbourne: Melbourne University Press.

———. 1988. *History's Anthropology: The Death of William Gooch.* (ASAO Special Publications 2.) Lanham, Maryland: University Press of America.

———. 1989. "History 'in' the Pacific." *The Contemporary Pacific: A Journal of Island Affairs* 1:134–139.

Douarre, Guillaume. 1843–1853. Journal, 21 December 1843–8 November 1846, 13 October 1848–17 November 1849, 15 April 1851—20 April 1853. MS copy. Archives de l'Archevêché, Noumea.

Douglas, Bronwen. 1972. "A History of Culture Contact in North-Eastern New Caledonia, 1774–1870." Ph.D. thesis. Australian National University, Canberra.

————. 1979*a*. "Bouarate of Hienghène: Great Chief in New Caledonia." Pp. 35–57 in Deryck Scarr (ed.), *More Pacific Islands Portraits*. Canberra: Australian National University Press.

————. 1979*b*. "Rank, Power, Authority: A Reassessment of Traditional Leadership in South Pacific Societies." *Journal of Pacific History* 14:2–27.

————. 1980. "Conflict and Alliance in a Colonial Context: Case Studies in New Caledonia, 1853–1870." *Journal of Pacific History* 15:21–51.

————. 1984. "Ethnography and Ethnographic History: Some Recent Trends." *Pacific History Bibliography and Comment* 19:36–42.

————. 1990. "'Almost Constantly at War?' An Ethnographic Perspective on Fighting in New Caledonia." *Journal of Pacific History* 25:22–46.

Dousset, Roselène. 1970. *Colonialisme et contradictions: Etude sur les causes socio-historiques de l'Insurrection de 1878 en Nouvelle-Calédonie.* (Le monde d'outre-mer passé et présent, troisième série, Essais 10.) Paris: Mouton & Co.

Dousset-Leenhardt, Roselène. 1976. *Terre natale, terre d'exil.* Paris: G-P. Maisonneuve & Larose.

Durand, Jules. 1900. "Chez les Ouébias, en Nouvelle-Calédonie." *Tour du Monde* (n.s.) 6:493–516.

Fabian, Johannes. 1979. "The Anthropology of Religious Movements: From Explanation to Interpretation." In Johannes Fabian (ed.), *Beyond Charisma: Religious Movements as Discourse. Social Research* 46 (special issue):4–35.

Foucault, Michel. 1966. *Les mots et les choses: Une archéologie des sciences humaines.* Paris: Gallimard.

[Gagnière, Matthieu]. 1905. *Etude ethnologique sur la religion des Néo-Calédoniens.* Saint-Louis: Imprimerie catholique.

Garnier, Jules. 1868. "Voyage à la Nouvelle-Calédonie." *Tour du Monde* 18:1–64.

Geertz, Clifford. 1986. "The Uses of Diversity." *Michigan Quarterly Review* 23:105–123.

Guiart, Jean. 1957. "Les modalités de l'organisation dualiste et le système matrimonial en Nouvelle-Calédonie." *Cahiers Internationaux de Sociologie* (n.s.) 22:21–39.

————. 1963. *Structure de la chefferie en Mélanésie du sud.* (Travaux et mémoires de l'Institut d'Ethnologie 66.) Paris: Institut d'Ethnologie.

————. 1966. *Mythologie du masque en Nouvelle-Calédonie.* (Publications de la Société des Océanistes 18.) Paris: Musée de l'Homme.

————. 1968. "Le cadre social traditionnel et la rébellion de 1878 dans le pays de la Foa, Nouvelle-Calédonie." *Journal de la Société des Océanistes* 24:97–119.

————. 1984. "La société traditionnelle des vallées de Bourail, côte ouest de la Nouvelle-Calédonie." *Journal de la Société des Océanistes* 40:51–61.

————. 1985. "Ethnologie de la Mélanésie: Critiques et autocritiques." *L'Homme* 25:73–95.

Hollyman, K. J. 1959. "Polynesian Influence in New Caledonia: The Linguistic Aspect." *Journal of the Polynesian Society* 68:356–389.

————. 1978. "La langue de relation entre autochtones et Français: Nouvelle-Calédonie avant 1854." *Te Reo* 21:35–66.

Jolly, Margaret. 1987. "The Chimera of Equality in Melanesia." *Mankind* 17:168–183.

Karp, Ivan. 1978. "New Guinea Models in the African Savannah." *Africa* 48:1–16.

Keesing, Roger. 1971. "Descent, Residence and Cultural Codes." Pp. 121–138 in

L. R. Hiatt and C. Jayawardena (eds.), *Anthropology in Oceania*. Sydney: Angus and Robertson.

———. 1987. "African Models in the Malaita Highlands." *Man* 22:431–452.

———. 1989. "Creating the Past: Custom and Identity in the Contemporary Pacific." *The Contemporary Pacific* 1:19–42.

Laferrière, Julien. 1845. *Voyage aux îles Tonga-tabou, Wallis et Foutouna, à la Nouvelle-Calédonie et à la Nouvelle-Zélande, exécuté du 1er novembre 1843 au 1er avril 1844*. Paris: Imprimerie royale.

La Hautière, Ulysse de. 1869. *Souvenirs de la Nouvelle Calédonie*. Paris: Challamel ainé.

Lambert, Pierre. 1900. *Moeurs et superstitions des Neo-Calédoniens*. Noumea: Nouvelle Imprimerie nouméenne.

Latham, Linda. 1978. *La révolte de 1878: Etude critique des causes de la rébellion de 1878 en Nouvelle-Calédonie*. (Publications de la Société d'Etudes Historiques de la Nouvelle-Calédonie 17.) Noumea: Société d'Etudes Historiques de la Nouvelle-Calédonie.

Leconte, François. 1847. "Notice sur la Nouvelle-Calédonie, les moeurs et les usages de ses habitants, par F. Leconte, capitaine de vaisseau." *Annales Maritimes et Coloniales* (32ᵉ année, 3ᵉ série) 2:811–869.

Leenhardt, Maurice. 1930. *Notes d'ethnologie Neo-Calédonien*. (Travaux et mémoires de l'Institut d'Ethnologie 8.) Paris: Institut d'Ethnologie.

Lyons, Martyn. 1986. *The Totem and the Tricolour: A Short History of New Caledonia since 1774*. Sydney: University of New South Wales Press.

Mathieu, Adolphe. 1868. "Aperçu historique sur la tribu des Houassios ou des Manongôés." *Le Moniteur de la Nouvelle-Calédonie* 433:9–11.

Maude, H. E. 1968. *Of Islands and Men*. Melbourne: Oxford University Press.

Moniteur impérial de la Nouvelle-Calédonie et dépendances, 1859–1861. Thereafter *Le Moniteur de la Nouvelle-Calédonie*. Noumea.

Newbury, Colin. 1980. *Tahiti Nui: Change and Survival in French Polynesia 1767–1945*. Honolulu: University Press of Hawaii.

Ortner, Sherry B. 1984. "Theory in Anthropology since the Sixties." *Comparative Studies in Society and History* 26:126–166.

Parkin, David. 1982. "Introduction." Pp. xi–li in David Parkin (ed.), *Semantic Anthropology*. (ASA Monograph 22.) London: Academic Press.

Patouillet, Jules. 1872. *Voyage autour du monde: Trois ans en Nouvelle-Calédonie*. Paris: E. Dentu.

Philipp, June. 1983. "Traditional Historical Narrative and Action-Oriented (or Ethnographic) History." *Historical Studies* 20:339–352.

Pigeard, Charles. 1846. *Voyage dans l'Océanie centrale, sur la corvette française le Bucéphale*. Paris: Arthus Bertrand.

Rivière, Henri. 1881. *Souvenirs de la Nouvelle-Calédonie: L'insurrection canaque*. Paris: Calmann Lévy.

Rochas, Victor de. 1862. *La Nouvelle-Calédonie et ses habitants: Productions, moeurs, cannibalisme*. Paris: F. Sartorius.

Rougeyron, Pierre. 1846–1849. Journal, 7 September 1846–1830, October 1849. TS copy. Archives de l'Archevêché, Noumea.

Sahlins, Marshall. 1981. *Historical Metaphors and Mythical Realities: Structure in the Early History of the Sandwich Islands Kingdom*. (ASAO Special Publications 1.) Ann Arbor: University of Michigan Press.

————. 1985. *Islands of History*. Chicago: University of Chicago Press.

Saussol, Alain. 1979. *L'héritage. Essai sur le problème foncier mélanésien en Nouvelle-Calédonie*. (Publications de la Société des Océanistes 40.) Paris: Musée de l'Homme.

Seneviratne, H. L. 1989. "Identity and the Conflation of Past and Present." In H. L. Seneviratne (ed.), *Identity, Consciousness and the Past. Social Analysis* 25 (special issue):3–17.

Service historique de la Marine, Paris.

Shineberg, Dorothy. 1967. *They Came for Sandalwood: A Study of the Sandalwood Trade in the South-West Pacific 1830–1865*. Melbourne: Melbourne University Press.

Sinclair, Andrew. 1977. *The Savage: A History of Misunderstanding*. London: Weidenfeld and Nicolson.

Stephen, Michele. 1979. "An Honourable Man: Mekeo Views of the Village Constable." *Journal of Pacific History* 14:85–99.

Strathern, Andrew. 1973. "Kinship, Descent and Locality: Some New Guinea Examples." Pp. 21–33 in Jack Goody (ed.), *The Character of Kinship*. Cambridge: Cambridge University Press.

————, ed. 1982a. *Inequality in New Guinea Highland Societies*. Cambridge: Cambridge University Press.

————. 1982b. "Two Waves of African Models in the New Guinea Highlands." Pp. 35–49 in Andrew Strathern (ed.), *Inequality in New Guinea Highland Societies*. Cambridge: Cambridge University Press.

Sydney Morning Herald. Sydney.

Ta'unga. 1968. *The Words of Ta'unga: Records of a Polynesian Traveller in the South Seas, 1833–1896*. Ed. R. G. Crocombe and Marjorie Crocombe. (Pacific History Series 2.) Canberra: Australian National University Press.

Thomas, Julian [James, John Stanley]. 1886. *Cannibals and Convicts: Notes of Personal Experiences in the Western Pacific*. London: Cassell.

Verguet, C. Marie-Léopold. 1854. *Histoire de la première mission catholique au vicariat de Mélanésie*. Carcassonne: P. Labau.

FOUR

Approaches to Articulation

James G. Carrier

In late November of 1978 Achsah Carrier and I arrived at Ponam Island, where we were to do fieldwork off and on for the next eight years.[1] What struck us then, as now, was that on Ponam the old ways stood together with the new: complex kinship and exchange coexisted with wage employment and commodity relations; elaborate fishing techniques coexisted with tinned fish; traditional markets and trade partnerships coexisted with trade stores, bank loans, and cash transactions between market partners. Islanders appeared to be part of two worlds: the modern West and the traditional village. They owned pots and pans, sheets, pillows and pillowslips, watches, radios, and tape players, in fact a surprising range of paraphernalia. They were interested in and knowledgeable about the larger world. They asked us about the success of Margaret Thatcher in becoming the Prime Minister of Great Britain, about Soviet activities in Afghanistan, about the governmental structure of the United States. At the same time, they lived in thatch houses and used fishing techniques that patently harked back to their precolonial past, and even continued the tedious and time-consuming manufacture of the shell money that they still used to make brideprice payments. And in everything they did islanders referred back to the ramified network of kinship relations that bound them to each other, shaped who did what, who they did it with, and how they did it, a network that they celebrated and recreated in the scores of ceremonial exchanges, gifts, and payments that filled their year.

How were we to come to some sense of which aspects of this mix of the traditional and the modern were worth our attention and efforts, and of how those aspects fit together? Certainly we knew that Ponam Island was in a region of Papua New Guinea that had a relatively long history of Western influence, and certainly we knew that Ponams were well-educated and that many were very successful government employees in Port Moresby and elsewhere. Yet the *reality* of this curious mixture of old and new was hard to grasp. While islanders did many things that were straight out of introductory anthropology courses, these were not embedded in the sort of society those same courses so often portray, subsistence societies relatively little touched by the outside world. How were we to make sense of this?

ARTICULATION

In stepping on to Ponam Island we confronted the problem of articulation, the problem that I will discuss in this chapter. By articulation I mean something very simple: the way that village societies are linked to and interact with the larger social, political, and economic orders in which they are embedded. For Ponam Island during the time we were doing fieldwork, this meant how this village society was linked with the national economy and state organization of Papua New Guinea.[2] This presented itself to us most visibly in the field in the form of the juxtaposition of inward- and backward-looking practices, local and traditional, together with the signs of a strong interest in and involvement with the outside national and even international world.

Observing life on Ponam Island brought home the importance of the issue of articulation, and I suspect that most anthropologists working in Melanesia experienced in their field sites the same sort of incongruous juxtapositions that Achsah Carrier and I witnessed, even if, perhaps, not to the same degree. However, if the criticisms of anthropology described in the introduction to this collection of papers have any common theme, it is that conventional anthropology has failed to address, and frequently has failed even to recognize, this issue. In Orientalizing the societies they study, the critics have argued, anthropologists deny that villages and the West are linked in any significant way, deny they occupy places in the same world at the same time, and deny they impinge upon each other. The observation that anthropologists tend to impose a radical separation between Us and the Other means that they deny, in effect, that there is any articulation worth mentioning.

In view of this criticism, it is appropriate to look at what anthropologists in Melanesia have had to say about the relationship between villages and the West.

This look at articulation will not be purely descriptive. Rather, it will be critical, based on the belief that an adequate understanding of articulation must exhibit two attributes. These attributes are relatively simple, though as this paper unfolds it will become clear that they are not necessarily characteristic of the approaches to articulation commonly used in Papua New Guinea ethnography.

First, it is necessary to have a conception of village societies as societies, as forms of social life, rather than as collections of individuals. I do not mean by this that one ought to focus on a clearly bounded and essentialized entity called The Village. Rather, I mean something much more modest. At the very least, it must be recognized that villages are social, comprised of sets of interrelationships among the people who are in them, sets of interrelationships that are significant for distinguishing one village from another, both in the mind of the analyst and in the minds of the people who live there.[3] This point may appear self-evident and uncontentious, but it has the important corollary that any approach that deals with articulation simply in terms of individual actions or as the passage of sets of individual people from one realm to another fails to deal adequately with the phenomenon. Those actions and passages may be important, but restricting attention to them reduces the likelihood of seeing their consequences for realms of village life that are less obviously a part of the response to colonization, such as relations of inequality, kinship, marriage patterns, and the like, described later in this paper.

Second, and related to my first point, a model of articulation should be so oriented that it allows one to look in detail at, and make sense in detail of, the processes and effects of articulation in village life. Again, this may seem self-evident and uncontentious. However, it means that an adequate model of articulation can not focus only on the macroscopic aspects of articulation, neither can it focus only on the effects of articulation on the Western, capitalist-oriented sphere. Instead, it needs to encompass as well the mechanisms and relationships that link the village at issue and the national sphere and the effects of those links on the village. Saying that one needs to encompass the processes and effects of articulation on the village society means that one needs to go beyond the mere demonstration of articulation: one should be able to identify how articulation occurs in the village and what difference it makes.

Activist Approaches

To return to my original question: How were we to make sense of Ponam society?

Had it been the 1950s or even the 1960s the answer would have been fairly simple, for common wisdom then suggested that the old ways were fragments of a precontact order that was being destroyed by colonization and the collision with Western capitalism.[4] In fact, the power of Western society was so great that even indirect exposure to it could transform the old ways, or at least that was the lesson W. E. H. Stanner drew from Richard Salisbury's study of the effects of steel axes on precolonial Siane society in what became Simbu Province in Papua New Guinea: "Steel drove out stone; the new cutting edges saved men's working-time; and from those beginnings, the whole design-plan and dynamism of their way of life changed" (in Salisbury 1962, vi). A few years later, C. D. Rowley, a distinguished and long-time observer of colonial Papua New Guinea, came to similar conclusions. From contact, Melanesia became "committed to a permanent process of change...from this point, the old order of society is doomed" (Rowley 1965, 94).

The reasons for this change were self-evident. No one would expect neolithic societies to survive the collection of British, German, and Australian colonial apparatuses that had governed Papua New Guinea. Cosmological upheavals appeared as cargo cults, the vehicles of religious and political reorientation (Lawrence 1964; Worsley 1957). Old trading systems collapsed, pulling down complex sets of economic dependencies and social relationships (Harding 1967; Mead 1968). Tribesmen were turned into peasants and big men into entrepreneurs (Finney 1973; Meggitt 1971).[5]

This faith in the power of colonization was not limited to Melanesianists, nor was it original with them. Over a century earlier Marx and Engels wrote that "the bourgeoisie... compels all nations, on pain of extinction, to adopt the bourgeois mode of production; it compels them... to become bourgeois themselves. In one word, it creates a world after its own image" (Marx and Engels 1976, 488). This view, of course, did not merely reflect an assessment of the potency of the productive forces that capitalism unleashed. Rather, it sprang as well from a belief that the falling rate of profit and the periodic crises of overproduction were inherent in capitalism; one forcing capitalists to search for new and cheaper sources of raw materials and the other forcing them to search for new markets; both, in other words, forcing capitalism to extend its grasp to ever greater areas of the world.

During the 1970s, assumptions about articulation in Papua New Guinea began to diverge. Even so, a number of researchers continued to use this activist approach, studying the ways in which the encroaching Western world affected village life and people. Noticeable here was a spate of studies focused on entrepreneurs, the innovative individuals who are one locus of the articulation of the money economy and village life. These entrepreneurs were most noticeable in the forward-thrusting Highlands region of the country. The best known of these studies is Ben Finney's *Big-Men and Business*. With Finney in particular, entrepreneurs are presented as unstable creatures, shuttling back and forth between the two social systems they inhabit, using their gains in one realm to shore up and extend their position in the other. While such studies clearly address the question of articulation, from my point of view they present two important problems. The first is their individual orientation, which makes them prone to the shortcoming described earlier in this paper. Because they are concerned primarily with the transactions and histories of individual people, they may ignore how these affect and even transform the organization of village societies in ways that may not be obvious. The second problem, particularly noticeable in Finney's work, is an orientation toward the urban, more Westernized sphere: people are selected for study precisely because they are doing well in the urban sector.

This is more apparent if we look at two studies that more clearly represent these two tendencies. The first illustrates the individualistic element. It is *Money, Motivation and Cash Cropping*, T. K. Moulik's analysis of cultural factors affecting cash cropping in various regions of the country. Moulik sees cash-crop entrepreneurs in terms of individual strategies and transactions, and does not attend to the more broadly structural factors constraining or facilitating these entrepreneurs or to the social settings in which they find themselves, though to be fair I should note that this individualism was ascendent more generally around this time among anthropologists concerned with Papua New Guinea (A. Carrier 1984, esp. 77–83). Thus, Moulik's explanation of variation in entrepreneurial innovation reduces to social psychology: where psychological constraints (e.g., a fear of sorcery) are strong, individuals will not be motivated to engage in cash-cropping. In failing to take us beyond the hopes and fears of individual villagers, however cultural the basis of these feelings, Moulik affords us little sense of how village societies are affected by this reorientation to a money economy.

The second of these studies is Rolf Gerritsen's description of Highlands entrepreneurs, which, though published relatively late (1981), was formulated in the early 1970s. Gerritsen avoids an individualistic orientation. Although he is concerned with studying a fairly small group of people, his model defines them not as innovative individuals but as the emerging elements of a new class. Thus, he takes a firm hold of sociological factors and processes. However, in doing this he embraces the second problem I mentioned, a strongly urban or national orientation. Gerritsen is concerned with establishing the existence of an emerging big peasantry, to plot its links with the state and its privileged access to state resources. Although Gerritsen's concern may be for issues that are important in understanding changes in the economic and political organization of Papua New Guinea, it does mean that he slights consideration of the social organization of the villages from which these big peasants have emerged and the way that articulation, which the big peasants embody, links these villages to the national economy and affects their structure.

Since the first wave of these studies around 1970, analysts have become better able to relate entrepreneurs or emerging big peasants, depending upon one's perspective, to village society. However, difficulties remain. The nature of these is illustrated by Lawrence Grossman's description, a decade later, of cattle projects in a village in Eastern Highlands Province. Grossman locates the emerging big peasants firmly in their village milieux, by the simple expedient of looking at village enterprises, cattle projects, rather than just the individual entrepreneurs who might initiate them. However, Grossman rejects a structural approach to articulation (1983, 59–60), arguing that structures themselves cause nothing, that it is necessary to consider "the strategies and aggregate actions of individuals and groups" if one is to understand articulation. While such an approach can command support, Grossman ignores structure altogether, and so does not investigate the ramifying effects of these strategies and aggregate actions on areas of social life not immediately related to the cattle projects. In other words, he does not consider how a village society, as opposed to certain individuals, articulates with the larger economy, and so fails to link these projects more than cursorily to the social organization of the village in which they occur.

The way that I think he fails to do this illustrates an important shortcoming in much of the recent literature on articulation in Papua New Guinea: the fact that even though the site of the study is the village, the orientation, the conceptual framework of the study, is firmly rooted in the national economy. Grossman focuses on village relationships, especially between leaders and participants in the cattle projects. However, his perception is shaped by his interest in commodity relations of the sort found in the national economy: thus, he describes how leaders and participants differ in terms of the labor and money they invest and the wealth they receive (1983, 67–70). In other words, while Grossman focuses on village relationships, he selectively perceives and recasts them in terms of the logic of the national economy. The consequence, certainly not what Grossman intended, is to elide all village relationships that cannot be reduced to this economistic calculus, and so obliterate differences between capitalist and precapitalist forms.

In sum, while these studies do identify and investigate the activities that link town and village, they adopt individualistic orientations. This problem is not as severe with the later studies as it is with the earlier ones, nevertheless it is there. In failing to consider villages as social units, these authors maintain an isolationist approach to Papua New Guinea villages even while they appear to be linking them to the outside world. They describe how individuals shuttle back and forth between more village-oriented and more Western-oriented activities and realms, but they leave largely unexplored the ways that village society itself, as a set of ordered interactions and practices, is touched by Western impact.

Persistence Approaches

I said that during the 1970s anthropological approaches to articulation in Melanesia began to diverge, and I have described what I have called the activist approach. Some other anthropologists used a different approach. To them, it became clear as the 1970s began to pass that the penetration of capitalist relations into village life was problematic rather than automatic. Tradition, custom, seemed more tenacious than many people expected. So, for example, Harold Brookfield (1973, 127) recanted his earlier belief that Chimbu society would be transformed by colonization, concluding instead that what was taking place was only "the partial acceptance of 'modern' innovations into a continuing system whose 'central variables' have not been transformed." Likewise, Mervyn Meggitt (1974, 182), speaking of the Mae Engan system of ceremonial exchange, the te, but probably reflecting a more general sentiment about traditional practices, said, "I for one would not assume its demise unless I actually attended the funeral."

Those anthropologists who, concerned to show the strength of village life, focused on durability, persistence, exposed themselves to a risk. They were especially likely to succumb if they accepted the idea, described in the Introduction to this collection, that Western influence appears as Westernization. In identifying some aspect of society as an element of an earlier, traditional order that survived into the present, they tended to focus on the sheer existence of such elements as culture traits, to use an old anthropological phrase. In doing so, they tended to slight the use and significance of such elements in society. As a result, they ignored the fact that the "same" institution can exist in two very different ways at different times. The te or kula of 1970 or 1980 may have entailed practices that resembled those in existence in 1910, but it would seem hasty to conclude from this evidence alone that the institutions survived in any but superficial ways.

This growing construction of the persistence of tradition in Papua New Guinea villages went hand-in-hand with two related tendencies that reduced the likelihood that those concerned with persistence would make the effort to situate socially the aspects of village life that concerned them, would attempt to see whether the "same" practices had the same social import. These tendencies were a conceptual isolation of village life from the intruding Western world and a principled unconcern with history.

This isolationism appears strikingly in the long-awaited volume of papers from the first kula conference (Leach and Leach 1983). Certainly many of the papers in that collection acknowledged the importance of colonization, the fact that, as C. A. Gregory (1983, 103) put it in his contribution, colonization had served "to integrate the [Milne Bay] province's 108,000 people well and truly into the world economy." Nonetheless, generally the importance of colonization was ignored once it was acknowledged, as the authors made no real effort to link the kula, an intensely economic and political system, with the economy and politics of Milne Bay Province. Thus, although notice was taken of the fact that kula voyages may be motorized and that money and other Western novelties may form part of the trade, the collection generally relegated the second half of the twentieth century to the role of a set piece, sparkling when ignited but not really linked to anything else.

Integration into the world economy is proclaimed, but its consequences do not form part of the substantive discussion of the kula. (A similar point is made by Michael Allen in his review of the collection [1985, 147], and indeed by Edmund Leach in his concluding chapter in the volume [1983, 537].) Illustrative of this is the fact that the book's index contains no entries for the following: government, labor, migration, Milne Bay Province, plantations, provincial government, remittance, or wage. Of course, one might argue, the kula conference was, after all, about the kula, so that the question of articulation with the outside world is beside the point. But such an argument only illustrates my point. Any institution of as much political and economic importance as the kula is almost certain to be influenced, both obviously and subtly, by the economic and political institutions of Milne Bay Province and Papua New Guinea more generally, and so cannot be understood without reference to them.

The tendency to ahistorical isolationism appears strikingly in some of Annette Weiner's work, also based on the study of indigenous society in Milne Bay. She laid out an anthropological version of reproduction theory, which, like its Marxist sociological cousins and its Durkheimian parent, was intended to explain how things remained the same over time. Weiner argued that ceremonial exchanges need to be seen as being linked together in long-running cycles that give logic and meaning to society generally and reproduce society itself over time. She argued that these cycles have the explicit objective of reproducing and regenerating people, objects, and relationships that are not eternal but necessarily decay through time. And she was arguing that this reproduction is not just a central value of the indigenous understanding of these exchanges. In addition, it is an essential element of society objectively perceived. Thus, she says, "In formulating a model of reproduction, my basic premise . . . is that any society must reproduce and regenerate certain elements of value in order for the society to continue" (1980, 71).

Weiner's formulation of reproduction theory illustrates both isolationism and ahistoricism, sharing them with the earlier functionalism that it recapitulates. This is manifest most clearly in the cycles that interest Weiner. Although these cycles may appear to inject an element of history, of the passage of time, into her model, this appearance is misleading. The time that is invoked is theoretical, not empirical. It is defined in terms of the essentialistic logic of her model, and as such does not involve the consideration of real historical events, both the momentous and the mundane, and the ways that these events can affect society.

To see the ahistoricism of this approach, imagine that in Weiner's fieldwork she saw the marriage of A in January, the funeral of B in June and the birth of C in November. From this she constructed a set of exchanges punctuating the life of a hypothetical x through his or her birth, marriage, and death over a period of seventy years. In other words, she constructed a logical structure of reproduction from the exchanges that both she and the villagers she studied saw, and concluded that reproduction over time really took place. But in the absence of concrete historical evidence it seems unreasonable to assume that the funeral of B in June of 1980 was really preceded by a marriage like A's in 1940, or a birth ceremony like C's in 1910; or that the birth of C in November of 1980 would culminate in a funeral like B's in 2050.

This assumption appears to rest on the prior assumption that Kiriwina villages are unchanging, which makes sense, even given Weiner's transmuted functionalism, only if it is assumed that those villages are untouched by the outside world.

Thus, in the shift to optimism about the durability of local social life there occurred as well a shift of interest away from the leading event in Papua New Guinea in the last century: Western penetration.[6] While that penetration may not have turned out to be the steamroller that some had anticipated, and while not everything that happened in Papua New Guinea was a direct response to it, its effects remain profound. Instead of trying to deal with these effects, instead of considering how village life might be something other than a pure reflection of indigenous social order, anthropologists like Weiner turned to a more ahistorical, isolationist approach, focusing on village life and shutting out the external world. Thus, an important part of Melanesian ethnography warrants Joel Kahn's (1980, 2) more general criticism:

> Pick up almost any monograph and you will find an introductory statement about the outside society, the total social whole in which the village is embedded, the importance of extra-local ties, etc. And yet I would argue that in most of such cases this holistic view is set aside, and the total social whole ignored in favour of detailed analyses of purely local phenomena.

PROGRAMMATIC STATEMENTS ON ARTICULATION

This optimistic view that Papua New Guinea villages were more persistent than the steamroller model of colonization allowed did not appear only in ethnography. As well, it surfaced in developments taking place at about the same time among Marxists, particularly in interpretations of the way the encroaching colonial capitalist mode of production articulates with the pre-existing traditional modes (see, e.g., Wolpe 1980). Like some Melanesian anthropologists, they too were beginning to think that the relation between the West and the rest was more problematic than it had first appeared.

Claude Meillassoux and Peter Fitzpatrick

Probably the most influential writer in this area has been Claude Meillassoux, especially in his *Maidens, Meal and Money*, and his model was applied to Papua New Guinea in different ways by Peter Fitzpatrick, in *Law and State in Papua New Guinea*, and by C. A. Gregory, in *Gifts and Commodities*.

Meillassoux argued that capitalist penetration need not lead to the eradication of precapitalist forms, but rather often results in their encapsulation and perpetuation. This occurs because the survival of a precapitalist sector benefits capitalism. This is because much of the labor in Third World countries is provided by circular migrants, and many of the costs of the reproduction of this labor force are born by the precapitalist sector, thereby reducing costs to the capitalist sector. Because circular migrants are reared in the village and will return to the village, their wages (both their direct wage and what Meillassoux calls their "social wage") need cover only the "sustenance of the workers during periods of employment" and perhaps "maintenance during periods of unemployment (due to stoppages, ill-health, etc.)" but not their "replacement by the breeding of offspring" (Meillassoux 1981, 100, emphasis omitted). This subsidy of the capitalist sphere exists as well in the goods that villagers produce to sell in the towns. Meillassoux said that "subsistence goods bought on the local market, if they are produced in the domestic sector, will be sold below their value because of the labor rent they also contain" (1981, 115). As a result, urban wage workers are able to eat for less than they could otherwise, further helping to keep labor costs down. Indeed, much of the power of capitalism to expand derives from this sort of subsidy by the domestic sphere (e.g., 1981, 138–144; for a description and criticism of this view, see Kahn 1980, chap. 10).

If it exceeds a certain level, this migration can have serious and accelerating consequences for the village. This Meillassouxian crisis occurs when the level of migration is so high that the village is no longer able to produce the means of its own reproduction. Village society begins to disintegrate. This can occur when villagers divert money from other uses to that of increasing their food supplies: "buying subsistence goods on the market or...employing seasonal workers to bring fallow land under cultivation" (Meillassoux 1981, 129). This staves off the immediate crisis, but it results in the destruction of the old ways and, apparently, the transformation of village social relations into monetized, Western-seeming relations: "The monetarisation of the economy which thus establishes itself further increases the need for cash by transforming goods, formerly bartered, into merchandise, thus inducing an irreversible process" (1981, 129). In other words, low levels of migration leave the village more or less intact, encapsulated by capitalist colonization. Beyond a certain point, however, these old ways are swept away as the village appears increasingly Westernized.

Meillassoux's model is based on his research in Africa. Peter Fitzpatrick applied it fairly mechanically to Papua New Guinea. Much of his analysis of *Law and State in Papua New Guinea* consists of arguing that colonial and postcolonial government policies served the interests of encroaching metropolitan capital by supporting and solidifying key elements of traditional Melanesian life. He says that the result was the continuation of village institutions that bore the costs of social reproduction, and thus that subsidized capitalism by allowing artificially low wages. Particularly pertinent for the points made in the introduction to this collection is Fitzpatrick's discussion of the concern within Papua New Guinea for village identity and ethnicity, for the image of the small and isolated village society. He says that this concern should not be seen merely as the recognition of an objective state of affairs. Rather, he says, this is part of an emerging capitalist-oriented national ideology. It helps assure the dominance of capitalism by making it difficult for a common consciousness to emerge among the growing urban proletariat.

The Meillassoux-Fitzpatrick model of articulation has some important virtues. It is macroscopic. This is a virtue because it encourages ethnographers to look beyond the immediate villages they study; because it encourages them to recognize the influence that capitalism has in Third World societies; because it emphasizes that an important fact about these diverse village societies is that they are related to a relatively uniform capitalist sphere. In other words, by shifting the ground of anthropological description, the model stresses the common and important colonial and postcolonial situation of rural societies in Papua New Guinea, and so helps combat the ahistorical isolationism that has attracted some anthropologists.

Only slightly less important, the model makes the point that the influence of capitalism on village societies does not necessarily appear in a familiar guise, does not necessarily turn village social relations into class relations, though this may occur as a result of the Meillassouxian crisis. This helps combat both the simplistic steamroller model of Western impact and the idea that the absence of Western-ness means the absence of Western impact. But, however useful this is, it is something negative, not something positive. It tells us that capitalist penetration does not necessarily turn Papua New Guinea villages into working-class suburbs of urban capitalism or into a collection of petit bourgeoisie. But it does not tell us what those villages become.

At this point the sweep and generality of the Meillassoux-Fitzpatrick articulation model become liabilities. In being so general that it obliges anthropologists to look to the common historical situation of the societies they study, the model becomes relatively unable to deal with the more detailed aspects or local consequences of that common situation. And once we try to use the model for more detailed descriptions of the nature of articulation, to get some clues about what villages actually are like and how they actually are affected by articulation, it loses much of its power. This is because the model orients itself in terms of the capitalist sector and constructs villages in terms of their links with capitalism. For Meillassoux and Fitzpatrick, then, the village is not an object of investigation in its own right. They do not attend to the inner workings of village societies, for the simple reason that there is no theoretical motive to do so.

Indeed, village societies often appear as little more than ill-understood entities hovering on the edges of Third World cities. For Fitzpatrick, Papua New Guinea villages often are reduced to the two-dimensional stereotypes embodied in his chapter titles, "The Colonized," "The Peasantry," and so forth, lacking any sensitivity to the differences between the sorts of people, situations, and relationships he condenses into these images. For Meillassoux, villages often are reduced to labor reserves, seats of the domestic mode of production that subsidize encroaching capitalism. There is little more to know about them, for once capitalism encroaches, they lose the sort of internal dynamic that was the focus of the whole first half of his *Maidens, Meal and Money*. Instead, they become passive, locked into their traditionalism and slowly drained of their vitality, unless they suffer the Westernization of the Meillassouxian crisis. Villages do not, then, respond to capitalism in a generative way by becoming something new; they do nothing but decay.

Thus, although these claim to be models of articulation, they are fundamentally isolationist. Instead of looking at two social groups and systems and seeing how they interact, these models reduce articulation largely to the shuttling back and forth of circular migrants between two otherwise unconnected social systems. They arrive in town full of the subsidy endowed them by the household economy that reared them and that they leave behind. They leave town drained of that subsidy and just about everything else. And when they get home, they return to villages that remain curiously untouched by the process of articulation. The upshot is that these models not only fail to focus on village societies, they also fail to conceptualize the ways that village and town are linked, for they describe little more than the flow of individual units of value: subsidized labor and subsidized goods. They do not allow anthropologists a perspective on the ways that articulation affects village life.

C. A. Gregory

The third writer that I mentioned who has put forward a programmatic statement of articulation is C. A. Gregory, primarily in *Gifts and Commodities*.[7] Although Gregory has been influenced strongly by Meillassoux, he appears to feel that an adequate model cannot construe articulation as Meillassoux did, only from the point of view of the capitalist sector. Instead, he pays more attention to how things look from the village.

This attention is apparent in his paper "Gifts to Men and Gifts to God." Here Gregory argues that Western capitalist and Melanesian precapitalist systems are oriented in fundamentally different ways, with the corollary that terms drawn from one are not adequate to describe the other. This sets him apart from those who, I argued, envisaged the effects of articulation as the emergence of capitalist relations in village life. Gregory characterizes the distinction between these two systems in terms of the distinction between gifts and commodities, between gift relations and commodity relations, between gift-debt and commodity-debt. He presents these two systems in ideal-typical terms and outlines four basic differences between them, elaborations of the classic Maussian point that in gift systems people are not distinguished from objects and transactors are not distinguished from each other in the way that they are in Western capitalist systems. Two of those differences concern me here.

One points to fundamental differences between objects and transactors in

the two sorts of systems: commodity-debt "is created by the exchange of
. . . objects between transactors who are in a state of reciprocal independence, whereas gift-debt is created by an exchange of. . . objects between people in a state of reciprocal dependence" (Gregory 1980, 640). Second, while
gift-debt "must be explained with reference to the social conditions of the
reproduction of *people*," such as "clan structure and the principles governing
kinship organization," on the other hand commodity-debt "must be explained with reference to the social conditions of the reproduction of *things*,"
such as "class structure and the principles governing factory organization"
(1980, 641).

Gregory's point in these observations is to stress that village societies are
dominated by the logic of gift relations and kinship. An example will help
illustrate the nature of this dominance. That example is "wok meri," perhaps
most briefly defined as a collective women's saving system around Goroka, in
the Papua New Guinea Highlands. As described by Lorraine Sexton (1982),
"wok meri" was an attempt by village women to adopt and adapt their own
version of important Western economic institutions.

It is apparent from Sexton's description that in adopting banking—in,
if you will, remaking banking into a more comprehensible and congenial
form—women recast it in terms of "the social conditions of the reproduction
of *people*," such as "clan structure and the principles governing kinship organization." Thus, women involved in the different "wok meri" groups were
recruited from the in-marrying wives of men's agnatic lineages. The groups
themselves were seen as elements of matrilineages: each was the daughter of
an earlier-formed group which was instrumental in founding it, and each was
expected to produce its own daughter in turn. Furthermore, the main transactions involving groups, one to mark the foundation of the daughter group
and one to mark the end of the main phase of the collection (i.e., saving) of
money, were modeled explicitly on marriage ritual, though Sexton notes
(1982, 177) that she detected in the rituals surrounding these transactions
elements of all rituals associated with the female life cycle except menarche.

My description of "wok meri" is cursory, but it is enough to illustrate the
point I want to make. Here, village women produced an economic institution
modeled on the introduced Western institution of the bank. These women
did not have to transform the institution they adopted; they could have simply set up informal village-based banks. However, they did transform it, and
they did so in a way that fits and illustrates Gregory's synoptic characterization of Melanesian precapitalist systems.[8]

In "Gifts to Men and Gifts to God" Gregory laid out a Maussian model of
the key distinctions between Western capitalist systems and Papua New
Guinea villages. In *Gifts and Commodities* he sets out to produce an overall
model of the articulation of these two realms, especially in chapters vi and
vii, "The Transformation of Gifts into Commodities in Colonial Papua New

Guinea" and "The Transformation of Commodities into Gifts in Colonial Papua New Guinea."

The first of these chapters performs its task admirably. It is a systematic description of how gift relations in the village affect commodity relations in the capitalist sector. Restating Meillassoux's point, Gregory shows how the domination of gift relations in villages so diffuses the cost of social reproduction that employers in the capitalist sector were able to pay wages well below the actual cost of the reproduction of the labor force, and hence well below the level of wages expected in wholly capitalist systems. Hence, Gregory argues that commodity relations in the capitalist sector of colonial Papua New Guinea were affected by articulation with precapitalist villages, and consequently were different from commodity relations in core capitalist areas where this sort of articulation does not take place. In other words, he has tried to describe the ways that articulation affects the operation of the commodity realm, and he does so in terms of the logic of the commodity system itself.

By its title, the second of these two chapters should be an inversion of the first, a systematic discussion of the ways that village precapitalist societies have their system of gift relations affected by their link to commodity relations in the capitalist sector. It should, in other words, bear most directly on the issues I have raised in this paper. Unfortunately, however, this chapter does not live up to its promise. Gregory contents himself with the proposition that "the gift economy of PNG has not been destroyed by colonization, but has effloresced. This is reflected in a tendency for European commodities to be transformed into gifts" (1982, 166). This is an improvement over Meillassoux and Fitzpatrick, for it suggests that articulation can result in more than just the encapsulated repetition of the old ways or the collapse of the Meillassouxian crisis. However, the first sentence of the proposition is defended primarily by describing a number of Melanesian exchange systems, while the second sentence, the one with the most interesting implications from my point of view, is left unexplored.

Although it goes beyond Meillassoux and Fitzpatrick, Gregory's model presents some fundamental problems. At the theoretical level, Gregory sees the need to consider the ways that articulation affects village life, and so rejects Meillassoux's and Fitzpatrick's bias toward the perspective of urban capitalism. However, in practice Gregory fails to carry out his own program. He does not analyze these consequences of articulation in the village with the same sophistication that he applies to the capitalist sphere. In principle, articulation may be generative in village societies; in practice, all that is described is more of the same.

Part of the reason for this may be the essentialist tendency in Gregory's typifications of gift and commodity systems. Although his idealized constructions of these two realms are useful for pointing out the ways that they involve different orientations and forms of social relations,[9] they can very easily take on a causal status, can become explanations rather than sensitizing concepts. At least this may be what happened with Gregory, for his description of articulation indicates that capitalist and village realms become more purely themselves, rather than being modified in any significant way.

ARTICULATION

Ponam Island did not behave as any of these models suggests. It did not freeze into traditionalism, as Fitzpatrick's model predicts; it did not decay in a Meillassouxian crisis; it did not even effloresce in the sort of sheer expansion of the old ways that Gregory's model predicts. The problem that Achsah Carrier and I confronted, how we were to make sense of what we saw on Ponam, remains. To resolve it, it is necessary to find a better way of approaching the problem.

In spite of my criticisms of Gregory's work, I think that it points in the right direction. Gregory identified a dominant realm in the capitalist and in the noncapitalist spheres: commodity-debt and the social conditions of the reproduction of things on the one hand, gift-debt and the social conditions of the reproduction of people on the other. This suggests that we look for the effects of articulation in the dominant realm of each sphere, look for the ways that the kin and exchange relations in the village sphere are affected by articulation, how they differ from such relations in village societies that are not so articulated, or how they change as a result of articulation. Until one can address this question, one cannot, I think, understand the relationship of the Western and village spheres in Papua New Guinea, and thus one cannot understand village society. After all, even if these villages are subordinated empirically to encroaching capitalism, there is no reason to assume that the terms and concepts used to describe them should be subordinated to the conceptual framework of capitalist commodity relations.

My point, put most simply, is that a rounded approach to articulation would have to try to trace out the links between the *commodity* relations of the national economy and the *gift* relations of the precapitalist village sector. It is this that underlies my objection to the urban and commodity-oriented terminology of some village-level studies of articulation. These do not look at gift relations in the village, they look at what are implicitly but the precursors of commodity relations. Failure to look for the signs and processes of articulation in the dominant village realm of gift relations constitutes a failure to see how articulation with the expanding national economy impinges upon the core elements of precapitalist society. Such a limited approach may contain interesting information and insights. However, it assumes that the capitalist sector displaces village social organization, not that it articulates with it, which is another way of saying that it assumes that the only consequence of Western influence worthy of notice is Westernization.

Ponam Articulation

I want now to give concrete expression to the general point I have made, by describing briefly the effects of articulation on Ponam society. This description will be highly condensed, for many of the points that I will make have been made at greater length elsewhere (esp. J. Carrier and A. Carrier 1985, 1989; A. Carrier and J. Carrier 1987, 1991). In condensing, I will focus particularly on the relationship between kinship and economics and on the ways that colonization affected kinship practices through its effects on economics. As will be apparent, Ponam society changed, but not in the direction of Westernization.

Before extensive colonial impact, Ponam society was linked to, and could be best understood with reference to, the regional system of which it was a part. In fact, it is likely that Ponam's integration in this larger system both shaped and made more visible its growing links to the emerging colonial, and later national, economy. We may, in other words, have found ourselves in a setting that was particularly suited to a consideration of articulation. Certainly it is reasonable to assume that more self-reliant agricultural societies less intensely dependent upon trade in subsistence goods and less tightly enmeshed in a regional system would experience colonial impact differently, that people in such societies would think about the encroaching colonial world differently, and that discerning the nature and consequences of articulation would be harder (these issues are addressed in Thomas 1991, chap. 3). But while Ponam may have been particularly likely to experience and exhibit systemic changes of the sort I will describe here, and while such changes may be less apparent elsewhere in Melanesia, it seems unlikely that any society in the area is free of such impact and articulation. If my comments about the isolationism of the discussion of the kula are at all accurate, then the absence of articulation in the literature is likely to reflect the predispositions of ethnographers rather than the isolated self-reliance of the villages they study.

Before marked colonial penetration, the economy of the Admiralty Islands, the area that is now Manus Province, contained an extensive division of production between villages, based on the ownership by patrilineal groups (called *kamal* on Ponam) of real property and of manufacturing and technique rights. Complementing this was a system of circulation that distributed local products through the region, most importantly through markets, trade partnerships, and ceremonial exchange. Because key elements of this circulation system were based on kin relationships and motivated by obligations between kin, and because property and production rights were owned by kinship groups, control over people was the key to control over production and circulation.

This had consequences for kinship practice. People sought to manipulate the system of kinship in order to secure access to valuable aspects of the production and circulation of goods through things like judicious adoption, patronage, and the arranging of marriages (see Mead 1934). Old men and women repeatedly stressed that their elders had arranged marriages in order to bring the greatest and most immediate economic gain without considering the wishes of their children or the personal characteristics of their partners.

For instance, Ponams reported that there had been a preference for girls to repeat the marriages made by their *asi* (FZs and FMs), and older women said that women preferred to arrange the marriages of their *natue-* (BDs, SDs—those to whom they were *asi*) this way when they could. They said that when a woman married, she moved on to her husband's land, worked for him and planted coconuts on his land. And when she died she wanted her natal kin to benefit. To ensure this she would try to arrange that a girl whose marriage was in her gift be married to a boy who had claims to the land on which she had worked. Likewise, men in particular said that there had been a strong political and economic marriage preference: "We married wealth." Men sought to marry their wards to the children of *lapan*, members of the elite stratum. After all, these were the people with the best access to land, sea, and trade partners, and no concerns of genealogy or reciprocity were more pressing or more legitimate than this.

What were the economic concerns that led elders to try to marry their children off to the children of lapan? Most immediately they expected to receive marriage prestations that they could distribute to their kin, and they expected to receive contributions toward other prestations: prestations to wife's kin, for children's marriages, and so on. Therefore men wanted to marry their wards to the children of families that would be valuable partners in exchange, that could make major prestations and return prestations, that could make significant contributions to their affines' prestations. To do this these prospective affines needed to have land and, more importantly, sea and fishing rights, and they needed wealthy trade partners with whom they could trade their sea produce for the other valuables needed for exchange.

Not only was wealth an important goal in marriage, men and women needed wealth for marriage itself. The wealth needed for marriage prestations was accumulated by the bride's and groom's families through contributions to the parents, primarily from the father's siblings, especially the father's sisters. Boys and girls from small kamal, with few men and few out-marrying sisters, were unlikely to be able to accumulate marriage prestations on their own. In order to marry, these children and their parents became dependents of other men who financed their marriages in return for the right to arrange the marriage, receive and distribute incoming prestations, manage the dependent's property, and direct the dependent's labor as they would the labor of any other child.[10]

Colonization brought changes that eventually undermined this system and undercut the lapan's power to dominate exchange and to manipulate and dominate kinship. This was because these changes undercut the value of the wealth that Iapan could control through their manipulations of kinship and exchange. The emerging colonial economy undercut indigenous production and made Manus a dependent outlier of the larger Papua New Guinea and Australian economy. Villages ceased to rely on one another to acquire the means of survival, but became oriented instead toward the world outside, dependent on government assistance, on the sale of food, copra, and other commodities in Lorengau (the provincial capital), on remittances sent back to Manus by migrant workers and on the purchase of imported replacements for what was once produced locally. The old articulated system of locality, production, kinship, and circulation was replaced as the location of the significant sources of wealth moved out of the region and out of the control of village societies. As a result villages shifted their orientation away from one another and toward the outside world, and shifted their economies away from specialist production and exchange and toward remittance and consumption.

However, colonization did not alter the ideology of kinship and ownership directly. Indeed, the descent-based system of ownership of resources and rights of production remained intact through the time of fieldwork. What colonization did change was the value of what was owned. The significant divisions of production ceased to lie between villages and kin groups within Manus and came to lie instead between Manus and people elsewhere.

Exchange continued to be important, and it continued to link production and kinship as it had done before, but it did so in the context of a new system of production of wealth, the system of education, migration, and remittance. Consequently, the place and practices of kinship and exchange underwent profound changes. Thus, although affinal exchange remained important, it no longer served to integrate Ponam with other communities in the region. This was so because exchange items ceased to be goods produced in other Manus villages and acquired through links to these villages. Instead, they became Ponam manufactures, cash, or commodities purchased in stores. This was so also because these exchanges took place almost entirely within Ponam. Islanders had always preferred to marry endogamously, and colonization made it easier for them to do so because it reduced the political and economic advantages of marriages made with people from elsewhere in Manus.

Also important was the influence of the Catholic Church, to which Ponams converted in the 1920s. The Catholic Fathers disapproved of marriages that were too close, particularly those between first and second cousins, and refused rites to any who were too closely related. With the passage of time, and with the decreasingly interventionist attitude of the Catholic mission, these specific injunctions became a general sense that marriages to more closely related Ponams were less desirable than marriages to those more distant. Thus, by the 1970s there was a preference for marrying kin who were as distantly related as possible. More particularly, Ponams preferred to marry into or beyond the most distant of the cognatic stocks that contributed to their families in exchange.

Furthermore, during the 1950s two of the practices so important in earlier marriages changed, the payment of brideprice and the arranging of marriages. These changes both reflected and furthered the decreasing domination of children by their elders. First, brideprice ceased to be paid by the groom's parents before his marriage, but came to be paid by the groom and his siblings many years later, so that couples married and set up house together but did not pay brideprice for five or even ten years, until the husband and his siblings were in a position to manage this themselves. Second, adults ceased to arrange the marriages of young people, saying that one must follow the Catholic ideal and marry for love (though they continued to attempt, with varying success, to prevent unsuitable matches). Of course, marriages did not occur at random, but the overt arrangement of marriages by elders, as well as most of the covert pressure on the young to marry specific partners, disappeared.

It was at about this time that the people who led exchanges became, almost invariably, the siblings of the individuals concerned. When they were not mature enough to do this, or were too weak-willed to do so, parents could be effective leaders. But when siblings were mature and willing they had authority over their parents in these matters. These siblings bore the major financial responsibility for the prestations. If they could not raise large sums, then prestations were small, but the prestations were not taken over and financed by outsiders. They received assistance from other kin, but the amount of assistance that others gave reflected their relationship to the married couple more than it reflected their personal wealth.

Because the exchanges following from marriage were dominated by the married couple's close kin, wealthy men did not undertake major responsibility for financing the marriages of distant kin or nonkin. Consequently, marriage was not used to set up competitive partnerships between men who married their children and dependents back and forth in order to keep up a constant flow of gifts between them. Marriage exchange was instead decentralized, and participation in it became highly constrained. The rules of exchange allowed each person to give to only a very limited range of immediate kin and affines, and there was no mechanism by which individuals could work themselves into exchange relationships not based on kinship.

With the change in production, then, Iapan ceased to manipulate marriage and affinal exchange to control productive labor. The rules of kinship and property that allowed this manipulation remained, but there no longer existed motive for ordinary people and financiers to seek each other out. Instead, marriage reflected the mutual attraction of two people, no less real for being influenced by their level of education and place of work or for being tempered by marriage proscriptions. No longer did parties to the marriage and its exchanges face each other as dependents of financiers to whom their financial obligation was overpowering. Instead, relatives of bride and groom faced one another directly, unaffected by the convenient fiction of adoption. No longer were their obligations shaped by their indebtedness to their patrons. Instead, they were shaped by their genealogical and affinal relationships with each other.

This brief summary of a much longer story should be sufficient to show that Ponam society underwent profound changes in a number of central areas of social life. Marriage and affinal exchange ceased to integrate Ponam with other Manus communities, ceased to be a vehicle for the control of juniors by elders, ceased to be a mechanism for gaining and controlling access to wealth, ceased to be dominated by leaders in the way that they were before. Following the deterioration of local production and trade, it was impossible for an island elite to dominate exchange, for they had no way to monopolize the key exchange valuable, cash. They therefore lost the means to control young people and make them into dependents by financing their marriages. Nor was there any advantage in doing so. Only childless couples had real need for extra children as producers, for there was little wealth to produce locally and less demand for it. There was no great need to develop a wide network of trade partnerships, for few Manus products were in demand. And there was no need for pawns in the game of affinal exchange, for the game no longer existed. Even so, the system of kinship and exchange remained closely linked to the system of the production of wealth. This was because affinal exchange, and particularly brideprice payments, became an important link between residents and migrants. As Ponams themselves recognized, a key function of affinal exchange was attracting money to the island from employed migrants and circulating it among residents.

Further, the elements of Ponam life that remained relatively stable did so in a setting that was itself undergoing substantial change, so that the part these elements played and the practices associated with them also underwent substantial change. For example, in 1980, as in 1920, and as in 1880, Ponams had named, property-owning agnatic groups, kamal. But if one accepts that kamal survived colonial impact, it is not clear that what survived was much more than a generic term and an ideology of agnation. Because extensive patronage and adoption disappeared, the practical aspects of kamal affiliation and membership changed: kamal in 1980 appear to have been more purely agnatic than they ever had been before.[11] Because of the economic impact of Western encroachment, the practical importance of kamal property changed: in 1980 this property figured largely as an element of the social identity of groups, the members of which increasingly relied for their subsistence on remittances from migrant workers, so that their property was no longer what it had been, an important prop for sheer survival and a manipulable key to prosperity. In the face of these points, it is not clear that the kamal that existed in 1980 were the same as those that existed in 1880.

Thus it is not correct to see Ponam in 1980 as a resilient society, reproducing social life in the face of colonization. Too much has changed. But equally, Ponam in 1980 did not look very much like the urban, industrial capitalist societies that had colonized it. Within Ponam itself kinship and descent were key forces shaping marriage choice, social life, and social structure; wage labor did not exist; no commodities were produced; affinal exchange was an important social and economic force. These factors and others meant that although Ponam had been changed by Western impact, it had not been converted by it.

Articulation in Papua New Guinea

My point in this recitation has been to provide an example of the sort of approach to articulation I have been advocating. Ponam's articulation with the colonial sphere had significant consequences on what Gregory identifies as the dominant sphere of village life, kinship and exchange, consequences that are not Westernization in any obvious sense. This example shows as well that the problem that Achsah Carrier and I first confronted when we clambered off the outrigger that took us to Ponam Island late in 1978 was not what it appeared at first glance. We were perplexed because we misunderstood. We were bedazzled by the juxtaposition of the Western and the non-Western, which we misrecognized as the juxtaposition of the Western and the traditional. But what we saw was not traditional in the way that we thought. The classic anthropological elements of Ponam life that we saw were not very old. They may have been descended from precolonial forms, but in that descent they were altered in important ways by colonization.

The approach to articulation that I have advocated is not entirely novel, though as my description of anthropology in Papua New Guinea at the beginning of this paper shows, it has not been common. Others have tried to identify and investigate the effects of articulation on kinship and exchange relations. I want to point to some anthropologists who have focused on an aspect that was important on Ponam, the way articulation affected inequality in kinship and exchange relations.

One is Deborah Gewertz, especially in her *Sepik River Societies*, a description of the Chambri Lakes people.[12] The people Gewertz studied were in many ways typical Melanesian villagers. They were relatively isolated from the outside world: they were far from towns, plantations, and mines. They engaged in no significant commodity production and were not dependent on remitted wages for their survival. Even so, Gewertz notes some important ways that village life had been affected by contact with the outside world.

The effect that concerns her most is indirect, brought about by the imposition of state control of the Sepik region. This changed relations between the

fish-producing Chambri and their starch-producing trade and market partners, and local trade deteriorated. This forced people to begin to look outside
the local economy for their necessities, and as part of this Chambri women
began to travel farther afield, to marry elsewhere and to become lost to the
village. The upshot of even this relatively mild articulation with the encroaching West was the deterioration of preexisting relations of inequality.
Gewertz (1983, 195) says the consequences

> have been destructive of the very relationships Chambri elders hoped to main-
> tain, and the texture of life within the three Chambri villages when I was last in
> the field can only be described as anomic. No one is sure any longer who is
> beholden to whom, or of how to establish and maintain social relationships.

The Gende people of upland Madang, described in Laura Zimmer's "The
Losing Game," are in a similar situation. Even though local production continued among the Gende, local trade networks decayed with colonization.
This made it harder for the Gende to maintain relations with neighboring
groups, relations that, significantly, included the giving and getting of
women in marriage. The Gende were not, at the time of fieldwork, close to
sources of wage labor, so that survival still depended overwhelmingly on
subsistence production. Even so, Zimmer notes that the deterioration of local
trade networks led to an increasing demand for cash and cash goods in exchange. Consequently, social success required access to both Western and
indigenous sources of wealth. The result was that Gende aspiring to full and
prosperous adult status had to have migrant relatives remitting money. The
net effect was that social success became, in terms of earlier Gende values,
capricious: virtue and reward no longer marched together, and the moral, as
well as the social, bases of Gende inequality was under threat.

Perhaps the best-known Papua New Guinea anthropologist interested in
this is Andrew Strathern, who has dealt with this issue a number of times (at
greatest length in 1984), particularly in "Gender, Ideology and Money in
Mount Hagen" and "The Division of Labor and Processes of Social Change
in Mount Hagen." In both papers he notes the way that exchange, and especially moka, is a crucial aspect of the maintenance and reproduction of social
relations among men and between men and women. He goes on to describe
the way that colonization has affected moka and the relations of which it is a
part. In particular, he notes that women's access to money through their
market activities, together with the growing importance of money in Hagen
exchange, was leading to tension in relations between men and women. Increasingly women were asserting their power to participate in exchange, and
even in moka, in their own right.

Gewertz, Zimmer, and Strathern have looked at a number of ways that
colonial and postcolonial penetration have affected village life and social relations. In my necessarily brief invocation of them here I have focused on one

simple, common theme: how penetration has influenced relations of inequality between people and groups. Each of them presents a case in which articulation seemed to produce relatively little in the way of simple Westernization, little sign of the simple displacement of noncapitalist by capitalist social relations. Further, for Gewertz and Zimmer at least, if not for Strathern, the changes that they describe occur in societies where the intensity and pervasiveness of Western impact is less than is the case for Ponam Island. Nonetheless, what all three authors describe demonstrates the point that social relations in these villages can be understood adequately only if one recognizes that village life can be affected in important ways by articulation with the expanding capitalist sphere in Papua New Guinea.

CONCLUSIONS

The point of this paper is fairly simple. In their published work, if not in their private thinking, anthropologists in Papua New Guinea generally have succumbed to an essentialistic conception of the societies they study. This has been manifest in the tendency to represent those societies in terms of a clear separation of Us and Them together with the assumption, sometimes explicit but often implicit, that the effect of Western impact is Westernization and that the absence of overt Westernization signals the absence of significant Western impact. These are the assumptions that characterize the activist and persistence approaches that I described in the beginning of this chapter.

Both of these assumptions contain part of the truth, but both are misleading. Certainly the articulation of the village with the expanding urban capitalist sphere can result in the displacement of elements of village life by Western introductions. However, in rural Papua New Guinea capitalism has signally failed to create Marx's "world after its own image." Equally, the absence of Westernization raises at least the possibility of the absence of significant Western impact: certainly the presence of Westernization would foreclose that possibility. However, that same failure of Western capitalism to create a world after its own image was not for want of trying.

It seems to be true, then, that anthropologists who have thought in terms of simple Westernization have been following a false trail, one that appears inviting because it accords with the tendency to see village societies in essentialistic terms and with the tendency to assume that the only way a village can change—especially faced with the onslaught of colonization—is to move toward Western modernity.

Instead, I have argued that we need to think in terms of a more subtle process, in which the effects of capitalist encroachment are transmuted into a form reflecting the dominant elements of village life, kinship and exchange. Certainly this is what happened on Ponam. Relations among islanders were not Westernized or capitalized, but neither did they continue as they had been. They changed, they changed profoundly, they changed as a result of colonization. These changes become apparent, however, only if we reject the essentialist view of village life and the ahistorical approach commonly associated with it, and only if we reject the unidimensionalist assumption that change means Westernization. These changes become apparent only if we are prepared to consider the possibility that Ponam society was changed in its own way.

The vehicle I have used to make this point is the idea of articulation. My main concern has been to use this to explore the ways that Western penetration can have systemic consequences that may appear in unexpected ways. However, at a more fundamental level articulation challenges an important feature of much anthropological work in Melanesia, the construction of the isolated and hypostasized village society. In saying this I do not mean to imply that one ought to abandon the notion of the village society: doing so would violate too much of what most anthropologists, and probably most villagers, see around them. However, it is clear that Melanesian societies generally have been apprehended primarily in terms of their internal structures or (less frequently) dynamics in a process that essentially looks inward to the "detailed analysis of purely local phenomena" that Joel Kahn criticized. That is, the focus has been on the village society as a unit, rather than as a location of intersecting processes, a variable number of which extend elsewhere.

A greater regard for the issue of articulation can sensitize researchers to the ways that villages are not simply societies that happen to engage in relations with societies elsewhere, but are societies that may be shaped by and even thoroughly dependent upon those relations. This was true for Ponam in 1980 and, as I have said, the insistent visibility of those relations made the notion of a self-contained Ponam society particularly suspect. However, as I have also said, this appears to have been true for Ponam for as far back as one can plausibly conjecture. Islanders claim that their ancestors never were independent, but always were enmeshed in regional trade, marriage, military, and religious networks.[13] This does not mean that they did not see themselves as distinct people and their village as a distinct social unit. It means instead that they situated themselves and their village within a broader context—first within a region, and later within a region within a nation. A really proper consideration of villages like Ponam, then, would involve not just the articulation with the national socioeconomic sphere that has been the focus of this paper. It would involve as well a consideration of Ponam's articulation with the regional system, one which itself changed as it too was affected by colonization and the emergence of the country of Papua New Guinea.

NOTES

1. Achsah Carrier was central to the fieldwork and thought that went into this paper. I am grateful also for comments by Fitz Poole. Sections of this paper are drawn from J. Carrier and A. Carrier, "A Manus Centenary," reproduced by permission of the American Anthropological Association from *American Ethnologist* 12:3 (August 1985), and from J. Carrier and A. Carrier, *Wage, Trade, and Exchange in Melanesia: A Manus Society in the Modern State*, reproduced by permission of the University of California Press. These permissions do not extend to further reproduction of this material.

2. Had we stepped on to Ponam Island a century or two earlier, the larger social, political, and economic order would have been regional. Up through the early part of this century, the Admiralty Islands contained a coherent, though certainly not unchanging, regional system, and understanding Ponam would have entailed understanding its place in that regional system. I illustrate this point later in this chapter.

3. For the Admiralty Islands, as for many parts of Papua New Guinea, the same points can be made about the need to see regions as more than collections of individual villages.

4. This discussion is not a comprehensive review of the literature. At every stage instances can be found that contradict my assertions, and I mention some of these later in the paper. Even so, it identifies an important aspect of anthropology in Papua New Guinea, an aspect whose importance is not dependent on the presence or absence of alternative and even competing intellectual developments.

5. Such studies often are an anthropological echo of the blinkered view of the process of colonization described in Bronwen Douglas's contribution to this collection, one that sees what villagers do solely as a response to European actions.

6. Ahistorical isolationism appears as well in the efflorescence of hypercultural ethnography in Papua New Guinea (e.g., Wagner 1986). This ethnography does not address the ways that village life is shaped by the world that surrounds it, but assumes that village life and beliefs can be understood as a pure form without reference to the outside world. The issue of articulation is not resolved, it is abandoned and nothing is learned. John Barker, Nicholas Thomas, and Margaret Jolly make this point in their contributions to the collection, Barker with reference to Christianity, Thomas with reference to gift relations, Jolly with reference to women's wealth.

7. Marshall Sahlins's work on the colonization of Hawaiian society (e.g., 1981, 1985) can be treated as a model of articulation. I will ignore this because he focuses on initial rather than significant contact, on how Hawaiians interpreted Captain Cook rather than how they coped with Dole Pineapple. Sahlins's model thus does not address the sort of articulation that concerns me in this paper.

8. Sexton (1983) has described a different form of economic organization that occurred among women who were more familiar with Western social and economic ways. This was the Goroka Women's Investment Corporation, a conventional women's investment group that ran small businesses around Goroka town. These women apparently did not feel the need of their less Westernized village counterparts to transform capitalist institutions to suit a precapitalist idiom.

9. In his contribution to this collection, Nicholas Thomas suggests that the dualism in Gregory's distinction between gifts and commodities can itself be an artifact of

colonization. However, I do not think this invalidates Gregory's model for the uses I make of it.

10. I describe this relationship in stark economic terms though this was not the way Ponams described it, at least in the 1980s. They said instead that the patron offered help and support to those who could not help themselves. He became a father and expected no more from the dependent than he would from any other child. This may be, but it is also clear that fathers expected, and seem to have received, absolute service and obedience from their children.

11. This echoes a point suggested by Simon Harrison (1984), that descent is more likely to be a determining factor in group formation where the political and economic significance of those groups is relatively mild.

12. Gewertz's interest in the effects of articulation predates *Sepik River Societies*. In an earlier paper (1981) she reanalyses Margaret Mead's description of gender relations among the Chambri. She shows how those relations, which Mead took to be traditional Chambri culture, were instead one of the consequences of articulation on Chambri social relations.

13. The classic statement of such networks in the Admiralty Islands is by Theodore Schwartz (1963). They appear as well in A. Carrier and J. Carrier (1987), and J. Carrier and A. Carrier (1985, 1989).

REFERENCES

Allen, Michael. 1985. Review of "The Kula: New Perspectives on Massim Exchange." *Oceania* 56:147–148.

Brookfield, Harold. 1973. "A Full Cycle in Chimbu: A Study of Trends and Cycles." Pp. 127–160 in Harold Brookfield (ed.), *The Pacific in Transition*. Canberra: Australian National University Press.

Carrier, Achsah H. 1984. "Structural and Processual Models in Oceanic Kinship Theory." *Research in Melaneaia* 8:57–87.

Carrier, Achsah H., and James G. Carrier. 1987. "Brigadoon, or; Musical Comedy and the Persistence of Tradition in Melanesian Ethnography." *Oceania* 57:271–293.

———. 1991. *Structure and Process in a Melanesian Society: Ponam's Progress in the Twentieth Century*. London: Harwood.

Carrier, James G., and Achsah H. Carrier. 1985. "A Manus Centenary: Production, Kinship and Exchange in the Admiralty Islands." *American Ethnologist* 12:505–522.

———. 1989. *Wage, Trade, and Exchange in Melanesia: A Manus Society in the Modern State*. Berkeley, Los Angeles, London: University of California Press.

Finney, Ben. 1973. *Big-Men and Business*. Canberra: Australian National University Press.

Fitzpatrick, Peter. 1980. *Law and State in Papua New Guinea*. London: Academic Press.

Gerritsen, Rolf. 1981. "Aspects of the Political Evolution of Rural Papua New Guinea: Towards a Political Economy of the Terminal Peasantry." Pp. 1–60 in Rolf Gerritsen, R. J. May, and Michael A. H. B. Walter, *Road Belong Development: Cargo Cults, Community Groups and Self-help Movements in Papua New Guinea*. (Working Paper 3.) Canberra: Department of Political and Social Change, Research School of Pacific Studies, Australian National University.

Gewertz, Deborah. 1981. "A Historical Reconsideration of Female Dominance among the Chambri of Papua New Guinea." *American Ethnologist* 8:94–106.

———. 1983. *Sepik River Societies*. New Haven: Yale University Press.

Gregory, C. A. 1980. "Gifts to Men and Gifts to God: Gift Exchange and Capital Accumulation in Contemporary Papua." *Man* 15:626–652.

———. 1982. *Gifts and Commodities*. London: Academic Press.

———. 1983. "Kula Gift Exchange and Capitalist Commodity Exchange: A Comparison." Pp. 103–117 in Jerry Leach and Edmund Leach (eds.), *The Kula: New Perspectives on Massim Exchange*. Cambridge: Cambridge University Press.

Grossman, Lawrence. 1983. "Cattle, Rural Economic Differentiation and Articulation in the Highlands of Papua New Guinea." *American Ethnologist* 10:59–76.

Harding, Thomas. 1967. *Voyagers of the Vitiaz Straits*. (American Ethnological Society Monograph 44.) Seattle: University of Washington.

Harrison, Simon. 1984. "New Guinea Highland Social Structure in Lowland Totemic Mythology." *Man* 19:389–403.

Kahn, Joel. 1980. *Minangkabau Social Formations: Indonesian Peasants and the World-Economy*. Cambridge: Cambridge University Press.

Lawrence, Peter. 1964. *Road Belong Cargo*. Manchester: University of Manchester Press.

Leach, Edmund. 1983. "The Kula: An Alternative View." Pp. 529–538 in Jerry Leach and Edmund Leach (eds.), *The Kula: New Perspectives on Massim Exchange*. Cambridge: Cambridge University Press.

Leach, Jerry, and Edmund Leach, eds. 1983. *The Kula: New Perspectives on Massim Exchange*. Cambridge: Cambridge University Press.

Marx, Karl, and Fredrick Engels. 1976 (1847). "The Manifesto of the Communist Party." Pp. 477–519 in *Karl Marx and Fredrick Engels Collected Works*, vol. 6. London: Lawrence and Wishart.

Mead, Margaret. 1934. "Kinship in the Admiralty Islands." *American Museum of Natural History Anthropological Papers* 34:189–358.

———. 1968 (1956). *New Lives for Old*. New York: Dell.

Meggitt, Mervyn. 1971. "From Tribesmen to Peasants: The Case of the Mae Enga of New Guinea." Pp. 191–209 in L. R. Hiatt and C. Jayawardena (eds.), *Anthropology in Oceania*. Sydney: Angus and Robertson.

———. 1974. "'Pigs are our Hearts!' The Te Exchange Cycle among the Mae Enga of New Guinea." *Oceania* 44:165–203.

Meillassoux, Claude. 1981. *Maidens, Meal and Money*. Cambridge: Cambridge University Press.

Moulik, T. K. 1973. *Money, Motivation and Cash Cropping*. (New Guinea Research Bulletin 53.) Canberra: New Guinea Research Unit, Australian National University.

Rowley, C. D. 1965. *The New Guinea Villager. A Retrospect from 1964*. Melbourne: Cheshire.

Sahlins, Marshall. 1981. *Historical Metaphors and Mythical Realities*. Ann Arbor: University of Michigan Press.

———. 1985. *Islands of History*. Chicago: University of Chicago Press.

Salisbury, Richard. 1962. *Stone to Steel*. Canberra: Australian National University Press.

Schwartz, Theodore. 1963. "Systems of Areal Integration: Some Considerations Based on the Admiralty Islands of Northern Melanesia." *Anthropological Forum* 1:56–97.

Sexton, Lorraine. 1982. "'Wok Meri': A Women's Savings and Exchange System in Highland Papua New Guinea." *Oceania* 52:167–198.

———. 1983. "Little Women and Big Men in Business: A Gorokan Development Project and Social Stratification." *Oceania* 54:133–150.

Strathern, Andrew. 1979. "Gender, Ideology and Money in Mount Hagen." *Man* 14:530–548.

———. 1982. "The Division of Labor and Processes of Social Change in Mount Hagen." *American Ethnologist* 9:307–319.

———. 1984. *A Line of Power*. London: Tavistock.

Thomas, Nicholas. 1991. *Entangled Objects: Exchange, Material Culture and Colonialism in the Pacific*. Cambridge, Mass: Harvard University Press.

Wagner, Roy. 1986. *Asiwinarong: Ethos, Image, and Social Power among the Usen Barok of New Ireland*. Princeton: Princeton University Press.

Weiner, Annette. 1980. "Reproduction: A Replacement for Reciprocity." *American Ethnologist* 7:71–85.

Wolpe, Harold, ed. 1980. *The Articulation of Modes of Production*. London: Routledge.

Worsley, Peter. 1957. *The Trumpet Shall Sound*. London: McGibbon and Kee.

Zimmer, Laura. 1985. "The Losing Game: Exchange, Migration and Inequality among the Gende People of Papua New Guinea." Ph.D. dissertation, Bryn Mawr College. (Also: Ann Arbor: University Microfilms.)

FIVE

Christianity in Western Melanesian Ethnography

John Barker

The photographs that conclude Gregory Bateson's *Naven* neatly frame a key problem in Melanesian ethnography.[1] Most of the plates portray exotic subjects: initiations, mortuary rites, portrait skulls, and so forth. Plate xxiv, however, is an instructive study in contrasts. The upper photo shows a man in native garb, whose face is painted white with pig tusks hanging from his nose, holding a long limestick on which dangle pendants indicating the number of men he has killed. The caption describes him as one of Bateson's chief informants and describes the nuances of his personality at some length. The lower photograph shows a man dressed in a white *laplap*. The caption is as austere as his dress: "Tshimbat, a native of Kankanamun, a product of culture contact." In the context of the ethnography, the message is clear: the Iatmul have a culture worthy of study while the "product of culture contact" does not. It is not only that the "product" has become more like Us and less like Them—he is a special kind of pretend Us. Tshimbat's culture, if he can be said to have one, is as much a mindless product of acculturation as the mass-manufactured white calico he is wearing. His culture is spurious, not capable of supporting ethnography.

It is quite possible that Tshimbat was a Christian. Certainly, many visitors to Melanesia have written about Christian converts in dismissive terms. Before World War II, however, anthropologists could still easily find the "real" natives, those who seemed more or less untainted by mission influence. This strategy has become increasingly difficult as the vast majority of Melanesians have associated themselves with the many Christian sects and denominations in the region. Yet few ethnographers have altered their assumptions about Melanesian Christians—these "products of culture contact." They have, instead, developed new strategies to write them out of

144

ethnographies, to reduce them to silence or inconsequence. As a result, ethnographers are presenting a picture that is more and more removed from reality.

Lest there be any doubt about the extent of Christian influence in Melanesian countries, consider the following: In a century and a half—considerably less in most places—the vast majority of the population has come to profess Christianity. The Pacific Council of Churches, for example, reported in 1980 that 85 percent of Papua New Guineans declared themselves Christian, while only 7.5 percent adhered to "indigenous religions" (1980, 3, 4). There are thousands of village churches, theological schools, religious radio services, and church businesses spread across the region. Christianity today exerts a powerful influence at all levels of Melanesian life. In rural villages, the churches have introduced a wide range of ideas and forms, from vernacular translations of Bible stories and Western-style education and health services to Pentecostal revivalism. At the regional level, Christian converts have moved through church networks to enter the working and middle classes in the postcolonial nations, while many villagers have appropriated Christian themes into millenarian movements and independent churches. Christianity also commands attention nationally. The first prime minister of Vanuatu, Fr. Walter Lini, is an Anglican priest. And the constitution of Papua New Guinea ranks "Christian principles" with "noble traditions" as values to be cherished and preserved. Finally, we also find Melanesians participating in international Christian organizations such as the Pacific Council of Churches and the Vatican. Christianity thus pervades Melanesia. Apart from Polynesia, one can find few places where Christianity has spread so quickly or permeated so thoroughly (see Forman 1982).

Anthropologists have a unique vantage point on the ways Melanesians have interpreted, modified, and incorporated Christian forms and ideas in local communities.[2] Yet only a handful seem interested.[3] In the first part of this chapter, I argue that anthropological ignorance of Melanesian Christianity is methodical, deriving on the one hand from a narrow conception of cultural authenticity and, on the other, from a simplistic conception of Christianity as a missionary imposition. I then critique the assumptions behind missionization models, and suggest a broader framework that places Christianity within the context of Melanesian popular religion. My aim throughout is to take Melanesian Christianity seriously as an ethnographic subject. I hope to show that meeting this goal requires not only removing obstacles to seeing Christianity but also rethinking assumptions about Melanesian religion in general. This chapter, then, shares several of the larger aims of this volume, especially the desire to situate ethnography in a shared world of historical experience rather than the romanticized and divided universe of Them and Us.

MELANESIAN RELIGION AND AUTHENTICITY

Ethnography in Melanesia began as a salvage operation undertaken by educated colonialists to record what they could of indigenous customs before they vanished under the juggernaut of "Christianity, commerce, and civilization." Most of the first ethnographers were missionaries (e.g., Codrington 1972; Brown 1910; Holmes 1924; Saville 1926; see Langmore 1989). Metropolitan anthropologists like E. B. Tylor and James G. Frazer depended upon these "men in the field" for most of their ethnographic facts. Beginning with the Cambridge expedition to the Torres Strait in 1898, survey anthropologists, notably A. C. Haddon and C. G. Seligman, developed even closer working relations with missionaries and administrators, relying upon their services as translators, hosts, informants, and writers (see Barker 1979; Haddon 1901; Seligman 1910). These kinds of partnerships broke down after Bronislaw Malinowski established intensive personal fieldwork as the basis of professional anthropological careers. The search for the traditional intensified, however, as anthropologists roamed remote high valleys for pristine cultures or delved ever deeper into the symbolic systems of missionized coastal peoples (see Lawrence 1988). This fixation on the traditional has nowhere been so pronounced as in the study of religion. It is ironic that while Christianity's success stimulated and provided the conditions for early ethnographic studies of Melanesian religion, Christianity, by virtue of its Western origins, has rarely itself been considered a reputable ethnographic subject.

Although students of Melanesian religion frequently acknowledge that Christianity has made inroads, their writings, taken in the aggregate, paradoxically leave the opposite impression. The best case studies describe topics such as initiation cycles, sorcery practices, and mythology, usually in societies where Christianity has as yet made limited inroads (e.g., Schieffelin 1976; Tuzin 1980; Williams 1940; cf. R. Smith 1980). Comparative studies also treat Christianity very briefly (if at all) as a foreign influence altering or replacing Melanesian religion (e.g., Brunton 1980; Chowning 1987; Lawrence 1973). It is rare, then, to see Christianity recognized as a legitimate aspect of Melanesian religious life despite its long presence in many areas.

The huge anthropological literature on millenarian movements would seem to provide an exception. Christian borrowings and syncretic formulations often form core elements in these movements. Yet the interest in the movements is itself revealing. Anthropologists tend to focus on the most exotic forms, notably cargo cults. Moreover, they concentrate on syncretist movements while neglecting revivals within Christian communities, although the latter have been very common (see Barr and Trompf 1983; Loeliger and Trompf 1985). In other words, anthropologists find most intriguing those religious movements most analogous to traditional cultures—those that can be regarded as exotic native productions (see Fabian 1981).

The convention of analyzing religious elements solely in terms of local cultures further obscures the presence of Christianity. This working assumption, elaborated in many forms since the days of Malinowski's functionalism, extends the primary aims of salvage anthropology: one not only reports indigenous exotica, one goes beyond them to discover supposedly primordial cultural systems. Whether drawing upon functionalist, symbolic, phenomenological, or cultural reproductive modes of analysis, models that posit autochthonous cultural systems are prone to oversystematization and over-interpretation of ethnographic data (Brunton 1980; Keesing 1989a). They create an essentialist fiction by denying history to Melanesian communities. The resulting insular images of Melanesian societies may seem plausible for communities in remote high valleys, but become contentious when applied to coastal societies with long-established and intricate ties to encompassing government, church, and economic systems.

Consider two recent ethnographies written by expert and highly respected anthropologists. *The Fame of Gawa*, by Nancy D. Munn, presents a symbolic analysis of value formation on a small Massim island. Munn investigates several topics of religious interest such as mortuary observances, witchcraft, and notions of time and space. Although a map shows the presence of a church, and Munn mentions Gawan preachers and sermons (1986, 247), she simply asserts that the Gawans treat Christian and other "new authorities" in the same way as traditional specialists, "on the fundamentally acephalous (separate and equal) terms of the indigenous order" (1986, 44).[4] We never learn whether the Gawans consider themselves Christians. Perhaps it does not matter. This seems to be Roy Wagner's assumption in *Asiwinarong*, a study of the Usen Barok people of New Ireland. In the opening chapter on Bakan Village, Wagner indicates that the villagers are deeply involved in the larger Papua New Guinea society: many have attained elite positions in business and government, and those left in the villages place much importance on economic development, schooling, and their membership in the United Church (1986, 20–23). These aspects of the Usen Barok's world vanish in the chapters that follow, where Wagner resolutely pursues *kastom* through a study of (presumably) traditional ideas and ritual actions. Both studies, then, fail to grapple with the presence of Christianity apparently because the authors (if not the villagers) consider the "new" religion to hold little intrinsic interest.[5]

Anthropologists pride themselves on their ability to grasp indigenous points of view. There is something ironic, therefore, about the widespread resistance to the fact that many Melanesians incorporate Christian ideas, rituals, and organizations into their religious lives. Clearly there is more at work here than assumptions about what is and is not really Melanesian. We need to look closer at how anthropologists think about the relation between Christianity and indigenous religions.

Models of Missionization[6]

While students of Melanesian religion have had little to say about Christians or Christianity, they have been more forthcoming about missionaries and missionization. There is a staggering literature on the missions in Melanesia, most of it written by missionaries, missiologists, and historians. But anthropologists have also made important contributions since the 1930s. In recent years, a number of ethnographic studies of missions and the missionary impact on indigenous societies have appeared.[7] These studies reveal much about the foundations of Christianity in various parts of the region. Yet their focus on the missionary as the agent of religious change, when combined with the essentialist perception of Melanesian cultures, presents a major obstacle to the recognition that Christianity has become part of Melanesian religion for a number of reasons. First, the study of missionaries is anachronistic in many parts of Melanesia where most foreign clergy have long departed (a point to which I return later). Second, those who focus upon the missionary tend to think of religious change in dualistic terms: missionaries versus natives, Christianity versus Melanesian religion, Western versus traditional culture, and so forth. This dualism, in turn, provides explicit arguments for denying a Melanesian-supported Christianity by portraying Christianity as irreconcilable with authentic indigenous religious beliefs.[8]

If one thinks of religious change as a contest between two incompatible religions and cultures then there can be but three possible outcomes to missionization: displacement of Melanesian religion by Christianity, temporary accommodation between the two sides, or rejection of Christianity by indigenous peoples. Each of these scenarios has gained favor at different times. The first was advanced by ethnographers in the 1920s, who loudly protested what they saw as the wanton destruction of native culture by missionaries. Such "dangerous and heedless tampering," Malinowski (1961, 467, 465) warned, inexorably led to the "rapid dying out of native races." F. E. Williams (1923, 1928) suspected that missionary mischief also lay behind the mass frenzies (as he saw them) of the Vailala Madness and Taro Cult in Papua. The second opinion formed in the 1940s and 1950s when it became clear that missionized people had not lost all of their traditional religion. Ian Hogbin (1939, 1951) and Kenneth Read (1952) described a kind of creeping Christianization and syncretism among the people of the Solomon Islands and New Guinea Highlands, respectively, in which new converts adopted Christian forms and ideas while maintaining a range of former beliefs and ritual practices. These authors assumed that eventually Christianity would become the dominant religious strain in this mix. The third perception formed during the explosion of new ethnographic research in the 1960s and 1970s, as several anthropologists working in the coastal regions discovered that many indigenous institutions were thriving despite the long period of colonial rule and missionary activity. Peter Lawrence and Mervyn Meggitt concluded that the religions of missionized coastal peoples "have proved far more durable than is generally supposed. The changes introduced impinged mainly on the superstructure of native life, the external form of the socio-cultural order" (1965, 21).[9]

Different as these scenarios appear, they are permutations of the same model of missionization. I will review the assumptions underlying this dualistic conception of religious change more closely in the second part of the paper. My concern here is to show how each scenario allows ethnographers to dismiss Christianity as not authentically Melanesian, while buttressing the essentialized notion of indigenous religion. Christianity appears as a threat, a recent innovation, or a rejected possibility. It is not allowed to emerge as an ethnographic subject in its own right. After looming ominously on the pages of an ethnography in the form of missionary activities and pressures, Christianity then disappears. Now you see it, now you don't.

Ethnographic writings on the Trobriand Islands, that "sacred place" in anthropology (Weiner 1976, xv), present a striking illustration of how assertions about missionization may bolster an essentialist perspective on traditional society. The Trobriands were among the first places in eastern Papua to receive missionaries. European and Fijian Methodists arrived in 1894, followed by Roman Catholic priests in 1937. According to historian David Wetherell, membership in the Methodist church "was small for a long time but eventually burgeoned" (cited in Forman 1982, 57). Anthropologists have not worked in the Trobriands as long as the missions, but the islands are almost unique in terms of the historical depth of the ethnographic record, stretching back to Bronislaw Malinowski's famous research in 1915–1918. Susan Montague and Annette Weiner, who worked in the islands in the 1970s, mention the Christian presence. It is interesting to compare what they say with Malinowski's comments and to consider the implications of these different assessments of Christianity on anthropological perceptions of Trobriands society.

Bronislaw Malinowski arrived on Kiriwina in the Trobriands more than twenty years after the Methodist missionaries. While providing few details about the Christian presence, Malinowski's tone in his published work is clearly hostile. Missionaries appear *deus ex machina* to account for missing or transformed customs. In *The Sexual Lives of Savages*, for example, he blames mission influence for the disappearance or corruption of several customs (1929, 61, 217–218, 230, 475) and for the encouragement of a "novel immorality": couples resting together in public view (1929, 403). Malinowski makes his reasoning clear: Christianity is utterly incompatible with Trobriand culture.

> We must realise that the cardinal dogma of God the Father and God the Son, the sacrifice of the only Son and the filial love of man to his Maker would completely miss fire in a matrilineal society, where the relation between father and son is decreed by tribal law to be that of two strangers, where all personal unity between them is denied, and where all family obligations are associated with mother-line. (1929, 159)[10]

In *Argonauts of the Western Pacific* (1961, 464–467), Malinowski unleashes a tirade against government and mission meddling and predicts the imminent collapse of Trobriand society. He thus sees his task in classic salvage terms: to make a record of a disappearing way of life.

Annette Weiner (1980, 1982), who returned to Kiriwina in the early 1970s, found that Malinowski had been unduly pessimistic. Trobriand society has successfully resisted colonial pressures (including missionization) for more than a century. Malinowski's first error was to regard the islanders as passive victims awaiting the colonial steamroller. Weiner claims instead the Kiriwinans eagerly embraced the new opportunities presented by church, state, and capitalism. Still, as Margaret Jolly shows in her detailed critique in this collection, Weiner consistently presents changes in the Trobriands as extrinsic and superficial; the core values and reproductive processes of the society remain intact. By exchanging yams and women's wealth, the Trobrianders "ultimately subvert any plans that touch at these core elements" (1982, 72); and so cooperative commercial ventures fail, school enrollments drop, and out-migration and remittances flag, while Trobriand culture endures. Working from the kind of unidimensional conception of European-Native contact that Carrier describes in the Introduction, Weiner not only uses indigenous institutions to explain cultural persistence, she presents them as evidence that Trobrianders really are traditionalists. Perhaps for this reason she finds it unnecessary to say whether there are churches in Trobriand villages or even if any islanders regard themselves as Christian or pagan. The acceptance of the new order by Trobrianders, then, turns out to be a mirage. They are, at their core, the same people described by Malinowski some fifty years earlier (see Carrier's and Jolly's discussions of this in their contributions to this collection).

Although Kiriwina apparently escaped the ravages of missionization, by the 1970s Kaduwaga village on Kaileuna island off the west coast of Kiriwina looked like Malinowski's nightmare come true. According to Susan Montague, the villagers had abandoned colorful yam houses, canoes, traditional ceremonies, and ritual deference to their chief in favor of numerous "Westernisms": manufactured clothes, cooperative stores, and ardent Christian worship. Rather than seeing this as the inevitable result of colonialism, however, Montague expresses surprise:

> It was one thing to find that Trobrianders, exposed to Western ways, have largely ignored them. But it was quite another to discover that a large, prominent Trobriand village, physically located well away from the Westerners who reside in the Trobriands, should move against the current of conservatism, and go out of its way to embrace Western life ways. (1978, 93)

Montague argues that the collapse of the traditional society has been more apparent than real. She takes the position I have described as creeping Christianization, implying that real change has not progressed much further than external forms. Unlike Malinowski, Montague believes that several key premises of Christianity and Trobriand cosmology are easy to reconcile (and the rest, presumably, can be ignored). These Trobrianders reinterpret Christianity to make it consistent with what they already know. They see Christianity as a source of power, as a means of access to the European wealth to be utilized in cultural reproduction. The Kaduwagans' purpose in converting, in other words, has been to appropriate the power of Europeans by adopting their mannerisms. Their conversion amounts to "a series of changes designed to perpetuate traditional life in the village" (1978, 100).

Unlike Malinowski or Weiner, Montague reveals some details about Christian practices and identity in one part of the Trobriands. Yet this is the exception that proves the rule. Montague does not provides the historical background on colonial and missionary activities in Kaduwaga that would allow one to evaluate her claims of cultural continuity. Nor does she investigate the connections between the various "Westernisms" and encompassing political, religious, and economic systems (it would be interesting to know, for example, if pastors receive training from the United Church or are even Kaduwagans). In an unintentionally revealing aside, Montague mentions that she refused to attend church services, despite the urgings of some Kaduwagans, because of her personal agnosticism (although this does not prevent her from commenting on the contents and significance of the services [1978, 98]).[11] The effect of such neglect, of course, is to deflect attention from Western introductions and innovations to the conceptual and social processes that form the authentic Trobriands culture. The key part of the article is thus taken up with an analysis of traditional cosmology and of how Christianity and other "Westernisms" have been appropriated and made Trobriandisms.

Malinowski, Weiner, and Montague assess the impact of the missions on Trobriand society differently, but they share the premise that Christianity and traditional culture do not mix. Because Christianity is a Western imposition that works to displace Trobriand culture, indigenous elements *ipso facto* represent rejection or subversion of Christianity. The premise thus provides a rationale for elegant synchronic interpretations of the traditional culture, and fends off—in ethnography if not in the actual Trobriands—the Christian influences Malinowski dreaded. Caught in crossfire between missionaries and indigenous culture, Trobriand Christianity never appears in its own right. Indeed, these anthropologists have little to say even about the missionaries.

The Problem of Religious Authenticity

Dan Jorgensen writes the following in a recent review: "If the study of Oceanic religions is to retain contemporary relevance it must take as its task an understanding of religious life harking back to Leenhardt's central problem: the retention of authenticity in the face of christianization [*sic*] of the Pacific" (Jorgensen 1987, 53).

I have shown in this section that many anthropologists identify authenticity with traditional religion. Christianity, by implication, is inauthentic. It may be ignored or considered a threat, but it does not receive the attention, esteem, and sensitive analysis reserved for "authentic" religion. Read this way, Jorgensen's call for relevance is in accord with mainstream opinion going back at least to the time of Malinowski.

There is another possible reading, however. This is to consider authenticity as a subjective problem at the heart of Melanesians' efforts to construct a satisfying religious response to their changing experience. The search for authenticity leads some Melanesians to reject Christian symbols and values. But many others conduct their search by combining Christianity with indigenous values and beliefs. This is nothing new in the history of Christianity. As Kenelm Burridge (1978) notes, Christianity poses the issue of authenticity rather sharply. It is a global religion potentially embracing all people, yet the Bible provides no firm guidelines as to the cultural makeup of a truly Christian social order. From this second perspective, then, Jorgensen's statement can be read as a challenge to take Christianity seriously as an integral part of modern Oceanic religion: to see Christianity as a constituent part of indigenous people's total religious dialogue with the forces affecting their world. In the remainder of this chapter, I want to explore the possibility opened by this second reading by enlarging the scope of Melanesian religion to include Christianity.

RETHINKING MELANESIAN RELIGION

If we grant that Melanesian Christianity should be considered seriously in ethnographic terms, the question remains of how to conceptualize it. James Carrier has suggested in the Introduction that many anthropologists take a selective unidimensional view of the articulation between traditional society and the West, a view that assumes that village societies are incapable of creative interaction with Western ideas and institutions. This is certainly true for the study of religious change in Melanesia. Pointing out the inadequacy of unilinear models, however, is not enough. One must also take into account the fact that Melanesians have had very different experiences of Christianity. By the 1980s, for example, many peoples on the coast had been active Christians for a century while many interior people were still in the process of receiving an introduction to the religion. This is, of course, to say nothing of the historical influences of sectarian divisions, missionary action, and local reinterpretations. The challenge is to move from unilinear and unidimensional models of missionization to more complex conceptions of religious innovation that simultaneously address a variety of factors and contexts: the history and organization of non-European and missionary religious ideas and actions in an area, popular religious practice and ideology, and the social circumstances in which combinations of religious elements are generated (cf. Laitin 1986). This wider approach rejects the narrowness of unilinear models of missionization. It also disputes the conventional opposition between Melanesian religion and Christianity, an opposition that finds its basis in essentialist distinctions between Them and Us rather than in empirical observation.

I have three aims in this section. First, I wish to show through a variety of examples that Christianity today forms a vibrant part of many Melanesians' religious experience. My second aim is to offer a systematic critique of missionization models. Finally, I wish to propose ways of conceptualizing religious innovation that include Christian and indigenous elements. I provide illustrations of Melanesian Christianity throughout the section, but the second and third goals require a more methodical approach. Missionization models rest upon an essentialist distinction between Us and Them, but analysts differ in where they situate this opposition. Some see it in terms of agency: the missionary versus the indigene. Others perceive religious systems in opposition: Christianity versus traditional religion. And still others suggest a cultural and political framework: Western colonial capitalism versus traditional subsistence societies. Sometimes these are presented as alternative theories of missionization, but they are by no means mutually exclusive. Indeed, from the perspective of religious innovation, each framework provides a complementary angle on a single complex process of change. In constructing my critique, then, I find it helpful to consider missionization models and alternative understandings of religious innovation in three stages: in terms of agency, popular religion, and finally political economy.

Agents of Religious Change

At the most basic level, missionization models highlight the encounter between missionaries and Melanesians. Missionaries, who leave extensive records, usually appear as the initiators of action—as "change agents." Eugene Ogan (1972), for example, compares the impact of different sects upon Nasioi economic performance on Bougainville, and A. H. Sarei (1974) argues that Catholic doctrines eroded the traditional marriage practices of the Solo on Buka. Such studies of missionary agency focus on the success or failure of a mission to bring about change.

Too often analysis stops there. Scholars who perceive Melanesian Christianity in terms of missionary initiatives tend to reduce complex and often ambiguous situations of change to a simple contest between missionaries and natives. This narrow perspective distorts understanding both of missionary activities and of the religious forms that emerge from them.

To begin with a very common distortion: Focusing on missionary pronouncements often leads scholars to exaggerate the consistency of a mission's policy and practice. Studies of Anglicans in Papua provide a good example of this confusion. Drawing from pronouncements by mission leaders, David Wetherell concludes that "The aim of the Anglican pioneers was the creation of village Christianity within the framework of Melanesian society. They wanted the convert to live beside his neighbors, differing from them in nothing but his religion" (1977, 131). Anglican leaders were indeed liberal in their attitudes—although not especially knowledgeable about Papuan culture. Yet Richard Davey (1970, 90) notes that liberal pronouncements on paper "did not stop [missionaries] imposing social habits on their catachumens in the guise of Christian moral teaching." The Anglicans were not particularly consistent in practice. The five missionaries who worked in the Collingwood Bay area on the northeast coast between 1898 and 1920, for instance, veered sharply between acceptance of indigenous customs and out-and-out condemnation (Barker 1987). But even those missionaries who sought radical change in converts found it difficult to enforce new rules. They simply did not have the resources to supervise widespread villages that they could only visit periodically from the head stations. Statements of aims by Anglican leaders, then, give only a crude indication of the direction of mission efforts. Missionaries' musings on their purpose may constitute a "theory of social change" (Beidelman 1982, 16), but it is hard to see what interest such a "theory" holds to students of religious innovation if it has not been consistently applied.

An analytic focus on the missionary has a second weakness: it tends to obscure the contributions of non-European evangelists and teachers. The vast majority of missionaries to Melanesia have been Polynesian and Melanesian converts recruited along the path of mission expansion. Leaving few if any writings of their own, and often downplayed or ignored in mission writings, they are only beginning to receive the attention they deserve (Crocombe and Crocombe 1982; Latukefu 1978; Wetherell 1980).

Teacher-evangelists have often been responsible for diffusing cultural traits between groups and for promoting the wholesale abandonment of elaborate traditional ceremonies and customs, often against the wishes of white missionaries. Ann Chowning points out:

Since local people usually have no reason to doubt the authority of the native missionaries, nor opportunity to check their dicta, they often believe that it is a necessary part of Christianity to abandon practices (such as wearing face paint, mortuary observances, avoidance between certain relatives) which strike missionaries from other areas as "pagan" or just distasteful. (Chowning 1969, 34)

Teacher-evangelists have frequently promoted unorthodox interpretations of Christian dogma, particularly in more remote areas where they escape the direct supervision of white missionaries. Peter Lawrence thought cargo-cult doctrines in Madang were preached by "the less reliable congregational elders and native members of [Lutheran] Mission staff" (1956, 86). "Convinced that the cargo would come only when everybody had embraced Christianity, they spared no efforts to hasten the event" (Lawrence 1964, 82–83). Chowning tells of a Tolai catechist who gained fame as a native healer: "He is sometimes reported to have been over-zealous, but the possibility of his reinterpreting doctrine, and the effects of his attitudes towards the people he is working with, have rarely been considered" (1969, 33). Reinterpretations made by teachers are thus difficult to unravel from those of converts.

Missionaries and teachers do not exhaust the list of those shaping Melanesian Christianity, however. Diane Langmore (1982) draws our attention to the important but neglected contributions of European women in the missions. In addition, government agents, traders, and other foreigners forged their own complex links with both the missions and indigenous people and thus influenced religious attitudes (cf. Burridge 1960).

This is to say nothing of the crucial part played by villagers, especially converts, in adapting Christian ideas and institutions into Melanesian settings. As we shall see in the next section, some anthropologists have examined cultural reformulations of Christianity. Few, however, have looked at the actions or interpretations of individuals. Studies of leaders, from the highly successful Paliau on Manus Island to obscure local prophets and healers, demonstrate a general willingness to reconceptualize and incorporate Christianity into local belief systems (e.g., Loeliger and Trompf 1985; Schwartz 1962; Trompf 1977; Tuzin 1989). It would be most interesting to know how indigenous clergy and lay people understand and attempt to live out Christian beliefs.

In the final analysis, the focus on the missionary encounter must be questioned because it is archaic. With the key exception of the Roman Catholic Church, almost all of the older missions have largely localized their staffs and have become nationally based churches. While the churches maintain many of the policies, rituals, and theological orientations of their missionary predecessors, they are no longer simply missionary extensions of Western-based churches.

It is worth considering for a moment why the figure of the missionary exerts such a strong pull on the imagination of scholars, attracting praise and condemnation alike. I suspect that the popular literary image of the heroic white missionary struggling to bring light into the pagan darkness accounts for much of this attention (and derision). The attitude, however, is not limited to outsiders. Many Melanesians also speak of religious change in terms of missionary initiatives. Maisin villagers on the northeast coast of Papua New Guinea, for example, told me that they had given up or greatly modified several traditional practices because the missionaries "told us to stop." They typically drew a striking contrast between the "ignorance" of their ancestors and the enlightenment of those who "obeyed the mission" (see Schwimmer 1973, 77ff.). This was puzzling to me, for a European missionary had not lived among them since 1920 and the local priests were Papua New Guineans who rarely intruded into local affairs. It was only after months of detailed research in the archives and extensive interviews with village elders and former missionaries and teachers that I realized that the people themselves had made most cultural modifications. The changes had less to do with mission initiatives than with the pressures deriving from the Maisins' increasing participation in the national economic system of Papua New Guinea (Barker 1985b). The Maisins' rhetoric, then, masked the very active role they had taken in shaping their conversion to Christianity. It also concealed (from themselves as well as outsiders) the degree to which religious innovations were influenced by the process of colonial incorporation (Barker n.d.).[12]

I do not mean to imply that missionaries have never forced change or that interactions between missionaries and converts have been unimportant. My point is simply that the missionary encounter forms too narrow a focus for understanding either the development or diversity of Christianity in Melanesia. What is required is a wider framework that includes the contributions of indigenous peoples, European missionaries, Melanesian teacher-evangelists and clergy, politicians, traders, and others to the totality of a people's religious ideas and actions. Such a framework should embrace different sorts of religious expression—traditional, syncretic and Christian—without reducing them to a contest between traditionalists and converts. The framework also needs to be wide enough to contain the different types and levels of social organization within which the actors participate, experience, and develop their religious ideas, rituals, and discourses. Christianity, in other words, should be examined as an ingredient within a people's popular religion—the totality of their religious experience.

Melanesian Popular Religion[13]

While the missions have had different receptions in different places, almost everywhere today we find people making use of both Melanesian and Christian forms and ideas. R. W. Robin (1982, 340) argues that this situation challenges anthropological interpretation:

The major source of contention appears to lie in two questions. First, to what extent does Melanesian society continue to adhere to traditional values and world-view? And second, to what extent does Melanesian society adopt the tenets and beliefs of Christianity (as taught by the mission) and make them their own?

Robin says, citing Lawrence (1956, 88), that most scholars "express the opinion that Christianity 'has been built into the framework of native society,' implying the pre-eminence of indigenous beliefs and values over Christian ones" (1982, 340). However, the Pacific Council of Churches has confidently declared that "Christianity is the predominant religion" (1980, 3).

The issue Robin raises is deceptively simple. It is not an easy matter to determine whether a person really is or is not a Christian, even among people who have had only a recent acquaintance with the religion. Writing of the relatively unacculturated Tauade of Papua, C. A. Hallpike (1977, 18) cogently remarks that "to estimate the sincerity and motivation of [a convert's] faith, motivations which may be obscure even to the believer himself, is a task for which the ethnographer has no competence." Indeed, even theologians have yet to come up with a mutually acceptable definition of Christian identity. It is little wonder, then, that fieldworkers studying peoples with similar cultures and religious histories may come to very different conclusions as to the relative strength of Christianity and tradition (cf., for example, McSwain 1977 and Michael French Smith 1984).

This kind of debate is a red herring. It draws our attention away from the key point that popular religion in Melanesia often consists of both Melanesian and Christian religious forms and ideas (cf. Ranger 1978, 487). Further, the debate rests upon a questionable premise: the notion that religions form coherent and mutually exclusive cultural systems. David Laitin has recently criticized this assumption in Clifford Geertz's (1973) influential definition of religion as a cultural system:

> By implying that there is a coherent religious interpretation of what is "really real," Geertz's definition misses the social reality that any religion encompasses a number of traditions that are in some degree in conflict. His definition ignores the historical dimension of religious dissemination, and the fact that religions pick up different baggage in different eras and areas. (Laitin 1986, 24)

It is important to note that Laitin's criticism holds not only for Christianity but for indigenous religions as well. There is abundant ethnographic evidence, for example, of Melanesian groups exchanging rituals and magic. Because they were highly permeable, Melanesian religions during the early contact period were likely far less coherent than some anthropologists suppose (Brunton 1980). Certainly the popular religion of today, which may encompass in some places secret male cults, nationalist ideals, and the Bible, is extremely mixed and fluid.

To say that Melanesian popular religion includes indigenous and Christian elements, however, is not to suggest that it is syncretic, at least in the usual sense of that term. "Syncretic religion" implies not only a middle position on an evolutionary ladder—the "creeping Christianization" of missionization models—but also implies a coherent system emerging out of the synthesis of Western and indigenous elements. Now it is clear that Melanesians do invent such creative combinations, but they also support many other ideas and forms which retain the distinct identities of their origins—garden magic and church hymns, for example. Melanesian popular religion, then, is heterogeneous, made up of distinct practices, ideologies, and organizations.

If we include Christian organizations within the compass of Melanesian popular religion instead of excluding them as foreign entities, a picture of dynamic religious pluralism emerges. In some places, the religious field has a sectarian appearance. In northern Malaita, as in many parts of the New Guinea Highlands, for example, numerous Christian sects compete with each other and with non-Christian traditionalists and syncretic religious movements (Burt 1982, 1983; Keesing 1967; Ross 1978). In contrast, many of the coastal people in Papua New Guinea belong to single denominations. But, as Miriam Kahn's (1983) study of Wamiran religion in Milne Bay shows, people with a single Christian identity also experience a type of religious pluralism. All Wamirans identify themselves as Christians, many regularly attend church, still more donate money and labor for the maintenance of the church buildings, and several have become evangelists and priests in the Anglican Church. Yet Wamirans express received ideas about spirits and sorcery and participate in garden rituals that clearly contradict church teachings. Suspended, as it were, between these two religious identities, Wamiran ideas about God and their own recent history merge traditional and Christian perspectives.

It is clear that some foci of religious identity among the Malaitans and Wamirans are more consciously organized than others. It is also obvious that leaders and members of different sects may compete against each other and denounce religious practices that go against the particular dogmas of their group. All the same, when we attend to the experiences of people instead of denominational rivalries, we find that it is impossible to separate Christianity from the totality of popular religion. Despite the foreign support that missions have received, churches succeed or fail on the basis of local participation. The sectarian rivalries on Malaita exist not simply between, say, Anglicans and traditionalists, they emerge *between Malaitans* who, while sharing common languages, cultures, and recent histories, have developed rivalries along the lines of religious affiliations.[14] In Wamira, such divisions have not developed and the same people participate in church and traditional rites. For the most part, Melanesians do not find either situation strange or contradictory. Why should they? We do not expect rigid consistency from Western Christians. It would be hard to imagine Malaitans (as a whole) or Wamirans (individually) abandoning Christianity for traditional religion or vice versa, for to do so would be to renounce a part of themselves (see Ranger 1978, 489).

My argument raises an important question. If churches, cults, and traditional rites are not autonomous religious systems that displace or resist one another, how do they maintain distinct identities in so many places? Outside support for missions and churches provide only a small part of the answer. One must also analyze the emergence and decline of religious organizations and ideologies within a religious field in terms of a people's cultural and historical points of concern: those crucial matters over which they argue and for which they seek solutions (see Laitin 1986, 29). Consider the following three scenarios. In the first, a group of people switches its allegiance from one kind of religious expression to another as they seek an answer to a pressing problem. Cargo cults and religious movements are one kind of situation in which a prophet formulates a unitary answer to a widespread and pressing point of concern: the moral relation between Melanesians and Europeans (see Burridge 1969). In the Madang movements described by Peter Lawrence (1964), leaders experimented with conventional Christianity before reviving aspects of the pagan religion and then, later still, developing syncretic millenarian movements. Northern Malaita illustrates a second sectarian scenario, in which religious groups simultaneously compete by proposing different solutions to the same point of concern. According to Burt, Kwara'ae sects share a common antagonism toward colonial rule which they oppose by "describing their present religion as the basis of the true and original *kastom* of the Kwara'ae people" (1983, 334). Each sect, however, promotes a different mix of Christian and indigenous elements and thus a different conception of kastom. And, of course, some pagan groups oppose any mixing of Christianity with received traditions. Finally, the situation of the Wamirans described by Kahn (1983) represents what may be the most common scenario of all. Here the points of concern addressed in the various religious activities of the people are so far apart that people are mostly unconcerned about the logical contradictions between, say, attending church and warding off sorcery attacks. They are "Sunday Christians, Monday Sorcerers." The cults, church organizations, or religious movements that emerge in all three scenarios, therefore, should be seen as variant expressions of a popular religion that includes them all.

The notion of religious pluralism enriches our understanding of the dynamics of religious innovation in Melanesia. It may lead to misleading models, however, especially if we identify particular organizations, rituals, or ideologies within popular religion simply as Christianity or as traditional religion. While traditional (or indigenous), syncretist and Christian elements are often concentrated in certain religious forms, they occur across the religious field. Moreover, if people are engaging in several types of religious activities, we would expect their experience from one context to affect their understandings of another. Despite the Western, indigenous, or syncretic appearance of a religious action or expression, one can often detect this sort of crossover. Thus Erik Schwimmer (1973) suggests that Orokaiva conceive of their relation with God in terms of traditional reciprocal cycles. Darrell Whiteman (1983) suggests that the concept of *mana* forms a crucial component of priestly authority in the Solomon Islands. And Carl Thune (1990) shows that seemingly conventional prayers and Biblical readings carry radically different connotations when they are reinterpreted in terms of the matrilineal cultural world of Lobodan villagers on Normanby Island.

Where there are real or perceived similarities between Christian, traditional, and syncretist activities and ideas, it may be very difficult to untangle one religion from the other. Take, for example, the fundamentalist Christians Ben Burt describes in northern Malaita who reject "heathen" indigenous rituals, betel chewing, smoking, and traditional costume.

> Such prohibitions may be legitimated by Biblical references and form a set of rules which define righteous living under Christianity, as pagan *tambu* did under the traditional ritual system. Even the strictly observed whole "day of rest" has parallels with the periods of enforced idleness which preceded major sacrificial feasts. . . . Hence, despite the conflicts between mission and *kastom* ideologies, between Christian and pagan ways of life, theological parallels between the two religions have enabled Christian Kwara'ae to sustain some of the underlying premises of the pagan religion. (1983, 337–338)

In speaking of various Christian, traditional, and syncretic organizations and ideologies in a religious field, then, we must be careful not to reintroduce essentialist notions. These identities represent constellations of religious elements which are subject to variant interpretations and influences from across the spectrum of popular religion.

The main point I wish to make is simple: all the forms of religious activity a people engage in need to be understood in terms of the specific historical and social conditions in which they emerge. Even the most Western of Christian forms may symbolize a pressing point of concern for local peoples. The Maisin of Oro Province in Papua New Guinea, for example, devote considerable money, food, and labor to their church, and completely accept the authority of the clergy to determine the liturgy, in large part because they associate the church with the education of their children and, beyond that, with economic prosperity (Barker 1985*a*). This concern is as important to Maisin villagers as the fertility of their gardens or the success of their cooperative store, practical areas in which indigenous and syncretist ideas respectively play more prominent roles. By the same token, even the most "traditionalist" religious forms may in part constitute a creative response to

external forces and certain forms of domination, as Jolly's analysis of Trobriand women's mortuary exchanges in this book suggests. Thus when people
follow "traditional" religious sects and forms this does not mean they are
incapable of responding to new situations any more than a people's embrace
of Christian forms necessarily entails capitulation to Western values. While
we probably cannot avoid categories like Christianity and traditional religion, we must resist the tendency to think of them as coherent and separate
systems (Keesing 1989*b*, 209). Ironically, the first step toward creating a
more inclusive view of Melanesian religion is to return to an old ethnographic principle and take what our informants tell us seriously, even
when they are Christians.

The Political Economy of Melanesian Religion

Melanesianists often see the missionary encounter as part of a much larger
drama: the confrontation between Western and indigenous cultures. In
Weberian terms, Melanesian religions are "traditional" or "ethnic"—highly
localized and parochial—while Christianity is a "world religion," universal-
istic in its theological scope and expansive ambition. Ian Hogbin suggests
that Christianity's impact is fundamentally ideological.

> Although pagan beliefs linger beneath the surface for so long, one great change
> follows immediately on conversion. The religion of any primitive people inevi-
> tably reflects the social structure of the community in which it develops. . . .
> Christianity reflects another type of social system in which genealogical rela-
> tionship is not so significant. Every Church asserts its universality, and those
> who belong to it offer the same kind of prayers to the one Deity. A mission
> native may continue to believe for many years that his chief obligations are to
> the members of his own society, but a basis is now provided for broadening the
> concept of brotherhood until it embraces not only the inhabitants of neighbour-
> ing settlements but also strangers. (Hogbin 1958, 182)

Several Melanesianists have also suggested that the missions played a
political role by simultaneously undermining local autonomy and intro-
ducing villagers to key organizations, forms, and ideas of Western society:
writing, mathematics, councils, legal codes, and money—to name but a few
(M. F. Smith 1982, 1984). Also: "Whatever their motives, and their other
concerns, the missions performed very similar functions to those carried out
by the administration in lightly controlled areas—they inculcated respect
for Western order, receptivity to the white man's domination and his values,
worship of the work ethic, and attention to hygiene" (Amarshi, Good, and
Mortimer 1979, 170). From the point of view of cultural confrontation, then,
missionary activities acted as a softening-up process for colonialism and
Westernization.

The expansion of Christianity in the Third World is inextricably mixed with the political and economic ventures of the Western powers. It is perhaps true, as Beckett suggests, that "Christianity in the South Seas must, in the final analysis, be understood in terms of colonialism" (1978, 209). However, it is misleading to think of colonization as a unilinear process inevitably leading toward a Westernized culture. While the colonial process has produced Westernized and relatively homogeneous social and political structures at the national level, Melanesia retains its famous cultural diversity in local communities. The continuing existence of local cultural variations does not necessarily imply that colonialist incorporation has failed. In Melanesia, as in the rest of the capitalist periphery, different political and economic systems and cultural patterns coexist within the capitalist hegemony (see Wolf 1982). Indeed, some students argue that aspects of indigenous systems have flowered under colonial domination (Gregory 1982). To understand the relation between religious innovation and wider social and political change in Melanesia, therefore, we need to consider how Melanesian religion is generated and articulated within a multileveled political economy.

Robert Hefner's (1987) research on Islamic conversion in southern Java provides valuable insights into the relation between religious discourse and political economy. Hefner notes that scale is a crucial factor in the generation of distinct religious discourses. Embedded in small-scale communities in which knowledge is woven into the fabric of everyday life, local religious expressions are relatively flexible and unarticulated, informed by tacit moral and cosmological assumptions. In contrast, regional religious expressions must contain more explicit general assumptions, for they "provide the discourse for the elaboration of a secondary moral and ideological identity beyond that given in the immediacy of local groupings." Regional and international religious organizations thus form "a kind of secondary community built above and between those given by local social circumstances" (Hefner 1987, 74–75).

We should therefore expect to find a general correspondence between the scale of social organization Melanesians are engaged in and the character of religious discourse. Most Melanesians engage in at least three levels of social and economic organization. Subsistence-peasant economies, based upon kinship and exchange networks, form the most immediate context for rural people. By selling crops at the market, securing jobs in government and commercial sectors, and sending remittances to the villages, Melanesians also participate in the wider networks of regional-urban economies. Finally, Melanesian nations form part of the network of the world economic order. The religious discourses that emerge from these encompassing levels can be distinguished as "local," "popular," and "global," respectively.[15]

The religious discourses differ not only in their tone and scale, they differ in what they discern as points of interest, as things worth caring about. International religious organizations, for example, direct attention to global issues: evangelization and revitalization of Christianity, the problems of poverty, pollution, and exploitation in the international system, and the expansion of literacy. National religions direct attention to regional problems such as the qualities (or lack thereof) of leadership in efforts to develop the economies of rural and urban areas, to create a unifying political and religious language, or to settle conflicts between districts. Local religious discourses focus on parochial moral issues: the meaning of death and suffering in a community or the securing of good crops. Each religious discourse addresses distinct problems that concern most people at one time or another, although rarely at once. Melanesian religion emerges, transforms, and is itself transformed in the intersection of these concerns.

Christian ideas and groups tend to dominate the broader levels of religious discourse and social organization while indigenous forms find their fullest expression in local communities. Christian theologies explicitly provide symbols that potentially unite large groups (an omnipresent and omnipotent deity), whereas indigenous religious discourses tend to build upon implicit knowledge shared by small groups of people who know each other well. In addition, churches have the benefit of rationalized organizations that have long associations with political regimes through schools, medical facilities, and other social services. All the same, we cannot assume that indigenous, syncretist, and Christian sects occupy fixed positions within the hierarchy of religious discourses. Indigenous idioms are capable of being made more universal and taken up in organized worship. The contrary is also true: Christianity may be appropriated by converts to address very parochial concerns. In other words, the essence of Christian or traditional ideas is of less importance than the potential of religious symbols to address and unify different levels of community. Melanesian religion combines indigenous and Christian elements at all levels of discourse.

Beginning at the level of local communities, we find that villagers often employ Christianity in support of preexisting norms. Ian Hogbin gives two interesting examples. The Busama of the Huon Peninsula traditionally condemned adultery and premarital intercourse. After converting, Busama elders forbad everything remotely immoral, from wearing flowers in the hair to dancing, but now in the name of Christianity. Hogbin compares them with the Trobriand islanders:

> These latter natives, unlike the Busama, were before marriage almost completely free—and in spite of fifty years of missionary endeavour they still are. During a visit to the Trobriands I asked the Court Interpreter why the islanders were so heedless of Mission morality. "There is nothing in the Commandments to say that unmarried people should avoid intercourse," was his reply. "We accept the Bible and follow it." I thereupon quoted...two passages..."That's only Paul!" he exclaimed. "God's orders and Paul's opinions are two different things." (1951, 253–254)

Many coastal Papuans, like the Mailu islanders and the Maisin, have adopted church-based organizations as political forums replacing kin groups and feasts, although the issues and moral values expressed in these newer contexts draw heavily on indigenous themes, especially reciprocity and egalitarianism (Abbi 1975; Barker 1985a, 1990). The A'ara people on Santa Isabel in the Solomons, for instance, construct images of Christian leadership that balance social harmony with social dominance, key themes in the local moral ideology (White 1980).

Turning next to the level of popular culture and religion in Melanesian nations, we find that the missions have played formative roles. They established networks of churches, educational institutions, and commercial ventures. Over time, these provided an important basis for the emergence of a class of people who moved between tribal groups and who eventually formed part of an educated and economically privileged elite (Oram 1971). As Michael French Smith (1982, 1984) shows in an important series of papers on Kragur village in the east Sepik, participation in mission practices—especially in the schools and on plantations—also formed one of the principle ways rural people begin to internalize hegemonic orientations to time, money, and work (although not without much ambiguity and reinterpretation). Yet, indigenous cultural elements and initiatives have also been important at this level, especially within millenarian movements, cooperative societies, and other micronationalist forms. One should also note the recent efforts of national governments and indigenous elites to blend a range of traditional customs with Christianity and thus invent an overarching cultural identity and political ideology for their multicultural states (Keesing and Tonkinson 1982).

As Pacific nations have gained independence, the churches too have been eager to associate themselves with Melanesian culture. Drums, indigenous dances, traditional costumes, and other traditional paraphernalia are now commonplace in the church services of many denominations (Dawia 1980). Theologians and their students are also exploring indigenous religious discourses in an attempt to create a Melanesian Christianity grounded in traditional understandings (Christ in Melanesia 1977, Deverell and Deverell 1986). There is more than a little irony in these developments. While traditional religious activities and ideas continue to be abandoned by villagers who find them increasingly irrelevant, many of them are being given a new lease on life in national churches as symbols of "the Melanesian Way"!

At the widest levels of global religion, we find various religious elements that link Melanesia with the rest of the world system. These include international church organizations, trends in Christian education, Pentecostal revivalism, and so forth. Christian influences dominate at this level, but to a growing degree non-Christian religious elements are also entering the global network. Books and films of the occult, for example, are becoming increasingly popular in urban Melanesia. In recent years, tribal religious elements have also entered the repertoire of international religion: New Guinean religious ideas, for example, receive attention in films, books, tourist brochures, and sermons. Elements from the global culture penetrate rural villages in a myriad of forms: as Evangelical radio broadcasts, American gospel cassettes, pamphlets, and comic books, to name a few (see Fabian 1981).

The three-tiered model of Melanesian religious discourse I have described helps to explain how anthropologists arrive at such varied assessments of missionary impact. Depending on the level of social organization one is dealing with, religious activities and ideologies look very different indeed. Those traveling throughout the region might conclude that Melanesians are a highly Christianized people who regularly go to church, bow to the Cross, and enjoy (in English or Pidgin) the latest American gospel hits. A researcher tracing the rise of micronationalist associations and movements might note how leaders creatively combine Christian and cargoist ideas to build regional religions in tune with the current aspirations of people from a wide number of sociolinguistic communities. Finally, the anthropologist studying a village society may discover that indigenous assumptions about bush spirits, ghosts, and power underlie local understandings of Christianity and conclude that the traditional religion has continued under a Christian veneer. In reality, of course, most Melanesians are involved in all of the three levels of discourse. As they move between them, they reshape each discourse according to the concepts and pressures they experience in the others. The limited perspective of the researcher, therefore, may obscure some of the forces that push and pull at the totality of a people's religious ideas and actions.

CONCLUSION

In the fifty years since Gregory Bateson's *Naven* was published, Christianity, already widespread in his day, has expanded into the most remote corners of Melanesia. The religion has developed, mutated, appropriated local cultural elements, and been itself appropriated in a myriad of forms. Yet most anthropologists still regard Christianity as foreign intrusion and continue to pursue the fading vestiges of uncontaminated traditional religions. Like Tshimbat, Bateson's "product of culture contact," Christianity cannot always be entirely ignored, especially in the coastal regions. But few anthropologists incorporate the Christian presence into studies of village societies. Christianity is the perennial outside force—threatening, corrupting, or merely dusting the surface of the authentic focus of anthropological concerns. In and of itself, it is of no interest. It can never become "cultural."

I have argued in this chapter that these sorts of assumptions have little basis in reality. They form part of a denial that has more to do with preserv-

ing a traditionalist notion of anthropology than with understanding traditional societies. There is no reason why ethnographic perspectives cannot be
applied to nontraditional aspects of people's lives. Indeed, I am convinced
that anthropologists have much to offer in understanding Melanesian Christianity and popular religion in general. But first they need to recognize that
most Melanesians have embraced Christianity and ponder the significance of
this shift in identity. While mission Christianity challenged indigenous religious ideas and practices it did not destroy them. Nor have Melanesian
Christians been forced to abandon a diversity of religious and cultural identities for a single Western religious form, as unidimensional models of missionization seemed to predict. In the years since initial mission contact,
Christianity and a myriad of indigenous religious forms have become resources for formulating innovative religious ideas, for taking on political
causes and even for conserving the status quo.

While I have been critical of anthropologists' lack of attention to Melanesian Christians, my main purpose in this chapter has been positive. Rather
than signaling the end of the ethnographic endeavor, Melanesian Christianity challenges us to create historically situated accounts of religious innovation. As we have seen, this will entail looking at the dynamics through which
different people accept, create, and combine Christian and indigenous forms;
the ways they interact with encompassing systems connecting them to the
rest of the world; and the ways they maintain their cultural distinctiveness.
In critiquing missionization models I have not tried to advance a model of
my own, choosing instead to place Melanesian Christianity within a loose
framework within which we can better appreciate its diffuseness, diversity,
and pliancy in a variety of settings. In emphasizing the dynamic qualities of
Melanesian Christianity within the larger popular religion, I have implied
that Melanesians must be regarded as the primary architects of their religions, even though they may import elements wholesale and often must construct their religions under conditions of domination by outsiders. All of
these points can be developed much further, most profitably through specific
case studies (several of which I have cited already). Such case studies would
also examine processes I have only touched on here, particularly the ways
Melanesians make sense of Christian forms and ideas and incorporate them
into indigenous conceptual schemes and cosmologies (e.g., Barker 1990 and
n.d.; Jolly 1989; Keesing 1989*b*).

These and other questions increasingly will engage anthropologists and
other students as we learn to address Melanesian religious life in the round,
not simply those aspects that, in the abstract, strike us as authentic. We shall
need to observe Melanesians as members of local communities, regional
associations and nations within the world system. We shall need to see how
concepts and pressures through these linkages are mediated by popular reli-

gion and made comprehensive by different groups of Melanesians. And we shall need to explore the pluralistic ways Melanesians are creating innovative religious ideas and forms from indigenous, Christian, and other sources.

NOTES

1. I would like to thank James Carrier, Robin Ridington, Anne Marie Tietjen, and Donald Tuzin for their helpful comments on earlier drafts of this chapter.

2. Missionaries, missiologists, historians, and Melanesian intellectuals have their own interests in this subject. This literature is huge and I do not consider it here. My impression, however, is that these scholars also tend to neglect indigenous adaptations of Christianity, largely because of their dependence upon missionary documents.

3. I am thinking here particularly of B. L. Abbi, Kenelm Burridge, Margaret Jolly, Michael French Smith, Geoffrey White, and Darrell Whiteman.

4. Munn implies that she was unable to provide an account of Gawa colonial history because of "sparse written documentation" (1986, 277), yet she provides clues that the government and church presence on Gawa is not all that new. She notes that the Methodist Mission purchased land for a church in 1920 and stationed a Fijian teacher there, although a permanent school was not established until 1974 (1986, 281). Other odd bits of information—forgetting the traditional cyclical calendar, the regulation of community projects under the councillor, and the presence of Gawan preachers—point to an extended interaction with Western institutions. It may be that Gawans encased these innovations within the received order, but Munn's assertion closes off any serious investigation of this important process.

5. I am not arguing for the opposite extreme in which all important aspects of indigenous societies are attributed to outside agencies—colonialization or the world system. There are obvious differences between peoples in the world, and these differences can be profitably explored through cultural analyses. Problems arise, however, when the Other is seen as both different and *separate*. I agree with William Roseberry, who views "the Other as different but *connected*, a product of a particular history that is itself intertwined with a larger set of economic, political, social, and cultural processes to such an extent that analytical separation of 'our' history and 'their' history is impossible" (1989, 13, original emphasis). Munn actually gives some indication of the potential richness of this latter kind of study with her sophisticated analysis of a speech concerning the founding of the island school. Rich in allusions to Gawan traditions, the speech ties these to Gawan historical experience and aspirations in the outside world (Munn 1986, 240–255).

6. My main interest here is with anthropological models. Melanesians, of course, form their own understandings of conversion and its implications. While drawing on indigenous narrative forms, these are often suffused with evangelistic tropes: from darkness to light, from cannibalism to peace (e.g., Kahn 1983; Young 1977), thus supporting the essentialist opposition of "pagan" and "Christian." Indigenous perceptions of the missionary period are fascinating but have as yet received little attention.

7. See, for example, Boutilier, Hughes, and Tiffany (1978), Huber (1988), Jolly and Macintyre (1989), Kahn (1983), Schieffelin (1981), Whiteman (1983), and Young (1977).

8. During some periods and in some places, Melanesians have divided into antagonistic traditionalist and Christian factions, a point to which I return below in a discussion of Malaitan sectarianism. To anticipate, I argue that such a situation is not best understood in terms of a universal contest between Christianity and indigenous religions. Rather the different factions should be seen as belonging to a single popular religion, albeit a sharply divided one (see Keesing 1989*b*). In other words, the opposition between Christianity and traditional religions is not a given, it has to be taken up by local people to be sustained. And local people, of course, may have a variety of reasons—many of which have little to do with the contents of the religious traditions—for fostering the divisions.

9. The first and last of these permutations correspond broadly to the "activist" and "persistence" approaches to the impact of colonization that Carrier describes in his chapter herein.

10. Carl Thune's (1990) analysis of a Methodist church service on nearby Normanby Island shows that the translation of Christian patriarchal concepts into a matrilineal culture does require considerable modification of meaning but is by no means impossible.

11. At risk of stating the obvious, one wonders if an ethnographer would so casually justify absenting themselves from "traditional" mortuary or fertility rituals because they did not believe in spirits!

12. James Carrier (1987) calls this form of historical consciousness a "constitutional" historiography. Maisin, like Wamirans to the east (Kahn 1983), characterize history in terms of momentous events, such as the arrival of missionaries, that shift the entire social order. The apparent agreement with the missionary impact model, then, is quite accidental and superficial. Unfortunately, statements by villagers that missionaries destroyed certain customs are often accepted at face value. Although such statements refer to historic events, not "traditional" institutions, they represent the kind of indigenous substantivization explored by Thomas in his contribution to this collection.

13. Terence Ranger's (1978) impressive critique of writings on African religion provides the inspiration for much of my analysis in this section.

14. Roger M. Keesing makes this point very effectively in an analysis of the ways traditionalist Kwaio women incorporate notions of competing Christian communities into their image of their own religion. "Christian and traditionalist communities," Keesing argues, "now belong to a single, albeit deeply divided, *ideological* system (as well as a single, albeit deeply divided, social system)." Therefore, "the struggle between Christian and 'heathen' cannot be viewed as one theology doing battle with another, but must be understood as a deeper and more subtle and complex struggle for political domination, and with it the power to define what Kwaio culture is to be" (1989*b*, 209).

15. My model draws on Fabian's (1981) rethinking of African religious movements.

REFERENCES

Abbi, B. L. 1975. *Traditional Groupings and Modern Associations: A Study of Changing Local Groups in Papua & New Guinea*. Simla: Indian Institute of Advanced Study.

Amarshi, Azeem, Kenneth Good, and Rex Mortimer. 1979. *Development and Dependency: The Political Economy of Papua New Guinea*. Melbourne: Oxford University Press.

Barker, John. 1979. "Papuans and Protestants: A Sociological Study of the London Missionary Society, Methodist and Anglican Missions in Papua, 1870 to 1930." M.A. thesis, Victoria University of Wellington.

———. 1985*a*. "Maisin Christianity: An Ethnography of the Contemporary Religion of a Seaboard Melanesian People." Ph.D. dissertation, University of British Columbia.

———. 1985*b*. "Missionaries and Mourning: Continuity and Change in the Death Ceremonies of a Melanesian People." Pp. 263–294 in Darrell L. Whiteman (ed.), *Anthropologists, Missionaries, and Cultural Change*. (Studies in Third World Societies 25.) Williamsburg: College of William and Mary.

———. 1987. "Cheerful Pragmatists: Anglican Missionaries among the Maisin of Collingwood Bay, Papua 1898–1920." *Journal of Pacific History* 22:66–81.

———. 1990. "Mission Station and Village: Cultural Practice and Representations in Maisin Society." In John Barker (ed.), *Christianity in Oceania: Ethnographic Perspectives*. (ASAO Monograph 12.) Lanham, Md.: University Press of America.

———. n.d. "'We are *Ekelesia*': Conversion in Uiaku, Papua New Guinea." In Robert Hefner (ed.), *Christian Conversion: Perspectives from History and Anthropology*. MS.

Barr, John, and Garry Trompf. 1983. "Independent Churches and Recent Ecstatic Phenomena in Melanesia: A Survey of Materials." *Oceania* 54:48–72, 109–132.

Bateson, Gregory. 1958. *Naven* (2d ed.). Stanford: Stanford University Press.

Beckett, Jeremy. 1978. "Mission, Church, and Sect: Three Types of Religious Commitment in the Torres Strait." Pp. 209–230 in James A. Boutilier, Daniel T. Hughes, and Sharon W. Tiffany (eds.), *Mission, Church, and Sect in Oceania*. Ann Arbor: University of Michigan Press.

Beidelman, T. O. 1982. *Colonial Evangelism: A Socio-Historical Study of an East African Mission at the Grassroots*. Bloomington: Indiana University Press.

Boutilier, James A., Daniel T. Hughes, and Sharon W. Tiffany, eds. 1978. *Mission, Church, and Sect in Oceania*. Ann Arbor: University of Michigan Preas.

Brown, George. 1910. *Melanesians and Polynesians: Their Life-Histories Described and Compared*. London: Macmillan.

Brunton, Ron. 1980. "Misconstrued Order in Melanesian Religion." *Man* 15:112–128.

Burridge, Kenelm. 1960. *Mambu*. New York and Evanston: Harper & Row.

———. 1969. *New Heaven, New Earth*. Toronto: Copp Clark.

———. 1978. "Missionary Occasions." Pp. 1–30 in James A. Boutilier, Daniel T. Hughes, and Sharon W. Tiffany (eds.), *Mission, Church, and Sect in Oceania*. Ann Arbor: University of Michigan Press.

Burt, Ben. 1982. "Kastom, Christianity, and the First Ancestor of the Kwara'ae of Malaita." *Mankind* 13:374–399.

————. 1983. "The Remnant Church: A Christian Sect of the Solomon Islands." *Oceania* 53:334–346.

Carrier, James G. 1987. "History and Self-Conception in Ponam Society." *Man* 22:111–131.

Chowning, Ann. 1969. "Recent Acculturation Between Tribes in Papua–New Guinea." *Journal of Pacific History* 4:27–40.

————. 1987. "Melanesian Religions: An Overview." Pp. 350–359 in Mircea Eliade (ed.), *Encyclopedia of Religion*, vol. 10. New York: Macmillan.

Christ in Melanesia. 1977. *Point*. Goroka: The Melanesian Institute.

Codrington, R. H. 1972 (1891). *The Melanesians: Studies in Their Anthropology and Folklore*. New York: Dover.

Crocombe, Ron, and Marjorie Crocombe. 1982. *Polynesian Missions in Melanesia*. Suva: Institute of Pacific Studies, University of the South Pacific.

Davey, Richard. 1970. "The Church of England in New Guinea until 1914." *Journal of the Papua–New Guinea Society* 4:89–98.

Dawia, Alexander. 1980. "Indigenizing Christian Worship in Melanesia." *Bikmaus* 1:63–84.

Deverell, Gweneth, and Bruce Deverell. 1986. *Pacific Rituals: Living or Dying?* Suva: Institute of Pacific Studies and Pacific Theological College.

Fabian, Johannes. 1981. "Six Theses Regarding the Anthropology of African Religious Movements." *Religion* 11:109–126.

Forman, C. W. 1982. *The Island Churches of the South Pacific*. Maryknoll, N.Y.: Orbis Books.

Geertz, Clifford. 1973. *The Interpretation of Cultures*. New York: Basic Books.

Gregory, C. A. 1982. *Gifts and Commodities*. London: Academic Press.

Haddon, A. C. 1901. *Head-hunters, Black, White and Brown*. London: Methuen.

Hallpike, C. R. 1977. *Bloodshed and Vengeance in the Papuan Mountains*. Oxford: Clarendon Press.

Hefner, Robert W. 1987. "The Political Economy of Islamic Conversion in Modern East Java." Pp. 53–78 in William R. Roff (ed.), *Islam and the Political Economy of Meaning*. London: Croom Helm.

Hogbin, H. Ian. 1939. *Experiments in Civilization: The Effects of European Culture on a Native Community in the Solomon Islands*. London: Routledge.

————. 1951. *Transformation Scene*. London: Routledge.

————. 1958. *Social Change*. London: C. A. Watts.

Holmes, J. H. 1924. *In Primitive New Guinea*. London: Seeley Service.

Huber, Mary Taylor. 1988. *The Bishops' Progress: A Historical Ethnography of Catholic Missionary Experience on the Sepik Frontier*. Washington, D.C.: Smithsonian Institution Press.

Jolly, Margaret. 1989. "Sacred Spaces: Churches, Men's Houses and Households in South Pentecost, Vanuatu." Pp. 213–235 in Margaret Jolly and Martha Macintyre (eds.), *Family and Gender in the Pacific*. Cambridge: Cambridge University Press.

Jolly, Margaret, and Martha Macintyre, eds. 1989. *Family and Gender in the Pacific: Domestic Contradictions and the Colonial Impact*. Cambridge: Cambridge University Press.

Jorgensen, Dan. 1987. "Oceanic Religions: History of Study." Pp. 49–53 in Mircea Eliade (ed.), *Encyclopedia of Religion*, vol. 11. New York: Macmillan.

Kahn, Miriam. 1983. "Sunday Christians, Monday Sorcerers: Selective Adaptation to Missionization in Wamira." *Journal of Pacific History* 18:96–112.

Keesing, Roger M. 1967. "Christians and Pagans in Kwaio, Malaita." *Journal of the Polynesian Society* 76:82–100.

———. 1989a. "Exotic Readings of Cultural Texts." *Current Anthropology* 30:459–479.

———. 1989b. "Sins of a Mission: Christian Life as Kwaio Traditionalist Ideology." Pp. 193–212 in Margaret Jolly and Martha Macintyre (eds.), *Family and Gender in the Pacific*. Cambridge: Cambridge University Press.

Keesing, Roger M., and Robert Tonkinson, eds. 1982. *Reinventing Traditional Culture: The Politics of Kastom in Island Melanesia. Mankind* 13 (special issue) (4).

Laitin, David D. 1986. *Hegemony and Culture: Politics and Religious Change Among the Yoruba*. Chicago: University of Chicago Press.

Langmore, Diane. 1982. "A Neglected Force: White Women Missionaries in Papua 1874–1914." *Journal of Pacific History* 17:138–157.

———. 1989. *Missionary Lives: Papua, 1874–1914*. Honolulu: University of Hawaii Press.

Latukefu, Sione. 1978. "The Impact of South Seas Islands Missionaries on Melanesia." Pp. 91–108 in James A. Boutilier, Daniel T. Hughes, and Sharon W. Tiffany (eds.), *Mission, Church, and Sect in Oceania*. Ann Arbor: University of Michigan Press.

Lawrence, Peter. 1956. "Lutheran Mission Influence on Madang Societies." *Oceania* 27:73–89.

———. 1964. *Road Belong Cargo*. Manchester: Manchester University Press.

———. 1973. "Religion and Magic." Pp. 201–226 in Ian Hogbin (ed.), *Anthropology in Papua New Guinea*. Melbourne: Melbourne University Press.

———. 1988. "Twenty Years After: A Reconsideration of Papua New Guinea Seaboard and Highlands Religions." *Oceania* 59:7–28.

Lawrence, Peter, and Mervyn Meggitt, eds. 1965. *Gods, Ghosts and Men in Melanesia*. Melbourne: Oxford University Press.

Loeliger, Carl, and Garry Trompf, eds. 1985. *New Religious Movements in Melanesia*. Suva: Institute of Pacific Studies, University of the South Pacific and the University of Papua New Guinea.

Malinowski, Bronislaw. 1929. *The Sexual Life of Savages in North-Western Melanesia*. London: Routledge.

———. 1961 (1922). *Argonauts of the Western Pacific*. London: Routledge.

McSwain, Romola. 1977. *The Past and Future People*. Melbourne: Oxford University Press.

Montague, Susan P. 1978. "Church, Government, and Western Ways in a Trobriand Village." *Anthropology* 2:91–101.

Munn, Nancy. 1986. *The Fame of Gawa: A Symbolic Study of Value Transformation in a Massim (Papua New Guinea) Society*. Cambridge: Cambridge University Press.

Ogan, Eugene. 1972. *Business and Cargo: Socio-economic Change Among the Nasioi of Bougainville*. (New Guinea Research Bulletin 44.) Port Moresby and Canberra: The New Guinea Research Unit.

Oram, N. D. 1971. "The London Missionary Society Pastorate: The Emergence of an Educated Elite in Papua." *Journal of Pacific History* 6:115–137.

Pacific Council of Churches. 1980. *Christianity in Papua New Guinea*. (Research Paper

1.) Port Vila, Vanuatu: Pacific Churches Research Centre.

Ranger, Terence. 1978. "The Churches, the Nationalist State and African Religion." Pp. 478–502 in Edward Fashole-Luke, Richard Gray, Adrian Hastings, and Godwin Tasie (eds.), *Christianity in Independent Africa*. London: Rex Collings.

Read, Kenneth E. 1952. "Missionary Activities and Change in the Central Highlands of Papua and New Guinea." *South Pacific* 6:229–238.

Robin, R. W. 1982. "Revival Movements in the Southern Highlands Province of Papua New Guinea." *Oceania* 52:242–320.

Roseberry, William. 1989. *Anthropologies and Histories: Essays in Culture, History, and Political Economy*. New Brunswick: Rutgers University Press.

Ross, Harold M. 1978. "Competition for Baegu Souls: Mission Rivalry on Malaita, Solomon Islands." Pp. 163–200 in James A. Boutilier, Daniel T. Hughes, and Sharon W. Tiffany (eds.), *Mission, Church, and Sect in Oceania*. Ann Arbor: University of Michigan Press.

Sarei, A. H. 1974. *Traditional Marriage and the Impact of Christianity on the Solos of Buka Island*. (New Guinea Research Bulletin 57.) Port Moresby and Canberra: New Guinea Research Unit.

Saville, W. J. V. 1926. *In Unknown New Guinea*. London: Seeley Service.

Schieffelin, Edward L. 1976. *The Sorrow of the Lonely and the Burning of the Dancers*. New York: St. Martin's Press.

———. 1981. "The End of Traditional Music, Dance, and Body Decoration in Bosavi, Papua New Guinea." Pp. 1–22 in R. Gordon (ed.), *The Plight of Peripheral People in Papua New Guinea*. Cambridge: Cultural Survival.

Schwartz, Theodore. 1962. "The Paliau Movement in the Admiralty Islands, 1946–1954." *Anthropological Papers of the American Museum of Natural History* 49:211–421.

Schwimmer, Erik. 1973. *Exchange in the Social Structure of the Orokaiva*. New York: St. Martin's Press.

Seligman, C. G. 1910. *The Melanesians of British New Guinea*. Cambridge: Cambridge University Press.

Smith, Michael French. 1982. "Bloody Time and Bloody Scarcity: Capitalism, Authority and the Transformation of Temporal Experience in a Papua New Guinea Village." *American Ethnologist* 9:503–518.

———. 1984. "'Wild' Villagers and Capitalist Virtues: Perceptions of Western Work Habits in a Preindustrial Community." *Anthropological Quarterly* 57:125–139.

Smith, Robert. 1980. "The Time that Ethnography Forgot." *Canberra Anthropology* 3:81–94.

Thune, Carl. 1990. "Fathers, Aliens, and Brothers: Building a Social World in Loboda Village Church Services." In John Barker (ed.), *Christianity in Oceania: Ethnographic Perspectives*. Lanham, Md.: University Press of America.

Trompf, Garry, ed. 1977. *Prophets of Melanesia*. Port Moresby: Institute of Papua New Guinea Studies.

Tuzin, Donald F. 1980. *The Voice of the Tambaran: Truth and Illusion in Ilahita Arapesh Religion*. Berkeley, Los Angeles, London: University of California Press.

———. 1989. "Visions, Prophecies, and the Rise of Christian Consciousness." Pp. 187–208 in Gilbert Herdt and Michele Stephen (eds.), *The Religious Imagination in New Guinea*. New Brunswick: Rutgers University Press.

Wagner, Roy. 1986. *Asiwinarong*. Princeton: Princeton University Press.

Weiner, Annette B. 1976. *Women of Value, Men of Renown.* Austin: University of Texas Press.

————. 1980. "Stability in Banana Leaves: Colonization and Women in Kiriwina, Trobriand Islands." Pp. 270–293 in Mona Etienne and Eleanor Leacock (eds.), *Women and Colonization: Anthropological Perspectives.* New York: Praeger.

————. 1982. "Ten Years in the Life of an Island." *Bikmaus* 3(4):64–75.

Wetherell, David. 1977. *Reluctant Mission: The Anglican Church in Papua New Guinea, 1891–1942.* St. Lucia: University of Queensland Press.

————. 1980. "Pioneers and Patriarchs: Samoans in a Nonconformist Mission District in Papua, 1890–1917." *Journal of Pacific History* 15:130–154.

White, Geoffrey M. 1980. "Social Images and Social Change in a Melanesian Society." *American Ethnologist* 7:352–370.

Whiteman, Darrell L. 1983. *Melanesians and Missionaries: An Ethnohistorical Study of Social and Religious Change in the Southwest Pacific.* Pasadena, Calif.: William Carey Library.

Williams, F. E. 1923. *The Vailala Madness and the Destruction of Native Ceremonies in the Gulf Division.* (Anthropology Reports 4.) Port Moresby: Territory of Papua.

————. 1928. *Orokaiva Magic.* London: Oxford University Press.

————. 1940. *Drama of Orokolo.* Oxford: Oxford University Press.

Wolf, Eric. 1982. *Europe and the People Without History.* Berkeley, Los Angeles, London: University of California Press.

Young, Michael W. 1977. "Doctor Bromilow and the Bwaidoka Wars." *Journal of Pacific History* 12:130–153.

SIX

Kwaisulia as Culture Hero

Roger Keesing

The nineteenth-century strongman Kwaisulia, in the Lau lagoons of northern Malaita (Solomons), parlayed his ability to deal with Europeans as an intermediary in the Labor Trade into substantial local power.[1] Kwaisulia's European contemporaries had characterized him as a "chief." Historians and anthropologists have corrected the record, showing Kwaisulia to have been an able opportunist whose power came from Europeans, not his chiefly status in "traditional" society. I show that contemporary Lau speakers, and even the elderly survivors of Kwaisulia's children's generation, retrospectively recognize and celebrate his powers and prestige: not because he was a traditional "chief," but because his powers came from Europeans. I use this paradox to reflect on implicit assumptions about "tradition" and authenticity in anthropological discourse, and on anthropological characterizations of the Melanesian big man.

Both Kwaisulia and his son Timi Kakaluae, who achieved considerable power and prominence as policeman and headman within the colonial state, exemplify the kinds of careers anthropologists have been prone to ignore or deprecate. In our focus on "traditional" arenas and styles of leadership, our preoccupation with pigs and shells, exchange and feasting—rather than innovative leadership styles using European presence and wealth and the power of the colonial state to explore new avenues to power and prestige—we anthropologists have been curiously blind to changing political realities.

The absence of the Kwaisulias and Kakaluaes from the anthropologically depicted Melanesian landscape represents more than a selective focus on what looks traditional and authentic. Our concepts of "culture" and "social structure" impose stasis and closure on communities whose boundaries were open, whose customs were being changed, borrowed, renegotiated. Placing closed universes of meaning and structure outside the flow of time and change left no room for agents of political transformation. Despite the changes of the colonial period, anthropologists have too often sought to preserve the conceptual closure and stasis. Those local leaders who pursued new opportunities and occupied new arenas belonged outside or on the margins of ethnography—dependent though anthropologists have been on them to get to fieldwork communities and gain acceptance there. A further irony, then, is that Kakaluaes have been our companions and colleagues in fashioning accounts from which they have often been expunged.

KWAISULIA OF ADAGEGE

Kwaisulia was a strongman who parlayed exceptional personal talents and charisma and a sophistication in things and ways European into great local political power, exercised over a period of thirty years. His extraordinary career, well documented by historian Peter Corris (1970, 1973), represented an expansion of leadership roles institutionalized among his people so as to seize on the new opportunities, political arenas, and sources of power presented by European invasion of the Solomons.

Among the Lau speakers of the shallow lagoons of the northern Malaita coast, living on densely packed islets and coral platforms dredged from the lagoon floor, the Malaita pattern of social structure and leadership was rigidified into strict patrilineal descent and chiefly titles, based on seniority within chiefly patrilineages, entailing control over fishing grounds and nets (Keesing 1985; Ivens 1930). Complementing the chiefs, whose power was considerable, were priests who acted as ritual officiants, and *ramo*, who acted as warrior-leaders, bounty hunters, and agents of chiefly discipline and punishment within the community.

Kwaisulia was born in the early 1850s, on the most populous of the Lau lagoon islands, Sulufou. Kwaisulia's father was from the interior, a man who had married into the chiefly family of Sulufou. Thus Kwaisulia, in this system where status was agnatically derived, was well placed in terms of proximity to power and prestige, but poorly placed in terms of formal status. However, two developments associated with the growing European presence in the southwestern Pacific in the 1860s and 1870s were to open new opportunities.

The first was the casting up in the Lau lagoon in 1868 of a Scottish sailor, John Renton. Renton was taken under the protection of the Sulufou chief and spent eight years there, learning the Lau language and customs; during this period, young Kwaisulia must have been close to him. The second development was the advent of the famous Labor Trade. In 1875, the *Bobtail Nag*, recruiting laborers, "saved" Renton. Kwaisulia went on the *Bobtail Nag* that year as a recruit to Queensland, where he stayed six years and acquired considerable sophistication in Pidgin, and in European ways. This early experience gave him an ideal opportunity to begin acting as an intermediary in the Labor Trade as recruiting intensified. As "passage master," he secured recruits and negotiated terms for them, receiving payment and trade goods in return. By 1883, only two years after his return from two terms in Queensland, "Kwaisulia. . . was already spoken of by Europeans as the 'coastal chief'" (Corris 1970, 257). By this time, he was "a person of authority amongst the islanders—his word carried weight with the recruits and the ships' Melanesian boat crew—and he was already forging the reputation as a 'friend of the white man' which he was to enjoy for almost thirty years" (Corris 1970, 257).

Kwaisulia's expanding powers as a ramo, at a time of political instability in northern Malaita as a result of European penetration, came partly from his access to firearms, and hence to followers. He "was successful in attracting followers. . . because the energy he displayed in his dealings with the labour recruiters in the years immediately following his return gave him access to arms and ammunition" (Corris 1970, 260).

> A vast stream of European goods [poured] into "Urassi," as the recruiters termed Kwaisulia's domain: rifles and ammunition, tobacco by the case, barbed wire, knives, axes, looking glasses, and cloth . . . and more exotic things such as a ship's boats, clocks, music boxes, and . . . a chest of drawers. (Corris 1970, 259–260)

His island stronghold of Adagege became a bastion, fortified with barbed wire (Ivens 1930, 191); and from it, he launched attacks both on the old enemies of the Lau in the adjacent bush and on the Lau chiefs of the northern islets of the lagoon.

Kwaisulia's power and authority grew when Kabou, the chief of Sulufou, the largest Lau island, died in the 1880s.

> That Kwaisulia's power reached beyond ordinary limits is further illustrated by the weighty evidence that his authority was supreme on Sulu Vou as well as on Ada Gege. . . . After the death of Kabbou no European visitor made mention of any "chief" in the set of islands comprised of Sulu Vou, Ada Gege, and Saua, apart from Kwaisulia. He was referred to indiscriminately as the chief of Sulu Vou and Ada Gege, and it is certain that, although new chiefs were installed on both islands in Kwaisulia's lifetime, he eclipsed them, not only to European ways of thinking, but in fact. (Corris 1970, 262)

By the turn of the century, when the British Protectorate had been established at Tulagi, Kwaisulia's power began to be transformed. Woodford, the first Resident Commissioner, sought to use him as an ally in establishing colonial law and order: "Qaisulia can put a large force of fighting men into the field, and if he proves to be what I expect he might be ready to arrange to keep the coast in order and to aid in the pursuit and capture of fugitive murderers who have taken to the bush" (Corris 1970, 259). A year later, in

1897, when Woodford was installed as Commissioner, Kwaisulia sent his formal greetings. In 1902 Kwaisulia's oldest son Kaiviti was deputed to arrest two murderers for the Protectorate administration. Woodford's assistant Mahaffy wrote that "it is quite plain that Qaisulia is able to keep order in this district and I impressed upon him that he would in future be held responsible for the peace in this part of Mala[ita]. There is probably no other chief in the island who could send nine or ten miles down the coast and effect without any disturbance, the arrest of two malefactors" (Corris 1970, 259).[2]

Yet European control and the establishment of mission stations in the Lau lagoon threatened and progressively eroded Kwaisulia's power. He remained obdurately pagan, and the imposition of a measure of law and order and the opposition of the missionaries threatened the power base he had built up and his means of maintaining it. "Some of Kwaisulia's private and profitable dealings—such as the holding of bush 'returns' [laborers repatriated from Queensland] for ransom, providing human expiatory sacrifices, and trading in guns—came quickly to the notice of missions, and through them the government, bringing reprimands and warnings" (Corris 1970, 264). His style of self-presentation had changed somewhat in the political climate of the Protectorate: "He appeared in a white drill suit, spotlessly clean, sun helmet, sash, and a broad smile" (Hopkins 1928, 155). Despite the partial erosion of his power in this century, in 1909, the year of his death, he remained a powerful and almost legendary personage.

What are we to make, in political terms, of such a remarkable figure? Was he genius or petty dictator, a man who seized a moment in history or an opportunist rogue? Ivens, who was in the lagoon in 1927, eighteen years after Kwaisulia inadvertently blew himself up dynamiting fish, went to some pains to document how Kwaisulia illegitimately arrogated the rights and powers of a chief, in waging war in the capacity of a ramo. In precolonial Lau society, Ivens pointed out, the ramo himself did not make war or initiate "foreign policy": he was an instrument of chiefly authority: "it was the chiefs . . . who decided upon the waging of war, or the making of reprisals for any insult offered them or their people" (Ivens 1930, 88). Ivens stressed Kwaisulia's lack of descent credentials for chiefly status:

> So far as his descent status goes, Qaisulia could not possibly be chief of an Ada Gege, for succession on Mala[ita] follows the father, the people being patrilineal. It is as well to make this point quite clear, since from the early days of the Labour trade white men have regarded Qaisulia as chief of Ada Gege (Urasi, as they called it). (Ivens 1930, 65)

Ivens pointed out that far from Kwaisulia being legitimate chief of Adagege, as the son of a bushman who had married into Sulufou (of which Adagege was a colony), he was not even among the "true owners" of the Adagege fishing grounds. Ivens observed that the elevation of warriors into "chiefs" in

European eyes represented both misunderstanding and the usurpation of power it made possible:

> When white men first began to visit Mala[ita] it was the ramo who forced himself upon their notice, and who by his forwardness and his truculent behaviour was considered by them to be the chief of the place. Kwaisulia of Ada Gege was of this type of ramo, and . . . he was constantly spoken of as "the Chief of Urasi.". . . It was only due to his reputation amongst white people, which he traded on, that he was not killed for his overbearing ways and his unjustifiable assumption of authority. (Ivens 1930, 199)

Corris, generally sympathetic to Kwaisulia as Ivens was not, concurs that he "appropriated [the rights of a chief] to himself of many occasions. . . . For most of his career Kwaisulia was acting *de facto* as a chief" (1970, 261).

But Corris aptly observes that Kwaisulia's rise to power represented an extraordinary extrapolation from and transformation of the precolonial Lau political system, not simply opportunist thuggery and a lust for power.

> Kwaisulia's influence . . . was due not merely to the possession of [European material wealth] and the prestige he acquired through his association with their providers, but also to the use to which he put them and the extent to which he was able to combine his new enterprises with the extension and exercise of more traditional forms of power. . . .
>
> So great was Kwaisulia's ambition that he over-stepped the traditional bounds, both in the means he used to widen his power and in the extent of the success which he achieved. . . . Kwaisulia came to combine in his own person many of the functions of priest and chief. In this way he introduced, if only for the span of his own lifetime, some novel features into the authority structure and politics of the Lau lagoon. (Corris 1973, 260, 261)

LAU INTERPRETATIONS OF KWAISULIA'S POWER

Political obstacles to research in the Solomons have precluded my exploring in as much detail as I had planned the retrospective interpretations of Kwaisulia's career by contemporary Lau speakers. In 1977, encouraging research by Solomon Islanders in a series of Honiara lectures, I had several long discussions about Kwaisulia with young, Western-educated Lau men (including some of Kwaisulia's descendants). I was struck by the interest and knowledge on the part of these young men, but also by the almost mythic celebration of his powers and deeds even among those who knew the facts of his life fairly well. And I was struck most of all by the way the retrospective construction of Kwaisulia's career concentrated *on his power in relation to Europeans*, and its material embodiment (his Western dress, his ship's boat). This interpretation, whether in its most factual manifestations or its mythic elaborations, left entirely unasked precisely the question that preoccupied

Ivens: the legitimacy of Kwaisulia's power in terms of the "traditional" system of chiefly authority, and descent credentials.

Corris, who had done research on Kwaisulia in the Lau lagoon a decade earlier, had been given apparently similar retrospective interpretations:

> Visitors to Ada Gege today can see the sacred grove in which Kwaisulia's body and the much prized whaleboat were deposited, and hear stories of the exploits of the "great chief." And 1500 miles away and sixty years after his death, . . . descendants of Lau people who went to Fiji as indentured labourers, readily recall the name and deeds of Kwaisulia, the strongman of Ada Gege. (1970, 265)

> People on Ada Gege—including a son and grandson of Kwaisulia—. . . are intensely proud of his renown. . . . Rather than leaving behind them a reputation as "enforcers," the passage masters [of Malaita, notably Kwaisulia] are remembered principally for the rapport they enjoyed with Europeans at a time when such things were rare. (1973, 62)

An interesting text, both in terms of the aura of myth that surrounded Kwaisulia even among Lau born in his lifetime and in terms of the celebration of his powers and authority in relation to Europeans (rather than in terms of "traditional" authority), is an account I recorded in 1974 from Usuli Tefu'i, a nephew of Kwaisulia who was on Adagege when the strongman's body was brought there.

> When I was a child I was at Adagege—Kwaisulia's place. They called him "Friend" (Firen), because he had been a friend of the King [of England]. When they started the work in Queensland.
> Kwaisulia was my uncle. He saved twelve men who came—from a ship that broke up at Ata'a. He saved the twelve men from the ship. They went back to England. And the King said, "Oh, you're my friend now, Kwaisulia." So that's how he came to be called "Friend." His real name was Kwaisulia, but the name the King gave him was "Friend."
> When he was alive he went around with his men to fight. He was a fighting man [*faetemane*, i.e., a ramo], someone who made war to attack and kill people.[3]

As will be seen, Malaitans themselves have done a good deal in the last forty years to invent and legitimate chiefs, including "paramount chiefs," in areas where they did not exist in precolonial societies, through spurious appeals to traditional custom. It would not be surprising to find Kwaisulia retrospectively promoted to a chiefly status he did not have. This makes it all the more striking that Kwaisulia is celebrated for his power over, and power from, Europeans—rather than his "traditional" status. Kwaisulia, who appropriated many of the powers of the real chiefs who were his contemporaries, is remembered for his guns, his whaleboat, his sun helmet, his com-

mand over trade goods, his ability to manipulate the whites and be accepted
by them on their ships as a powerful equal. His "legitimacy" in terms of
"authentic" custom was an issue for the anthropologist/linguist Ivens and
later for Corris, but apparently not for the Lau people themselves (except, no
doubt, for the "real" chiefs who were his rivals).[4]

We have, then, a paradox in terms of "authenticity" in anthropological
discourse. We glimpse further facets of this paradox if we look at the succeeding generation of Lau leaders, including Kwaisulia's children.

THE TRANSMISSION OF POWER

Did Kwaisulia succeed in transmitting his power and influence through his
children and descendants? Kwaisulia's oldest son Kaiviti and nephew Kaa
acted as his lieutenants, and achieved some recognition. It was Kaiviti who
arrested two murderers on Kwaisulia's behalf when a request came from the
colonial powers in Tulagi in 1902.

> Kaiviti and Kaa carried on Kwaisulia's policy of co-operating with European
> authority: in 1909 one of them earned commendation. . . . However, they must
> have realised that opposition to the Christian missions was inexpedient. . . . In
> the years following his father's death, Kaiviti (and probably Kaa also) must
> have joined the S.S.E.M.[5] . . . In this way Kaiviti and Kaa were able to wield
> influence by adapting to a new force in their society rather as Kwaisulia had
> done. The authority and prestige associated with the name of Kwaisulia, some-
> thing of which was passed on immediately after his death to his elder son and
> nephew, have endured until more recent times, for in the 1940s his last surviv-
> ing son, Kakaluae, was appointed government headman of Lau and subse-
> quently chosen by the Lau people as their Marching Rule "chief." (Corris
> 1970, 265)

The case of Kakaluae deserves closer inspection. If Kaiviti and Kaa
emerged in a transitional period when mission influence was becoming
strong, Timi Kakaluae's career developed in the period when effective colonial administration was established on Malaita, complementing yet in competition with the power of the S.S.E.M., the dominant mission on the island.
Whereas Kaiviti became a Christian, Kakaluae remained pagan, following
his father's commitment to custom. Kakaluae was picked out by W. R. Bell,
the first District Officer to become a strong presence on Malaita (Keesing
and Corris 1980), to join the constabulary—no doubt partly because, as
Kwaisulia's son, he carried some prestige as well as a potential for forceful-
ness and bravery. Kakaluae rose to seniority within the constabulary, and
played a prominent part in the punitive expedition in 1927, after Bell was
assassinated by Kwaio strongmen (Keesing and Corris 1980).

A retrospective sketch of Kakaluae's career written by the District Com-

missioner, Malaita, apparently in 1952 (BSIP 28/VII/B/1), sums up his
career and shows how it was connected to Kwaisulia's:

> T. Kakaluae, Adagege Village, Age 58, Heathen.
>
> Decorated with Jubilee Medal in 1935, and Certificate of Honour in 1951.
>
> One of the great heathen chiefs of the Lau Lagoon he succeeded his father
> Kwaisulia as such in 1937. He entered the Armed Constabulary in 1920 and
> rose to the rank of corporal in 1927 when, after the death of Mr. Bell, he was
> appointed a Government headman for the entire area Lau-Baegu-Baelelea and
> Makwanu. He was confirmed as chief headman of the Lau Lagoon and
> achieved the rank of Sgt. at Tulagi. Since, he has done invaluable work as
> Government headman on the most senior scale, standing aloof from MR
> [Maasina Rule] activities in 1947–1950. He is greatly respected far outside his
> domain of indigenous authority and his aristocratic connections throughout the
> Central Solomons are considerable. So far as sectarianism allows he may be
> regarded as an elder statesman of Malaita and certainly of the Northern areas.
> Self-educated, reserved, the complete snob, yet a die-hard Tory, his value to
> the [Malaita] council will be considerable even if it does spring from the respect
> in which he is held generally and not from his own peculiar brand of enlight-
> ened despotism.

This account requires some unpacking: Timi Kakaluae's career as agent
of the colonial state did not run a totally smooth course.

As early as 1935, S.S.E.M. missionary Norman Deck referred to Kakaluae
as "the most prominent District Headman on Malaita" (BSIP 1/III/F. 36/9/
pt. 1). Yet Kakaluae's role as Headman and his interest as a strongman in
customary terms were sometimes in conflict, as Government reports from the
1930s show. In 1936, he was pressing claims for the title to Basakana Island,
in rivalry with a fellow north Malaita strongman, Irobaua (Malaita Quarterly Report, 6/30/36; BSIP 29/I/1/1936).[6] In 1937, he was locked in a conflict
with his deputy, Salaimanu (BSIP 14/36); and in the investigation, Kakaluae's demands for customary compensation for an unintentional desecration
of his daughter's death—seemingly taking advantage of his colonially conferred power—were upheld: "I think that Kaluae[7] acted in the correct
manner. Had there been any suggestion of a fine in English money it would
obviously been [sic] wrong but the whole thing is strictly in accordance with
their old custom and the people concerned are pagan" (BSIP 14/39). The
District Commissioner's report to the Resident Commissioner portrayed
Salaimanu as a man of vastly lesser status than Kakaluae: "Naturally, apart
from his government appointment, he can not expect to be treated with the
respect shewn to a man of Kaluae's influence." To suggestions that Kakaluae was using his power as Headman to advance his personal and factional
interests, the District Commissioner noted that "the man suspected of [a]
murder is the chief of Saua Is.: and a friend of Kaluae's." He pointed out that

in asking the District Commissioner to hold an inquiry, "Kaluae acted in an absolutely straightforward manner."

The British were clearly bending over backward to rationalize the acts of a man they had backed so strongly, and in whose loyalty they had placed so much faith—and a man whose status and legitimate authority in "traditional" society they apparently never questioned. But both the times and the colonial cast of characters were changing. By 1940, accusations that Kakaluae was using his power as Headman to advance his own factional interests could no longer be ignored. He was accused of condoning and covering up an assault by men from Sulufou and their allies on a group from Funaafou, in a quarrel growing from an insult and a customary curse. (Recall Kakaluae's father's wars to establish hegemony over the lagoons.) Kakaluae did not report the assault, but was persuaded that it should be settled by the exchange of compensation. The District Officer (BSIP 29/I/5) wrote that "District Headman Kaluae was undoubtedly extremely negligent in not reporting the matter immediately and was severely censured by me. I am not prepared, however, to comment on his fitness to carry out his duties since I have so little knowledge of him." The subsequent investigation (1/III/19/3, 1941) led to a triumph for Kakaluae's old rival Salaimanu: "As a result of an administrative inquiry held on his activities, District Headman Kaluae of Tai was dismissed from his post by His Honour, the Resident Commissioner, who subsequently approved the appointment on probation of Salaimanu in his place. Salaimanu is a man who is both liked and trusted by the people of Tai."

An account from a District Officer's report in 1946 (Laracy 1983, 123) notes: "For many years [Kakaluae] was Government Headman but lost his job when he used his position to have a number of Sulufou people sent to prison and at the same time protected the Adagege and Funafou people who were at least as blameworthy if not more so."

This was a time of political conflict in northern Malaita. Enilana ("England") Kwaisulia[8] had led a Lau delegation to 'Are'are in 1944 to find out about the new political movement there. Enilana had come back strongly supporting Maasina Rule (Laracy 1983, 117–118; 132). Kwaisulia initially accepted appointment as a Maasina Rule Head Chief for Lau, then backed off when he discovered the degree to which this committed him to an antigovernment position incompatible with his role as Headman. Maasina Rule presented a quandary to the Headmen, whose considerable local power depended on loyalty to a British administration that had scattered in the face of the Japanese invasion, and had been dramatically upstaged by the massive American presence. Some, like Maekali of Malu'u, remained unambiguously loyal—partly because the Maasina Rule leaders in their communities were their old adversaries in local power struggles, the S.S.E.M. elders. Others, like Kakaluae, had more difficult tasks of retaining both local power and colonial patronage in the face of massive support for Maasina Rule. The District Officer's 1946 report (Laracy 1983, 123) goes on to comment:

> Until his appointment as Masina Law chief Kakaluae had lived quietly and refrained from taking an active part in politics. During the war he gave useful and loyal service on Tulagi. . . .
>
> Kakaluae determined to win his district for the Government and not the Masina Law. He found difficulties. Although his name carried a great deal of weight among the older men it did not have the same force with the young men. He found his Masina Law position less and less congenial.

Although he was reappointed Headman in October 1945, Kakaluae's political influence was never fully reconstituted, either vis-à-vis the colonial government or the people of the Lau area. His prestige with his own people had been eroded by the turbulent events of Maasina Rule, when the Lau lagoon was split into pro- and antigovernment factions and the loyalist Headmen had acted as agents of mass arrests and political repression. His standing in the eyes of the government had never been fully restored, given both the blots on his record and his initial support for Maasina Rule.

Perhaps, however, the most important factor in his political decline was simply that times, and modes of colonial administration, had changed. The old style of heavy-handed direct rule of the prewar period had given way to local experiments in indirect rule and limited representation of indigenous interests. A "native Headman" deemed by the colonial rulers to be a mighty chief, proud and dictatorial to his own people—and still holding fast to pagan custom—no longer served the needs of gradual democratization in an island becoming dominated by Christianity. In 1954 Kakaluae was still Headman; but the District Commissioner, Malaita, reported the following:

> Chief Headman Kakaluae would not be a good member for the Lau Native Court. I have the greatest of admiration for him as a stalwart supporter of Government and direct administration but he . . . just cannot find his feet in an indirect administration. . . . I believe that [he is] only waiting for the day when [he] can draw a pension and retire from public office. Kakaluae commands little influence in Lau although his standing with the government is respected. . . . He is regarded as a man of the past, which he unfortunately is. (Letter from District Commissioner, Malaita, to Senior Assistant Secretary for Native Affairs, 29 April 1954; BSIP 12/I/29)

Kakaluae's historical moment, and the mode of leadership he emulated—combining the style of his father and the style of Bell—had passed.

It is worth pausing to reflect on some issues of interpretation and agency. It would seem that whereas Ivens and Corris sought to demystify Kwaisulia's supposed chiefly status, on which his son Kakaluae's claims to chiefly status so clearly rested, the colonial administration took as beyond doubt the customary legitimacy of the mantle of authority Kakaluae inherited. The

British in the Solomons, as in Africa and India, had a vested interest in establishing a congruence between the indigenous elites they empowered and the structures of rank and authority in precolonial society. It served their interests to accept and sustain the illusion that the lad Bell had plucked from Adagege as a police recruit a decade after his father's death, a figure created by and in the colonial state, was legitimate successor to his father's exalted rank and fame.

This, then, raises squarely the problem of agency. Was Kakaluae architect of his own destiny, or a colonial puppet? The question is too-simply posed. We see here a process in which an able and gifted man seized opportunities to gain and use power in ways congruent with his customs and the ways of the ancestors to whom he still sacrificed. To him, his British masters were to be used and deceived, as well as respected and feared.

We find this manipulation as early in Kakaluae's career as 1927, when as a corporal in the constabulary he led patrols scouring the mountains of central Malaita for Kwaio fugitives implicated in the massacre of District Officer Bell. In 1975, Kakaluae told anthropologist Ian Frazer how he had ordered his patrol to shoot unarmed prisoners, to avenge tenfold his own Lau kin who as native police had been killed during the assault on Bell and his party. Kakaluae and his fellow corporals Maekali and Ba'etalua, who also became Headmen after the assassination of Bell, spoke proudly, late in life, of these deeds which customary honor had demanded; but they had maintained staunchly at the time to the District Officer that only a few prisoners had been killed, and that these had been "shot trying to escape."

We see fragmentary evidence in the record I have set out of the way Kakaluae sought during his career as Headman to use the power and authority conveyed by the colonial state to pursue his personal interests and those of his kin and allies (continuing his father's projects of political domination, but carefully staying within a framework of "custom" in order to avoid violating Protectorate laws or his duties as Headman). Controlling wealth in shell and dolphin-teeth valuables, partly by virtue of his power and influence as Headman, Kakaluae had reinforced a traditional status that in turn reinforced his aura of customary legitimacy vis-à-vis the colonial state. This aura of customary legitimacy and great hereditary authority—the mantle of his father—enabled him to maintain an empire within the lagoons and along the coast of northern Malaita, where the colonial administration then needed to make only sporadic appearances: entrusted to Kakaluae, things were in good hands.

As I read the record, his undoing in 1940 came partly because he eventually miscalculated, usurping too much colonial authority in running his own empire according to "custom"; but it may have come partly because a new and excessively zealous District Officer intruded on this empire more than his predecessors had—perhaps induced to do so by the scheming rival Salaimanu.

Kakaluae and his fellow Headmen, then, like their counterparts in colonial India and Africa, were throughout their careers both users and used, both agents of manipulation and objects of manipulation. It served both Kakaluae's interests and those of the administration for him to be both a powerful traditional chief and a loyal colonial servant, and for the contradiction between these roles to be disguised.

What, in the longer run, has come of Kakaluae's project? For it would seem that in colonial Melanesia, such leaders have characteristically sought to convert what for them was a contingent and rather precarious power into a longer-term and more solidly based advantage for their children and other close kin. The first generation of "native" functionaries of the colonial state (and their counterparts in mission empires) knew full well that they— uneducated and speaking only Pidgin, subjected to racism and cultural prejudice—were ultimately only petty subordinates far down the social scale of colonial society. Their close contact with Europeans and their potential access to patronage gave them means to attain for their children what they knew they could never attain for themselves.

Melanesian leaders who gained their power as intermediaries with Europeans, as functionaries within the colonial state, or as leaders of millenarian or political resistance, have in many cases been successful in securing a prominent place for their children and grandchildren, as political biographies in modern Melanesian states attest.

Kakaluae was notably less successful in transmitting advantaged status to his children. One of his sons, Kakui, married the sister of Enilana Kwaisulia, and then divorced her in 1954. Two and a half weeks later, Kakui and Enilana came to blows at a Lau market-ground, and Kakui was knocked down and his face scratched. Kakui accepted a *tafuliae* shell valuable as compensation, but remained bitter about his public humiliation. Shortly afterward, Kakui and his half-brother Sada (also Kakaluae's son) encountered Enilana at the market, apparently conspiring to kill him. Kakui killed Enilana in front of a large gathering, with Sada intervening "after England had been struck down by Kakui" (Criminal Case no. 17/54, report of Judicial Commissioner, BSIP). Kakui and Sada were sentenced to death and hanged— the last prisoners to be executed in the Protectorate. That "both accused are . . . sons of Timi Kakaluae, a senior district headman," carried no weight in the trial—a fact that greatly embittered their father after decades of service to the colonial government (Ian Frazer, personal communication). A surviving son works in the Ministry of Transport, Works and Utilities, in charge of allocating furniture for government houses.

Whether the more general patronage established through Kakaluae helped his other kin to more successful careers is unclear. A generation of leaders prominent in the late stages of the colonial period and in the postcolonial period, including one of the country's first two Anglican bishops, have emerged from Sulufou and Adagege. However, I have not been able to establish the degree to which direct connections can be traced from Kwaisulia through Kakaluae and into the following generation, in terms of the perpetuation of power through patronage and elite education.

An interesting question[9] is whether the retrospective representations of Kwaisulia and Kakaluae by contemporary Lau people reflect the old lines of factionalism and family interest that emerged during the careers of the father and of the son. Do Irobaua's descendents, or the family of Salaimanu, represent the two strongmen in less positive terms? I have only fragments of information on this,[10] but I strongly suspect that representations of Kwaisulia and Kakaluae are very much matters of political contention within the Lau Lagoon. A sign of this sort of contention is the controversy in which I became involved, regarding the representation of Kakaluae's police comrades-in-arms Ba'etalua and Maekali, from neighboring To'abaita. The book on the Bell massacre (Keesing and Corris 1980) documents at some length how Ba'etalua, Maekali, and Kakaluae ordered the shooting of prisoners by the constabulary patrols that they led. Contemporary To'abaita politicians, including Ba'etalua's son, attempted to ban the book from circulation in the Solomons (see Keesing 1990).

Kakaluae's career does serve clearly to illustrate the way Melanesian leaders have used the power of the colonial state to achieve prominence. The new political arenas, the new paths to power, were no less real than those of "traditional" society, with its pigs and shell valuables; but to the anthropological eye, they have always smacked of opportunism and lacked the "authenticity" of the cultures we have come to Melanesia to study. It was not the Kakaluaes of Melanesia that anthropologists have written about.[11] Their contemporaries who led millenarian cults have received some attention; but most of all, we have focused on "big men" doing what big men should do: giving feasts, exchanging valuables, presenting pigs. That leads us to some wider questions.

THE MELANESIAN BIG MAN IN ANTHROPOLOGICAL DISCOURSE

For decades, anthropological discourse embodied a set of premises about the peoples around the frontiers of the colonial world it took as subjects and objects. These premises, which can be subsumed within the general framework of "Orientalism" as characterized by Said (1978), took "primitive" societies to be static, self-contained, self-reproducing: a series of separate experiments in human and societal possibility it was anthropology's task to catalogue, characterize, and analyze in terms of their internal functional logic. In this framework, the precolonial histories of tribal societies were essentially unknowable and irrelevant and for all practical purposes non-existent (Fabian 1983).

The histories of European penetration and colonial incorporation were relevant, if it all, only in an introductory chapter. The ethnographer's task in subsequent chapters was to filter out extraneous elements—the missionaries, the colonial officers, the trade stores, the plantations—and depict the "authentic" cultural elements and social structures as if they were intact, self-reproducing, and timeless. Implicit in this task was a denial of history and the political economy of the colonial states within which the peoples under study were encapsulated.

This special anthropological version of Orientalism is implicit in 75 years of social anthropology in the southwestern Pacific. The Melanesian big man, as a stereotypical figure in comparative anthropology and in ethnographic accounts, is a case in point. In our accounts, the big men of the colonial (and now postcolonial) period have been embedded in contexts of "traditional" social structure and economy, even though the social worlds in which Oliver's Siuai *mumi* and Hogbin's To'abaita *ngwane inoto* (and their counterparts in the subsequent three decades) operated were partly creations of colonial pacification, European hegemony, Christianity, and cash economy. The big men of seaboard Melanesia[12] are, it is increasingly clear, in substantial measure a product of the colonial era, with its forced pacification and the disruption of warfare and external trade as avenues of political leadership. In many areas, leaders in warfare were transformed into, or upstaged by, leaders in production and exchange. Warfare and exchange, it would seem, had long been complementary arenas for power and prestige; the closing off of one arena opened up the other for intensified and escalating competition.

Recent linguistic and archaeological research suggests that the processes that produced the Melanesian big man had in fact been operating through the millennium preceding European invasion, as an older system of hereditary chiefdoms, in which the power of chiefs was based partly on external trade within political supercommunities, devolved into more involuted, fragmented, egalitarian social systems where competitive internal exchange prevailed. In many parts of seaboard Melanesia, hereditary chiefs were still significantly powerful when Europeans invaded; but they were mainly in coastal areas where they commanded external trade and exchange systems, and hence their power was quickly eroded by European penetration and economic manipulation.

Modes of leadership and arenas for power were historically constituted, and changing. Leaders seized on the resources and opportunities at hand to build power, extend influence, and forge alliances across societal boundaries; in Melanesia as everywhere else, political processes were characterized by flexibility and opportunism.[13] Power, once gained, could sometimes be institutionalized, legitimated, given cosmological charter, hence reproduced; but where actual political ascendancy rested on success in warfare and prosperity, the structures and charters could imply a stability that was in fact illusory (as was the case in much of Polynesia).

Into this scene we came as ethnographers, crystallizing what was transitory and recent into systems, structures, and stereotypes. Yet the colonial situation that brought us as anthropologists also created new arenas for power. As middlemen and brokers in dealing with Europeans, as leaders in anticolonial resistance—whether millenarian or military—as functionaries of the colonial state or local mission empires, Melanesians found ways to seize on the European presence for their own purposes.[14]

Moreover, as with others who achieved political power, these leaders along the interface of the invading and the invaded sought ways to reproduce their power. Sometimes they used their gains in a newly emerging arena—wealth, followers, patronage—through "traditional" idioms (feasting, exchange) to give their power a cultural acceptability it might otherwise have lacked. And obviously, such leaders used older Melanesian political styles and idioms in enacting new roles. The careers of Kwaisulia and Kakaluae illustrate both phenomena.

One interesting question we can pose is whether, in bringing together the roles of warrior-leader and chief and expanding the regional span of power and authority, Kwaisulia in effect permanently transformed Lau political structure. That is, even though Kwaisulia's ascendancy was based partly on his access to European resources and his control over indentured labor, perhaps we can best view him as transforming a political system, not abusing it.[15] The question becomes more relevant if we look at Kakaluae's position. If we examine him with reference to the pre-Kwaisulia political system of Lau, he was just as fictional a chief as his father; but if we examine him with reference to the new political system his father created, then he emerges as hereditary claimant to his father's ("non-existent") position. I raise the question because I believe that this is precisely how, in the precolonial tribal world, political systems changed. The precolonial equivalent of a Kwaisulia extended existing political possibilities and roles through successful conquest or diplomacy; the precolonial equivalent of a Kakaluae, in succeeding to a new status, clothed it in cultural symbols of permanence and legitimacy.[16]

Too often, I fear, we anthropologists have either denigrated or ignored the new forms and arenas of political power catalyzed by European invasion or made possible by colonial power as extraneous to our concerns, as opportunism, as lacking cultural sanction. We have worked hard to show that the local "chiefs" or headmen invested with power by the colonial state, or the middlemen who gained power through their access to Western weapons and wealth, were not "real," not sanctified by "traditional culture." We have been quick to point out how those who held real traditional power in Melanesian communities often themselves put incompetent or marginal characters forward to serve as colonial puppets, or how the incompetent and marginal put themselves forward and were empowered, out of ignorance, by colonial officers.[17]

We have not only been naive about the nature of the political process, and the labile nature of the "structures" we have studied, within wider contexts of political economy and history. In denigrating or ignoring the new styles of leadership and power, we have been less astute than these "opportunistic" and "illegitimate" leaders of the colonial frontier themselves about the way this power gained in new arenas could be reproduced: not by the old means, but by the new ones offered by the colonial state and missions. Limited, local, and contingent status gained in the colonial situation has been secured and expanded through privileged access of the succeeding generation to education, English, patronage, and opportunity. If we look at the sons and grandsons of the early "opportunist" leaders of colonial Melanesia, we find them as the parliamentarians, senior public servants, and entrepreneurs of postcolonial Melanesia. The "big men" we have taken as our focus, and enshrined with cultural legitimacy, have sometimes been able to reproduce their power in their children's generation, and in the new channels and idioms colonialism offered. But more often, I think, they have been outstripped by those whose power came from dealing with Europeans, not shells and pigs.

What is striking about the retrospective construction of Kwaisulia in Lau oral tradition is that the legitimacy of his leadership and power in terms of "traditional custom" is not an issue. But "traditional custom" itself may be elevated as a political symbol, with little concern for the "authenticity" of the customs so invoked. I have recently reflected on the paradoxes this poses (Keesing 1989). As anthropologists we may see wide gulfs between the cultures documented ethnographically and the versions of the past being invoked in cultural nationalist rhetoric. Clearly, "culture" is a highly flexible and multivalent symbol (Keesing 1982a, 1982b, 1989). Yet if we invoke our version of a people's ancestral past, more accurate and authentic than their contemporary ideologies, we may be attributing to that past greater coherence and stability than ever existed. The mythical "ethnographic present" was a moment in time and change. The static, self-contained, self-reproducing "authentic" ancestral cultures of the past are themselves in some ways fictions, ideological renderings (ours and theirs) of what was always opportunistic, flexible, and situationally adaptable.

NOTES

1. I am grateful to Ellison Suri for clarifying some points, to David Akin, Ian Frazer, and Hugh Laracy for providing historical documents and useful comments, and to Fitz Poole for helpful suggestions for revision. An earlier version of the paper

was presented at the American Anthropological Association meetings in November 1987; Paula Brown and James Watson, organizers of the symposium on "Big Man, Strong Man, Culture Hero," and participants in the symposium, particularly Theodore Schwartz, gave helpful comments.

2. However, Mahaffy, who had just overseen the destruction of a settlement in Suafa inlet, detained Kwaisulia on HMS *Sparrow* while the latter sent Kaiviti to make the arrests on behalf of the government (Australian Archives A1108/56).

3. Although Kwaisulia's identity as a "chief" would have been very much a matter of contention among his contemporaries, his identity as a ramo would not. Even though in Malaitan ideologies (see Keesing 1985) becoming a ramo was thought to entail special personal powers and aggressiveness of personality conferred by ancestors, any man who *demonstrated* these powers and traits was attributed ancestral support. The proof of the power lay in the doing, and Kwaisulia's deeds were beyond question.

4. Ian Frazer (personal communication 26 April 1988) comments that "considering that Kwaisulia remained a pagan all his life, it could be argued (from a Malaitan perspective) that he really owed all his success to his ancestors anyhow rather than Europeans, and so was a big man in traditional terms!"

5. South Sea Evangelical Mission.

6. Ian Frazer notes (personal communication 26 April 1988) that in the 1936 claims to Basakana Island, Kakaluae presented a genealogy showing that Kwaisulia's grandfather was a man from Sulufou, while Irobaua (who seems to have been Ivens's principal informant) claimed that Kwaisulia's connection to Sulufou was through his father's mother. The court was unable to decide between the two versions. Hence, even Kwaisulia's nonagnatic status in relation to Sulufou and Adagege is a matter of contention and competing claims.

7. Kakaluae's name is rendered this way frequently in administration documents.

8. I have been unable to verify Enilana Kwaisulia's relationship to Kwaisulia and Kakaluae; he apparently was Kakaluae's cousin, distantly enough related for one of Kakaluae's sons to marry his sister (see below).

9. Raised by Fitz Poole (personal communication).

10. From Ian Frazer and Ellison Suri.

11. There are, of course, a number of individual exceptions in the writings of earlier decades, such as Ian Hogbin's account of Bumbu in *Transformation Scene* (1951). In later years, some writings on Papua New Guinea (such as Brown [1963] and Finney [1973]) and other parts of Oceania (see, e.g., Rodman and Counts 1982) have begun to fit into the gaping lacunae in the literature. This problem is not confined to Oceania, as indicated by James Clifford's comments (1988, 48–49) on Victor Turner's schoolteacher assistant, Windson Kashinakaji.

12. Much of what I say applies equally to the big men of Papuan-speaking New Guinea, but I am speaking most directly of seaboard Melanesia, and particularly zones in which Austronesian languages are spoken. My doubts about "Melanesia" as an ethnological category and "culture area" are expressed in the Epilogue to this collection.

13. In discussion of the version I presented in Chicago, an objection was raised that in emphasizing the opportunism of politics, I was elevating a Machiavellian model of self-interest and manipulation. My point is not that political claims and

strategies are best analyzed in terms of cynical self-interest; but rather the point Marx emphasized, that to act effectively, groups and individuals must seize a moment in history, must analyze opportunities and arenas for power so as to grasp and control them.

14. Indeed, we may note how leaders have used ethnographers for their political projects, as we have used them for our academic ones. Ongka's relationship with Andrew Strathern and my own with Jonathan Fifi'i (Fifi'i 1989) come to mind, but there are many more examples.

15. In a recent thesis, Jeffrey Crowe (1989) suggests that I overemphasize the individual opportunism of Kwaisulia and Kakaluae by giving insufficient weight to the new needs of groups and communities for which they provided leadership, and for which they buffered against the demands and manipulations of the colonial state. I acknowledge this imbalance and the importance of collective, as well as individual, interests in generating new modes of leadership. Maasina Rule provides vivid evidence of the collective character of confrontations with colonial power.

16. Ian Frazer, who interviewed Kakaluae and has done ethnohistorical research on Lau, comments (personal communication 26 April 1988): "Kwaisulia was able to take advantage of new opportunities but there was nothing new about his political ambitions; he was only doing what many had done before him, whether or not they were agnates! In this respect, the Lau might have been strongly patrilineal, but I would be surprised if patrilineality dictated political fortunes. I wonder whether the picture given by Ivens is overdrawn, representing a view from the top and underplaying the dynamics of Lau politics."

17. As Theodore Schwartz pointed out in discussion of my paper, leaders in the colonial context themselves claimed legitimacy in customary terms (as witness both Kwaisulia's and Kakaluae's styles of leadership). And, as the conflict between Kakaluae and Salaimanu illustrates, a colonially appointed official whose "traditional" status was recognized often had higher status in local communities than one whose "traditional" credentials were suspect. But on close examination, as Hobbes pointed out, almost all credentials of legitimacy are ultimately suspect.

REFERENCES

Brown, Paula. 1963. "From Anarchy to Satrapy." *American Anthropologist* 65:1–15.

Clifford, James. 1988. *The Predicament of Culture: Twentieth-Century Ethnography, Literature, and Art.* Cambridge, Mass: Harvard University Press.

Corris, Peter. 1970. "Kwaisulia of Ada Gege: A Strongman in the Solomon Islands." Pp. 253–265 in J. W. Davidson and D. Scarr (eds.), *Pacific Islands Portraits.* Canberra: Australian National University Press.

———. 1973. *Passage, Port and Plantation: A History of Solomon Islands Labour Migration, 1870–1914.* Melbourne: University of Melbourne Press.

Crowe, Jeffrey. 1989. "The 'Sweet' Talk of Brotherhood: Hierarchy or Ideology on Malaita?" M.Sc. dissertation, London School of Economics.

Fabian, Johannes. 1983. *Time and the Other: How Anthropology Makes Its Object.* New York: Columbia University Press.

Fifi'i, Jonathan. 1989. *From Pig-Theft to Parliament: My Life Between Two Worlds.*

Honiara: University of the South Pacific and Solomon Islands College of Higher Education.

Finney, Ben. 1973. *Big-Men and Business*. Canberra: Australian National University Press.

Hogbin, Ian. 1951. *Transformation Scene: The Changing Culture of a New Guinea Village*. London: Routledge.

Hopkins, Arthur I. 1928. *In the Isles of King Solomon*. London: Seeley, Service and Company.

Ivens, W. H. 1930. *The Island Builders of the Pacific*. London: Seeley, Service and Company.

Keesing, Roger M. 1982*a*. "Kastom in Melanesia: An Overview." *Mankind* 13 (Special Issue):297–302.

———. 1982*b*. "Kastom and Anticolonialism on Malaita: 'Culture' as Political Symbol." *Mankind* 13 (Special Issue):357–373.

———. 1985. "Killers, Big Men and Priests on Malaita: Reflections on a Melanesian Troika System." *Ethnology* 24:237–252.

———. 1989. "Creating the Past: Custom and Identity in the Contemporary Pacific." *Contemporary Pacific* 1:16–35.

———. 1990. "Colonial History as Contested Ground: The Bell Massacre in the Solomons." *History and Anthropology* 4:279–301.

Keesing, Roger M., and Peter Corris. 1980. *Lighting Meets the West Wind: The Malaita Massacre*. Melbourne: Oxford University Press.

Laracy, Hugh. 1983. *Pacific Protest: The Maasina Rule Movement, Solomon Islands, 1944–52*. Suva: Institute of Pacific Studies, University of the South Pacific.

Rodman, William, and Dorothy Counts, eds. 1982. *Middlemen and Brokers in Oceania*. Ann Arbor: University of Michigan Press.

Said, Edward. 1978. *Orientalism*. London: Routledge.

SEVEN

Gone Native in Isles of Illusion
In Search of Asterisk in Epi

Michael W. Young

We live, as we dream—alone.
— CONRAD'S MARLOW, *Heart of Darkness*

. . . and he went off, not without misgivings, not without regrets, to seek no fortune, but to find the substance of a dream.
— BOHUN LYNCH OF ASTERISK, *Isles of Illusion*

. . . viewed from a certain angle the island resembled a female body, headless but nevertheless a woman, seated with her legs drawn up beneath her in an attitude wherein submission, fear and simple abandonment were inextricably mingled.
— MICHEL TOURNIER, *Friday or The Other Island*

DOUBLES AND JANUS-FIGURES

Anthropologists in the field, observes Malcolm Crick (1989, 39), "have to use 'working fictions' to pursue their research; they have to maintain a balance between involvement and detachment."[1] There is, moreover, a good case to be made for the duplicitous nature of fieldwork practice being one of its most singular features. Let me caricature a little. We anthropologists are not what we pretend to be to the alien people whom we elect to be our hosts. Conversely, we put our (usually) Western identities at risk when we try to assimilate to our adopted communities. We make friends but rarely take them home with us; we try to learn the vernacular of our hosts but rarely manage it well enough to persuade them we can share their lives; we take time off to visit other European exiles, relieved to find we still remember our table manners. We practice hypocrisy, approving of things that privately appall us. We undertake diplomatic maneuvers, not with the innocent aim of improving our personal relationships, but with the devious end of using those connections to gain information. In the name of rapport and enhanced research opportunities, we commit these and many other acts of bad faith. We are driven, hectic and impatient, pressed to theorize prematurely, for we have so little time to learn. Our vaunted objectivity, as Michael Jackson (1989, 4) remarks, is but "a synonym for estrangement."

Like Janus, then, anthropologists are two-faced and two-tongued; and we too look in two directions at once—at the culture under observation and at the culture that bred us as observers. We have to be duplicitous yet friendly, agreeable if not liked. Yet how we yearn to be loved—loved for ourselves and not just for what we can give to or do for our hosts! Although we are uneasily aware that they too might be engaging in duplicity, we have all relished those gratifying moments when our hosts grant us the accolade of a kinship designation, and, over a shared plate of yams, a bowl of kava, or a betel nut chew, they pronounce us white natives: *olsem hapkas.*

Janus is not the only apt emblem of our professional predicament: we are also "half-castes." Born of one culture, adopted by another, we hope to learn somehow to be equally at home in both. This is accomplished by very few anthropologists, and most of us end our days in the culture of our birth, recollecting in comfortable tranquillity the culture of our adoption which now lives only in our nostalgic writings.[2] Marginal natives, half-castes, double-agents, ambivalent Janus-figures—anthropologists are yet further bifurcated by the very attempt to live with these contradictions of role and identity.

Although I have apostrophized my anthropological colleagues in these paragraphs, the compromised condition applies to any profession or activity in which a dual identity needs to be cultivated and maintained. These characterizations of the fieldworking anthropologist also applied in large measure to Robert James Addison Gerard Fletcher, alias Asterisk, who was born seven years before Malinowski and preceded him by two years to Melanesia. The Janus-theme of the Double haunted his life and writings.

Under the pseudonym "Asterisk," Robert Fletcher inadvertently authored what is among the most compellingly honest and justly celebrated books about colonial life in the Pacific, *Isles of Illusion: Letters from the South Seas.* Fletcher was born in 1877 and (amazingly, in view of the ravages the tropics wrought upon him), died in 1965 at the ripe age of 87. An Oxford-educated Englishman who wearied of preparatory school teaching ("bum-brushing" as he called it), Fletcher, at the age of 33, sought a more adventurous life abroad, first in South America, then in the New Hebrides, and finally in French Polynesia. His longest sojourn was in the New Hebrides, where he spent seven and a half years: first as a court interpreter in Port Vila; then as a land surveyor in the central and northern islands; lastly, for a period of five years, as a coconut plantation manager on the island of Epi. Fletcher (like Malinowski in Papua) thereby evaded the horrors of World War I in Europe, though he found enough complementary horrors in the colonial backwaters of the New Hebrides. It was on the island of Epi, where I did fieldwork in 1985 and 1986, that I first read Asterisk's book and uncovered faint traces of Fletcher's life there some seventy years earlier.

A number of puzzles lie at the heart of *Isles of Illusion,* the most obvious being its ambiguity of authorship.[3] These puzzles obscurely mirror the ambiguities and ambivalences at the heart of the anthropological enterprise—at least, as it has been (and still is) pursued in small-scale communities in the Pacific. It was as if Fletcher, although not an anthropologist himself, experienced many of the discomforting contradictions we practitioners face while in the field.

At least two French ethnographers, Michel Leiris and Jean Jamin, have claimed a special place for Fletcher's letters in the annals of anthropology (see n. 6). They amount to an ethnographic journal which reflexively comments as much on the white intruders as on the black indigenes. The contradictions Fletcher reveals (and ironically relishes) are those of colonialism, racism, miscegenation, and the divided being of Western man. (Dr. Jekyll and Mr. Hyde, we might note, were the imaginary children of R. L. Stevenson, Fletcher's first literary hero.) *Isles of Illusion* can thus be read for the kind of social, moral, and psychological circumstances under which anthropology has been historically conducted. It can also be read by contemporary anthropologists of Melanesia as an exemplary warning. For during his petulant, literary yearnings for the "authentic" South Seas, Fletcher committed every one of the seven ugly sins of anthropological discourse listed by James Carrier: orientalism, temporalism, essentialism, primitivism, isolationism, unidimensionalism, and mirroring. He committed them with no more conscience than a beachcomber, but his ironical vision and ludic style undermined his reifications even as he inscribed them.

Increasingly, nowadays, our concern is to understand the conditions and contingencies, social and intellectual, under which anthropology is done: its dual practice as data collection in the field and writing in the study. Under the first rubric are the social relationships in which the anthropologist becomes enmeshed; under the second are the means and methods of ethnographic construction: guiding theories and techniques of authorship. The catch, of course, is that we must rely mainly on what anthropologists themselves write to discover what they did. They present their masks, their literary personae, to fabricate (and fabulate) their practice in the field. On this widened view of what anthropology studies, Fletcher has something of historical importance to say to us. Like Malinowski's notorious *Diary* (1967), Fletcher's epistolary "intimate journal" is a model of reflexive observation: it records an interior journey.

I invoke Malinowski a number of times during the course of this essay. This is not simply because he is the precursor of modern fieldwork methods in Melanesia (to which we are all direct heirs), but because he flirted with fictional modes of representation (derived from Conrad among others), because he explored a similar colonial space to Fletcher's, and because his Trobriand fieldwork experience was, in Robert Thornton's words, "among the most deliberate of personal and intellectual confrontations between the

'European' and the 'Savage' that had yet been attempted" (1985, 14). An objective of my essay is to situate Robert Fletcher in the ambit of this anthropological tradition. What Fletcher grants me, in turn, is an allegory of representation: not James Clifford's "ethnographic allegory" but "biographic allegory."

A LONELY, LOQUACIOUS MAN

Isles of Illusion, as I have mentioned, is ambiguously authored. It comprises a collection of letters edited by their recipient: fellow old-Oxonian Bohun Lynch. Known to Fletcher as "John," Lynch was himself a prolific writer, though quite forgotten today. Without the knowledge or express permission of their author, Lynch prepared the letters for publication by Constable, censoring them to disguise persons and places. Pseudonyms and dashes conspire to impart a fictional air by implicitly questioning the authenticity of the letters. Today, however, most of the locations and people can be identified by anyone with a local knowledge of the ex-New Hebrides and its dismal colonial history. "Asterisk" is Fletcher (publicly unmasked in 1929 by his new publisher, John Murray); "Mowbray" is the English lawyer and author Edward Jacomb (another old-Oxonian to whom Fletcher also wrote lengthy letters); "Muller," the brash and burly entrepreneur, is Nicolas "Tiby" Hagen, whose plantation on Epi Fletcher managed; "Bernhardt," who adopted Fletcher's son, is Zeitler, a business partner of Hagen's; Mosquito Bay can be readily identified as Ringdove (latterly Rovo) Bay on Epi; and the unnamed site of Fletcher's plantation is Lameru, at the northern-most point of Epi.

Asterisk's letters, Lynch confides in his Introduction, "were not real letters, but the outlet of a man who has no one to talk to. I was the safety-valve" (1923, xiii). Elsewhere, their author excused them as "the confidential whimpering of a loquacious man condemned to months of intolerable silence" (1924, xi). He admits that he does not always tell the truth in any plain and simple way. His is an anthropological stance: "You—with me—surely look upon 'truth' somewhat from a pragmatistic standpoint. Truth is what is best for us to believe. Furthermore we must not forget the question of subjective idealism. What is, isn't always. What is for A. is not necessarily for B." (1923, xiv). The letters are self-revelatory, passionate, cynical, paradoxical, bitter, brutal, disconsolate, and grimly humorous. Partly because they are so painfully self-honest, the "self" they express is contradictory and hopelessly divided.

If the book tells a story it is that of a cultivated and sensitive man's progressive disillusionment with the sad tropics, the enchanted South Sea isles of Stevenson. It is a record of his deteriorating health, his increasing loneliness and his growing distaste for the purulent colonial milieu. In its unschematic way, and with its flippant echoes of Conrad, the book is a harrowing indictment of British and French imperialism. Not that Fletcher believed the pristine state of the "savage Kanakas" to have been any better, but he utterly despised the hypocrisy of his kind: the sanctimonious missionaries, the rapacious planters, the incompetent government officers. He was clear-sightedly Swiftian concerning their "civilizing mission" to produce law-abiding, God-fearing, hard-working natives who would serve their invaders' interests. But Fletcher's greatest contempt was reserved for half-castes, the métis, who symbolized for him the odious success of the colonial enterprise. He was equally scathing about "Biche-la-mar" (as he called it), the "bastard" English which served as the trade language of the colony; he regarded it as a linguistic "throwback" which impoverished and vulgarized the cultural worlds of indigenes and colonists alike. Ironically, Fletcher too met with odious success in fathering a child by a native woman, both of whom he adored, communicated with in Bislama, played with happily for a few years—and then abandoned.

A subplot is discernible in the temporal progression of the letters (just as in the temporal sequence of Malinowski's diaries). Their author becomes reconciled in some measure to his hymnic proposition that "only Man is vile," and the Kurtzian "horror" of the colony is ameliorated to a degree. Some of his own prejudices dissolve with the passing years, and following his breakdown and flight from the New Hebrides he finds restored health on Makatea in the Society Islands. There he learns once more to celebrate natural beauty, which represents for him the quintessential happiness of lotus-living: "the true life, the solitude, the forest."

So against the descending scale of disenchantment in the New Hebrides (lightened by the coda of his recovery in French Polynesia), is counterpointed a rising scale of tolerance for the savagely exploited indigenes. In his love for a native woman and their child he finds a qualified redemption. It is qualified, he realizes, because his intellect will not allow his feelings to rule him. His ambivalent attempt to go native is soured by his yearning for educated conversation and subverted by a sneaky bourgeois conscience that tells him he has betrayed, not so much his race or his class, but his finer sensibilities. Fletcher, for all his heretical views, was something of an intellectual snob.

There is much blatant racial prejudice, class and male chauvinism in the letters. Fletcher sometimes expresses revulsion for the natives, the Christianized ones more so than the pagans. He rails against English snobbery and conformism, French ill-manners and cowardice, Australian philistinism and crudeness (nowadays called "ockerism"). English class prejudice aside, white superiority was self-evident in this era, a political fact of colonial life. It is no mystery, then, how an intelligent and convention-hating spirit like Fletcher could have subscribed to the colonial ideologies of race that were flourishing during the first half of the century. They have wilted only slowly after all, and some have been reborn in new guises. The fact that he was appalled by the evils of colonialism did not shake his belief in "natural" racial hierarchies. His general attitude to the morality of colonialism was close to that of his friend Edward Jacomb ("Mowbray"), the maverick English lawyer who did much to protect indigenous New Hebrideans against unscrupulous French land-grabbers and labor-hirers. In *The Future of the Kanaka*, Jacomb had argued: "All we are morally entitled to do is to offer them the benefits of civilization, but they are entitled to refuse them, and we have then no moral right to use force to make them abandon their decision" (1919, 24). Nor do we need to excuse Fletcher's squeamishness concerning the social acceptability of his native wife and half-caste son. He would need to have been uncommonly thick-skinned to evade the censure that operated through the prevailing "codes of discrimination" (see Keesing 1988).

"ISLES OF ILLUSION"

It hardly does justice to the range of Fletcher's preoccupations (still less to the exuberance of his style) to offer a mere handful of sample quotations. But the following passages give some flavor of what was, in 1923, an unusually forthright and introspectively "modern" text. In its literary merit also it greatly outpaced the humdrum run of covertly sensational adventure tales told by bluff colonial officers and greatly outshone the pious memoirs of humorless missionaries. The passages focus on lotus-eating and Fletcher's Janus-like predicament of love and disgust, but they serve to highlight some of his opinions on race and miscegenation—topics relevant to the theme of this essay.

First, however, let me establish that Fletcher was not simply a homesick aesthete, haughtily aloof from the colony's culture of terror. Passages from a letter written on 24 May 1914 from a surveying camp on the coast of Malekula reveal a mock heroism, a boy-scout bravado, as he reports his first (and last) engagement in the common colonial sport of "nigger hunting." His account verges on parody—of C. A. W. Monckton's New Guinea Resident Magistrate and any number of other swashbuckling colonial officers who relished punitive raids.

"Why weren't you here yesterday? I have had such fun," Fletcher wrote to Lynch. He had learned that "bushmen" had attacked a tradestore on the coast, wounding the French owner. ("He had a bullet in his thigh which I skilfully [he will probably die] extracted, and having put him within reach of his Pernod Fils we started off for the bush village.") His party comprised just three natives and himself, armed with "two Winchesters, two Colts Police Positive Special revolvers, two Browning automatic pistols." After floundering through the bush for six hours they reached their destination. "We crept in, but it was no good; the birds had flown. They had probably heard us for hours." Exhausted, Fletcher "turned into the least filthy of the huts and slept till daybreak." Still enraged, "We burned their village, cut down their 'God'-tree, and then found their gardens and uprooted and stole all their yams. That means that they will starve during the winter." If the villagers had not driven off their pigs he would have slaughtered them too, and he "naturally" purloins the chief's dancing mask ("garnished with real human teeth"), which he promises to send to Lynch. Fletcher concedes that what he has done is illegal ("if the Government get to hear of my goings on there will be a row"), even foolhardy ("every tree might hide a dozen cannibals"), but he is far from remorseful and wishes Lynch could have been back there to join the fun ("we would have hunted the swine"). Back at the coast, Fletcher's assistant, a Scotsman, is furious at what he had missed and wants to return and "massacre some of the beggars"; but "20 hours' walking inside 36 hours" had left Fletcher feeling rather weary. As for the wounded Frenchman: "I feel no sympathy at all with the man. He sells the niggers grog and Winchesters, and then wonders that he gets shot" (1923, 112–114).

The letter goes on to revile "beastly" England and its suffocating conventions, to wax nostalgic about "the joys of a wandering caravan life," to quote (from memory) Dante's *Inferno*, and to conclude with what he had eaten for dinner: "I have filled my belly with duck and finished the repast with wild honey which I like to think came from scarlet hibiscus" (ibid., 118).

The wild and woolly aspect of life in the New Hebrides was part of its dubious charm for Fletcher, but this letter is one of the last from the wilderness. He went to Sydney to visit a dentist, and had returned by October 1914 (possibly on the same boat that brought anthropologists W. H. R. Rivers and John Layard to Malekula), and by the beginning of 1915 he is established on a cotton plantation in Epi as his own master, quite alone, with a hundred-odd "servants" (i.e., male and female labor), nine horses, and two cows. He works from sunrise to sunset on the plantation and spends two hours a day in his small surgery, "treating many things from malaria to elephantiasis." In the evenings he reads "of pleasant things pleasantly written in a pleasant tongue." On Sundays he writes to Lynch. The "happy hedonist," as he referred to himself on one occasion, had begun to create a lotus-land that would need an effort of will to sustain. The quotations that follow plot the zigzag course of his journey into this new colonial self.

> October 26th 1915. I found out many things at first hand, and you have the better part in that you only imagine them. . . . My valuation of coral islands would be brutal but correct. . . . Of such things as O——ns [i.e., Australians], tropical diseases, niggers, half-castes, iron houses in the tropics at midday, tinned food, scabies, fleas in herds, nerves and jumps, and the wonders of solitude, I can speak in an authoritative manner—and I wish to God that I couldn't. (Ibid., 137)

Fletcher confects his imaginary idyll: "A return to the beast" on "Muller's island." He builds it to a dreamy perfection, then without breaking rhythm turns the idyll over and inspects its underside:

> And the flies would crawl over my sores and feed on the crust around my eyelids. And the sea would boom on the coral reef outside and the palms would wave gently in the trade wind and the brown folk would laugh and chatter and scratch themselves quite in the proper R.L.S. way. And I would get up and look lovingly at my dear little Webley and Scott and wonder when I would have the pluck to do it. And I never would. Sperat infestis, metuit secundis. (Ibid., 138)

He disarms the shocking import of this suicidal temptation with a casual aside, followed by the bathos of another anticlimax:

> I got a "prize" for translating that into English verse . . . just think of it and laugh. And about an hour ago I was scraping dirt off a tuberculous Kanaka in order that I might lance an abscess and prolong his beastly existence for a few weeks. La diddle di iddledy, umpty i. (Ibid.)

Loneliness gnaws and the climate enervates. An outbreak of dysentery on the island stretches his resources to the utmost: "This week I have tended single-handed 28 cases and buried five under conditions which even war could not beat. . . . The filthy things that I have had to do would be nauseating in a cold climate and among civilized creatures. Here they are unspeakable" (ibid., 144).

A few months later he consoles himself by taking a native mistress, a fifteen-year-old Aoba (a later name for Omba) girl he names Topsy. The tide of disillusionment ebbs for a while, but it is not long before he resumes the tone of a cynical, clinical realist lancing romantic illusions:

> No, you are a sentimentalist who invests the unknown with charms which exist only in your imagination. What have I said before? I repeat it. Touch not, taste not, handle not. Keep your distance and you will keep your enchantment. (Ibid., 165)

Lotus-eating begins to give him moral indigestion:

> September 1916. I am afraid that I have eaten too much lotos already. The effects show in the deterioration of one's morals and one's mentality. I realized the other day when she [Topsy] was ill, how absurdly and disgustingly attached I have grown to my little brown woman. And what is she? A little nut-coloured savage less than five feet high. Her body certainly is beautiful in its doll-like tininess. Her face and hair are quaint. She behaves to me just like a very nice Persian kitten or a terrier pup would behave. . . . It is only when I find that she has stealthily filled up my shoe with sugar . . . that I realize what an absolute baby she is. . . . She spends the whole afternoon in the sea swim-

ming and diving, and in every way is much cleaner than a good proportion of the white women I have "met." And yet six months ago I was lampooning her to you as a savage beast. . . .

But do you think I could tolerate her in civilisation? Not for a week. That is the difference that the islands make. (Ibid., 166 and 167)

Some months later:

January 9th 1917. I simply must shift from here. I have miscalculated the effect of lotos eating; I mean of my last meal. That wretched little brown slut has tied me up a dam sight tighter than I could ever have imagined. . . . If I were to give way now, it would mean the renunciation of all that I really love. And I'm not such a fool as that. (Ibid., 179)

The dilemma becomes acute:

May 1917. I saw the absurdity of what I had proposed to myself. I was going to be worse than a missionary. I was going to say to a quite primitive savage: "You are fit mate and equal for complex twentieth century me." It would have been hopeless. . . . It's true that plenty of "white men" here have lived happily for many years with Aoba women and have brought up half-caste kids. But, to begin with, the white men were the mental and physical inferiors of their brown wives and, to end with, their kids were unspeakable. That was no use to me as comfort. I could never grow native. (Ibid., 204 and 205)

He devises a painful solution:

The Topsy and Man Friday question I can solve by sending them back to Aoba. She will weep her heart out until the anchor's up and perhaps have wistful half regrets for even longer. There is a quite nice French half-caste who lives close to Topsy's passage. I shall arrange with him to take the pair into his ménage. Then if after a year or two Topsy forsakes the kid—as Aoba women generally do—Monsieur Métis will adopt him and he will become a citoyen français. If Topsy sticks to him and he grows up to be a "man Aoba," he will probably be much happier. I am afraid that I have spoiled her, but the spoiling is less than skin deep. (Ibid., 205–206)

Fletcher's ethnographic observations on New Hebrideans are infrequent but trenchant. Marcel Mauss would have appreciated this one:

Of course their [Aobans'] code [of manners] is not the same as ours, but they are very strict. I used to be annoyed at the way Topsy received gifts, I looking for the "Oh, thank you *so* much, darling; where did you manage, etc." That was my ignorance. Gifts should be presented in the most utterly careless manner and received with the most stately indifference. It is only the vulgar, ill-bred, missionaries who deviate from this rule. The inner meaning of the manner is that friendship ought to be quite independent of gifts. And gifts must be returned strictly ad valorem. (Ibid., 226)

On his frank Orientalism and the canker in the rose:

> November 25th 1917. Having viewed these last three years of Europe from a leisurely remoteness, I must say that I prefer Cathay. That is the fact of it. It is hard to express in words, but I am possessed with a loathing for civilisation and its humbugs and mockeries. Here I have practically no contact at all with the sham. Here I have what elemental man needs, a woman (who is not a lady), a man-child (who has doubtless enough of his father in him to make an interesting subject for experiment, and most certainly has not inherited any love of convention), food, shelter, earth to be buried in. Do I want anything more? Yes, I do. I want friendship—with my intellectual equal. (Ibid., 215)

Fletcher's yearning is also for fatherhood, to rear a child who will not "from babyhood be loaded with the barnacles of convention." He defends his way of life, his mixed ménage, and his anarchic freedom:

> My own individual existence is bound to be less hampered here than in, say, London. Why should it necessarily be brutish because it is not British? . . . Topsy is far less of a bore to me than would be a white woman. She does not expect "attentions," and would not understand them if she got 'em. The thought of the upbringing of the child in my own free way pleases me tremendously. . . . My fear is due to my ignorance of what really composes Friday's distaff half. I know little enough of my own congenital gifts; naturally, I know still less of Topsy's. Of some things, however, I am quite certain. From his ma Friday will not have inherited snobism, gluttony, Christianity or any other of the sweet legacies to which we are victims. At present he shows rather frightening precocity both of mind and body. The clay is very promising. I am itching to have it on the wheel. (Ibid., 218 and 219)

His growing love of Man Friday (baby Bilbil) brings agonizing indecision:

> October 1st 1918. My wretched mind simply will not be quiet about Bilbil. I get him and his future nicely settled—and then comes a shock. It is literally and lamentably true that I love him now. But shall I always do so? (Ibid., 244)

Fletcher is "physically repelled" by the French métis he meets, despite their being well educated, well behaved, and well dressed. He laments:

> You see I am absorbed in my little Kanaka world; I very rarely meet any whites and those only such people as are very little better than Kanakas. You don't know how the island blight eats into one. . . . I tolerate the happy-go-lucky kind of life, but I am more than ever resolved not to give way to the soiled-lotos temptation. I am so afraid that, if I take Bilbil away and get him among whiter things, I shall straightaway begin to hate him. (Ibid., 245)

Later he broods, "I have sinned against nature . . . and I am going to pay the price" (ibid., 260). His last reference to his son is made from the distance of French Polynesia:

September 18th 1920. Bilbil. Cold logic can't cure that wound. I fear that it is incurable. Another case of the great wisdom of keeping well away from one's ideals. I cherish only the reality that I knew and that was charming. The ideal that could never, never have been realised exists with me. (Ibid., 302)

Fletcher is not without hypocrisy himself:

> Although I pine for that savage simplicity which, as you may remember, I once agreed spelt degeneration, I simply can't stand the sight of it in other white men. There are plenty here, both British and French. They are quite decent folk—but they have gone native. They wear a wreath of tiaré round a native-made straw hat. They go bare-footed except on Sundays. They sit more easily on their "hunkers" than on a chair. They expectorate when and where the fancy dictates. When they are frightened they say so. That is the complete gone native. (Ibid., 291 and 292)

So in the last analysis he was compromised by his ideals. He confesses that he is not cut out for the half-life of going native:

> But there can be no half-way for me. For that reason the sooner I am out of the S.Seas the better. In my quality of white man, and educated white man at that, these Tahitian women do not appeal to me at all. I should have to give free play to the savage that is in me. And . . . that game does not seem worth the candle. (Ibid., 302 and 303)

A LITERARY LOTUS-EATER[4]

When Fletcher returned to England in 1923 he discovered himself to be a "literary lion"—if an anonymous one. *Isles of Illusion*, according to Fletcher's own recollection, "went into many editions, both in England and the U.S.A., with translations into French, the Scandinavian languages and braille."[5]

It is instructive to note a contemporary English reviewer's opinion of Asterisk's book, for it indicates the ideological context of its reception. The anonymous reviewer for the *Times Literary Supplement* was grudging of praise and high-mindedly moralistic, and wondered if *Isles of Illusion* was a literary hoax. It is only the happy ending that "sustains, what might otherwise be regarded as yet another illusion, the existence of a real person as writer of the letters. The conventional end for the writer was the beach, the hospital, or the asylum." Unimpressed by Asterisk's rebellion, the reviewer draws a stern moral from the book in defense of the civilized norms that Asterisk ("obviously an egoist") flaunts: "at the back of conventions, absurd and hypocritical though they may be in form, there lies the unconsciously acquired wisdom of the race."

The reviewer chides him for his "chilling vanity and self-absorption," and takes particular objection to Asterisk's failure to concern himself with the war that was ravaging Europe. It is as well that Asterisk was marooned, the reviewer dryly suggests, considering his disregard for conventional morality:

> In the island where he is regarded as a God, he is in his way a just God and a benevolent God. He is kind to the childish native girl whom he has taken into his household, and for a time a devoted playmate to their half-caste child. . . . The conclusion of the whole matter may be found in his relations to these two. He, too, is subject to the law of nature against the mixing of kinds that is formulated in the Pentateuch. . . . In the end he cuts loose from island ties as from others. (*Times Literary Supplement*, 28.6.1923)[6]

Times change, and the novelist Penelope Mortimer had only the fondest memories of "Uncle Bertie," as she called her father's brother, despite the knowledge that "He had returned home to find himself erased from the Family Bible." In her autobiography, *About Time*, Mortimer recalls the "air of disgrace" that hung around Fletcher during her childhood:

> for he had not only betrayed his country, keeping his distance in its time of need, but he had betrayed an entire ethic (and, perhaps, himself) by having a liaison with a native woman, siring a number of indeterminately coloured children, and by making the whole unsavoury business public, so that my grandmother could never hold up her head in Deal again. (1979, 81)

Bilbil had multiplied in her imagination: "Perverse of me, perhaps, but these unknown cousins—I always imagined them beautiful, hibiscus in their hair, noble and lithe and the colour of sandalwood—became my favourite contemporary relatives" (ibid.).

*

Fletcher's predicament had been unusual but far from unique.[7] Many others lived the dream of going native, and many wrote passionately about it. One of "the quite decent folk" Fletcher referred to in his characterization of lotus-eaters in Tahiti could have been S. W. Powell, another adventurous Englishman, who published *A South Sea Diary* more than thirty years afterward.[8] Born in London in 1888, Powell traveled and worked in South Africa and Australia as well as Polynesia. He married a Tahitian girl in 1911 and worked a small coconut plantation near Papeete. His diary, which covers little more than a year, is prosaic and pedestrian compared to Fletcher's letters, though his ethnographic observations are astute. Of interest in this context, however, is the "anthropological" transference of identification the author underwent. On the very first page of his diary (begun a year after his arrival in Tahiti), he makes a simple declaration of his switched identification, from "white" to "black." Powell visits Papeete one day and is appalled by the white tourists. He sees his own kind as if for the first time:

I said to myself: Can these people really be of my race? Was I, but a year ago, one of them? I asked Tehiva [his wife] if I resembled them. She said: No, not at all. . . . Now you are quite different—in colour and look and everything, you are more like us. All the same, you are a white man, though not one of these. (1945, 5)

It is this very experience of culture shock in reverse, a variety of Janus-effect, that prompts Powell to keep a diary. For the duration of his idyll he succeeds (as did Fletcher) in being happy with very little amid surroundings of great natural beauty; he also finds the pace and style of Tahitian life conducive to contentment. The lotus-dream is short-lived, alas, for his wife dies of "consumption," aggravated when her canoe capsizes in a squall. The erotic identification of woman with island is then revealed as the very heart of the romantic idyll.

Now that she is gone I cannot stay here. . . . She made this place what it was for me. Without her it is just a dead body—lovely but dead. One cannot live with that. She made all my life for me here; she was the spirit of it. I did not clearly know that before. When I say "this place," I mean not only this little place that was home, but all Tahiti. (1945, 143)

Powell might just as well, of course, have said, "all the South Seas."[9]

"GONE NATIVE"

Since the turn of the century there had been a steady market for colonial fiction in general and for South Sea tales in particular. Much of this literature was pulp fiction, mercifully short-lived. For example, Jack London (born the year before Fletcher)—whose mad, mock-heroic cruise around the South Pacific in the ironically named *Snark* ended in his physical collapse—wrote violently racist stories out of the experience (Sinclair 1977). The romances of Beatrice Grimshaw extolling race pride and race purity are even more typical of the genre. Her heroes (with one exception) "never besmirch themselves" by consorting with native women (Inglis 1974, 13–14). The exception is the planter Hugh Lynch (educated at Harrow and Sandhurst) of *When the Red Gods Call* (1911). This misguided hero commits "the unforgivable sin of folly" by marrying a Papuan girl, but "after much suffering and remorse" he is redeemed by a white woman (Laracy and Laracy 1977, 170). I turn now to Fletcher's contribution to this genre of colonial novel.

Although Robert Fletcher was "extremely annoyed" about having his private life exposed in a book published during his absence, it sold so well that Constable urged him to write a novel. Of this he was to say in 1957, "I blush, even now, when I think of it."[10] *Gone Native: A Tale of the South Seas* appeared in 1924, also under the alias Asterisk. It was the year that Conrad died and also the year that E. M. Forster's *A Passage to India* was published, arguably the best English colonial novel since *Heart of Darkness*. Hastily written though it was, *Gone Native* gave Fletcher scope to romanticize and objectify his experience. Asterisk's life became his fiction. But as a confessional novel, a vehicle for his bruised conscience, it is less compelling than the raw immediacy of his letters. Anthropologists, of course, suffer similar problems of representation. Once returned to the comparative comfort of their own culture, they turn the hotly remembered images of ethnographic experience into coldly ornate texts from which autobiography is methodically expunged.

In Fletcher's case there was an additional mirror effect. Here was an eccentric man reflected in private letters to his friend, an alter ego of similar tastes and temperament, who publishes the letters (not the correspondence, so there is no dialogue with the reflection) under a pseudonym. This disguised author then writes a novel that fictionalizes what was already a distorted mirror-image of himself. The ambiguity of authorship of *Isles of Illusion* is thereby compounded in the novel. In an ironic prefatory page ("To the Wise") Asterisk risks his literary identity by acknowledging that he authored the letters, but promptly distances himself from the self who wrote them: "When I first read *Isles of Illusion* I was amazed at some of the things that I had apparently said even so few years ago" (1924, xi). The opening sentence of the novel also flirts with dual identity: "Her name was not Topsy yet; it was Ouela Kohkon."

Although the novel is so much inferior to the letters (Jamin called it "banal"), Fletcher seems to have been attempting another version of the "writing cure" that had served him as a "nerve balm" in the sick and lonely tropics.[11] Through the devices of fiction he could divide and conquer himself, and finally be healed through a personally redemptive ending. At any rate, deploying this doubly reflexive mode of letters and novel, Fletcher vitalized what was a tired colonial cliche: the doomed union between a civilized white man and a savage black woman. The metaphors of white-man-gone-native and miscegenation (black islands ravished by white invaders) are "natural" images of the tragic imperial process.[12]

Gone Native is explicitly titled, and the subtitle evokes similar titles of Robert Louis Stevenson, Louis Becke, Jack London, Beatrice Grimshaw, and, more recently, James Michener. It is a moral tale, the story of an English planter of educated sensibilities who "marries" a spirited Melanesian girl, has a son ("Monday") by her, and suffers gradual demoralization. The action begins in about 1914. The theme of the novel is marriage, or more precisely, miscegenation, and the cost it exacts when it is held to be "a sin against nature." The tripartite structure of the novel presents three short periods in the protagonists' lives. Part I ("The Woman") recounts the adventures of Ouela Kohkon after she leaves her village husband on Omba to the moment when she marries George Donaldson on Uma (Paama) and is renamed Topsy. The main interest of this part is Ouela's induction into the glamorous life of a stately coconut plantation on Tasiko (Epi). Part II ("The Man") recounts George's attempt to put away Topsy and their child and regain his civilized white status. After testing his fitness for this status by spending a month with a missionary doctor (Angus Macdonald) and his lovely sister (Hilda), George's plan is thwarted by his son's illness, a crisis that evokes in him such compassion for his family that he decides to go native in more thoroughgoing fashion. Part III ("The Conclusion") presents the tragic dénouement, some years later, when Topsy abandons the now demoralized and drunken George, and George sacrifices his own life to save his son's.

*

Like much ephemeral fiction, *Gone Native* has long been out of print. I lack space to examine the story in detail but some critical points are worth making. The narrative is not without its pleasing symmetries and recursions. There is, for instance, the repeated pattern of the heroine's escapes: first from her blind Omba husband and second from a prospective Pentecost husband. On both occasions the escapes are effected by blatant trickery, by sea, and with the connivance of an Omba crew. The pattern is repeated for a third time when Topsy leaves George to return to her beloved island.

At least four types of marriage are depicted in the novel: traditional Omba marriage, European marriage, plantation marriage, and "mixed" marriage, of which there are at least two kinds depending upon whether the mission had given its sanction. All the Omba women in the novel appear to be intent upon hypergamy. If they cannot marry whites, then half-castes will do. Repeatedly, Fletcher depicts Ombans as the superior indigenes of the New Hebrides: more handsome, more noble, more refined. In contrast to Uma men, for instance, who "savagely guard" their womenfolk, Omba men appear to permit whites to mingle and mate with them.[13] One is reminded of the unique status of Trobrianders in colonial Papua as the most beautiful, erotic, and culturally refined people: a noble savage myth which Malinowski endorsed but by no means invented.

The kind of "labour marriage" that Ouela fled Tasiko to avoid was described by Fletcher in *Isles of Illusion*:

> We have a fairly large number of women labourers, and from these the boys are allowed to select a wife to have and to hold during their three years' service. All marriages have to be first sanctioned by the white man in charge, and it is here that the fun comes in. (1923, 58)

After explaining how he marries a shy couple (the ceremony consists of writing their names on a piece of paper), Fletcher denounces the exploitative aspect: "The shameful part is that from the day of the marriage the wretched couple are bound to serve for another three years, quite irrespective of whether their real time is nearly finished or not" (ibid., 59).

*

The central part of the novel explores George's dilemma as a man torn between two irreconcilable ways of life. During the course of a few weeks, George oscillates from one to the other, or rather from a "noxious compromise" (in which he continues to live with his partner Harry, and mates with—but never sleeps alongside—Topsy), to a flirtation with the civilized (in the guise of the lovely white woman at the mission station), and to the final committed state of "gone native." The compromise he had tried to live proved to be insufferable; his half-hearted embrace of the "primitive" as symbolized by his marriage to Topsy was soured by vacillation and pretense.

The child of their union is the means by which he comes to recognize his dilemma, for the child is a half-caste, a marginal being for whom George feels the awakening of a particular horror. His progeny symbolizes the "noxious mix" of civilized and primitive, the "squalid," "sordid" mingling of races. His son will grow into a despised epitome of colonialism. It is this perception that persuades him to rid himself of his family, though later, having responded as a father to the child's need of him, he recognizes his "natural" love of the child (and its mother). He then decides to renounce the dream of civilization, personified by the white woman (whom he does not desire sexually, "naturally"), and commit himself to the lotus-eating life the "primitive" part of him so desires. The new commitment entails sharing a bed with Topsy and Monday, living in reduced means, planting gardens, and—like authentic "natives"—making a little copra when Western commodities are required. Along with civilized comforts he will renounce the exploitation of his fellow men. But a family does not make a society, and George suffers for this decision too.

Let me sketch the third and last part of the novel to give the full flavor of the melodrama. I do so without deliberate parody, but it will be evident that the *mise-en-scène*, the clichés, and the narrative resolutions are now the stuff of magazine stories, B-grade movies, and television soaps.

Four years have passed since George joyfully accepted his destiny as a lotus-eater. A trading vessel anchors reluctantly off George's Uma beach. The supercargo is utterly contemptuous of the white man gone native, for George is now transformed: shabbily clothed, bearded, thin, sickly, and depressed. He goes aboard the ship to buy stores (mainly whisky), and is humiliated by the Scottish supercargo's demand that he "put some decent clothes on" and leave his "native slut and half-caste brat" ashore. A further humiliation awaits him on the ship, for one of the passengers is Macdonald. The missionary speaks to him sympathetically, but on hearing news of Hilda (now in China), George is flooded with remorse at all that he had lost: "his birthright, his manhood, his very soul." Later, Macdonald pieces together the story of George's decline. It was the unaccustomed garden work that had broken his health. His attempt to be self-sufficient and his principled refusal to employ native labor ("the thin end of the capitalist wedge") were his undoing. He became a prey to fevers and the enervation of the climate. Sheer isolation too had demoralized him and driven him to drink.

Left on the beach, a disgruntled Topsy broods about the changes in her man: how once he would have defended her right to board the boat. She suspects he is mad, for he talks to his "devils" each night. Topsy already begins to think of herself as a widow, and goes off to visit Charlie, an Omba man who used to be George's servant. Charlie reminds her of the "call of Omba," and impulsively they decide to steal the Uma men's whaleboat and return to their island. George blunders upon the scene too late, and is confronted by enraged Uma men, grotesquely masked, who blame him for the loss of their boat. George scares them off with his crazed laughter—the irony of Topsy running off with an Omba man (almost as naked as when she had first come to him) seems perversely to delight him.

George returns to his hut to find Monday unconcerned about his mother's departure. George broods about the emerging "half-caste" characteristics of his son, and his growing distaste for him. He visits Père Douceret, the Marist priest, who commiserates with George, but reminds him that he did not take his advice given so long ago. He warns him of the "evil" he senses; they are both uneasily aware of the pounding drums in nearby Uma villages. He tells George, finally, that to put his life in order now there must be redemption: a sacrifice.

Back at his hut George cannot sleep for the infernal heat. His whisky has been stolen by Uma men, and as the drumming booms in the distance, George contemplates the horror of advancing madness and the alternatives of life-long remorse or suicide. The place "reeks" of evil: "And this is Lotos-Land! He laughed aloud as he thought of the fatuity of his young man's dreams" (1924, 294). The drums and "raucous, inhuman yells" conjure for him the image of a cannibal victim clubbed and butchered in an "unholy orgy."

George is awakened by his own scream of terror. In the predawn light he glimpses a leering face in the open window. Then there is a deafening shot. He has been wounded in the shoulder by the musket, and his son is lying inert across his legs. George binds his own wound and injects the child with morphine to dull the pain of a stomach wound. He realizes he has to get him to Burumba, and with an immense effort lifts him aboard his canoe and sets sail for Epi. It is dawn by now and the choppy waters of the strait begin to swamp the canoe.

Attracted by his own trailing blood, sharks appear and begin to circle menacingly. George sights a launch ploughing toward them. It is the doctor!

Rescue is only minutes away, but the canoe is heavy and the sharks are waiting. George lowers his sail, props up his unconscious son more securely in the prow of the canoe, and slips over the side: "And as he left the side and struck out savagely but hopelessly for the onrushing launch, Père Douceret's words sang in his mind like a refrain: 'Salvation . . . sacrifice'" (ibid., 303).[14]

*

"Gone native" is a state of mind, like "gone mad." It is also a degraded social state, which is what George Donaldson cannot come to terms with. Fletcher did not, like his hero, succumb quite so drastically to the lure of the lotus; he escaped, but there was remorse mingled with the relief. On the surface, *Gone Native* is an exploration of the temptations and consequences (some imagined, others lived) of going native; but the author also seems to be expiating his guilt for abandoning his wife and child. The novel is thus a wish fulfillment, a fictional exploration of the alternative fate he had in fact renounced for himself. Fletcher allowed Donaldson the noble and quasi-Christian resolution of self-sacrifice to save his only begotten son, though the salvation is uncertain at the novel's end, and the sacrifice possibly futile. The half-caste son, ambivalently cherished and despised, represents a rather vain hope. Mortally wounded, he might die after all, or be saved—albeit orphaned—by the succoring mission.

George's relationship with Topsy, his child's mother, is no less interesting. Although as an Omba woman she is depicted as a cut above the other Melanesians, she is still moved by atavistic, even animal "instincts." The author denies her mature thoughts and motivations, though he must be given some credit for trying to get inside her head and let her speak for herself in the first part of the novel. But she is a feckless creature of whim: amoral, vain, easily delighted, and just as easily discontented; indeed, she is thoroughly childlike in her wants and in her capacity for amusement and boredom. She is likened to various animals: in a playful, sensual mode she is a kitten, cat, or puppy; in a maternal, breeding mode she is like a cow or mare. Of her seductive hold on George almost nothing is said, for the popular conventions of the day did not permit more than veiled reference to sexuality. So the focus of their relationship is rather blurred and abstract, sentimental rather than sensual. Technically, a saving decorum is executed by the author's device of letters to an alter ego, for it is in these that George is permitted to explore his own relationship to his mistress. His embrace of the "native" life-style is the effective consummation of their "marriage." George seems not to differentiate between the woman and the way of life entailed by loving her: Topsy *is* lotus-eating in the South Seas. She is Topsy to his Turvey, his Melanesia and his Nemesis. But this requires some qualification.

I have suggested that the novel's moral scheme is indicated by the varieties of "marriage" that it depicts. Insofar as it might be said that *Gone*

Native doubles as a domesticated *Heart of Darkness* (George is to Asterisk is to Fletcher, as Kurtz is to Marlow is to Conrad), there are tempting parallels to be made between Topsy and Hilda on the one hand and Kurtz's African mistress and English "Intended" on the other. But the "wild and gorgeous," "savage and superb" African woman who stands silently on the riverbank has little in common with the chirpy and kittenish Topsy who frolics in the sea between her sulks. The two white women, though equally idealized, are also made of different stuff; Kurtz's guileless Intended has to be protected from the awful truth with a "noble lie," whereas Hilda has the islands "in her blood" and daily confronts the horrors of a tropical hospital. The image of Topsy's body is not at all evocative of the unspeakable dark desire that was Africa to Kurtz (and Marlow). Topsy is voluble, girlish, and playful; her very name is toylike. Fletcher, in short, did not inscribe on her body the lineaments of the dark and vicious New Hebrides. She represents, rather, the spirit of the islands as animal amorality or as something innocent won for a while from the darkness.

George Donaldson's name, we should note, is also significant in pointing to a level of covert meaning. He is literally divided, as was his author who was "authored" by John (Bohun) Lynch as Asterisk. Robert Fletcher had studied medicine, and in the novel he projects himself also into the character of Dr. Macdonald. Since both Donaldson and Macdonald mean "son of Donald" we are invited to suspect that the English planter and the Scottish doctor are twin aspects of the same authorial figure.[15] If we regard them as "brothers," it is understandable that George has no physical desire for Hilda, for she would then be his "sister" too. But at a more profound level, Donaldson and Macdonald are one: a divided self, a split character. On this reading, George Donaldson is the "black," primitive self, who takes a native wife and lives in Lotus-Land. This aspect of the composite figure is the id (Fletcher had indeed read some Freud). Macdonald, by contrast, is the "whiter," civilized self, cerebral and celibate, who dedicates his life to curing sick natives and leading them to the "light" (though the emphasis is all on his doctoring, and little is said about his evangelizing). He represents the superego, the part of himself that George (alias Fletcher) fails to cultivate and feels guilt about betraying.

On this reading of a black-white Janus-figure, George's son is also Macdonald's son: the "black" half sacrifices himself to deliver up his son to the "white" half; for if the story is projected beyond its ending, it is implied that the doctor will save the boy's life, nurse him back to health, and adopt him. The irony, of course, is that the son is a half-caste and Janus-figure too, a physical embodiment of the psychic tension of the Double. The son is thus doomed to perpetuate for yet another generation, and in an even more acute form, the divided self of his parent(s).

The analysis can be pushed a stage further. The moral confusion of

George's ménage reflects the moral confusion of the colony; so the double moral scheme of the novel also embraces the colonial situation. The New Hebrides was doubly colonized, and there is a demonstrable split between the permissive French and the puritanical British. George leans to the French side in this (as in truth, Fletcher found the worldly Marists far more congenial than the intolerant Presbyterians). An additional twist here is that George would have had his own son adopted by Père Douceret's adopted "son," the half-caste of Ambrym. Adoption replaces paternity in the novel, and "natural" patrimony is thereby denied. George—or Fletcher—goes even further in suggesting that paternity is an evil in the colonial mixed ménage: his natural son comes to stand for the "sordid mixture" that is the colonial New Hebrides. Although it is not explicit, Fletcher possibly intended a parallel to be drawn between the ménage and the colony: an ineffectual and degenerate white man who fails to be self-sufficient, an increasingly resentful black wife who refuses to be "raised" or learn cultivated ways, and a half-caste child who, despite the father's best efforts, will "follow the mother" and never achieve civilized white status.

So George's anguish also concerns the failure of his civilizing mission. His child, after all, is "illegitimate" and an object of great ambivalence. The Janus-image may then be seen to hover behind the colonial situation of the novel, for the New Hebrides was a condominium of joint Anglo-French rule. There is a third face, of course, in the exploited Kanakas whose lands are stolen and whose bodies and souls are enslaved. At this level, however, the Janus conceit loses definition, and Fletcher introduces necessary complexities in depicting the social composition of the New Hebrides. A dichotomy reappears in Fletcher's classification of the natives, for there are only Omba and the rest. His own racism motivates this opposition, and it is notable that every instance of miscegenation in the novel involves Omba women—as if white men never cohabited with women from other islands. Had he wanted to degrade his hero even further, one supposes, Fletcher would have had George marry an Uma, Epi, Pentecost, or Santo woman. In giving him an Omba girl, it seems, Fletcher thought to allow George some rags of white dignity.

LIKE FATHER, LIKE SON

If Fletcher's chief claim to posthumous fame was the inadvertently fathered *Isles of Illusion*, *Gone Native* was a more deliberate progeny, a remorseful surrogate, perhaps, for the flesh-and-blood son he left behind in the South Seas. So let us revert again from fiction to fact, though the "facts" may seem to be compromised by coincidental fictions. It remains to tell what became of Asterisk/Fletcher and his son Bilbil/Friday (nothing is yet known of the fate of Ouela/Topsy).

When he finally returned to England in the late 'twenties, Fletcher tried to make a living by writing (under his own name) a series of thrillers for the publisher John Murray. They featured a hero called Gilbert Davison and their titles are curiously evocative of Fletcher's self-division: *Half Devil, Half Tiger* (1929), *By Misadventure* (1930a), and *The Missing Doctor* (1930b). (Oddly, too, the first of these was "co-authored" by Fletcher's business partner, Alexander McLachlan, and the last was provisionally entitled *The Missing Partner!*) Although the books went into second or third editions they did not make Fletcher's fortune. Following a number of rejections from Murray he abandoned his literary career and resumed teaching at a prep school in Cornwall.[16] Before retirement he engaged in at least two more business ventures: a photographic studio in Bude, and an Angora rabbit farm in Kent. Neither were successful. Fletcher never married, and during the last decade and a half of his long life he lived with his widowed sister in Deal. A self-confessed lonely and almost friendless man (Lynch had died in 1928, Jacomb in 1960), he amused himself, until his death in 1965, by transcribing books into Braille. Disillusionment had dogged him in England as in the South Seas.

His son's life appears to have followed a more agreeably social and locally successful course. In 1919, two years after the birth of John James Friday (alias Bilbil the Bulbul, for his "neck like a bull calf"), Fletcher had lamented the depopulation of Epi:

> Ten years ago there were seven flourishing native villages within a half mile radius of this house [at Lameru, north Epi]. Today the villages do not exist. The same thing is happening all over the islands. Cheery sort of place to live in, eh? (1923, 262)

The people were being decimated by dysentery and poisoned by high-proof alcohol supplied by land-greedy Frenchmen; the remnants were scattered by their own sorcery feuds. From an estimated five thousand people at the turn of the century, barely a thousand were left by the early 'forties. But in 1986 I found on Epi an island of thriving communities with burgeoning, healthy populations fully in control of their own affairs. The survivors of the colonial era have shrugged off the nightmare, and now live under an independent Vanuatu government, an elective local government council, and a council of chiefs. Decolonized and virtually decustomized, Epi people engage enthusiastically in any number of modernizing associations: village cooperatives, sports clubs, church-based women's and youth groups, to name only the most prominent. Fletcher's Epi, in short, was very different from the one that I found; but it was his son who had witnessed the changes.

Bilbil had been legally adopted in 1919 by a German called Zeitler, who had married a native woman and was a business partner of Tiby Hagen at Ringdove Bay. Zeitler called the boy Jimmy. After reading *Isles of Illusion* and identifying most of the places mentioned in it, I discovered that many people in the area did indeed remember Jimmy Zeitler, though only one or two knew of Robert Fletcher. Elder Yoan Omawa, of Moriu, was one of the few. An itinerant "dresser" who used to perform dentistry and circumcisions, Yoan had also worked for Jimmy for many years. Now well into his sixties, lame and almost blind, Yoan nonetheless guided me to the overgrown ruins of the old plantation house at Lameru where Fletcher had stared at the lonely sea and written his anguished letters. Yoan had once perused a copy of *Isles of Illusion,* and told me he had met, on the wharf in Port Vila in 1945, a bald and bulky Englishman who claimed to be Jimmy's real father. The man had asked about his son, was pleased to hear he was well and sorry he was unable to visit him. According to another source, Jimmy well knew who his real father was, but he did not care to talk about him; he believed that he had been "lucky" to have been adopted by Zeitler, who had made "sacrifices" for his education and upbringing (Stober 1985, 23).

Zeitler had brought up Jimmy at Mapuna (a tiny bay a few miles south of Lameru), where he had started a small coconut plantation in 1922. He had duly sent the boy abroad to be educated, to Norfolk Island and Australia (some say New Caledonia). The old man died about 1928 while Jimmy was at school, but his fees were paid by a Mr. Mitchell of Malekula for whom Jimmy worked after he returned to the islands. He surveyed land, said Yoan, "like his father." Jimmy then married Salome, a woman from southeast Ambrym, and she bore two daughters. After World War II Jimmy returned with his family to Zeitler's abandoned plantation at Mapuna and worked hard to rebuild it; it was, after all, his inheritance. Just as it was coming into production a disastrous hurricane struck, destroying the family house and devastating the crops. This was the notorious hurricane of 1951 which killed over fifty Ambrym people on Epi, hapless refugees from an earlier disaster (Tonkinson 1968). Jimmy replanted coconuts and cocoa, then lived and worked in Malekula until his trees matured. When he returned he planted peanuts and corn and reared pigs and cattle. He acquired a boat, a truck, and a tractor, and during the 'sixties opened branch stores in neighboring villages. His business thrived and he was widely admired—and generally liked.

Yoan worked as his captain, driver, storeman, and bossboy at various times during the late 'fifties and 'sixties. He remembers Jimmy as a large, muscular man; not very tall, but stocky with a prominent belly; another man described him as the biggest man he had ever seen, with thighs as thick as a normal man's waist. Concerning his size, Fletcher had written that "48 solid hours" of parturition had all but killed the teenage mother, but as a "fond father" seven months later he was boasting of Bilbil's 12 kilos and 8 teeth (1923, 194, 231).

Jimmy died in 1972, afflicted by cancer. One of his daughters died in 1979, at the age of twenty-five. The other daughter married an Australian and now lives in Queensland. His widow lives alone in the rambling and ramshackle house at Mapuna; the plantation too is derelict and has scarcely been worked since Jimmy's death. Inside the house there are photographs of the children and grandchildren among the ornaments (but none of Jimmy), while outside the hulk of a whaleboat rots in the unkempt grass. To one side of the house are two solid cement graves of Jimmy and his daughter; Jimmy's monumental black headstone is unmarked.

Since Vanuatu's Independence in 1980, the original landowners of Mapuna plantation have been trying to reclaim the land. For the moment Salome has influence in Vila and will probably be permitted to stay; but when she dies the land will doubtless revert to the customary owners living in nearby Moriu. Ironically, in view of Fletcher's contempt for *métis*, even had Jimmy sired a dozen sons it is likely that his inheritance would have been denied them, for the postcolonial ideological climate of Vanuatu is not favorable to land-owning nonindigenes, or even to those of part ni-Vanuatu descent. A failed dynasty, Fletcher's doubly fathered line on the island of Epi has now ended.

AN ANCESTOR

The Janus-predicament I referred to at the beginning of this essay is a way of interpreting the social and historical situation of the social anthropologist. So far as individual fieldworkers are concerned, however, Janus-like duplicity is more often inadvertent than intentional. After all, a sense of integrity is as important to our personal well-being in the field as it is anywhere else: it is just that much harder to achieve. I find that it helps to use (in Crick's phrase) "working fictions."

My first reading of *Isles of Illusion*—during the midday ennui of Epi's doldrum heat—moved me to reflect upon such matters. I appreciated how my own Janus-predicament superficially resembled Fletcher's: an educated Englishman, often lonely and dispirited, cut off from the identity-confirming mirrors and self-affirming interactions of his own cultural environment.

But there were more obscure affinities at work, currents of attraction for Fletcher which pulled against the repulsion I felt for his tetchy misanthropism. It took me a while to cognize these feelings and hazard a guess about the meaning of the warm intellectual comfort he provided. I could admire him as a brilliant diarist and protoethnographer, and I could empathize with his disenchantment with the tropics and his weariness of their physical discomforts. (Though doubtless he had been more comfortable in his sturdy, mosquito-proofed plantation house on the hill than I was in a one-roomed and windowless bamboo village hut a few miles down the coast.) But our social and historical situations were worlds apart. So much had changed in eighty years, and so much of Epi life was open to me that had been closed to him by virtue of his colonial circumstances. The gravitational pull of our massive Western civilization has, for good or ill, brought all traditional South Pacific cultures into closer alignment. There are no savages any more, no customs that we cannot at least partly understand. Black and white now articulate in a worldwide political economy in ways that would have seemed unthinkable to Fletcher's generation. Racism persists in more or less subtle forms, of course, but the Other is not constituted in such grotesque terms as hitherto. This is partly as a result of anthropology's own efforts to make the exotic familiar by comprehending it (notwithstanding our enduring tendency to exoticize our subjects for professional reasons).

There were other differences. I enjoyed social and moral supports unavailable to Fletcher. After all, anthropological fieldwork is more vocational than plantation management, and to the extent that they go native, anthropologists do so with a sanctioned professional purpose that insulates them from the kind of demoralization suffered by Fletcher. Why, then, did I derive such comfort from reading him, and why did I feel impelled to search for his traces?

My empathy with Fletcher was clearly personal and had much to do with finding myself on Epi. I doubt that I would have read him so avidly had he lived on some other New Hebridean island, however close. This was a clue to my easy identification with him. I felt obscurely that he legitimized me (just as in writing about him I am repaying his posthumous patronage). Chance rather than choice had brought me to Epi, and for a time my morale was sapped by the lack of any sound rationale for my being there rather than on any of a dozen other islands of Vanuatu. I felt like Robinson Crusoe before he met Friday (or Fletcher before he met Topsy and fathered *his* Friday). I struggled to accept this arbitrary trick of fate, and unwittingly recruited Fletcher as a means. Though I could not see Epi through his eyes (we were too far apart in history and in temperament for that), he could help me to adjust to my life there. In short, I adopted him as an ancestor: the only other white man who had suffered thoughtfully on Epi and tried to tell the story of what it was to go native. My discovery of him (in his writing, in his ruined house, and in the memories of those who knew his son) somehow eased the nagging problem of my contingent existence.

Also at issue was my own "search for ceremony" in a new social environment (a phrase I was using to describe Epi people's restless reinvention of their culture). Such was the death rate on Epi during the first half of this century that many lines became extinguished, local migrations were common, and group identities became confused. I found it intellectually disorienting to work with people whose roots were so shallow, tenuous, and tangled, but their pragmatic need to recreate themselves was undeniable. In this fieldwork context I too needed an ancestral charter, a semilegendary figure whose story I could tell. I could then fancy that Fletcher, colonial interloper and failed patriarch though he had been, furnished me with local roots, a putative descent line and a borrowed identity. By imaginatively situating myself thus in relation to him, my sense of contingency was countermanded. Epi became more of a home to me by this act of imagination. Yet my link and anchor line to Fletcher was not unlike Epi people's anchoring claim on their own elusive ancestors.

I cannot expect this "biographic allegory" to be as poignant to others as it is to me. It would therefore be impertinent to draw too many general conclusions from the story I have told about another man's stories about himself. The mirroring of his life in his texts, my mirroring of my fieldwork in his life-as-text, and the mirroring of both in *this* text, intimate an infinity of refracted images—illusory reflections of reflections. But Fletcher's cultivated irony (and the reflexive ironies I have teased from his life-story) do comment indirectly upon the existential predicament of the anthropologist in the field: we live there, as we dream—alone. My story of his story points to our felt need: not only for sexual companionship (not all islands can be eroticized and seduced) but also for the security of precursors, ancestors, father-figures. Like Asterisk's letters, the pages of Malinowski's *Diary* are replete with such fleeting, heroic identifications, remote yet comforting. Each of us must find our own imaginary sustenance and succor while attempting to construe the social landscapes in which we find ourselves, "standing uneasily," as Carrier puts it, "between the Village and the West." The search becomes all the more pressing, it seems, when such simplistic essentialisms are discarded.

My adoption of Fletcher was fortuitous but apt, for some of the tenets of postmodern ethnography are strikingly exemplified by his starred alias: that authorship (representation) is an act of contrivance; that genres can be blurred; that ethnographic realism (insofar as it ever existed) is flawed to the degree that it denies the subjectivity of the observer; that Others' voices should be heard.[17] Fletcher's allegory, in short, speaks to the difficult, compromised birth of miscegenated, textual progeny that follow our anthropological ventures into Melanesian isles of illusion.

EPILOGUE

A final allegory of illusion. "When I was in Vila," wrote Fletcher to his friend in December 1913,

> two enterprising fellows ran up an iron shanty and installed a cinematograph with the idea of astonishing the Kanakas at a dollar a head, and making a fortune. The first night a few natives rolled up and were not in the least impressed. "Something b'long white man," was the contemptuous verdict, and the promoters had to declare themselves bankrupt in a month. My heart rejoiced exceedingly. It is the unemotionalism of the Kanaka that makes me like him. (1923, 99 and 100)

It happened that mine was not the only quest for Asterisk in Vanuatu in 1986. Herbert Brödl, an Austrian filmmaker from Hamburg, had traveled much farther and with more ambition. He too had been captivated by Fletcher's *Isles* and was intent on making a television feature about a quest for its author. He had learned only recently (through correspondence between his partner, Jobst Grapow, and Will Stober) that Fletcher had not, as French legend had it, died young of disenchantment and alcohol in Tahiti, but less romantically, of ennui and old age in Kent. Brödl flew to Epi and visited me in Nikaura. I introduced him to Yoan and Salome in Moriu, and together we made a pilgrimage to the ruined plantation at Lameru Bay. Several months later Brödl brought his team to Vanuatu and made a film.[18]

Inseln der Illusion is a colorful and subtle contrivance, neither documentary nor yet wholly fiction; it is languorously fragmented, with a sad undertow of tropical melancholy. Brödl's star actor, Ulrich Wildgruber, plays himself in search of Asterisk—recapitulating Brödl's own search a few months earlier. He mournfully identifies with Fletcher ("big and bald, with a bit of blonde hair, small eyes—one of which twitched; he always carried an umbrella and sweated profusely"), and other characters (playing themselves or actors' parts in the story) variously confirm or deny this physical resemblance. The travels and recursive local encounters of Wildgruber echo incidents in Fletcher's letters, from which Wildgruber recites apposite snatches in German voice-over. There are brisk sequences depicting modern rural Vanuatu: copra boats, taxi-trucks, and even a gold-prospecting helicopter animate the scenes. Counterpoised are dreamy sequences of village life evocative of a more "primitive" past: kava-drinking, cooking *laplap* in an earth oven, whipping young initiates, and shaping and hauling a wooden slit-gong.

The film's highlights are, for me, its anthropological and biographical ironies. When Wildgruber lands at Norsup airport on Malekula, a bespectacled customs officer examines the contents of his suitcase. She flips through a copy of *Isles of Illusion* and asks, "You're an anthropologist?" "No," he replies. "An actor." A young village boy, Mikael, becomes attached to him (and likewise sifts through his suitcase), and when he suffers a malaria attack Wildgruber keeps vigil by his bedside. Mikael obviously represents Fletcher's son, cherished then abandoned. When the actor finally departs, the boy requests a gift from the suitcase; significantly, he chooses a toy telephone and a photograph. On Epi, lame Elder Yoan conducts Wildgruber to the ruins of Fletcher's house (as several months before he had conducted Brödl and myself). Next morning, Yoan giggles hysterically as he uses his crutch to awaken the kava-drunk actor, asleep on the sand. The crumpled Wildgruber rises, a stupefied beachcomber, and shuffles after Yoan. (Fletcher's George Donaldson in *Gone Native* must have looked like this.) Wildgruber then visits widow Salome and her daughter Madeleine (visiting from Australia) in Jimmy Zeitler's ramshackle house. Yoan borrows a camera to take photographs of them all. As she pours the actor's coffee, Madeleine is scathing about her grandfather. She claims that she knew nothing about him until Will Stober sent her a copy of *Isles of Illusion*. "This man Fletcher! He gave a funny name to his Omba woman, my grandmother—Topsy! What kind of rubbish name is that! And Bilbil, my father, another funny name! So Fletcher is nothing to me." A sad but not unjust repudiation of her ancestry. Then she dismisses him with the most damning irony of all: "He just came here to enjoy himself." (How Fletcher would have loved her for that!) Wildgruber sits at Bilbil/Jimmy's old desk and poignantly intones Fletcher's ambitions for his son seventy years earlier; but then the impecunious Salome asks him for $50 ("for visiting Jimmy's grave"). "I paid willingly," says the actor cheerfully, "and was immediately cured of my sentimentality." Shades of Fletcher indeed.

Like tourism (that peculiarly Western mode of Janus-looking), television induces the dreamy, unreflecting gaze. Insofar as it visually exploits the spectacular exotic, it is tourism by proxy. Such visualism "denies coevalness" (in Fabian's phrase) and partakes of the persistent anthropological delusion that we step out of time when we visit other cultures. I found it richly ironic, then, to observe Epi people watch themselves and other Others on the video shows which began to circulate around the island in 1985. Unlike Fletcher's blasé Kanakas of 1913, they were mightily impressed. Men even curtailed their kava-drinking to view the video machine in the community hall or men's house (as I discovered for myself, one is apt to suffer disorienting optical illusions if one imbibes kava while watching the screen).

But when Brödl's film ultimately reaches the Epi circuit people will see little of themselves, and even less of Fletcher's Janus-life in the wicked colonial era. Unable to understand German, they will also be denied the poetry of his dissidence. What little understanding they achieve will be mediated by images of foreign actors. *Samting blong waetman* yet again. The isle of Epi, it seems, is destined to be confounded by another of the West's clever deceptions and doubly authored illusions.

NOTES

1. I thank the following readers for helpful and encouraging comments on earlier drafts of this essay: James Batley, Elizabeth Brouwer, Michael Jackson, Margaret Jolly, Martha Macintyre, John Morton, Ton Otto, Caroline Ralston, and Will Stober.

2. A striking recent account of an ageing anthropologist's nostalgic return to "his people" (after an absence of thirty years) is Kenneth Read's *Return to the High Valley* (1986).

3. There were obviously a number of puzzles at the heart of the man, too, but in this essay I deal principally with the paradoxes of his literary persona. I am particularly grateful to Mr. Will Stober of Birmingham University, a dedicated scholar of Fletcher, for generously providing me with his unpublished essays and notes on

Fletcher's life and writings. Unless otherwise acknowledged, however, Will Stober is not responsible for the interpretations that appear in the present essay.

4. In Homeric legend the Lotus-eaters (*Lotophagi*) were a people who ate the fruit of the lotos tree. It made them dreamily forgetful of their relatives and friends, and it banished the desire to return home (see *Odyssey* IX).

5. Will Stober (1985, 2) cites this from a letter (dated 5.5.57) Fletcher wrote to his niece, Penelope Mortimer. Fletcher himself, in lonely old age, transcribed his book into Braille, an interesting hobby in view of his acutely visual style. Fletcher was also to claim that Paramount had approached him for the film rights of his book, but since these rested with Lynch (who also received the royalties) the film was never made.

6. Again, I am grateful to Will Stober for bringing to my attention the French commentaries on *Isles of Illusion*. It appears to have been received even more warmly in French intellectual circles than in England, despite the curious fact that some passages (presumably too risque or too Francophobic) were suppressed by the translator. Appearing in 1926, it directly inspired Michel Leiris—the Dadaist, ethnographer, and diarist—while writing his classic *L'Afrique Fantôme* (surely, in 1934, among the very first experiments in reflexive anthropology). In 1957, the noted biographer and bibliographer of the Pacific, Patrick O'Reilly, had proclaimed *Isles of Illusion* to be "le seul ouvrage proprement littéraire inspiré par les Hébrides" (1957, 69). More recently, Leiris encouraged Jean Jamin of the Musée de l'Homme to publish a new translation, which appeared in 1979. For Leiris and Jamin (to cite Stober), "Fletcher is the guilty conscience, or accursed poet, of the social anthropologist who hides behind the elegant structures of his monograph . . . " (1985, 12). Daniel Defert gave this new edition a lengthy review in the *Journal de la Société des Océanistes*, claiming for Fletcher a literary lineage that included Melville, Stevenson, Loti, and Conrad, each of whom had propagated the legend of "a new land of lotus-eaters, an isle of oblivion of the last imperial Odyssey." Fletcher documents the colonial transformation of the self. It is not an exotic, "phantom" Oceania that Fletcher evokes but the island of his interior self. He chronicles the slow shedding of civilized conventions, a process facilitated by colonial "transgressions" and "profanations." The gradual "exoticization" of the self leads him to sensual abandonment in the arms of a native woman. Fletcher, according to Defert, anticipated by fifteen years Gregory Bateson's observations concerning the processes of dual differentiation (schismogenesis) observable between blacks and whites in the colonial relationship, and more generally in the complementary fashioning of the sexual ethos. Fletcher's colonial world is constituted of such pairs, the elements of which mutually fashion one another: French/English; English/Australian; whites/blacks; whites/Melanesians; whites/Polynesians; missionaries/indigenes; missionized indigenes/bush indigenes; Catholics/Presbyterians, etc., etc. "Authenticity" is diluted when each person is defined by his or her "vis-à-vis": for example, the native white and the Christian native are "l'horreur symétrique" to which the innocent, "mythical" primitive is opposed. Defert concludes: "It is true that if the letters revive the atmosphere and a moment of Oceanian history, they above all provide an astonishing archive of colonial subjectivity and of the disturbing process of its constitution" (1981, 131).

7. Statistics concerning mixed marriages in the New Hebrides during this period are unreliable, and it would be even more difficult to estimate the far greater frequency of casual concubinage. The Australian colony of Papua, however, offers a his-

torical comparison (see Inglis 1974, 17–18). Between 1896 and 1924 thirty-seven interracial marriages were recorded, all of them between European men and Papuan women. All of the men were traders, seamen, or miners, that is, of lower-class origin, and they were much older than their wives "who were mostly young girls." Without giving figures, Inglis adds that "many of these marriages were impermanent," and "if children resulted from the marriages, they must have taken Papuan names and disappeared into the Papuan communities of their mothers." The 1921 census of Papua recorded a half-caste population of 91 males and 67 females, but those who lived with their mothers in the villages were not counted. More realistically, the Annual Report for 1915–16 gave the figure 341 (of whom 231 were children), as the total number of half-castes in Papua.

8. Published by Penguin Books in 1945, it is quite possible that Fletcher read Powell's book, though less likely that he ever met him.

9. The ambivalent, eroticized landscapes of Malinowski's *Diary* have been remarked by Harry Payne (1981, 431–433); see also my epigraph from Michel Tournier.

10. Cited by Stober (1983, 1) quoting a letter from Fletcher to Mortimer dated 9.5.57. He added, "My only plea . . . is that I did not want to write it at all, Constable pestered me and poverty urged."

11. James Clifford (1986) has claimed that both Conrad and Malinowski administered their own "writing cures" (Mark Kanzer [1951] earlier made a similar claim for Stevenson). There are further parallels with Fletcher, triangulating what Clifford has demonstrated to be "general, thematic and structural parallels" between *Heart of Darkness* and Malinowski's *Diary*:

> Both books are records of white *men* at the frontier, at points of danger and disintegration. In both sexuality is at issue: both portray an other that is conventionally feminized, at once a danger and a temptation. Feminine figures in the two texts fall into either spiritual (soft) or sensual (hard) categories. There is a common thematization of the pull of desire, or excess, barely checked by some crucial restraint. (Clifford 1986, 153)

All of this may be said of *Isles of Illusion* and *Gone Native*, though Fletcher takes the "thematization" a stage further, so to speak, by succumbing to desire and finding himself unable to live with the consequences. There is no analogue to the problem of half-caste progeny in these works of Conrad and Malinowski.

12. See Abena Busia on sexuality in the colonial novel: "Sex becomes deeply symbolic, with miscegenation the bête noire of a deep, dark colonial nightmare always threatening to raise not so much her head, as her tail" (1986, 363). Miscegenation is therefore treated as a transgression: "The combination of the two factors of sex and race serves to make miscegenation the ultimate taboo, abrogating to itself the suggestion of taintedness or evil" (1986, 366).

13. In 1913 the German ethnographer Felix Speiser wrote the following about Aoba (Omba) women:

> The position of the women, so much better here than elsewhere, is not without effect on their behaviour. They are independent and self-possessed, and do not run away from the stranger nor hide in dark corners when a white man wants to speak to them. Because of their intelligence they are liked on plantations as house-servants, and so many of them have gone away for this purpose that Aoba has been considerably depopulated in consequence; few of these women ever return, and those who do are usually sick. Some Aoba

women have made very good wives for white men. . . . The women are very pretty, slim and strong; their faces often have quite a refined outline, a pointed chin, a small mouth and full but well-cut lips; their eyes are beautiful, with a soft and sensual expression; and the rhythm of their movements, their light and supple walk, give them a charm hardly ever to be found in Europe. The men, too, are good to look at. Considering the intelligence and thriftiness of the race, it is doubly regrettable that alcoholism, recruiting and consumption have had such evil effects of recent years. (1913, 242–243)

14. In "The Heathen," one of Jack London's less objectionable *South Sea Tales* (published in 1911), a Tahitian man sacrifices himself to the sharks to save his white companion when their boat capsizes. It is conceivable that Fletcher had read the story.

15. As well as its intimation of the doppelganger, the name Macdonald is perhaps another of Fletcher's identity-switching jokes. The Reverend Daniel Macdonald was the first Presbyterian missionary to live on Efate (between 1872 and 1907), and Alexander Macdonald was an Australian who had also written "A Tale of the South Seas" about the New Hebrides (1909). Fletcher's penchant for Scottish names was owing, no doubt, to the fact that all four of his grandparents were Scots.

16. Fletcher told Mortimer that he had written another South Seas novel (of which he was "really proud") about "a little Kanaka tart" who worked in a brothel in Noumea. Constable considered it too risqué to publish (Stober 1985, 22).

17. Concerning the last of these, the Appendix to *Isles of Illusion* is a ten-page sketch or one-act play called "On the Beach," which Asterisk based on the sworn declaration of a witness to a near-lethal quarrel that took place in Paama. He intended it as farce or parody, but it is historically remarkable as the first extensive published record of dialogue in Bislama ("Biche-la-mar"), now the national language of Vanuatu. We must remember, of course, that it was written primarily to amuse Bohun Lynch, and that it was he who had the acumen to publish it.

18. Brödl's 99-minute film, for which Jobst Grapow wrote the script, takes its title directly from the book: *Inseln der Illusion: Briefe aus der Südsee.* I am most grateful to Will Stober (once again) for sending me a copy in late 1988, several months after I wrote this essay.

REFERENCES

"Asterisk." 1923. *Isles of Illusion: Letters from the South Seas.* Edited by Bohun Lynch. London: Constable & Co. (Reprinted in 1986 by Century Classics, Hutchinson, with an Introduction by Gavin Young.)

———. 1924. *Gone Native: A Tale of the South Seas.* London: Constable & Co.

———. 1926. *Lettres des Îles-Paradis.* (Translation by Marthe Coblentz.) Paris: F. Rieder.

———. 1979. *Îles-Paradis, Îles d'Illusion: Lettres des Mers du Sud.* (Translation by Nicole Tisserand; Preface by Jean Jamin.) Paris: Le Sycomore.

Busia, Abena. P. A. 1986. "Miscegenation as Metonymy: Sexuality and Power in the Colonial Novel." *Ethnic and Racial Studies* 9:360–372.

Clifford, James. 1986. "On Ethnographic Self-Fashioning: Conrad and Malinowski." Pp. 140–162 in T. C. Heller, M. Sosna, and D. E. Wellbery (eds.), *Reconstructing Individualism.* Stanford: Stanford University Press.

Conrad, Joseph. 1973 (1902). *Heart of Darkness*. Harmondsworth: Penguin.

Crick, Malcolm. 1989. "Shifting Identities in the Research Process: An Essay in Personal Anthropology." Pp. 24–40 in John Perry (ed.), *Doing Fieldwork: Eight Personal Accounts of Social Research*. Geelong: Deakin University Press.

Defert, Daniel. 1981. Review of *Îles-Paradis, Îles d'Illusion*. *Journal de la Société des Océanistes*, 70–71:129–131.

Fletcher, Robert J. 1930a. *By Misadventure*. London: John Murray.

———. 1930b. *The Missing Doctor*. London: John Murray.

Fletcher, Robert J., and Alexander McLachlan. 1929. *Half Devil, Half Tiger*. London: John Murray.

Grimshaw, Beatrice. 1911. *When the Red Gods Call*. London: Mills & Boon.

Inglis, Amirah. 1974. *"Not a White Woman Safe": Sexual Anxiety and Politics in Port Moresby 1920–1934*. Canberra: Australian National University Press.

Jackson, Michael. 1989. *Paths towards a Clearing: Radical Empiricism and Ethnographic Enquiry*. Bloomington: Indiana University Press.

Jacomb, Edward. 1919. *The Future of the Kanaka*. London: P. S. King & Son.

Kanzer, Mark. 1951. "The Self-Analytic Literature of Robert Louis Stevenson." Pp. 425–435 in George B. Wilbur and Warner Muensterberger (eds.), *Psychoanalysis and Culture*. New York: John Wiley & Sons.

Keesing, Roger. 1988. "Colonial Discourse and Codes of Discrimination in the Pacific." TS.

Laracy, Hugh, and Eugenie Laracy. 1977. "Beatrice Grimshaw: Pride and Prejudice in Papua." *The Journal of Pacific History* 12:154–175.

London, Jack. 1911. *South Sea Tales*. New York: Macmillan.

Macdonald, Alexander. 1909. *The Island Traders: A Tale of the South Seas*. London: Blackie and Son.

Malinowski, Bronislaw. 1967. *A Diary in the Strict Sense of the Term*. London: Routledge.

Mortimer, Penelope. 1979. *About Time*. London: Allen Lane.

O'Reilly, Patrick. 1957. *Hébridais: Répertoire Bio-Bibliographique des Nouvelles-Hébrides*. Paris: Musée de l'Homme.

Payne, Harry C. 1981. "Malinowski's Style." *Proceedings of the American Philosophical Society* 125:416–440.

Powell, S. W. 1945. *A South Sea Diary*. Harmondsworth: Penguin.

Read, Kenneth E. 1986. *Return to the High Valley: Coming Full Circle*. Berkeley, Los Angeles, London: University of California Press.

Sinclair, Andrew. 1977. *Jack: A Biography of Jack London*. New York: Harper & Row.

Speiser, Felix. 1913. *Two Years with the Natives in the Western Pacific*. London: Mills & Boon.

Stober, Will. 1983. "A Note on R. J. Fletcher's Novel 'Gone Native'" (1924). TS.

———. 1985. Draft introduction to *Isles of Illusion*. TS.

Thornton, Robert J. 1985. "'Imagine Yourself Set Down . . .' Mach, Frazer, Conrad, Malinowski and the Role of Imagination in Ethnography." *Anthropology Today* 1(5):7–14.

Times Literary Supplement. London.

Tonkinson, Robert. 1968. *Maat Village, Efate: A Relocated Community in the New Hebrides*. Eugene: University of Oregon Press.

Tournier, Michel. 1974. *Friday or The Other Island*. Harmondsworth: Penguin.

Epilogue

Roger Keesing and Margaret Jolly

INTRODUCTION

James Carrier's Introduction and the papers of this volume aptly characterize the lens through which anthropologists have seen and portrayed the Melanesian communities where they have done fieldwork. Of course, the critiques apply in different degrees to the work of individual anthropologists: they characterize a discursive mode, a conceptual framework we inherited from the pioneers of Melanesian anthropology and we have, in varying ways, perpetuated and modified.

It would serve no useful purpose to recapitulate the arguments so strongly made in the Introduction and the papers that follow. We believe the ultimate implications of these critiques to be positive, not negative. There is a different Melanesia to be seen, explored, characterized; and anthropology is beginning to develop modes of representation that can serve us well in responding to this challenge. We will focus on these alternative modes of perceiving and representing Melanesian social life and experience.

In these new modes, the position of the observer is highlighted, questioned, bracketed with epistemological doubt and reflexivity. We urge not a narcissistic concern with our own experiences in fieldwork, or a fetishization of ethnography as the quintessence of anthropology; but rather, self-conscious reflection on the processes, and the politics, of representation in Melanesian anthropology.

In contemporary Papua New Guinea, Solomon Islands, Vanuatu, Fiji, and New Caledonia, the position of the observer is politically situated, too, in relation to questions of sovereignty, cultural nationalism, and indigenization. Contemporary Pacific Islanders view anthropology in the light of the historical association of our project with colonial power, and with representations of their cultures as primitive or exotic. We see problems not only in the ways we perceive and represent contemporary Melanesian communities, but in our *being there*, and our very project of representing the Melanesian Other.

An important first question is scarcely raised in these essays. The category "Melanesia," the culture-area on which we focus, is itself at issue. In the light of the accumulating evidence of linguistics and prehistory, a distinction originally drawn on lines of "race" is now deeply problematic (see Jolly n.d.*b*; Thomas 1989). "Melanesian" lumps together speakers of Papuan languages[1] and speakers of Oceanic Austronesian languages, and separates the latter from their close linguistic relatives in "Polynesia" and "Micronesia."[2]

We do not claim privileged status for genetic connections between languages as defining appropriate anthropological categories. Rather, our concern is with the self-perpetuating and self-reinforcing character of our construction of "Melanesia" in discourse. We have typified Melanesia in terms of big men, pigs, and shells: the centrality of exchange, the personalistic and decentralized character of politics, and extreme sociolinguistic diversity. Yet our typifications reflect our expectations and representational modes as well as our data. The "Melanesia" we have created is hermetic and timeless. Viewed in the *longue durée* of the prehistorian and the shorter spans of the historian, these islands have been characterized by regional trade systems, apparent widespread political hierarchy, and pervasive warfare.[3] Localized exchange systems and big men seem in many areas to have been a product of political devolution in the centuries preceding European invasion, a process greatly accelerated by European intrusion and pacification. The sociopolitical organization and religious systems of the Solomons, Vanuatu, New Caledonia, and Fiji as documented at the onset of the colonial period show striking cultural as well as linguistic connections to those of peoples to the east and north,[4] in contrast to those of peoples to the west with which we have traditionally classified them. Yet "Melanesia" as category endures, seemingly impervious to the tides of evidence that erode its foundations.

We turn now to the fundamental problems of representation raised by Carrier in his Introduction and by the essays in the volume.

RECONCEPTUALIZING ANTHROPOLOGY'S PROBLEMATIC

A first needed step, we believe, is to broaden and transform conceptions of anthropology's scope and problematic, beyond the representation of exotic Otherness. The established anthropological quest for alterity has been heightened by some recent developments in popular and intellectual culture.

One, deriving from popular culture, is a depiction of "primitive" peoples as wise ecologists, holistic healers, or mystical spiritualists. Native Americans, Aboriginal Australians, the mythical Tasaday, and African "pygmies" and "Bushmen" have all been candidates. Anthropologists have had an ambivalent relationship with popular idealizations of the "primitive," but in the public eye these have at least validated anthropology's long engagement with exoticism and difference.

Second, in the heady intellectual climate of critical theory, postmodernism, poststructuralism, feminism, and cultural Marxism, a concern with radical alterity has become highly fashionable in the last fifteen years. Huyssen (1986, 185), assessing postmodernism in the arts, writes of "this nostalgia for the past, the often frenzied and exploitative search for usable traditions, and the growing fascination with pre-modern and primitive cultures."[5] The currently fashionable anthropological stress (especially in North America) on cultural symbols and the cultural construction of reality—concepts of the person, agency, causality, the emotions—give a renewed impetus to anthropology's long commitment to characterizing radical Otherness (see Keesing 1989*a*, n.d.*c*; Marcus and Fischer 1986).

Here a major qualification is in order. In many, perhaps most, North American anthropology departments, and in much of Europe, the view of anthropology as primarily the study of "traditional" societies, particularly tribal ones, has long since been left behind.[6] Radical political questioning, limited fieldwork funding and access, and the demands of the marketplace in a generation where few academic jobs have been available have exerted a very strong pressure to bring anthropology "back home" to the contemporary First World,[7] and to characterize the Third World not in terms of residual tribalism, but of development, urbanization, and neocolonialism. Medical anthropology and diverse forms of applied anthropology have flourished, and in many places a concern with ritual, exchange, or kinship has become a nostalgic anthropological memory rather than a flourishing practice.

The anthropology of Melanesia is in crisis, then, not because anthropology is everywhere conservative in questing for the vanishing primitive and residual traditionalism, but because New Guinea and nearby islands are imagined as places where peoples practicing their ancestral cultures can still be found. Even in anthropology departments and professional communities where classic ethnographic problems are no longer predominant concerns, studying the culturally exotic may still have a strong mystique, and be regarded as the "real" anthropology most scholars can no longer do. Hence, in the last twenty years anthropological research in Melanesia has been subject to an intense selective process. Students and established researchers seeking to study ritual, kinship, exchange, myth, or, nowadays, gender relations— who may be a small minority in their home anthropological milieux—turn toward New Guinea, the Solomons, or Vanuatu as the last frontiers where anthropology's classic problems can still be pursued. Having come thousands of miles to find rituals or exchange, and finding coffee gardens, wage labor, Toyota trucks, and South Pacific Lager, the researcher may change the focus of research and write about the encountered present rather than the anticipated one. But we ethnographers have had an extraordinary capacity to find what we came to find, whatever tricks of vision and representation this has required.

Our quest for the culturally exotic and authentic not only leads us to filter out exogenous elements but of course guides us in our choice of fieldwork sites and problems. As ethnographers who have gone to the most strikingly traditionalist enclaves in Vanuatu and Solomon Islands, the authors are in no position to moralize. Both of us were drawn to remote regions in island Melanesia, partly because of the romance of working with people seemingly little "touched" by colonization and Christianity. Our initial ethnographic accounts highlighted the seemingly traditional and culturally pristine. In the last decade, each of us has been led not only to examine questions of process, politics, and transformation, but also to reassess what had seemed enduring and pristine. As A. Carrier and J. Carrier (1987) and Thomas (this volume) emphasize, what looks most culturally conservative and traditional in a hinterland community may represent a reaction to colonial domination, not historical insulation from outside influences.

Anthropology's core concepts abet us in finding what we came to find. The concepts of "society" and "culture" as bounded, self-contained, internally coherent, and self-reproducing universes of structure and meaning focus our vision on closure and stasis (see Keesing n.d.c). If we take a more processual, dynamic view of how human populations create order and meaning, a view that focuses on internal contradictions and cleavages as well as on coherence and consensus, and on the production and reproduction of symbols, then the engagement of contemporary Melanesians with capitalism, the world system, postcolonial states, and Christianity poses anthropological questions and problems no less important than those of the past (a point well developed by Barker, this volume).[8] A false antithesis between the stasis and coherence of precolonial societies and the complexities, changes, contradiction, and bricolage[9] we encounter in contemporary Melanesia can be laid to rest. As Marcus and Fischer observe (1986, 78), complexity, change, and adaptation to external constraint are the "normal" human condition, not a recent transformation.

> Most local cultures worldwide are products of a history of appropriations, resistances, and accommodations. The [present] task . . . is . . . to revise ethnographic description away from [a] self-contained, homogeneous, and largely ahistorical framing of the cultural unit toward a view of cultural situations as *always* in flux, in a perpetual historically sensitive state of resistance and accommodation to broader processes of influence that are as much inside as outside the local context.

Such a reorientation at the level of theory and concept, as well as practice, is needed if Melanesia as land of the vanishing primitive is to lose its mystique, and if the phenomena of the present and the historical transformations of the colonial past are to be given adequate representation.

THE CONSTRAINTS OF ETHNOGRAPHIC NARRATIVE

We have "seen" in the field not only what we came to find, but what we have been taught to regard as important and anthropologically salient. Most of us have filtered out as extraneous, inauthentic, or uninteresting other elements in the lives of those we have studied. Yet there is more to it than that. We have been neither blind nor stupid. Many of the constraints on our representations come from a discursive tradition of how ethnographies are written, and what is supposed to be in them. A tradition of ethnographic writing going back to Malinowski (and with much older roots in travelers' accounts; see Pratt 1986) which Marcus and Cushman (1982) characterize as "ethnographic realism" has guided and channeled us in our representations of the communities where we have worked.

We prefer the alternative term "ethnographic narrative" to refer to the discursive conventions and narrative strategies used in conventional ethnographic monographs.[10] To characterize ethnographic narrative as a representational genre is not to imply any *theoretical* uniformity of ethnographies. While recognizing considerable diversity in individual style, we see an underlying uniformity in narrative strategy running across dozens of well-known ethnographic accounts of Melanesia.

The authority of the ethnographer is first validated, by a characterization of fieldwork that establishes prolonged and sustained immersion in the social life of the community and intimate firsthand knowledge of local language and custom.[11] The substantive account characteristically begins by describing the geography, the linguistic and cultural affinities, and the history (since European contact) of the people under study. The fieldwork community is then described. The narrative move that characteristically follows, and is a foundation of ethnographic narrative, abstracts from the particularities of this community in time and space: the community is taken as microcosm of (and representationally transformed into) "a society." Its inhabitants then represent not themselves, but roles, positions within social structures.[12] Moreover, the individuals are placed outside of present time, a narrative device characterized by Fabian (1983) as "the denial of coevalness." The classic ethnographic monograph not only abstracts individuals into typifications but renders them as representations of their ancestors, living in the ethnographic present. The Melanesians of our monographs live not in the Papua New Guinea or Vanuatu of 1976 or 1985 but in a timeless world of "culture" (see Carrier's and Jolly's critiques of Weiner, this volume).

If they are disengaged from historical time, they can be disengaged from the postcolonial state, the plantation economy, and the world system: the village as microcosm of "a society" can be bounded. This allows a further narratological sleight of hand, an editing out of intrusive elements: trade stores, village schools, politicians, transistor radios, trucks, and coffee beans. We are reminded of the way Edward Curtis, in his classic photographs of American Indians as a "vanishing race" (Lyman 1982), air-brushed intrusive elements—clocks, frying pans, suspenders—from the negatives.[13]

Time, change, and the outside world appear in the first chapter or the introduction; they then recede into the shadow. And so, too, does the ethnographer. The confusions and doubts, moral, political, and existential dilemmas of the fieldwork encounter are touched on only in an obligatory introduction—usually one that establishes that by the end of fieldwork, despite the inevitable initial tribulations, the observer had been culturally and linguistically calibrated into a reliable instrument. The authorial eye and I of the ethnographer, as humanly engaged, are carefully edited out.[14]

These narrative conventions and the genre they sustain have been remarkably resilient and self-perpetuating, considering how dramatically the settings for our work have changed since the days of Malinowski, Fortune, and Mead. There are some elements of initiatory ritual in this perpetuation of a genre: fledgling ethnographers undergo their initiatory tribulations, then emerge from the field to demonstrate that they have learned the secrets of the profession—most centrally, how to write an ethnography. Here Michael Young's insightful reflections on Asterisk and the ethnographer come further to mind: "Once returned to the comparative comfort of [her] own culture, [the anthropologist] turns the hotly remembered images of ethnographic experience into coldly ornate texts from which autobiography is methodically expunged" (this volume).

How, then, do we get individuals, time, outside forces, and *ourselves*, back into the picture? How do we transcend the limits of conventional ethnographic narrative without succumbing to narcissism? In what follows, we will examine several alternative ways of representing the individuals whose lives we have shared, the communities within which we have worked, and the wider systems that impinge on them which transcend the limits of conventional ethnographic accounts. These genres include self-accounts, anthropological history, and postmodernist montage, all of which can potentially combat our tendency to essentialize and eternalize the other.

SELF ACCOUNTS

One genre that holds promise as an alternative to conventional ethnographic narrative and its abstracting of lives into roles and structures (Young's "coldly ornate texts") is the "anthropological autobiography," or "life-history." For Melanesia, we have as exemplars Andrew Strathern's rendering of Ongka's self-account (1979), Keesing's of 'Elota (1978), and a handful more.

Self-accounts lie at the heart of Young's study of Kalauna myth and self-realization (Young 1983*a*); and fragments of women's self-accounts have been published by Young (1983*b*), Keesing (1985, 1987, 1989*b*) and others.

Such self-accounts can revealingly complement other ethnographic descriptions, and can effectively individualize lives and personalities and convey a sense of motive, experience, and emotion too often filtered out. Through the prism of one life, they can convey a sense of collective change and history. But in highlighting the promise of self-accounts, some caveats are in order about the "selves" that are accounted.

First of all, the self-accounts must be very carefully, reflexively, and analytically contextualized. What is presented as a self-account is effectively interpretable only in terms of the historical, political, and interpersonal context in which it was recorded. Keesing's account (1985) of why and how Kwaio women finally spoke as freely, forcefully, and rhetorically as they did underlines the urgency of probing both the micropolitical and the broader historical contexts in which our subjects talk about themselves. Young found Kalauna women reluctant to talk about themselves, as Kwaio women had been at first; Kwahihi's long account was recorded in Young's absence, in the company of her male kin. Such contexts of telling are crucial. The pseudo objectivity and depersonalization of the standard ethnographic monograph can too easily carry over into self-accounts, if they are presented as if subjects were speaking for and by themselves.

Second, as Keesing (1985) and Young (1983*b*) further warn, what are presented as self-accounts or autobiographical narratives may have been construed in quite different terms by the individuals whose lives we recount on their behalves. That is, the genre of autobiography as self-explication rests heavily on our own notions of individuation, motive, and agency, and on a tradition of folk psychology (and genre of published autobiography) that inevitably colors self-explication. The Kwaio women from whom Keesing and Shelley Schreiner recorded accounts perceived their task as primarily to chronicle customs relating to women (particularly pollution taboos) and women's virtues, using events of their own lives as moral texts. Similarly Kwahihi (Young 1983*b*) uses her life as an exemplary moral tale of service to men, one in which she portrays herself as acted upon more than acting. To construct "autobiographical" narratives from such texts introduces considerable cultural distortion.

This then leads to questions of narrative convention. The relationship between conversations with an ethnographer as they actually unfolded and the narrative conventions with which we edit, organize, and present them is fraught with difficulty. It is almost irresistibly tempting to the ethnographer as editor/agent/author to structure self-accounts according to Western logics of time, sequence, and causality, and to impose on them our own narrative conventions (see, e.g., Shostak 1981). Moreover, if we do not do so, they

become less comprehensible and interesting to the great majority of readers
than they otherwise would be. Young (1983*b*, 479) suggests that Kwahihi's
text is too prolix, too opaque, to be interpretable without the accompanying
exegesis of the ethnographer. If we are faithful to Kwaio, Hagen, or Kalauna
cultural logic and narratology, who will read and understand the texts? Who
will buy the book? How literally do we translate a local language, and with
how much explication?

Keesing and Schreiner are presently wrestling with these problems in
translating and editing the rich texts elicited from Fa'afataa, a Kwaio pagan
woman who is a powerful ideologue and gifted raconteuse. Is Fa'afataa's
account to speak to Western feminists? To urban Solomon Islands women?
To the lay public? To anthropology students? To purists wanting to analyze
Kwaio logic and narrative conventions? How submerged or explicit should
our authorial voice and role be? Should the verbatim texts be published, as
well as the edited version—and if so, in what language? Do we begin, as she
did, by rhetorically pronouncing on women's virtues (which immediately
and probably appropriately distances her account from the Western genre of
autobiography) or do we begin with "I was born in . . . "? The very disjuncture of "Do we begin?" and "she began" highlights the problem of authorial
voice here, and the critical role of the editor/interpreter in imposing narrative
structure.

It may be no accident that in contemporary Melanesia men's self-
accounts can be constructed more easily and directly into the genre of autobiography than women's. Both the character of men's political activities and
their greater mobility in traveling beyond village communities may facilitate
their construing their lives and cultural traditions from an external point of
view, and attributing agency and significance to themselves (see Young
1983*b*, 483). Diane Johnson's superb account of women in the higher eche-
lons of the Papua New Guinea public service (1984), much of it based on
autobiographical materials, underlines the importance of life experience,
mobility, and political position—rather than "gender" as an essential
quality—in shaping self-perceptions and self-accounts.

This then raises further important questions. Who do we choose as
appropriate subjects to recount their lives? Ongka and 'Elota were longtime
friends and allies of the ethnographers who edited their self-accounts; it is no
accident that both were men, and both were prominent leaders. Even a be-
lated corrective ethnographic focus on women's lives, where it catalyzes an
engagement with women as subjects, agents, and narrators of self-accounts,
leaves us with nagging questions of selective perception. The assumptions
about "tradition," "authenticity," and the proper concerns of ethnography
that have led us to work in the most culturally conservative communities we
can find, and depict them in the most culturally traditional ways we can
manage, implicitly guide our choices of subjects. It is not the headmen of the

colonial state, or contemporary politicians or entrepreneurs, whose life-histories we have chosen to record (see Keesing, this volume), but feast-giving big men.[15] Where we do focus on women's lives, whether as ethnographic or autobiographical subjects, there is a danger—as Jolly (this volume) warns—of locking women into a timeless realm of culture (and effectively denying *them* coevalness) even if we accord our male subjects a place in the postcolonial state and capitalist economy.

This leads us to the urgency of historical perspectives, and to another set of alternatives to the conventional ethnographic monograph.

WRITING ANTHROPOLOGICAL HISTORY

A conventional ethnography often begins with a chapter that sets out in a few pages the history of the "society" whose culture is explicated in the chapters that follow. This chapter describes early contacts, missionization, incorporation into the periphery of a colonial state. Having done with history, and situated the community to be described in time and in space, "culture" and "society" can be analyzed in a discursive mode minimizing extraneous elements and change. (Douglas [this volume] points out the irony that accounts by Pacific historians use a mirror-image narrative convention of having a first chapter on the "culture" before plunging into "history.")

Anthropologists are now taking history more seriously. Increasingly, we place the peoples we have encountered in, not outside of, time. This helps us transcend the flat time perspectives we so often have taken vis-à-vis Melanesian communities. But again, we feel some cautions are in order.

First, (some) historians are now critically reconsidering their conventional discursive practices, just as anthropologists are. History as a discipline is in ferment. Anthropologists, however sophisticated in regard to the frontier issues of their own discipline, may enter a neighboring territory with insufficient appreciation of how slippery and contested the ground now is. Anthropologists doing history have in many instances been insufficiently trained and experienced, and therefore insufficiently cautious or zealous, in their excavation and interpretation of archival sources—for the same reasons that historians doing ethnography may have inadequately interpreted local languages, marriage systems, exchange, or politics. If it were not so, this would reflect ill on the disciplines in which scholars' primary training lies. The problem of an inadequate grasp of the theoretical and epistemological debates on the frontier of a neighboring discipline is deeper and more serious.

Keesing, in an ethnohistorical paper, used the unfortunately chosen phrase "what actually happened" (Keesing 1986, 269) in referring to an event a hundred years earlier.[16] Theoretically minded historians would tend to view all historical accounts, and indeed all contemporary reportage of "events," as perspectival, constructed, interpreted, a position well explicated by Douglas (this volume) and by Dening (1988).

In contemporary theoretical debates, the bracketing is becoming more radical (see Neumann, n.d.). As the work of Foucault and Guha makes inescapably clear, issues of representation cannot be separated from issues of power and interest. Nicholas Thomas's interpretation of a Fijian politico-religious movement in the early part of this century (n.d.*a*) highlights the newer concerns. Noting the "interested contrivance of representation" both in contemporary British accounts of the movement and his own counter-account, Thomas reflects on both

> the "distortions" of various perceptions of [the] movement and the constituted character of my own analysis. The claim behind this denial of any history outside recontextualization is not the relativist proposition that "we have different histories for different occasions" (Dening 1988, 99) but that both the hands of others and one's own hand ought to be disclosed. The cultural differences between different narratives emerge from political situations, from interests in particular constructions of the past. What confronts us is not merely a plurality of accounts, but a contested field. I do not put forward another history merely to add to those already in circulation, or to succeed those which have been forgotten, but to intervene in debate about the Fijian past. I would not write if I did not have an argument.

Seeing the anthropologist or historian as politically implicated in representing the past in relation to the present illuminates contemporary scholarly debate with regard to Fijian and Tongan history. The past is contested ground because of the uses made of it in the present.[17] Here we must see ourselves—as Foucault (1973, 1977) would have us do—as historically empowered to represent the past for the present; attacks on our representations by indigenous historians constitute challenges to this hegemonic position, as well as scholarly debates.

The anthropologist as historian may "culturalize" the past, invoking a unitary, coherent conception of "culture" that itself hides contradiction, contestation, and subaltern interest and perspectives. As Thomas (n.d.*a*) comments, "anthropology can domesticate history by establishing that events are incorporated into a cultural order . . . while neglecting the politically fractured and contested character of culture." Conceptions of "structure" and culture that essentialize enduring qualities are dangerous in this regard, as critics of Sahlins's interpretations of Pacific history, pre- and post-European (1985), and Geertz's interpretations of Bali as "theater state" (1980) have noted. Hegemonic ideologies are too easily taken as "culture."

An alternative approach to "culture" and "meaning" takes the production and reproduction of symbolic systems as political processes, examines the hegemonic force of cultural symbols, and seeks counter-hegemonic ideologies, subaltern representations, and contestation. Guha's accounts of Indian subalternity, and recent writings of feminist historians, illuminate further issues regarding what is hidden in conventional historical accounts and in archival sources. The problem is not so much a reading of texts (though as Douglas shows, that is problem enough) but a hearing *through* texts of silent voices, and an exploration of submerged perspectives, lives, worlds of experience, and acts.

Jolly, in her present work on the colonial history of Vanuatu, is seeking to recover the silent voices of indigenous women, doubly muted by the European and masculinist character of most documentary sources. There is polyphony of voices talking *about* ni-Vanuatu women—navigators, travelers, labor recruiters, missionaries, and colonial officials. This is not surprising: observing the debasement of ni-Vanuatu women and improving it was central to the colonial project. And as Guha (1987, 1989) stresses, a critical reading of such sources yields fascinating insights into colonialism and colonial discourse. Excesses or lacunae internal to texts, disjunctions between texts, and the contexts of texts can reveal much about the experience of subalterns—those who lack the historical voice afforded by authoring a letter, a journal, a report.

Jolly discovered this in her study of the relations between Presbyterian missionaries and indigenous women in the southern islands of Vanuatu in the period 1850–1880. The missionaries' obsessions were all too obvious—women's hard agricultural labor, maternal indifference or incompetence, the brutality of infanticide and widow strangulation. The lacunae were also telling: no detailed appreciation of women's place in indigenous structures of kinship or religion, and absolutely no reference to sexuality. Disjunctions between the accounts of missionary women and their husbands, and between the intimacies of daily journals and private correspondence as compared with the public proselytizing and fund-raising literature were also revealing.

Only very rarely were the words of local women reported, and then in dramatic contexts. In one instance, when Presbyterian missionaries were once again trying to stop a widow from being strangled, the widow herself is quoted as saying: "If I can't be strangled, I will do it myself" (Geddie 1975 [1848–1857], 65). What does the author do with a voice such as this—suddenly surfacing only to demand its own extinction? The difficulties of dealing with such a statement go beyond a confrontation with self-inflicted death. They derive from the conjunction of power relations between men and women, and colonizer and colonized.

This conjunction has been searchingly examined by Gayatri Spivak, who takes as text the self-immolation of Indian widows.[18] Spivak warns that the search for the hidden consciousness of the "subaltern woman" may subtly perpetuate imperialist and patriarchalist projects, and inflict "epistemic violence" on the women for whom we claim to speak. "And the subaltern woman will be as mute as ever" (Spivak 1988, 295). The assumption of identity between woman as object of study and woman as author is clearly at issue: First World feminists claiming to speak *for* (rather than *about*) "Third World women" may perpetuate the imperial character of much patriarchal discourse (cf. Jolly 1991; Mohanty 1984; Moore 1988, 10).

Recognizing these difficulties inherent in the enterprise, there is great challenge and promise in expanding historical understandings of contemporary Melanesian communities. Macintyre's analysis (1983) of warfare and exchange in the southern Massim at the time of European intrusion, and the transformations of the colonial period (including those that made it possible for "the kula" to function as Malinowski encountered it), provides an excellent model.

This growing engagement of anthropologists with history will continue and deepen in theoretical sophistication through dialogue in both directions. It would be an unfortunate irony if, as Peter Lawrence suggested with tongue in cheek in *Don Juan in Melanesia* (1967), it was all just a passing fad.

We will go on to consider other genres that might be used to capture the complexities of contemporary Melanesia, the juxtapositions of the new and the old, of exogenous and endogenous elements, of lives spent in villages and in urban centers. First, it will be useful to examine more closely these movements and juxtapositions, and the disjuncture of experience they seem to imply.

EXPERIENTIAL DISJUNCTURE AND LIVES OF COLLAGE

Carrier (this volume) points to the striking juxtapositions of the old and the new, the exogenous and the endogenous, in contemporary Manus. Within villages, we find trucks and trade stores and schools and political institutions of the postcolonial state coexisting with exchange, shell valuables, "traditional" objects, and obligations. The images of contemporary Melanesia are of collage, disjuncture, anachronism.

Moreover, our friends and neighbors in fieldwork are themselves coming and going, traveling to plantations, to town and back again. At any time, part of the "society" is not there. In many parts of Melanesia, this is no new phenomenon. For decades, often for more than a century, young men (and sometimes women) have been going off to distant plantations, where they have interacted with Europeans and fellow islanders from distant communities, have learned Pidgin and acquired technological skills and modes of dress and behavior foreign to their home communities (Jolly 1987; Keesing 1986).

We doubt whether Melanesian communities are unusual, in the spectrum of the Third World, in the radical juxtapositions of old and new, "traditional" and "modern," or in the experiential disjunctures of lives spent in village communities and in urban or plantation settings.[19] Our readings on Africa, Latin America, the Mediterranean, and southeast Asia suggest that radical disjunctures of the sort Melanesianists have encountered are systematically engendered along the capitalist periphery of the contemporary world system. And indeed, Clifford suggests that the mobile character of cultural forms, the process of hybridization or creolization, constitute *the* contemporary predicament of global culture (1988, 20).

There surely are striking disjunctures in life experience in contemporary Melanesia, with people from rural hinterlands communities circulating through growing urban centers and plantations. A Kwaio anecdote may bear relating. In 1974, Keesing was chatting outside a Kwaio men's house high on the coastal slopes when a seaplane landed in the harbor below. Half an hour later, a young man walked into the clearing, clad in long trousers, a Hawaiian shirt, dark glasses, and shoes. He greeted Keesing[20] in Kwaio, explaining that he was on Christmas holiday from a job in town; he and a friend had chartered a mission seaplane. At a mortuary feast in the bush the next day, the young man was stark naked but for a traditional fighting belt, and was sitting in an orchestra playing panpipes. Such disjunctures have been part of Kwaio experience since the nineteenth-century labor trade, although the transitions have been less abrupt. A grizzled, blind octogenarian pagan priest, who had been a feared warrior, once started speaking to Keesing in Fijian, then talked of the railroad trains he had ridden on during his ten years there. Our mode of ethnographic writing has failed, with very few partial exceptions, to capture these disjunctures. (We need also to bracket as problematic our own sense of wonder at the transitions involved and the extreme experiential dislocation they seem to imply. They seem to be quite taken for granted by the people we study. So do the juxtapositions of the old and new, local and alien, in which we see anachronism and inauthenticity.)

It is not that we have no knowledge of what happens to our friends and informants when they are in towns. Ethnographers pass through the urban centers on their way to and from the field, encountering their *wantoks* and sharing experiences with them. Yet the few serious studies of urban life and developing urban cultures are much less well known, less commonly cited, and less prestigious than the accounts of "traditional societies" (see Jourdan 1990). Not only is the urban side of contemporary Melanesian life relatively undocumented anthropologically. Our mode of ethnographic writing has failed, with very few partial exceptions, to capture these movements, these seeming disjunctures of experience.[21]

How do we bring such experiential disjunctures, lives of collage, into our accounts? How are we to capture vividly the experience of moving between worlds, while at the same time analyzing the systemics of political economy, of centers and peripheries, capital accumulation, power and pauperization, that create and sustain the disjunctures?

POSTMODERNIST MODES OF REPRESENTATION

A current wave of anthropological interest, inspired by postmodernism in the arts, has begun to explore alternative representational modes that bypass conventional constraints of ethnographic narrative. We believe that recent experiments with ethnography as literature and with techniques of montage, and an increasing self-reflexivity that places the ethnographer squarely in the picture, hold considerable promise for capturing present and past complexities of Melanesian life, and our engagement with them. We must again begin with some qualifications.

Ethnographic accounts that introduce the fieldworker as a crucial participant who has an impact on observed events and social relations, that are self-reflexive about the process of culture-learning and the shaping force of the ethnographer's own cultural constructions, can too easily become narcissistic and politically unreflective. What is lost in many "first-person" literary accounts of fieldwork is the political and economic relationship between hinterland villagers in a poor and peripheral Third World country and a scholar from a rich First World country, backed by the power and prestige of academic credentials. An account that explores the *Angst* of the fieldworker, her doubts, agonies and linguistic traumas, her self-delusory early triumphs, can too easily leave unasked critical questions about why the researcher presumed the right to invade other people's lives, and to represent them to the academic world, in genres about which they know or care little and over which they exert little or no control. (Young's sensitive and searching interrogation of himself and/as Asterisk [this volume] is a striking exception.) The fieldwork process perhaps inescapably perpetuates colonial power relationships. We will come back to these difficult political questions.

A second initial reservation is that postmodernist discursive styles can be used to evoke the same timeless, essentialized Melanesia as older styles of ethnographic narrative. As Carrier and others note in their chapters, a postmodernist argument regarding the contextual character of experience, the diversities of meaning from individual to individual, can be advanced (see, e.g., Wagner 1986) while still editing out the missionaries, the cash crops, the absent wage-labor force, the trade stores, the school, the state.

Many rhetorical pronouncements regarding postmodernist anthropology valorize ethnography as the core project of the discipline. But to celebrate local ethnography, and personal experience in its creation, can entail a retreat to local perspectives. The view from the village is limited and partial; the outside forces that shape local conditions too easily remain hidden.

A third reservation is that postmodernist styles of representation, in

emphasizing the ethnographer's personal experiences and the dialectical processes of understanding, and in avoiding spurious objectification and ab-
straction of "data" concerning the community under study, may not provide
forms of information—who was living where, what they were cultivating and
eating and buying and selling—that in future years could prove important in
assessing change and transformation. We are reminded of various recent
restudies of Pacific communities in which what has proved most valuable
have been the most "objective" and least interpretive records of an earlier
ethnographically recorded moment.[22]

We believe that these experimental representational modes can be used
effectively in characterizing lives spent in town or plantation settings and
villages, the hypostatization of *kastom*, the political economy of postcolonial
states, the new urban cultures, and the evanescent creation of meanings in
changing circumstances. Some anthropologists have been writing about
Africa and Latin America in ways that dramatically represent the juxtapositions and bricolage in local experiences of the contemporary world system.
We find Taussig's portrayal (1986) of the Amazonian frontier—his interpretations of the cultural constructions of jungle and Indian that sustained
terror—gripping and compelling. Taussig has recently advocated "montage" as a representational device as against "narrative"; conventional
strategies of story-telling, he argues, imply false unities and coherences.
"Montage," he argues, presents a multiplicity of views or voices, and this is
more open to the reader's reinterpretation than a closed text which tends to
unify the eyes of observer with the "I" of author and reader.

Such modes of representation are more problematic than their most
enthusiastic advocates have so far acknowledged. Paradoxically, the un-
intended variety, contestations and contradictions in such experience of
social life, evoked in these newer modes of anthropological writing, need to
be authorially *created*. The selectivity and manipulation with which anthropological author creates a desired effect—the effect *she* seeks—may be disguised
with the claim that one is presenting a multiplicity of views and perspectives,
and letting others "speak for themselves" (see Kapferer 1988).[23] Moreover,
few of us could aspire to the literary brilliance that makes Taussig's writing
so compelling. Despite our reservations, however, we welcome the new experimental spirit and see in alternative modes of writing possibilities of opening texts, capturing experiential disjunctures and diversities, and enlivening
conventional ethnographic narrative. Whatever their success, experiments in
ethnographic writing at least bring to awareness the usual realist artifices of
representation in which the author and reader of a conventional ethnography
are complicit.

But how do we show the articulation of local communities into wider systems of political economy without depicting indigenous peoples as passive

objects of external agency? As Carrier (this volume) and Jean Comaroff (1985) powerfully argue, local communities interact with outside "forces"[24] creatively, not passively. What emerges in this dialectical process is not necessarily "Westernization" of Manus villagers, or proletarianization of a Tswana wage-labor force, but distinctive local syntheses and adaptations. The agency indigenous peoples are able to exercise in the face of capitalist domination and state power may be limited, but it is still significant. The Carriers' recent book on Manus (1989) and Comaroff's book on the Tshidi Tswana (1985) exemplify a growing capacity of anthropologists to show this creative and dialectical process, the interplay of outside and inside "forces," and of "culture" (Comaroff's "structure") and action ("practice").

Comaroff (1985) offers other salient messages for contemporary Melanesianists. The Tshidi Tswana she studied in the 1960s and 1970s, locked in a vicious system of mine and industrial wage labor under the manacles of apartheid, could hardly be represented as preserving their "traditional" culture. Yet the rituals of modern Zionist cults (ultimately derived from early twentieth-century American Christian revivalism) are products of the same symbolic dynamics as pre-Christian Tshidi rituals. Their semiology creatively synthesizes indigenous and exogenous elements in cultural bricolage. In Melanesia, as Barker (this volume) reminds us, few of us have taken indigenous Christianity seriously. Insofar as it is acknowledged, Christianity is usually depicted as an invading foreign ideology, which either triumphs over ancestral religion or is resisted by it, or coexists with it in an uneasy syncretism. Such a model of missionization devalues the agency of Melanesians in the process of conversion, and presumes that Christianity perforce cannot be indigenous. Comaroff provides compelling evidence that the implicit distinction many of us have made in practice between genuine (indigenous, authentic) and spurious (exogenous, inauthentic) culture is meaningless (see Handler and Linnekin 1984).

THE POLITICS OF RESEARCH

Much has been written about the politics of anthropological research, both in the heady days of the New Left and, with less passion if more reflection, in response to Said's critique of Orientalism (1978) and other contemporary debates. We will not rehearse these arguments in detail. A good deal has been achieved in recent Melanesian anthropology in decolonizing research practice—partly in response to debates and heightened awareness within the discipline, partly in response to pressures exerted by postcolonial governments and local communities, more aware than they used to be of the political-economic context within which we ourselves work. Nonetheless, many of the contradictions that underlay field research in Malinowski's day remain. The asymmetries of power and wealth that allow us to be there and empower us to represent their lives remain. The gulfs between our projects and local perceptions of our projects remain wide.

We believe that indigenous critiques both of our project of representing Melanesian "culture" to the world of Western scholarship and of our practice must be taken seriously. Some elements of these critiques parallel the one we have advanced in the preceding pages. As Keesing (n.d.*b*) observes, one theme

> is a challenge to the way anthropologists filter out of their accounts what is not "traditional"—Christianity, cash crops, schools, tradestores, contemporary state politics, an absent elite and labor force—and concentrate on rituals, exchanges, and kinship, that may be of diminishing concern to local populations. . . . Another element. . . is the way we characterize indigenous cultures and worldviews through a kind of lens of exoticism, [portraying] mystical world views and exotic logics. These interpretations often violate both the intuitions and the . . . ideologies of those we study.

By engaging the problems and experiences of contemporary Melanesian life, rather than representing a vanishing past, ethnographers can make themselves more useful to, and welcome in, the countries and communities where they work.[25]

We believe that it is urgent for anthropologists to be deeply reflective about the political context of their work and the implicit assumptions that guide their projects. Although there have been plenty of pronouncements regarding a decolonization of research practice in Melanesia (as elsewhere in the Third World), and many commendable individual attempts to redress and avoid anthropology's sins of the past, the underlying asymmetries of power and wealth that make our research possible, and the assumption of the right to represent the lives of others to the world, remain problematic. We are certainly not urging an abandonment of research by Western academics. But the premises on which it rests and the practices by which it is carried out can no longer be taken for granted. Our work will now be continuously assessed by indigenous people with the right and the power to terminate our access to fieldwork areas; it is both prudent and appropriate that critical self-reflection and self-monitoring guide and govern our work, from planning to writing, and beyond.

SOME FINAL THOUGHTS

In questioning the very category of "Melanesia," in advocating alternatives to conventional narrative strategies and representational modes, in urging a more serious engagement with the transformations of the colonial period and the predicaments of the present, we do not mean to dismiss the possibility of anthropology of Melanesia. At the time of European invasion—whether (as in Vanuatu) it came very early or (as in parts of the New Guinea Highlands) it was recent—the island populations of the southwestern Pacific represented marked diversity in sociopolitical systems, modes of social organization, gender relations, economy, and cosmology. We regard it as a quite legitimate anthropological enterprise to explore the human diversity of Melanesia. Indeed, as Marilyn Strathern (1988) has brilliantly shown, in examining that diversity we can interrogate our own assumptions and categories, subjecting Western conceptual systems to deconstructive scrutiny. We further recognize that one of anthropology's most enduring and, we think, important concerns is with the ultimate depth of human differences: how radically diverse are culturally constructed realities and experiences.[26] The cultural diversity anthropologists have encountered in "Melanesia" provides a fertile field for such questioning, with all its attendant dangers and imponderables (see Keesing 1989a). Such comparative explorations and engagements with alterity may be Orientalist in Said's (1978) sense, but they lie at the heart of our discipline and it would be futile to call for their abandonment.

But this does not mean that these questions should continue to be pursued by conventional strategies of fieldwork and by perpetuating ethnographic narrative as a genre. There are now masses of ethnographic data on sociocultural variation on the library shelves, and they can be used effectively to pose comparative and interpretive questions, as M. Strathern (1988) and Barth (1987) have shown. Nor do we best ask questions about the depth and nature of cultural difference—say, in the constructions of time or space—by editing out of our account the fact that our subjects are wearing wristwatches or traveling by plane to Port Moresby. Finally, as Comaroff (1985) and Barker (this volume) argue, our humanness and the cultural process of creating meaning and order are, if anything, *more* strikingly manifest in the bricolage of the present than in the neater structures we have imputed to the past.

NOTES

1. Which themselves fall into a number of typologically rather similar but not demonstrably related families.

2. And their slightly more distant linguistic relatives in southeast Asia.

3. The literature on prehistory and sociopolitical systems in long time perspective is now too voluminous to bear citation; on political hierarchy, see, for example, Douglas (1979), Hau'ofa (1971), and Jolly and Mosko (n.d.).

4. The concepts of *mana* and *tabu* distributed widely in seaboard "Melanesia" will serve to exemplify.

5. Of course there have been earlier moments of fascination with primitivity, as with the celebration of African cultures centered in Paris in the 1920s.

6. There are, however, enduring concerns with non-Western systems of thought

and social formations in some national anthropological traditions. Much effort in French anthropology, for instance, remains devoted to characterizing *la pensée sauvage, mythologiques, rituels,* and *structures sociales.*

7. Although bringing anthropology back home has often meant the study of marginal or powerless communities in these developed countries.

8. We recognize that there has for decades been an alternative, but always subordinate, theme in the anthropology of Melanesia concerned with change, conflict, and the engagement of local populations with the world system, pioneered by such scholars as F. E. Williams, Ian Hogbin, and Peter Lawrence, and continued by such later researchers as Finney (1973) and Ogan (1972).

9. See Carrier, this volume.

10. We avoid the term "ethnographic realism" because "realism" may be taken to imply epistemological assumptions most ethnographers writing in this genre would not intend. Marcus and Fischer (1986), in developing the concept of "ethnographic realism" introduced by Marcus and Cushman (1982), note their allusion to Dickensian "realism" in nineteenth-century novels (as presenting a rounded, detailed description of the social world of its characters). But realism as a mode of novel-writing or film-making depends on the prior understanding that the reader/viewer is entering a world of "fiction." The power of realism in this sense lies in the illusion of reality created within a fictional frame (in Bateson's [1955] sense). Most anthropological monographs, insofar as they claim to represent "reality" scientifically, depend on a kind of reverse illusion.

11. Although fieldworkers do not all claim mastery of vernacular, even those who have worked mainly in Pidgin validate their characterizations by extensive citation of vernacular terms. On the pitfalls of cultural translation involved, see Keesing (1989a) and Heine (1985).

12. They may of course reappear as individuals in case studies, but usually are deployed to sustain typifications of roles, such as the big man.

13. Jonathan Friedman told one of us of his surprise and horror when, after reading a monograph on politics, ritual, and sorcery in a Papua New Guinea society, he visited the village where the ethnographer worked and discovered that the photographs showing the towering portals of traditional cult houses had been carefully framed so that the trucks parked underneath them were cut out. Jolly recalls a similar strategy employed by an ethnographic film-maker, shooting the famous "land dive" ritual in South Pentecost, who instructed participants to wear only "traditional" attire—grass skirts, penis wrappers, bark belts. Off came the shirts and trousers, Mother Hubbards, wristwatches, and safety-pin earrings. In the case of Curtis, not only were the negatives air-brushed in the interests of cultural purity; both the still photographs and cinematography were staged using a traveling wardrobe of "authentic" props and costumes.

14. Perhaps even more systematically in the ethnography of the 1960s and 1970s than they were by Malinowski, who speaks in the first person and who even has "confessions of ignorance and failure" (Malinowski 1935 [I], Appendix II; see Young 1979, 5, 13).

15. Keesing's recent translation of the autobiography of Kwaio political leader Jonathan Fifi'i, *From Pig Theft to Parliament: My Life Between Two Worlds* (1989), is a

rare exception, though one prefigured in work of such scholars as Schwartz (1962) and Finney (1973)

16. Although the infelicitous phrase was qualified by "albeit from the perspective of the crew of a European ship . . . ."

17. See Keesing's (1990*a*) account of controversies regarding the representation of the 1927 Malaita massacre and its aftermath and Thomas (n.d.*b*) on Fijian history and the coups.

18. It is illuminating to juxtapose Jolly's interpretation of widows' suicide in Vanuatu (n.d.*a*, n.d.*c*) with Spivak's (1988) reflections on *satī* and her final interpretation of the suicide of the revolutionary Bhuvaneswari Bhaduri.

19. We raise the point because it was suggested to one of us recently that Melanesia was distinctive in these respects.

20. Who hadn't recognized the young man, grown up and thickly muscled, as the gawky, spindly adolescent he had known.

21. Keesing's account of a recent murder in the Solomons (n.d.*a*), in which ancestrally empowered Kwaio warriors, killing for a blood bounty of shell valuables and pigs, flew to Honiara and assumed their alternative guise as urban thugs, probes this engagement with two cultural worlds and the contradictions it generates. In even more recent research (September 1989) Keesing has been exploring urban theft by Kwaio pagans, and the cultural disjunctures it generates (e.g., ancestors inducing the arrest of thieves because stolen goods have been stored in houses polluted by women); his paper "Foraging in the Urban Jungle: Notes from the Kwaio Underground" (Keesing 1990*b*) sets out and interprets a self-account from the leading Kwaio thief of his generation.

22. Restudies of communities documented by the Beagleholes in Tonga (1941) and Pukapuka (1938), by Morgan (1985) and Borofsky (1987), will serve to exemplify. We have heard the observation, in which we see some sobering truth, that now anthropologists have stopped writing descriptions of social structure, economy, and ecology, and devote themselves to interpreting cultural symbols and writing literary accounts, researchers in other disciplines such as human geography are having to take their place. We note a parallel irony in linguistics: the old descriptive grammars written by missionaries and other traditionally oriented field linguists that were so contemptuously regarded in the heyday of transformational theory are turning out to be much more useful in the long run than highly formalized and theoretical accounts that have become unintelligible with the demise of the paradigms that motivated them.

23. We doubt the inherently magical effects of montage in opening the anthropological text; montage can open, but it can also close. Helen Grace has tellingly commented (personal communication to Jolly) that Eisentein's montage was the ancestor of the video rock clip and the television advertisement.

24. We use quotes here to highlight the potential dangers of reification in metaphorically attributing agency to "forces" or "structures."

25. Although political difficulties may obviously arise in studying phenomena of the present; in one sense the traditional past may be partly safe and noncontroversial precisely because it is increasingly irrelevant.

26. From ours, and—in the "tribal" world—from one another.

REFERENCES

Barth, Fredrik. 1987. *Cosmologies in the Making: A Generative Approach to Cultural Variation in Inner New Guinea.* Cambridge: Cambridge University Press.

Bateson, Gregory. 1955. "A Theory of Play and Fantasy." *Psychiatric Research Reports* 2:39–51.

Beaglehole, Ernest, and Pearl Beaglehole. 1938. *Ethnology of Pukapuka.* (Bernice P. Bishop Museum Bulletin 150.) Honolulu: Bishop Museum.

————. 1941. *Pangai: Village in Tonga.* (Polynesian Society Memoir 18.) Wellington: Polynesian Society.

Borofsky, Robert. 1987. *Making History: Pukapukan and Anthropological Constructions of Knowledge.* Cambridge: Cambridge University Press.

Carrier, Achsah H., and James G. Carrier. 1987. "Brigadoon, or, Musical Comedy and the Persistence of Tradition in Melanesian Ethnography." *Oceania* 57:505–522.

Carrier, James G., and Achsah H. Carrier. 1989. *Wage, Trade, and Exchange in Melanesia: A Manus Society in the Modern State.* Berkeley, Los Angeles, London: University of California Press.

Clifford, James. 1988. *The Predicament of Culture: Twentieth-Century Ethnography, Literature, and Art.* Cambridge, Mass: Harvard University Press.

Comaroff, Jean. 1985. *Body of Power, Spirit of Resistance: The Culture and History of a South African People.* Chicago: University of Chicago Press.

Dening, Greg. 1988. *History's Anthropology: The Death of William Gooch.* Lanham, Md.: University Press of America.

Douglas, Bronwen. 1979. "Rank, Power, Authority: A Reassessment of Traditional Leadership in South Pacific Societies." *Journal of Pacific History* 14:2–27.

Fabian, Johannes. 1983. *Time and the Other: How Anthropology Makes its Object.* New York: Columbia University Press.

Fifi'i, Jonathan. 1989. *From Pig-Theft to Parliament: My Life Between Two Worlds.* Trans. and ed. Roger Keesing. Honiara: University of the South Pacific and Solomon Islands College of Higher Education.

Finney, Ben. 1973. *Big-Men and Business.* Canberra: Australian National University Press.

Foucault, Michel. 1973. *The Birth of the Clinic: An Archaeology of Medical Perception.* Trans. A. M. Sheridan. London: Tavistock.

————. 1977. *Discipline and Punish: The Birth of the Prison.* Trans. A. M. Sheridan. London: Penguin.

Geddie, John. 1975. *Misi Gete. John Geddie: Pioneer Missionary to the New Hebrides.* Ed. R. S. Miller. Launceston, Tasmania: Presbyterian Church of Tasmania.

Geertz, Clifford. 1980. *Negara: The Theater State in Nineteenth-Century Bali.* Princeton: Princeton University Press.

Guha, Ranajit. 1987. "Chandra's Death." Pp. 135–165 in R. Guha (ed.), *Subaltern Studies V: Writings on South Asian History and Society.* Delhi: Oxford University Press.

————, ed. 1989. *Subaltern Studies VI: Writings on South Asian History and Society.* Delhi: Oxford University Press.

Handler, Richard, and Jocelyn Linnekin. 1984. "Tradition, Genuine or Spurious." *Journal of American Folklore* 97:273–290.

Hau'ofa, Epeli. 1971. "Mekeo Chieftainship." *Journal of the Polynesian Society* 80:152–169.

Heine, Bernd. 1985. "The Mountain People: Some Notes on the Ik People of North-Eastern Uganda." *Africa* 55:3–16.

Huyssen, Andreas. 1986. *After the Great Divide: Modernism, Mass Culture, Postmodernism.* Bloomington: Indiana University Press.

Johnson, Diane D. 1984. "'The Government Women': Gender and Structural Contradiction in Papua New Guinea." Ph.D. thesis, University of Sydney.

Jolly, Margaret. 1987. "The Forgotten Women: A History of Migrant Labour and Gender Relations in Vanuatu." *Oceania* 58:119–139.

———. 1991. "Soaring Hawks and Grounded Persons: The Politics of Rank and Gender in North Vanuatu." Pp. 48–80 in Marilyn Strathern and Maurice Godelier (eds.), *Big Men and Great Men: Personifications of Power in Melanesia.* Cambridge: Cambridge University Press.

———. n.d.*a.* "Engendering Colonialism: Women and the History of Vanuatu." MS.

———. n.d.*b.* "Ill-Natured Comparisons: Racism and Relativism in European Perceptions from Cook's Second Voyage in Vanuatu." MS.

———. n.d.*c.* "To Save the Girls for Brighter and Better Lives." MS.

Jolly, Margaret, and Mark Mosko. n.d. "Transformations of Hierarchy." The Comparative Austronesian Project, Department of Anthropology, Research School of Pacific Studies, Australian National University. Forthcoming.

Jourdan, Christine. 1990. "Masta Liu." Presented at the Association for Social Anthropology in Oceania meeting, Kauai, Hawaii (March).

Kapferer, Bruce. 1988. "The Anthropologist as Hero: Three Exponents of Postmodernist Anthropology." *Critique of Anthropology* 8(2):77–104.

Keesing, Roger. 1978. *'Elota's Story: The Life and Times of a Solomon Islands Big Man.* St Lucia: University of Queensland Press. (2d ed., 1983, New York: Holt, Rinehart and Winston.)

———. 1985. "Kwaio Women Speak." *American Anthropologist* 87:27–39.

———. 1986. "Plantation Networks, Plantation Culture: The Hidden Side of Colonial Melanesia." *Journal de la Société des Océanistes* 82/83:163–170.

———. 1987. "Ta'a Geni: Women's Perspectives on Kwaio Society." Pp. 33–62 in Marilyn Strathern (ed.), *Dealing with Inequality.* Cambridge: Cambridge University Press.

———. 1989*a.* "Exotic Readings of Cultural Texts." *Current Anthropology* 30:459–477.

———. 1989*b.* "Sins of a Mission: Christian Life as Traditionalist Ideology." Pp. 193–212 in Margaret Jolly and Martha Macintyre (eds.), *Family and Gender in the Pacific: Domestic Contradictions and Colonial Impact.* Cambridge: Cambridge University Press.

———. 1990*a.* "Colonial History as Contested Ground: The Bell Massacre in the Solomons." *History and Anthropology* 4:279–301.

———. 1990*b.* "Foraging in the Urban Jungle: Notes from the Kwaio Underground." Presented at the Association for Social Anthropology in Oceania meeting, Kauai, Hawaii (March).

———. n.d.*a.* "Murder on Mount Austen: Kwaio Framing of an Act of Violence." In

Gilles Bibeau and Ellen Corin (eds.), *The Order of the Text: Asceticism and Violence in Interpretation*. Berkeley, Los Angeles, Oxford: University of California Press. Forthcoming.

——. n.d.*b*. "New Light on Old Shells: Changing Perspectives on the Kula." In Jukka Siikala (ed.), *Culture and History in Oceania*. MS.

——. n.d.*c*. "Theories of Culture Revisited." In Robert Borofsky (ed.), *Assessing Developments in Anthropology*. New York: McGraw-Hill. Forthcoming.

Lawrence, Peter. 1967. *Don Juan in Melanesia*. St. Lucia: University of Queensland Press.

Lyman, Christopher. 1982. *The Vanishing Race and Other Illusions: Photographs of Indians by Edward S. Curtis*. Washington, D.C.: Smithsonian Institution.

Macintyre, Martha. 1983. "Changing Paths: An Historical Ethnography of the Traders of Tubetube." Ph.D. thesis, Australian National University.

Malinowski, Bronislaw. 1935. *Coral Gardens and Their Magic*, Vol. I: *Soil-Tilling and Agricultural Rites in the Trobriand Islands*. London: Allen and Unwin.

Marcus, George, and Dick Cushman. 1982. "Ethnographies as Text." *Annual Review of Anthropology* 11:25–69.

Marcus, George, and Michael Fischer. 1986. *Anthropology as Cultural Critique: An Experimental Moment in the Human Sciences*. Chicago: University of Chicago Press.

Mohanty, Chandra T. 1984. "Under Western Eyes: Feminist Scholarship and Colonial Discourses." *Boundary* 2/12 (special issue):333–358.

Moore, Henrietta L. 1988. *Feminism and Anthropology*. Oxford: Polity Press and Basil Blackwell.

Morgan, Robert C. 1985. "Circuits in the Vava'u Social Economy." Ph.D. dissertation, Department of Anthropology, Research School of Pacific Studies, Australian National University.

Neumann, Klaus. n.d. "Not the Way it Really Was: Writing a History of the Tolai (Papua New Guinea)." *Journal of Pacific History*. Forthcoming.

Ogan, Eugene. 1972. *Business and Cargo*. (New Guinea Research Unit Bulletin 44.) Canberra: Australian National University.

Pratt, Mary Louise. 1986. "Fieldwork in Common Places." Pp. 27–50 in James Clifford and George E. Marcus (eds.), *Writing Culture: The Poetics and Politics of Ethnography*. Berkeley, Los Angeles, London: University of California Press.

Sahlins, Marshall. 1985. *Islands of History*. Chicago: University of Chicago Press.

Said, Edward. 1978. *Orientalism*. London: Routledge.

Schreiner, Shelley R. 1977. *The Kwaio Pagan Women of Malaita*. Honiara: Women's Centre of Solomon Islands.

Schwartz, Theodore. 1962. "The Paliau Movement in the Admiralty Islands, 1946–1954." *Anthropological Papers of the American Museum of Natural History* 49:211–421.

Shostak, Marjorie. 1981. *Nisa: The Life and Words of a !Kung Woman*. Cambridge, Mass: Harvard University Press.

Spivak, Gayatri C. 1988. "Can the Subaltern Speak?" Pp. 271–313 in Cary Nelson and Lawrence Grossberg (eds.), *Marxism and the Interpretation of Culture*. Urbana: University of Illinois Press.

Strathern, Andrew. 1979. *Ongka: A Self-Account by a New Guinea Big-Man*. (Andrew Strathern, trans.) London: Duckworth.

Strathern, Marilyn. 1988. *The Gender of the Gift: Problems with Women and Problems with Society in Melanesia*. Berkeley, Los Angeles, London: University of California Press.

Taussig, Michael. 1986. *Colonialism, Shamanism, and the Wild Man*. Chicago: University of Chicago Press.

Thomas, Nicholas. 1989. "The Force of Ethnology: Origins and Significance of the Melanesia/Polynesia Division." *Current Anthropology* 30:27–42.

———. n.d.*a*. "Alejandro Mayta in Fiji: Narratives about Millenarianism, Colonialism, Post-Colonial Politics, and Custom." In Aletta Biersack (ed.), *Clio in Oceania*. Washington, D.C.: Smithsonian Institution. Forthcoming.

———. n.d.*b*. "Taking Sides: Fijian Dissent and Conservative History-Writing." MS.

Wagner, Roy. 1986. *Asiwinarong: Ethos, Image, and Social Power among the Usen Barok of New Ireland*. Princeton: Princeton University Press.

Young, Michael. 1979. "Introduction." Pp. 1–20 in M. Young (ed.), *The Ethnography of Malinowski: The Trobriand Islands 1915–18*. London: Routledge.

———. 1983*a*. *Magicians of Manumanua: Living Myth in Kalauna*. Berkeley, Los Angeles, London: University of California Press.

———. 1983*b*. "'Our Name is Women: We are Bought with Limesticks and Limepots': An Analysis of the Autobiographical Narrative of a Kalauna Woman." *Man* 18:478–501.

CONTRIBUTORS

John Barker, "Christianity in Western Melanesian Ethnography."
Barker received his M.A. from Victoria University, in Wellington, New Zealand, and his Ph.D. (1985) from the University of British Columbia, where he is presently assistant professor of anthropology. He conducted field research on Christianity and tapa cloth among the Maisin people of Oro Province, Papua New Guinea, in 1981–1983 and 1986, and has also undertaken historical research on missionaries and pioneer ethnographers in Melanesia and British Columbia. He has published several articles and chapters on Maisin religion and is editor of *Christianity in Oceania: Ethnographic Perspectives.* Address: Department of Anthropology and Sociology, The University of British Columbia, 6303 NW Marine Drive, Vancouver, B.C., V6T 2B2.

James G. Carrier, "Approaches to Articulation."
After receiving his M.A. in sociology from the University of Virginia, Carrier studied the sociologies of science and education as a research student at the London School of Economics, receiving his doctorate in 1977. He accompanied his wife, Achsah Carrier, as she did fieldwork on Ponam Island, in Manus Province, Papua New Guinea, in 1978 and 1979 and intermittently from then until 1986. His main areas of interest were economics, education, and migration. From 1980 to 1986 he was in the Department of Anthropology and Sociology at the University of Papua New Guinea. With Achsah Carrier he has written extensively on Ponam society, most recently *Wage, Trade, and Exchange in Melanesia* and *Structure and Process in a Melanesian Society.* Address: 29, University Circle, Charlottesville, Virginia, 22903.

Bronwen Douglas, "Doing Ethnographic History."
Douglas received a doctorate in Pacific history from the Australian National University in 1973 and currently is a senior lecturer in history at La Trobe

University. Her main research interests are leadership in south Pacific societies, culture contacts, fighting, symbolism, and ritual in New Caledonia, and writing ethnographic history. She has done extensive research in Marist archives in Rome and the Pacific and in the French national archives, and has done repeated fieldwork in New Caledonia. She has published extensively, especially in the *Journal of Pacific History* and the *Journal of the Polynesian Society*.

Address: History Department, La Trobe University, Bundoora, Victoria, 3083.

Margaret Jolly, "Banana Leaf Bundles and Skirts."
Jolly studied anthropology and history at the University of Sydney, completing her doctorate there in 1979, a study of the effects of colonialism on the gender relations of the *kastom* communities of South Pentecost, Vanuatu. Since her fieldwork in Vanuatu, she has done archival work in Australia, Britain, and France, and is currently writing *Engendering Colonialism: Women and History in Vanuatu*. She has published extensively both in anthropological and feminist journals, and she is editor, with Martha Macintyre, of *Family and Gender in the Pacific: Domestic Contradictions and the Colonial Impact*. Since 1975 she has been a member of the Department of Anthropology and Comparative Sociology at Macquarie University, Sydney, where she is presently a Senior Lecturer teaching on Pacific colonialism, Melanesia, feminist anthropology, and women and development. She was a Research Fellow in Anthropology in the research groups on gender (1983) and the Comparative Austronesian Project (1989–1990) at the Research School of Pacific Studies of the Australian National University.

Address: Department of Anthropology, Macquarie University, Sydney, New South Wales, 2109.

Roger Keesing, "Kwaisulia as Culture Hero."
Keesing was Professor and Head of the Department of Anthropology, Research School of Pacific Studies, the Australian National University, at the time this collection was being organized. More recently he has taken a position at McGill University. Trained at Stanford and Harvard, he formerly taught at the University of California at Santa Cruz. He has done extensive research in the Solomon Islands and the Indian Himalayas. He is author of *Kwaio Religion, Melanesian Pidgin and the Oceanic Substrate, 'Elota's Story: The Life and Times of a Solomon Islands Big Man,* and, with Peter Corris, *Lighting Meets the West Wind: The Malaita Massacre.*

Address: Department of Anthropology, McGill University, 855, Sherbrooke Street West, Montreal, Quebec, H3A 2T7.

Nicholas Thomas, "Substantivization and Anthropological Discourse."
Thomas was a research fellow at King's College, Cambridge, and is now a Queen Elizabeth II Fellow at the Australian National University. He studied

archaeology, anthropology, and Pacific history at the Australian National University, completing a doctorate on early Marquesan society in 1986. He has conducted archival research on the culture and history of Polynesia, Fiji, and the Solomon Islands in Australia, the United States, Britain, France, and Italy, as well as various repositories in the islands themselves. He has done field research in the Marquesas and western Fiji. His research interests include indigenous social dynamics, gender, exchange, colonial history, and the history of anthropology. His publications include *Planets around the Sun: Dynamics and Contradictions of the Fijian* matanitu, *Out of Time: History and Evolution in Anthropological Discourse*, and *Marquesan Societies: Inequality and Political Transformation in Eastern Polynesia*. As well, he is a coeditor of *Sanctity and Power: Gender in Pacific History*, a special issue of the *Journal of Pacific History*.

Address: Department of Prehistory and Anthropology, Faculty of Arts, The Australian National University, GPO Box 4, Canberra, ACT, 2601.

Michael W. Young, "Gone Native in Isles of Illusion."
Young was born in Manchester, England, in 1937. After indifferent schooling he fled to the South Seas. On his return he narrowly escaped being absorbed into his father's ironmongery business, and studied anthropology instead. After five years at University College, London, he returned to the Antipodes to study for a Ph.D. at the Australian National University. He then taught at Cambridge for four years, returning to the ANU in 1975, where he remains today as a Senior Fellow in the Research School of Pacific Studies. He has conducted fieldwork in the islands of Goodenough and Ferguson and in Milne Bay in Papua New Guinea, Halmahera in Indonesia, and most recently Epi Island in Vanuatu. He is the author of *Fighting with Food, The Ethnography of Malinowski, Magicians of Manumanua*, and *Malinowski among the Magi*. Young lives in Canberra and edits *Canberra Anthropology*. He enjoys climbing small mountains, cooking exotic meals, and listening to Mozart and Pink Floyd.

Address: Department of Anthropology, Research School of Pacific Studies, The Australian National University, GPO Box 4, Canberra, ACT, 2601.

INDEX

Designer:	U.C. Press Staff
Compositor:	Asco Trade Typesetting Ltd.
Text:	10/12 Baskerville
Display:	Baskerville
Printer:	Bookcrafters, Inc.
Binder:	Bookcrafters, Inc.